Guerrilla Or

Guerrilla Oracle®

The Succinct Windows Perspective

Richard J. Staron

Addison-Wesley

Boston • San Francisco • New York • Toronto • Montreal
London • Munich • Paris • Madrid
Capetown • Sydney • Tokyo • Singapore • Mexico City

The publisher offers discounts on this book when ordered in quantity for bulk purchases and special sales. For more information, please contact:

U.S. Corporate and Government Sales
(800) 382-3419
corpsales@pearsontechgroup.com

For sales outside of the U.S., please contact:

International Sales
(317) 581-3793
international@pearsontechgroup.com

Visit Addison-Wesley on the Web: www.awprofessional.com

Library of Congress Cataloging-in-Publication Data

Staron, Richard J.
Guerrilla Oracle : The Succinct Windows Perspective / Richard J. Staron.
p. cm.
Includes bibliographical references and index.
ISBN 0-201-75077-5 (alk. paper)
1. Oracle (Computer file) 2. Relational databases. 3. Microsoft Windows (Computer file)
I. Title.

QA76.9.D3 S722 2002
005.75'85—dc21

2002028034

ISBN: 0-201-75077-5
Text printed on recycled paper
1 2 3 4 5 6 7 8 9 10—MA—0706050403
First printing, January 2003

*To my wife and best friend,
Kristina, who stayed with me through
all the computer disasters, late nights
when the servers went down, weekends when
scripts and code just wouldn't run, and
who listened to my litany of excitements and
frustrations. Without Kristina's belief in me
this book would have never been written.*

Contents

Preface

Try to make things as simple as possible; but not simpler.

— Albert Einstein

Simplicity is very difficult.

— Ray Ozzie,
software inventor

Read the following two sentences and choose the one that suits you:

1. Oracle is a rather complex subject, and this book will give you a close, detailed examination of its many intricacies. Intrinsic to our study is absolute concentration.
2. Welcome to the incredible world of Oracle databases!

If you voted for the first candidate, I regret that this book is not for you.

This book belongs in the hands of those who are intrigued by the Oracle environment and are looking for a complete view before they decide to focus on one particular area in depth. Yes, there is a lot to learn in the Oracle world, and it is a world that is continually changing. But certain basics are common to all Oracle installations, whether the scenario is a small Oracle shop with only three people or a large data center with several hundred. This book is aimed at those who are interested in a complete view of these basics—that is, those who are willing to do the work to turn a business idea into a functioning database.

In other words, this book is good material for both the newcomer to Oracle and the seasoned veteran. If you're a newcomer, you will be guided through all the steps you need to develop a working system. If you're a veteran (someone who has specialized in one or two areas of the Oracle database environment), you will be introduced to some exciting areas that you may have missed.

This book easily fits the bill for an intensive week-long seminar, a college class, a series of classes, or a self-study guide. If a company can make available a couple of servers, the book can be a do-it-yourself guide for employees, who can then work through the chapters on their own or in small, informal groups.

This book is *not* meant to be the one, definitive reference resource on every bit and piece of an Oracle installation. Rather, it gives you just what you need to get the job done. You will constantly be referred to other in-depth sources to complete your knowledge.

I believe that there is no knowledge like *experience*, and that is what this book will give you—*the complete Oracle experience* from the idea of a database through all the steps that are required to turn the idea into reality.

Be persistent and good luck! I look forward to working with you.

A Note about Typography

Some typographic conventions used in this book should be noted.

- First, a word about script annotations: Sample scripts are often accompanied by notes in the left-hand margin. For convenience each note is numbered, with a corresponding number shown at the end of the relevant line of code.
- In the sample scripts, system output is indicated in **bold** type.
- In the text, **bold** type is used to indicate key terms being defined.

—Richard Staron
Mansfield Center, Connecticut
July 2002

Acknowledgments

It is always amazing, isn't it, how a small turn here or there can lead to a major development. Taking that unmarked road may lead to a wonderful site or experience that we would otherwise just pass by. So, too, with this book. If it weren't for being naive enough to think I could teach an Oracle database class, I never would have seen the blank looks on the faces of the students in front of me when I showed them examples of "native" Oracle documentation, and I never would have thought, "There must be a better way," which is what led to writing the class syllabus, then to creating a couple of handouts, and finally to authoring this book.

So, I thank those brave and very bright students whose blank looks were the start of this project: Soju Daniel, April DeMartino, Syed Husains, Michael Sweet, and Chris Szewczyk. However, I never would have set foot in that classroom if it weren't for a dreamer and resident creative sparkplug, Dr. Gary Rommel of Eastern Connecticut State University. He pushed me into the classroom and constantly encouraged me, challenged me, and kept me aware that Eastern Connecticut State University exists for the sake of the students.

No manuscript ends up the way it starts, and many thanks go to those who patiently walked through page after page of acronyms, jargon, diagrams, and prints, making corrections and offering their advice: Dr. Richard Saley, Mr. Roman Baltram, Mr. William Becker, Mr. Declan Brady, Ms. Heidi Thorpe, and Mr. Fred Zarnowski.

Thanks to my parents, Joseph and Helen Staron. Little did they ever imagine that all those trips to the library when I was a little kid would ever result in this!

And finally, thanks to Tyrrell Albaugh, Mary O'Brien, Alicia Carey, Patrick Cash-Peterson, Chanda Leary-Coutu, and Brenda Mulligan at Addison-Wesley and Jimmie Young at Tolman Creek Design for their organizational and scheduling talents. Thanks to Cecile Kaufman, Joeth Barlas, and Nancy Fulton for their work during production, and a very special and sincere thank you to Stephanie Hiebert, whose editing talents and dedication transformed many a page into clear, readable text.

Chapter 1

Introduction

Welcome!

There isn't a backpack large enough to carry all the reference books you would need to build an Oracle8*i* or 9*i* server, create users, write programs, interface to the Web, and perform database administrator (DBA) tasks. And, at least in most states, it is still illegal to take shopping carts out of bookstores. Besides, how would you get the carts up and down the steps at your office or university?

Instead, we offer you this succinct, step-by-step manual for the entire Oracle cycle. You don't have to go out and build a new bookcase for your office, you don't have to start weight training to carry the reference manuals around. Start with this source, build your system and get it operational, and then you can consult other books for details on specific areas. By that point you will know enough to ask the right questions, and you will also know where to look in the application-specific guides and manuals for the information you need.

Enjoy, have fun, and get frustrated once in a while. Make contacts on list servers and bulletin boards, and be proud once your system is up and running.

Oracle8*i* and 9*i* the Guerrilla Way

In this book you will play all the professional roles necessary to turn an NT or Windows 2000 server into an Oracle server, configure both the Oracle server and client PCs, enable remote access, work with your customers on designing the database, normalize the data, turn the concepts into a real relational database, design the GUI forms, write the code, produce the reports, and then Web-enable your system. You will be the DBA, programmer, business analyst, and everything else that it takes to build a fully working database system.

Chapter by chapter you will be led through the necessary steps to ultimately produce a fully functional database system. In fact, you may end up selling your creation as is, or simply modifying it to fit other business environments.

What will you be building? Let's suppose that your goal is to produce a system that will test incoming students on the basics of computer literacy. The company, school, or college that has hired you currently offers a class, Computer Science 101, that is mandatory for all personnel. Many students who have taken the class have complained that it is boring and too simple, that they already know the material.

Your job is to produce an online, graphical user interface (GUI), user-friendly system that will let the students take an exam, will automatically grade the exam, will log the test, will allow professors to add additional questions, will provide online inquiry for the professors, and will produce reports, in addition to allowing the exam to be taken over the Web. You will learn more details on the system specs as we go along, but these are the overall goals. If you are successful, you will make life a little better for incoming students, and you will demonstrate your technical skills.

Oh, I forgot: There is one other requirement. The company or university has lots of information about its legacy system, and it wants you to migrate the data to your new Oracle system. Don't panic; we'll cover a neat utility called SQL*Loader that will make this task much more manageable. (Get used to hearing "Oh, I forgot" and "Oh, by the way" statements. These have been and always will be part of the environment in which we live and work.)

We encourage you to think of other uses for the system that you will be building. For example, with a little modification it could become an online, Web-based system for a video store that would allow customers to check availability as well as reserve videos, and that would give store employees access to all sorts of information. In this instance you could have some additional fun tying a bar code reader into the database to allow easy inventory of the films.

Our starting point is the idea that Oracle SQL*Plus, PL/SQL, relational database management systems (RDBMSs), and Oracle Server are all about databases. And databases are all about transforming data into information.

However, moving from raw data to a database information system in a Windows environment, especially a relational database system such as an Oracle database, is a complex process. First a computer environment must be built that will support the database, the programming, the applications, and the Web access. This includes (1) starting with the Windows NT or 2000 server, (2) installing the Oracle database server, (3) installing and defining the Oracle database software, then (4) creating the basic database security schema, and (5) formalizing the database backup plans.

Once the hardware and software foundation has been established, the database can be defined, created, and manipulated. (6) Data has to be defined around a concept, a business need, or in many cases, a migration from a legacy system to the Oracle relational database model. (7) Then the concept becomes solidified as the data is organized according to the principles of relational database theory. (8) Next the now formalized data becomes tables, and (9) SQL*Plus programs and user interfaces are created against the tables. A further extension is (10) to make the relational database Web accessible and even move the application into the e-commerce world.

This book will take you through these major steps. If you now have an NT or Windows 2000 server and your Oracle8*i* or 9*i* licenses, along with an operational local area network (LAN), you will be able to use the explanations and instructions in this book to build your own Oracle database environment. You will learn how to configure the server, configure the security, and define and build the database. Then, using SQL*Plus, PL/SQL, Oracle Forms, Oracle Reports, and Oracle Web tools, you will create systems that your business, customer, or students can use. By duplicating the examples in this book, you can gain hands-on experience with all the major steps in creating a successful Windows Oracle environment.

As you gain expertise and confidence, we encourage you to go further and consult other books, read the extensive Oracle documentation, join Oracle Web groups, and visit Oracle's home page. And as I just mentioned, duplicating what is shown in this book in your own work environment or classroom is an excellent way to become familiar with the steps necessary to successfully install and program an Oracle database.

Where, you may be asking, did the *guerrilla* in *Guerrilla Oracle* come from? There is an approach to systems development, programming, or just about any project that emphasizes rapid development. In this approach we know the intended goal, we have a limited amount of time (usually less than a year), and we do not have all the specs. But we're confident that we will complete the missing parts as we go along and that we will complete the project; that's the *guerrilla* part—an attitude that we will get the job done even though we're starting with somewhat insufficient information.

And that's what this book is about. I expect you to jump right in, even though you do not yet have much, if any, information about Oracle. But I believe that you have the initiative and tenacity to stay with the book and get the whole overview.

Chapter 2

The Three Most Important Dates

There must be over 20 million pages written on the Civil War, double that on World War II. A safe guess would be that over 500,000 pages have already been written on database history. As fascinating as history buffs might find a historical look at databases to be, I will devote only a few pages to the topic. I'll give you my version of the three most significant dates and events. If you're a history buff, I encourage you to delve further. For most of you, though, a few pages will be enough.

I hope you will see that the development of the RDBMS (relational database management system) and SQL (Structured Query Language) was not a smooth, clinical event. Rather, it was filled with radical thinking, corporate dissension, competition, market pressures, and ultimately the persistence of a very small group of scientists who dared to challenge the status quo.

Dr. Edgar F. Codd, Radical Thinker

The first date is 1970. In about 20 pages, in the June 1970 issue of the *Journal of the Association for Computing Machinery*, Dr. Edgar F. Codd, an IBM researcher, presented his theory on the structure of a relational database system. He proposed that the way data is stored, manipulated, and organized should be totally transparent to the user. He went on to show the inadequacies of existing database structures, and he proposed a system based on normal forms and a universal language.

That is, he believed that all existing data structures built on hierarchical (tree) structures, commonly known as parent-child relationships, were inadequate. They did not reflect the true nature of how the data is related. One side note is that Dr. Codd introduced the notion of **data normalization**. In brief, this means reducing something to its simplest form, and it is a familiar term for mathematicians. I will cover data normalization in more depth in Chapter 4.

In 1985, Dr. Codd wrote his 12 rules for a relational database management system:

Rule 1: Information. Data should be presented to the user in table form.

Rule 2: Guaranteed access. Every data element should be accessible without ambiguity.

Rule 3: Systematic treatment of null values. A field should be allowed to remain empty for future use.

Rule 4: Dynamic online catalog based on the relational model. The description of a database should be accessible to the user.

Rule 5: Comprehensive data sublanguage. A database must support a clearly defined language (SQL) to define the database, view the definition, manipulate the data, and restrict some data values to maintain integrity.

Rule 6: View updating. The user should be able to change the data through any available view.

Rule 7: High-level insert, update, and delete. Users must be able to add, delete, or change all data in a file—whether it is a single row in a single table or multiple rows in multiple tables—with a single command.

Rule 8: Physical data independence. Changes in how data is stored or retrieved should not affect how the user accesses the data.

Rule 9: Logical data independence. The user's view of the data should be unaffected by its actual form in files.

Rule 10: Integrity independence. Constraints on user input should exist to maintain data integrity.

Rule 11: Distribution independence. A database design should allow for distribution of data over several computer sites, and the user should be unaware of whether or not the database is distributed.

Rule 12: Nonsubversion. The only way to modify the database structure should be through the language mentioned in rule 5 (SQL).

Storage Technology Becomes System R

A second historical period that I consider very important is IBM's research from 1973 through 1976. During those years, IBM staff at the San Jose Research Center (Dr. Codd's base), worked on **System R**. System R was the experimental relational database they were trying to build according to Dr. Codd's theories. Codd's team did develop a successful prototype relational system that could do ad hoc reporting and transaction processing. SEQUEL (Structured English Query Language) was the database language that they created as the interface to the experimental System R database. Because of trademark laws, the name *SEQUEL* was changed to *SQL*.

Interestingly, the System R scientists were initially at odds with IBM. At that time, IBM had a very popular and successful database, IMS. IMS was a true hierarchical database, the very design Dr. Codd had called inadequate. During the mid-1970s there was quite a disagreement at IBM over which database should take precedence. IBM had already gone its own independent way in 1968, when it decided not to support the CODASYL[1] product, instead going ahead with its own IMS product. IMS became a solid commercial success and a major IBM product.

In reality no one, including Dr. Codd, realized that his first paper, and the subsequent laboratory experiments with System R, were the beginning of a revolution within IBM and within the technical community. In the early days of investigation of his RDBMS, Dr. Codd and his work were actually labeled as contrary to IBM's company goals. Dr. Codd eventually went head to head with Charles Bachman, spokesman for the CODASYL database design, and the outcome was a government-sponsored project (funded by the military and the

1. CODASYL is the acronym for Conference on Data Systems Languages. Founded in 1957 by the U.S. Department of Defense, it was created to develop computer programming languages, and it was the group responsible for developing COBOL. The group no longer exists.

National Science Foundation [NSF]) at the University of California at Berkeley. The two groups, Dr. Codd's at IBM and the UC-Berkeley group, both competed with each other and reinforced each other's efforts.

Although System R did eventually prove to be a data-independent, high-level database, as Dr. Codd had predicted, it did not on its own convince IBM to abandon IMS in favor of relational databases. IBM was still promoting IMS as the corporate database, in spite of the successes at UC-Berkeley and at San Jose. After all, wasn't San Jose supposed to be IBM's center for disk storage development, not database research?

It took the dissemination of source code from the UC-Berkeley group to get IBM's attention. As we all know, once source code gets out into the technical community, unexpected things start to happen. By then, Larry Ellison, founder of Oracle, had learned of SQL through publications from the System R team, and he had developed and was already marketing his version of SQL. Simultaneously, other companies began to appear, such as Ingres and Informix, along with established companies such as Software AG, all promoting the RDBMS, along with SQL.

Finally, in 1980, under the threat of being bypassed in the marketplace, IBM came out with its own version of SQL: SQL/DS for mainframes. During the same year Codd was awarded the Association for Computing Machinery's (ACM) Turing award. And the world of databases has not been the same ever since. Today, SQL is accepted as the standard RDBMS language.

Beep Beep! Here Comes Oracle Passing IBM on the Information Highway

The third important date is 1979. In that year, Relational Software Inc. (now Oracle Corporation), introduced the first commercially available implementation of SQL. As already mentioned, Larry Ellison took quick advantage of the IBM System R research, and he became an early leader in the RDBMS field. Oracle and IBM are currently the major RDBMS vendors. All other RDBMS vendors have a minuscule market share.

Many other dates are considered to be watersheds or true technological shifts. The invention of the transistor, the PC, client/server technology, and the Internet—to name a few examples—all have played an important role in getting us to where we are today. However, I believe that the three dates discussed in this chapter signify the most important milestones in the development and commercialization of RDBMSs.

Chapter 3

Concepts

If you're already familiar with the concepts and terminology associated with Oracle and RDBMS and SQL, then feel free to skip this chapter. For the rest of us, I'll try to be as brief and clear as possible while covering what I consider to be the basic information that you will need to make sense out of the remainder of this book.

I will cover the following five topics: databases, the Oracle Server environment, SQL programming languages, development tools, and the Web. Each topic builds on the previous one, and you need this basic understanding to successfully build your guerrilla database over the next few chapters.

To start, here's a quick review of some of the fundamental concepts for relational databases.

Relational Databases

RDBMS

RDBMS is an abbreviation of *relational database management system*. The history of databases is fascinating, and the reader is encouraged to spend some time researching. For our purposes here, know that the major hallmarks of an RDBMS are the following:

- Data storage and retrieval are transparent to the programmer and the end user. Oracle's RDBMS handles where and how the data is stored, and how it is gathered for reports, views, and screen functions.
- Data is contained in what are called **tables**, which arrange the data in rows and columns. A row contains all the data for a particular entity. Another way to look at it would be to consider each row a *record*, and the columns *fields* in the record. Proper terminology, however, is **row** and **column**, and these will be the terms used from now on. A row for a person's data might include name, address, phone, age, sex, and so forth. The row would contain all these pieces of data for a single person, and the columns would be name, address, and so forth:

COLUMNS

	Name	Address	Phone	Age	Sex
ROWS	Jon Adams	23 Michigan	877-654-3421	55	M
	Doris Adams	23 Michigan	877-654-3421	54	F
	Pete Seever	677 North Street	Unlisted	65	M

Relationships

The next concept we have to be clear about is the RDBMS idea of **relationships**. The idea is actually very simple because we all naturally make relationships between bits of data every day of our lives.

As a concrete example, think about summarizing all the courses you and your friends have taken over the years. Some were at workshops, some online, some from books, some in formal classes. You would naturally want to just jot your name down, and then list the courses one after the other, then the next name and all of that person's courses. However, this approach would be pretty messy in a couple of years after all of you had taken several more courses, wouldn't it? You would run out of room and have to start writing in the columns and margins.

So almost intuitively you would create two tables—one for names and other personal info, and the other for courses that were taken. The information would now look like this (italic typeface identifies the primary keys, which we will discuss shortly, in the section on constraints):

PERSON Table	**COURSE Table**
Person ID	*Course ID*
Date of Birth	Date Taken
Address	Location
Phone	Number

Again, what you've done is to make a natural connection, or *relationship*, between the two sets of data. This is very important for your understanding of how we will later create and link all the tables in your demonstration database.

To summarize, there are only a couple of types of relationships commonly used in the RDBMS world:

- **One-to-many**. One person has taken many courses, one exam has many questions, one building has many rooms, and so on.
- **Many-to-many**. For example, you as an Oracle expert work on many projects, and each project has many Oracle experts working on it. To create the relationship between the two tables—the one with you and all the Oracle experts and the one with all the projects—we need what is called an **intersect table**:

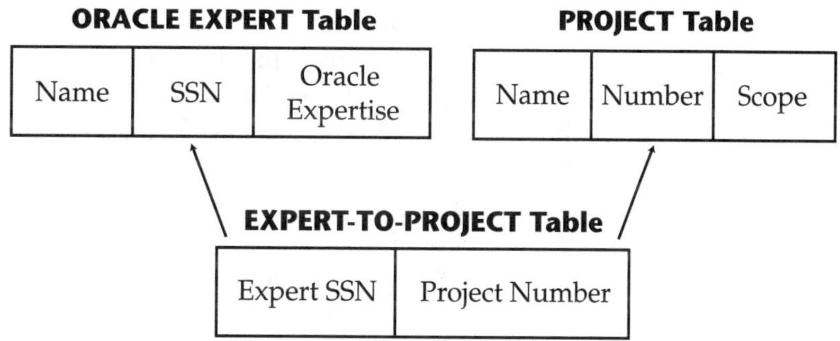

In this example of a many-to-many relationship, we have three tables: (1) the ORACLE EXPERT table, (2) the PROJECT table, and (3) the EXPERT-TO-PROJECT table. Think about this. We want to know which projects each of our experts has, and we want to know who all the experts working on a particular project are. So we can try to list all the projects for an expert in the ORACLE EXPERT table, and we can try to list all the experts on a project in the PROJECT table.

This approach quickly becomes a nightmare when project staffing changes or projects are added or dropped. If we did it this way, we would be constantly changing the two tables just trying to keep up. Instead, we create another table, the EXPERT-TO-PROJECT intersect table. Using this table, we can quickly get a list of all projects and who is working on them, and using just that little bit of information, we can go to the bigger tables and get detailed information on each expert and each employee.

This idea may be somewhat new to you, but try to work at grasping the general concept. You will see it again in later chapters, where we actually use it. For example, we will have a link table that is used to get information from both a question table and a test table. So stay tuned; Chapter 5, where this theory is put into practice, is just around the corner.

This is how tables link to each other, through relationships. To summarize, basic storage in an RDBMS is in *tables*. Tables have *columns* (Name, Address, Phone Number, and so on) and *rows*, where the data is stored. All the columns of a row represent an **instance** of that row. A column can have additional qualifications. For example, it can be a key, and constraints can be added.

Tables and relationships are the heart of an RDBMS.

Constraints

Constraints are another important piece of the RDBMS picture, one that you will be using as you develop your guerrilla database. In brief, a **constraint** is a rule or set of rules that apply to a column or combination of columns.

Before we terrorize you with the various kinds of constraints, let's take an English-language look at one that you've already done automatically. In the preceding PERSON table, notice the Person ID column. Without thinking, you knew that this had to be a unique column, or the table would not make any sense, right? Making this data element unique is a constraint. What you actually did was create a primary key for the table, and one of the characteristics of a primary key is that it is unique.

A Quick Word about Primary Keys

All the other pieces of data in a row must depend on the primary key column. In the PERSON table example, not much besides the person ID is unique. For example, several people can share the same phone number and address. Hence the person ID is the logical key, and because it is really unique for each person, it can be the primary key.

Here are some other constraints:

- **Foreign key**. The *foreign key* refers to the primary key of another table. Using the PERSON and COURSE tables above, let's add another table called COURSE DESCRIPTION. Why? Well, suppose that you and five of your friends took the Oracle DBA course. You could enter the course number and description over and over for each of you, or you could put the description in another table, like this:

PERSON Table	**COURSE DESCRIPTION Table**	**COURSE Table**
Person ID	*Course ID*	*Person ID*
Name	Description	Course ID
Date of Birth	Cost	Date Taken
Address		Location
Phone Number		Grade
		Hours

Look at the Course ID column in the COURSE table. It is the same as the Course ID column in the COURSE DESCRIPTION table. Since, as we just learned, the primary key must be unique, the Course ID column in the COURSE DESCRIPTION table has to be unique, and it is the primary key for that table. In the COURSE table, the Course ID column is a foreign key that refers back to the Course ID column in the COURSE DESCRIPTION table.

By linking both tables through a foreign key, you have also set the stage for what is called *referential integrity*. The *value* of the foreign key in the COURSE table depends on and exactly corresponds to the *value* of the primary key, which is the course ID in the COURSE DESCRIPTION table. Hence when you go to add a Course ID to the COURSE table, Oracle will automatically check to make sure that the ID exists in the COURSE DESCRIPTION table. This is referential integrity.

You can add the phrase "on delete cascade" to a foreign key. When you do this, Oracle will automatically delete any foreign-key rows in the table when the primary table row is deleted. For example, if you had taken a course called Intro to Oracle, with course ID 001, and decided to delete course ID 001 from the COURSE DESCRIPTION table, the "on delete cascade" statement would delete the entries for any course ID 001 in the COURSE table. If you didn't do this, you could end up having entries in the COURSE table with no match in the COURSE DESCRIPTION table.

- **Uniqueness**. This concept was covered with the primary key. Just be aware that you can make other columns unique without making them keys.
- **Check, including NOT NULL.** This powerful feature allows you to establish ranges for data. In the preceding example, you could say that you wanted only courses taken after 1979, when Oracle first appeared. You would then define the Date Taken column as a `DATE` and add `CHECK` (Date Taken greater than January 1, 1979).

A Word on NULL

NULL is a unique concept. It is the *absence* of any value; it is *not* zero or spaces. Adding the constraint NOT NULL to a column means that data must be entered when the row is created that uses that column. The NOT NULL constraint is a good way to make sure your users do not skip important columns when adding information to a table.

Jumping ahead a bit, you can get a look at the constraints on a table by checking the data dictionary. Appropriate commands are:

- `SELECT * FROM USER_CONSTRAINTS . . .`
- `SELECT * FROM ALL_CONSTRAINTS where . . .`
- `SELECT * FROM DBA_CONSTRAINTS`

The data dictionary is introduced on the following page and will be covered in more detail in Chapter 10.

The Server Environment

Over the years, with the various releases, Oracle Corporation has done a very good job of streamlining the installation of Oracle Server and the building of Oracle databases. In fact, using the wizards—as you will see in later chapters—has made these functions much easier because you have good, clear instructions.

There are a few server concepts I want to cover. First is the **data dictionary**. Repeat, "The data dictionary is my friend." This is where you will go time after time to find out the nitty-gritty information on tables, views, security, and so forth. In general, the data dictionary stores all the information for all the **objects** in the database. These objects include tables, indexes, views, PL/SQL stored procedures, constraints, and so forth.

Fortunately, there is a simple trick when you're looking for information. Almost all data dictionary views start with `ALL`, `USERS`, or `DBA`. For example, running the query `SELECT * FROM ALL_CONSTRAINTS` produces a list of every constraint for all tables in the database.

The second server concept is an **index**. This is a shortcut to information in a table. Think of the back of this book, where you quickly use the index to find what you need. If you specified an index for a column in a table, Oracle would maintain a separate table with that data. If you wanted to know all courses you took in which you earned a score over 90 percent, Oracle would use the index to quickly find those records instead of having to look at every course and grade for you.

The last server concept that I'll cover is just a little detail on **server configurations**. I include this information just to give you a mental picture of what we'll be doing very shortly when we build our database. If you built only one database on your Oracle Server, it would be seen as a single Oracle instance, with a single database. Alternatively, and this is the more common approach, you could have multiple databases on the same server—one for production, one for testing, and perhaps another one for development. This would be a configuration of multiple Oracle instances and multiple databases. For our purposes, we will have one production database and one test/development database, both on the same server.

There are other possible configurations, such as remote databases, clustering, and so forth, but they will not be covered in this book. Rather, I will take you through the steps necessary to get your own Oracle server/database system up and running as quickly as possible.

SQL Programming Languages

SQL

SQL was a product of the original RDBMS development efforts back in the 1970s. Since then, SQL has grown into a mature language that has three major categories—Data Definition Language (DDL), Data Manipulation Language (DML), and transaction control:

1. DDL contains verbs such as CREATE, ALTER, and DROP.
2. DML has SELECT, INSERT, UPDATE, and DELETE.
3. Transaction control is a subset of DML and contains the verbs SET TRANSACTION, SAVEPOINT, COMMIT, and ROLLBACK.

These are the expressions you would expect in a language. With DDL you will create. Then, using DML commands, you will insert and update your tables, and using the transaction control commands, you will either commit your modifications to the database, or do a rollback and not commit them.

Here's an example of SQL from the PERSON table. We want all the information for the person who has ID 0001. The SQL command is:

```
SELECT * from PERSON_TABLE
        where Person_id = 0001;
```

This query will return all the data (or the entire row) for the person with ID 0001, as shown here:

ID*	**Name**	**Date of Birth**	**Address**	**Phones**
0001	Harry Gould	06/04/62	14 Overlook, New Hartford, MI	611-432-5543

*Across the top are the names of the columns, and below is all the data that met the SELECT criteria.

Suppose that you wanted to know just the names and phone numbers for everyone. Using the query

```
SELECT NAME, PHONE_NUMBER from PERSON_TABLE;
```

you would get the following information:

Name	**Phone Number**
Harry Gould	611-432-5543
Nancy Stankov	611-531-9987
Damian Stern	611-769-3211
John Turin	514-899-5567
.	
.	
.	

and so forth, until the end of the table was reached.

Table 3.1 briefly summarizes the SQL commands that have been introduced already, as well as some additional basic commands that will be introduced later. These commands are covered more fully in the Oracle documentation and in the many excellent reference books available.

Table 3.1 Basic SQL Commands

Command	**Purpose**	**Format**
CREATE TABLE		CREATE TABLE table_name (Column name datatype, Column name datatype, . . .);
ALTER TABLE		ALTER TABLE table_name ADD (column name datatype) or MODIFY (column name datatype);
DROP TABLE		DROP TABLE table_name;
CREATE VIEW		CREATE VIEW view_name (view column name1, view column name2, . . .) as QUERY;
DROP VIEW		DROP VIEW view_name;
CREATE INDEX		CREATE INDEX index_name on Table_name (column1, column2, . . .);
DROP INDEX		DROP INDEX index_name;

Continued

Table 3.1 Basic SQL Commands *(Continued)*

Command	Purpose	Format
CREATE SYNONYM		CREATE SYNONYM *synonym name* FOR Object_name;
DROP SYNONYM		DROP SYNONYM synonym_name;
DELETE	Delete rows from a table	DELETE FROM table_name WHERE qualifiers . . . ;
INSERT	Add new rows to a table	INSERT INTO table_name (column1, column2, . . .) VALUES (value1, value2, . . .);
UPDATE	Change rows in a table	UPDATE table_name SET column1 = value, column2 = value, . . . WHERE qualifiers . . . ;
RENAME	Rename a table	RENAME old_name TO new_name;
COMMIT	Make changes permanent	COMMIT;
ROLLBACK	Roll back the changes (actually, undo the changes)	ROLLBACK; ROLLBACK TO savepoint_name;
SAVEPOINT	Mark a point to roll back to	SAVEPOINT savepoint_name;
SELECT	Get rows from the database	SELECT column1, column2, . . . (or * for all columns) FROM table_name WHERE qualifiers for rows;

Now that you have a little taste for SQL, let's take a walk through some basic SQL **syntax** (Table 3.2). These are symbols and formats that you will be using for the rest of your career, and they form the foundation of your programming. When you perform a test against something, such as a letter, number, column, or literal, you will use these symbols.

Table 3.2 SQL Syntax

Symbol[a]	Meaning	Example
=	Is equal to	PERSON_ID = 123456789
>	Is greater than	SCORF > 90
>=	Is greater than or equal to	SCORE >= 90
<	Is less than	SCORE < 90
!=	Is not equal to	SCORE != 90
<>	Is not equal to	SCORE <> 90
^=	Is not equal to	SCORE ^= 90

a. Must use 'is' or 'is not' when checking for NULLS.

You will also constantly be comparing other values, looking for things in lists and so forth, so here is some more SQL syntax that you will have to digest. Suppose you have created users whose names you can't quite remember, but you know they're something like Neuman, or Sunman, or something similar. With SQL you can search on a column using the LIKE statement:

- To find any name, for example, that begins with *Sun*, use this command: `Select NAME from PERSON_TABLE where name LIKE 'Sun%'`
- To find a name that has *man* anywhere in it, use this command: `Select NAME from PERSON_TABLE where name LIKE '%man%'`
- To find a name that has, for example, two *a*'s in it, use this command: `Select NAME from PERSON_TABLE where name LIKE '%a%a%'`
- If you know that the name you want has a *z* in the second position, you can get fancy by using an underscore. Each underscore stands for one space, so the following command would look for *z* in the second position of the name: `Select NAME from PERSON_TABLE where name LIKE '_z%'`

You will also find yourself using **lists** of things to compare values. For example, you may want all the students whose scores are not within the range of 70 to 90 for a certain exam, or for all exams. Or you may want to find the students who are from certain states—say, Alabama, Connecticut, and New York. Or you may want to exclude students from certain states, by using either the state name or letters of the alphabet. There is much flexibility with these commands. Here are the formats:

For numbers:

- Use the IN command when you want to check if something is *in* a list. For example, `Score IN (90, 91, 92, 93)` gives all scores that match anything in the list.

- Reverse the command to exclude a list. For example, Score NOT IN (90, 91, 92, 93) gives all scores that don't match anything in the list.
- To check for a range, use the BETWEEN command. For example, Score BETWEEN 90 and 95 gives all scores from 90 to 95.
- To exclude a range, use the NOT BETWEEN command. For example, Score NOT BETWEEN 90 and 95 excludes all scores above 95 and below 90.

For letters:

- Use the IN command when you want to check if something is in a list. For example, State IN ('AL', 'CT', 'NY') gives all states that match anything in the list contained within the parentheses.
- Reverse the command to exclude a list. For example, State NOT IN ('AL', 'CT', 'NY') gives all states that don't match the list.
- To check for a range, use the BETWEEN command. For example, State BETWEEN 'A' and 'D' gives all states between A and D.
- To exclude a range, use the NOT BETWEEN command. For example, State NOT BETWEEN 'AA' and 'DZ' excludes all states between A and D. (Note: The IN command ignores NULLS!)

Finally, you can use AND and OR just as you would think:

- Select Name from PERSON_TABLE where NAME LIKE 'Man%' AND STATE = 'CT';
- Select Name from PERSON_TABLE where NAME LIKE 'Man%' OR STATE = 'CT';

SQL*Plus

Oracle's extensions to SQL are called **SQL*Plus**. In general, the SQL*Plus commands are very useful when you are writing queries and generating reports. They give you control over headings, page breaks, totals, and other reporting format issues.

Here's an example of creating a simple SQL*Plus report to list all the phone numbers for everyone in the PERSON table:

```
spool c:\CHAPTER_3_REPORT
set echo off
```

```
set pagesize 55
set linesize 132
set newpage 0
ttitle left   'All Employees and Phone Numbers' -
      right  'Pg: ' format 999 sql.pno  skip 1 -
      center 'Guerrilla Oracle University' skip 1 -
      center 'As of &&date' skip 2
column PERSON_ID  format 999999999 Heading 'Person ID'
column Name       format a20 Heading 'Name'
column Phone      format a12 Heading 'Phone Number'
break on PERSON_ID skip 2 -

SELECT  PERSON_TABLE.PERSON_ID,  NAME, PHONE_NUMBER
                        from PERSON_TABLE,
TEMP_PERSON_TABLE
WHERE PERSON_TABLE.PERSON_ID = TEMP_PERSON_TABLE.PERSON_ID
order by 1;
spool off;
```

And here's what the report looks like:

```
All Employees and Phone Numbers
                                                        Pg:   1
                      Guerrilla Oracle University
                           As of 04-APR-02
Person ID   Name                Phone Number
-------------------------------------------------------------
111111111   Harry Gould         611-432-5543
222222222   Nancy Stankov       611-531-9987
333333333   Damian Stern        611-769-3211
444444444   John Turin          514-899-5567
```

Just to give you a quick synopsis, when this report runs, it prompts for the date; that's the **&&date** field. It then gets every record in PERSON_TABLE and TEMP_PERSON_TABLE and produces a simple listing with the column names of Person ID, Name, and Phone Number. (I'm about to show you why and how to create TEMP_PERSON_TABLE, so don't worry that you've missed something.)

PL/SQL

In addition to SQL*Plus, Oracle has developed **PL/SQL (Procedural Language/SQL)**, which supports more traditional programming, such as loops and `IF..THEN` statements. When you write PL/SQL statements, you will be creating **blocks**. These blocks generally have three distinct sections:

1. **DECLARE**. In this section you define any variables and cursors that you will use in the block. (I will discuss cursors later in this chapter.)
2. **BEGIN**. This section contains your commands, such as loops and `IF..THEN` statements.
3. **EXCEPTION**. As the name implies, this is where you put any exception handling you may want.

In addition to including these three sections, you must complete the block with an `END` command or you will have errors. Here's a simple example from our PERSON table:

```
DECLARE
  Per_ID                  NUMBER (9)
  Per_Name                VARCHAR2(20)
  Per_Birth               Date
  Per_Address             VARCHAR2(20)
  Per_Phone               VARCHAR2(10)

BEGIN
  Per_ID              := 000000123
  Per_Birth           :=  '06091950'
  Per_Name            := 'Jerry Dubois'
  Per_Address         := '54 Durham Rd'
  Per_Phone           := '7543228769'

  INSERT INTO PERSON_TABLE    VALUES
    (Per_ID, Per_Birth, Per_NAME, Per_ADDRESS, Per_PHONE);

EXCEPTION
  When DUP_VALUE_ON_INDEX
    Then . . . create a short report with the error and Student ID that
                       caused the error

END;
.
```

In this example, the data for the row in PERSON_TABLE is declared as variables in the DECLARE section, values are given to these variables in the BEGIN section, and a simple INSERT is done to add the new row to the table. We have added an EXCEPTION section to check for duplicates, and if one is found, a quick listing is produced and processing ends. Be aware that once your program goes into the exception-handling routines, it does *not* return to the program. If you wanted to process more records, you would have to trap the errors by checking for them within the executable code, using a series of IF statements.

Now you probably want to know about **cursors**. Think of a cursor as a holding tank for a query. It is where the results of a single row returned from a query are kept. Once you have the data from a row, you can manipulate the row, use the data to update other tables, and so forth.

Suppose that once a week you have to produce data showing all the hours that students and staff have spent on various courses. You are not concerned about the exact courses, rather just the total hours.

In the programming world, there are a couple of considerations. First, in general you do not store data in a table when that data can be calculated from other columns. So, you would not store a column called Total Hours in the PERSON table because you already have a column called Hours in the COURSE table, right? To get the total hours for a person, or all hours for a certain time period, you would just query the COURSE table.

Sometimes, however, some information might be needed by several programs, or the information might be exported to another system. Suppose that one department wanted you to provide the total hours so that they could chart staff development trends. Another department might want the same information to predict training requirements. Another might want to calculate training costs. They all want the same basic information, but in different reports, and perhaps at different times.

Here's where it gets interesting. If it makes no difference when the data is pulled, you can simply use the same code in various programs. However, if it does make a difference when the data is pulled—for example, suppose they all want the data at 9:00 AM on Friday—then you may want to pull the data and put it into a **temporary table**. This is often done when statistical reporting is necessary and timelines are crucial. By *temporary table,* I mean a working table that is refreshed periodically. The next example will show you how to use a cursor to update TEMP_PERSON_TABLE with the total hours for each person. Once TEMP_PERSON_TABLE has been updated, other scripts can use the data for reporting, exporting, or anything else.

TEMP_PERSON_TABLE has three columns: TEMP_PERSON_ID, TOTAL_HOURS, and DATE. The date is the current system date.

As usual, I'll attempt to show you several things at once. To start, take a look at the two tables we'll be working with. We're starting with 20 entries in COURSE_TABLE and 4 entries in PERSON_TABLE:

COURSE_TABLE

```
SQL> select person_id, hours
from course_table
  2  order by person_id;

PERSON_ID        HOURS
-----            -----
111111111          7
111111111         24.3
111111111         24.3
111111111         24.3
111111111          7
111111111          7
222222222         18
222222222          9
222222222         18
222222222         18
222222222          9
222222222          9
333333333         20
333333333         15
333333333         20
333333333         20
333333333         15
333333333         15
444444444         18
444444444         15
444444444         18
444444444         15
444444444         18
444444444         15
```

PERSON_TABLE

```
SQL> select person_id, name
from person_table;

PERSON_ID   NAME
-----       -------
111111111   Harry Gould
222222222   Nancy Stankov
333333333   Damian Stern
444444444   John Turin
```

Now follow this logic. We want a **temporary work table** that will have just the total hours for each person (temporary in the sense that it is only valid at a certain point in time).

What we have to do is first clean out anything in the temporary work table, create it with entries for the four employees in the PERSON table, and then calculate the total hours for each employee and update the employee record. We'll do all this using two scripts, where one script will drop, create, and load the person IDs into TEMP_PERSON_TABLE, and then call a second script that will run a cursor to load the table with the hours.

Here's our first script:

```
/*  This script is used in this chapter and has two parts.
    In the first part, we show you how to drop and then create
    TEMP_PERSON_TABLE, followed by loading the table with data.

    Part two runs a script that updates TEMP_PERSON_TABLE
    with the total hours per person.

*/
```

❶ First drop the table.

```
/*  First DROP the table just in case it exists  */ ❶


DROP TABLE TEMP_PERSON_TABLE;
COMMIT;
```

❷ Then create it.

```
/*  Now CREATE the working table   */ ❷

CREATE TABLE TEMP_PERSON_TABLE   (
PERSON_ID           NUMBER(12),
HOURS               NUMBER(9,2),
RUN_DATE            DATE
)
;
```

❸ Now insert the person_IDs from the PERSON table.

```
/* Now insert a row for every person in PERSON_TABLE ❸
```

```
    Take a close look at how this is being done. Notice that all
    we want are PERSON_ID instances in the table, so we use some
    fancy SQL to take the person IDs from PERSON_TABLE.

*/

INSERT INTO TEMP_PERSON_TABLE

(PERSON_ID) (SELECT PERSON_ID FROM PERSON_TABLE)

;


/*  Finally, run the cursor script to update the total hours for
each person.

NOTE - and this is important - that we run this script from the
C: drive.
You can move this script anywhere; just change the location
in the line below.

*/

@C:\CHAPTER3_SCRIPTS\CHAPTER3_CURSOR_SCRIPT.SQL ❹
```

❹ This command runs another script.

Once TEMP_PERSON_TABLE has become available, the second script runs, and here is where the cursor logic is used:

```
/* ----------------------------------
--
--  This script is an example of using PL/SQL to update rows
--  in one table from data in another table.
--
--  It is used in this chapter and is the second part of the
--  script that drops and creates the TEMP_PERSON_TABLE.
--
```

❶ Point to a file for your output.

❷ Sometimes when you code you have to do some debugging. The dbms_output shown below is a good tool. To enable it, you must first set the server output on.

❸ Increasing the buffer gives you more space for the dbms_output lines.

❹ The DECLARE section has the variables . . .

❺ . . . and the CURSOR definition. Here the cursor is called COURSE_TAKEN_CURSOR, and rows are retrieved from COURSE_TABLE and put into a holding area called COURSE_DATA, which has been defined as ROWTYPE data from the cursor. All the columns in the row go into the COURSE_DATA line, one row at a time. The forthcoming FETCH command actually gets the rows. (Yes, you can have more than one cursor in the DECLARE section.) Read on.

❻ The area where the actual processing takes place starts with BEGIN. The word BEGIN is mandatory.

```
--  Included are programming examples of the dbms_output command,
--  creating a cursor, processing first and last records, and
--  updating TEMP_PERSON_TABLE after calculating all the hours
--  for a given person ID.
--
--  There are several ways this could have been done. I wanted
--  to show you the power of PL/SQL, and I hope that you will
--  now go to some of the many excellent reference books
--  available.
--
------------------------------------
*/
spool c:\cursor.lst     ❶

set echo on;
set serveroutput on;     ❷
set buffer (1000000);     ❸

DECLARE          ❹

          XCOUNTER            NUMBER(1);
            OLD_PERSON_ID      NUMBER(9);
            NEW_PERSON_ID      NUMBER(9);
            XHOURS             NUMBER(6,2);
            IN_HOURS           NUMBER(6,2);

      CURSOR ❺
    COURSE_TAKEN_CURSOR     IS
    SELECT * from COURSE_TABLE          Order by PERSON_ID;

    COURSE_DATA  COURSE_TAKEN_CURSOR%ROWTYPE;
BEGIN   ❻
```

❼ The first step in processing is to open the cursor and initialize variables.

❽ LOOP means that we will now start processing rows of data using all the logic between LOOP and END LOOP.

❾ The FETCH command retrieves a row of data from the table. Notice that we have an EXIT command. EXIT tells the system to exit out of the processing loop when there aren't any more records. %NOTFOUND is a system-generated attribute of cursors.[1]

❿ The dbms_output.put_line( ) command prints whatever you put in the parentheses. It is a good debugging tool.

⓫ XCOUNTER indicates when the first record is read. You have to do some special processing with the first record, in this case move the person_ID into both the old and new person_ID variables. You need these variables to know when the new row retrieved does not have the same person_ID as the previous row because the COURSE table will have multiple entries for each person. XCOUNTER is set to 1 for the first row

```
OPEN COURSE_TAKEN_CURSOR;  ❼

XCOUNTER := 0;

   XHOURS := 0;

LOOP   ❽

    FETCH COURSE_TAKEN_CURSOR INTO COURSE_DATA; ❾
    EXIT WHEN COURSE_TAKEN_CURSOR%NOTFOUND;
    NEW_PERSON_ID := COURSE_DATA.PERSON_ID;

--dbms_output.put_line('Fetch person is  ' || course_data.
person_id); ❿

--dbms_output.put_line('Fetch hours  is  ' ||
course_data.hours);

    IF XCOUNTER = 0      ⓫
        Then XCOUNTER := 1;
        Old_Person_ID := Course_DATA.person_ID;
        New_Person_ID := Course_DATA.person_id;
      ELSE
        XCOUNTER := 2;
      END IF;

      IF XCOUNTER = 1
        THEN
          GOTO get_the_hours;
      END IF;
```

processed. All other rows will set XCOUNTER to 2.

⓬ We're giving you quite a bit with this UPDATE section. The important thing to understand is that what we're doing is updating the PERSON_TABLE rows with the total hours for each person.

⓭ After the row has been updated, set the variables back to zero.

⓮ GET_THE_HOURS is a "paragraph" that GOTO referred to earlier.

⓯ You must end with these commands. If you use a cursor, you have to close it. The same is true if you use a loop. And you need the END; and the period. Notice the final UPDATE section, which handles the last row. Remember that we told the system to exit when there weren't any more records? If we just exit, we won't do the final update for the last row we processed.

⓰ The final slash ("/") tells the SQL editor to go ahead and run the script. Without the final slash, the script would be loaded into memory but it would not execute.

⓱ Finally it is good practice to close your spool file.

```
      IF NEW_PERSON_ID = OLD_PERSON_ID
        THEN
          GOTO  get_the_hours;
      END IF;
⓬

    UPDATE TEMP_PERSON_TABLE
          SET HOURS = XHOURS,
          RUN_DATE = SYSDATE
         Where
           TEMP_PERSON_TABLE.PERSON_ID =  OLD_PERSON_ID;


         XHOURS := 0;     ⓭
         OLD_PERSON_ID := NEW_PERSON_ID;


 <<GET_THE_HOURS>>     ⓮
       XHOURS := XHOURS + COURSE_DATA.HOURS;

END LOOP;   ⓯
  UPDATE  TEMP_PERSON_TABLE
            SET HOURS = XHOURS,
            RUN_DATE = SYSDATE
          Where
            TEMP_PERSON_TABLE.PERSON_ID =  OLD_PERSON_ID;
CLOSE COURSE_TAKEN_CURSOR;
END;
.
/ ⓰
spool off; ⓱
```

----

1. There are four such attributes: (1) %ROWCOUNT gives the number of rows returned so far. (2) %NOTFOUND signals that there aren't any more rows to get. (3) %FOUND means that a row has been returned into the cursor. (4) %ISOPEN means that the cursor has been opened. You get an error if you try to open an already opened cursor. This is a way to check for an open cursor.

The preceding example contains a lot of code. This example has shown how to use one script to call another, how to drop, create, and load a table, and how to use a cursor. At first look, the scripts might appear complicated and somewhat unique. And they are a little strange to anyone who is starting to learn PL/SQL, so don't be dismayed. You're not expected to get it all at once. Rather, as I have said, take this example, get yourself a good book on SQL, PL/SQL, and SQL*Plus, and start coding.

I suggest that you start with this basic script, add another CURSOR section and some exception processing, and then take a look at creating procedures from your SQL and PL/SQL scripts. There's an enormous amount to learn, but just take it one step at a time and you'll be successful!

These scripts are on the CD that accompanies this book, so copy them and make your modifications. What you want to see is the successful message at the end:

```
.
.
.
                 THEN
                    GOTO  get_the_hours;
           END IF;
           UPDATE  TEMP_PERSON_TABLE
                    SET TOTAL_HOURS = XHOURS,
                    RUN_DATE = SYSDATE
              Where temp_person_table.TEMP_PERSON_ID =
                    OLD_PERSON_ID;
              XHOURS := 0;
               Old_Person_Id := New_Person_Id;
                New_Person_Id := 0;
      <<GET_THE_HOURS>>
            XHOURS := XHOURS + COURSE_DATA.HOURS;
      END LOOP;
      CLOSE COURSE_TAKEN_CURSOR;
      END;

PL/SQL procedure successfully completed.
```

This example is meant to show you how English-like and intuitive SQL, SQL*Plus, and PL/SQL are. In coming chapters we will cover additional SQL*Plus and PL/SQL commands, but just cursorily so that you can start programming immediately.

We're not quite finished with this chapter. There are two more major topics—Oracle Forms and Oracle Reports—to cover, and I'll do so in fast, guerrilla fashion. You will be using these two Oracle tools in your career. I'll also give a quick overview of a couple of other important Oracle modules: Web DB and Data Warehousing.

There are a few other important concepts you should also know:

- **View**. A view is a customized presentation of a table or tables. Usually it does not contain all the columns in the parent tables. In the PERSON table example, a view might contain the Name and Total Hours. Because a view has its own name, the actual table names are hidden from the users.
- **Synonym**. A synonym is another name for a table, view, or other object. The idea is to create short, easily remembered names, or to hide the actual name, such as *Payroll Table*, from the end user.
- **Sequence**. This powerful Oracle tool automatically assigns the next unique numeric value to a column. This is a great feature when you want sequential numbers for a column. You specify the starting number and range, and then use `NEXT.VAL` when adding data. This will be clear in Chapter 9, where data is loaded into tables.
- **Database triggers**. Database triggers are activities that happen automatically when something happens to a table. For example, if a student charges a meal in the cafeteria, a trigger will cause the available balance in her account to be reduced. A **trigger** is really code that you create and is "fired" when a particular event happens. You'll see examples of triggers in Chapters 13 and 14.

Development Tools

Oracle Forms

Oracle Forms is part of what is now called Developer 6*i*. This is Oracle's tool for developing the GUI front end, or screens—what customers see on their client PCs. Behind the forms is the Oracle database, including all the tables, security, and so forth that you have already built. Forms is your tool for presenting the data to your clients in a graphical, friendly way.

With Developer 6*i*, Forms now has a pretty nifty wizard:

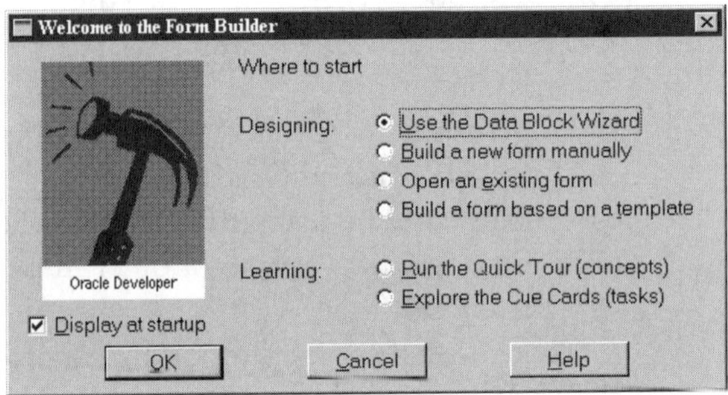

This wizard greatly streamlines the process of creating a good-looking screen. Here's an example of a simple screen, produced with the wizard, that shows each person in the STUDENT table, and automatically shows the first course that each person took by taking that information from the TEST_HISTORY table.

WINDOW1
Guerrilla Form
Person Id 111111111
Name Harry Gould
Person Id 111111111
Course Id 1
Grade 95.5
Hours 12.25

Some people have taken more than one course, but our example shows only the first one. Using Forms 6*i*, we are able, in a matter of a few seconds, to change the form to list ten courses at a time, so the screen now looks like this:

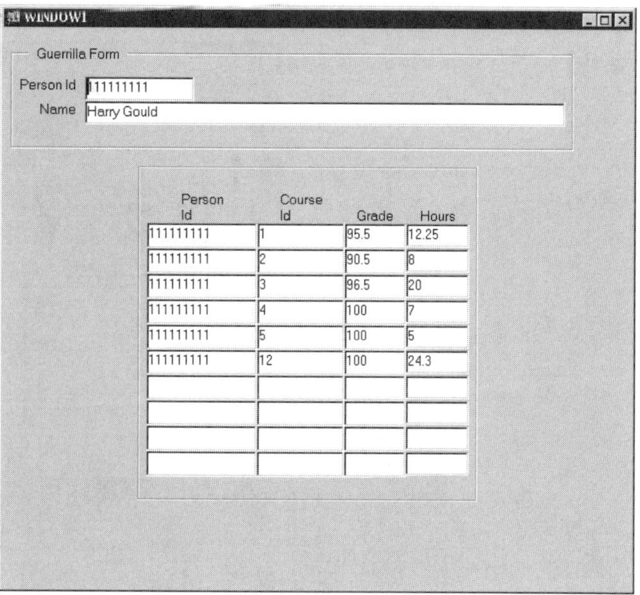

Look at Oracle Forms this way: It's your chance to show off your artistic talent, make your users happy, and have something unique to show for your efforts. Even more, with Oracle 8*i* and 9*i* and Developer 6*i*, you can now move your forms into the Web environment, giving you the best of the client/server world and the Web world.

Oracle Reports

Oracle Reports is your tool for publishing reports from your database. As with Oracle Forms, you can also deploy your reports over the Web. Along with being fully integrated with Oracle Web, Reports comes with quite a bit of pizzazz. Besides creating standard columnar or tabular reports, you can include charts and graphs using the Developer Graphics Builder. You also have several other powerful tools, such as Procedure Builder to add PL/SQL commands, and Query Builder to add queries from your database. Furthermore, you can easily turn your report files into XML (Extensible Markup Language) documents with a couple of quick, simple steps. And just as with Forms, you can add video, audio, or images to your report. Oracle Reports has taken us many steps beyond the old green-bar computer printouts that used to be delivered twice a day!

As with Forms, there is a wizard to assist:

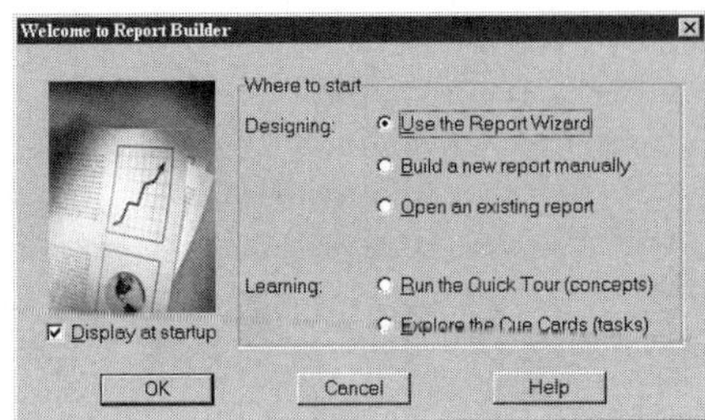

Here's a report we created in just a couple of minutes using the wizard:

Guerrilla Sample Report

Report run on: May 18, 2002 9:53 AM

Person Id	Course Id	Grade	Hours	Name
333333333	2	72.5	18	Damian Stern
444444444	2	67.5	18	Damian Stern
222222222	3	82.25	20	Damian Stern
333333333	3	71.25	20	Damian Stern
444444444	3	100	20	Damian Stern
444444444	4	100	15	Damian Stern
333333333	4	100	15	Damian Stern
222222222	4	100	9	Damian Stern
111111111	4	100	7	Damian Stern
111111111	5	100	5	Damian Stern
111111111	12	100	24.3	Damian Stern
222222222	12	100	20	Damian Stern
333333333	12	100	32	Damian Stern
111111111	1	95.5	12.25	John Turin
111111111	2	90.5	8	John Turin
111111111	3	96.5	20	John Turin
222222222	1	98.5	8	John Turin
333333333	1	82.5	8	John Turin
444444444	1	100	8	John Turin
222222222	2	81.5	18	John Turin
333333333	2	72.5	18	John Turin
444444444	2	67.5	18	John Turin
222222222	3	82.25	20	John Turin
333333333	3	71.25	20	John Turin
444444444	3	100	20	John Turin
444444444	4	100	15	John Turin
333333333	4	100	15	John Turin
222222222	4	100	9	John Turin
111111111	4	100	7	John Turin
111111111	5	100	5	John Turin
111111111	12	100	24.3	John Turin
222222222	12	100	20	John Turin
333333333	12	100	32	John Turin
Total:			**1222.2**	
Average:		**91.925**		
80	**80**			

If we wanted to send out this report as an XML, HTML (HyperText Markup Language), or other type of file, we would just select **File | Generate to File**:

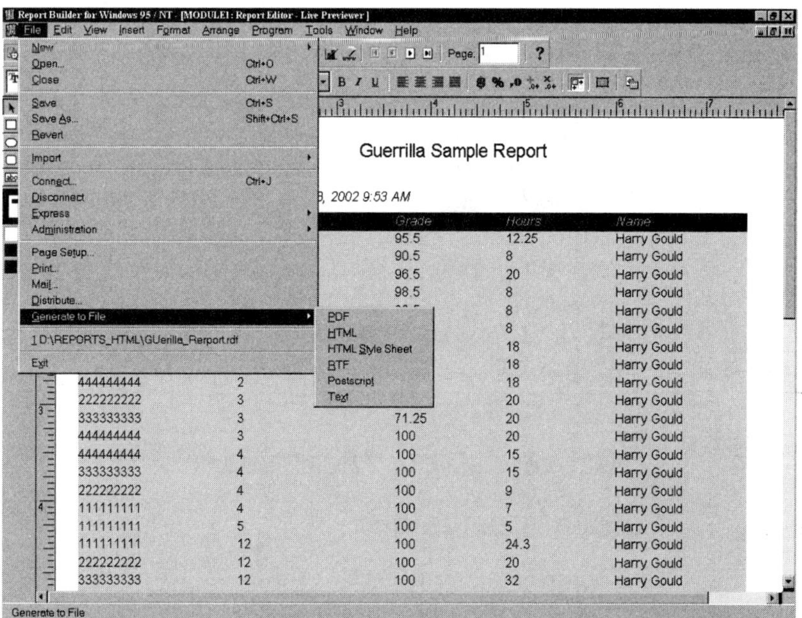

And here's what the report looks like in a browser:

C:\MODULE1.htm - Microsoft Internet Explorer

Address C:\MODULE1.htm

Guerrilla Sample Report

Report run on: May 18, 2002 10:05 AM

Person Id	Course Id	Grade	Hours	Name
111111111	1	95.5	12.25	Harry Gould
111111111	2	90.5	8	Harry Gould
111111111	3	96.5	20	Harry Gould
222222222	1	98.5	8	Harry Gould
333333333	1	82.5	8	Harry Gould
444444444	1	100	8	Harry Gould
222222222	2	81.5	18	Harry Gould
333333333	2	72.5	18	Harry Gould
444444444	2	67.5	18	Harry Gould
222222222	3	82.25	20	Harry Gould
333333333	3	71.25	20	Harry Gould
444444444	3	100	20	Harry Gould
444444444	4	100	15	Harry Gould
333333333	4	100	15	Harry Gould
222222222	4	100	9	Harry Gould
111111111	4	100	7	Harry Gould
111111111	5	100	5	Harry Gould
111111111	12	100	24.3	Harry Gould
222222222	12	100	20	Harry Gould
333333333	12	100	32	Harry Gould

Done | My Computer

There are some good reference materials available; please take a look at them. For now, I hope that I've gotten you interested in the power of Oracle Reports.

Oracle Web

Oracle Web is now part of Oracle's integration philosophy. Instead of offering its Web capabilities as a stand-alone product, Oracle now bundles them with its 9*i*AS server. The 9*i*AS is truly a middle-tier product that includes the Apache server and automatically gives you the Oracle Forms and Reports servers.

In Chapters 13 and 15 I will take your database and Forms efforts out to the Web and show you how to use the power of the 9*i*AS product. I think you'll be impressed. It is the crowning touch for the system that we're going to build in the next chapters. (No matter how hard things may get from time to time in this book, don't give up. You will have an impressive system to show off at the end!)

Other Oracle Modules

Data Warehousing

Data warehousing is one of those concepts that we can easily picture, but we may start to tremble when we hear terms like *artificial intelligence*, *architectures*, and *nonvolatile*. Putting all the mathematics and buzzwords aside, a *data warehouse* is a database that is designed not so much for user input and transaction processing, but rather for analysis.

Another way to look at it would be to think of what the research arm of your organization needs versus what the accounting arm needs. Even though it's all the same data, the two departments seek different information from it. The researchers don't really care that you've purchased five cartons of read/write CD-ROMs. They are interested in how many employees use the on-line and Web-based systems that you have created versus the old mainframe systems. Their job is to analyze and make projections. Members of the accounting department, however, do want to know how many boxes you purchased, what your budget code is, and who gets paid. They're not so interested in the wonderful screens and Web sites that you have developed. Their job is to balance the books.

A data warehouse usually has quite a bit of historical information, and often it runs in its own environment (on its own server). What makes the data warehouse distinct from being just a repository of transactions is that the data undergoes some kind of analysis and integration.

Lest you think this is a simple task, actually designing and then building a data warehouse is a complex, time-consuming project. What we want to convey here is that Oracle has included data warehouse documentation with 8*i* and 9*i*—documentation that covers all the major parts that go into designing and building a data warehouse.

Wireless

Oracle 9*i*AS also includes Oracle's Wireless Edition technology, which is Oracle's entry into the blossoming e-commerce and wireless world. In general, Oracle Wireless has the tools to make any Web content available to any device by using XML to move data from any source and deliver it to any target. Using this technique, Oracle Wireless has the capability to allow wireless devices access to both Web and database applications.

In Chapter 7 you will see some general references to Oracle's Wireless products when we step you through installing the 9*i*AS server. Because wireless technology is a highly specialized subject right now, it is beyond the scope of this book. However, I want to alert you to the fact that Oracle does have such products available. We will not be installing the Wireless products with 9*i*AS, so you can rest easy!

Thin and Thick Clients

Let me sneak in one more important concept: the idea of **thin** and **thick clients.** The thin-client environment is the Web; the thick-client environment is the standard client/server world. However, what we're really talking about is *presentation.*

The databases themselves—and the programs, views, and so forth—are still RDBMSs, and all the rules for SQL, SQL*Plus, and PL/SQL apply. What the Web does is make the data available through a browser. You will see some examples later in this book; just be aware that behind the scenes is still the Oracle database, Oracle Server, and all the necessary programs, views, security, and so forth. Everyone thinks the Web makes things really easy. You and I know that it still takes a lot of work. In fact, the Web has added another piece of complexity, but I'm sure you're ready for it.

So fasten your seatbelts, ladies and gentlemen. Here we go!

Chapter 4

Business Opportunity

All computer system projects, such as the Oracle database project we're about to start, begin with a business opportunity. Someone who has identified a problem that may or may not be a good candidate for automation comes to you, looking for potential solutions.

Imagine that you have arranged to meet with the director of computer training, or the chair of the Computer Science department, or the coordinator for a large consulting firm. The meeting stems from a phone call you received two weeks ago about a problem with the training classes. On the phone you were told that many of the people taking the introductory class turned in rather poor evaluations, and your ideas for improvement are needed.

So the meeting starts, and being a good business analyst, you ask directly what the poor evaluations say. Is the problem a lack of equipment, mediocre instructors, a very difficult syllabus? The answer surprises you: The class was boring for many of the students! And it was boring because the students already knew the material, but this was a mandatory class; they had to attend.

This immediately gets you thinking. If the students know the material, the real issue is how to test them easily and let those who are adept move on to the next level of classes. You modestly present this idea, it is received very well, and you find yourself charged to produce the system immediately. Nothing like pressure!

Your first step is to find out what is covered in the introductory class. This means patiently talking to the instructors of both the introductory class and the class at the next level. You need to know what is covered in the intro class and what level of expertise is expected as a prerequisite for enrolling in the second-level class.

You find that the goal of the first-level, or intro, class is to teach the basics of computer concepts and office software, so that the students will be able to use word processing for papers, include graphs and graphics in reports, and use e-mail and the Internet. Armed with this information, you now start to probe for the level of expertise.

Should students be able to create complex word processing documents, formula-rich spreadsheets, and fantastic slide shows, or should they know just enough to get a term paper done, create simple graphs, and insert graphics when necessary? You go through this exercise several times as you clarify the types of questions you need to adequately test the student's knowledge. After repeated meetings with the educational staff, you have finally developed a list of questions that everyone agrees with. You think that now you can run back to your desk and start coding.

"Aha," one of the instructors says, "What about . . . ?" This is a phrase that strikes fear into a systems person's heart. Actually, when users start to ask questions like this, you are really moving into the next step of system design (that's what you've been doing so far without knowing it). Once you've clearly identified the business problem—and I mean clearly—you have to test your ideas against the real world. That's what the What about means.

"What about mixing up the questions?" "What about adding new questions?" "What about one person taking the test for someone else?" "What about seeing the scores on the 'Net'?" "What about someone taking the test over and over?" These are the real business questions that will help refine your system into something truly useful, and you must probe over and over until you have uncovered all such issues.

The rule here is to design carefully. It is very difficult to change the basic design once you've started building your database. A suggestion is to run your ideas past knowledgeable users, especially those who will be using your new system. Do not be critical: rather listen, listen, and listen more. Ask questions such as, "What problems do you currently have with testing students?" "How soon do you need to know the results?" "Would you like a report each morning, or would you want to run reports on demand?"

Although this is not a book on system design, let me share with you a "best practice." Find out what your customers expect to get out of the system. What reports do they want, what charts, graphs, and online information? How timely must the data be, and what will it be used for? Are there weekly or monthly cycles?

A good place to start is to see what the current output is—any reports, screens, and charts that your customers now have or always wanted to have. Take a close look at them and you will start to see the data elements that your customer needs. The more time you spend digging into their needs, the more complete your final system will be. This is, in effect, working from the output back. If you know what they must get out of the system, you can be pretty certain that you will be able to determine what has to go in to produce those results. Just look at the output from your system design and see if the data is contained somewhere in your tables or can easily be calculated. If not, then redo your design.

Now you have a list of questions, and you have the system specifications:

- It will run online as a series of screen-based questions.
- Students will be allowed to take each level only once.
- There will be a way to authorize and identify the student.
- The student will see the results immediately.
- There will be several different tests so that students cannot memorize the questions.
- Anyone on the teaching staff will be able to create tests and to add, delete, or modify questions.
- Questions are not really deleted; they are marked as inaccessible for tests. This feature is necessary for historical purposes.
- All changes to questions will have an audit trail.
- There will be checking against the student database to ensure that the right test is being given for the level of the student.
- The system will be Web-accessible.

- A record will be kept for every student taking each test, showing the question, answer, and score.
- As more tests are developed, a full history for each student will be available.
- Inquiries can be by date, test, students, or a particular student.
- Basic reports will be available to show the activity against the tests.
- Once a student starts the test and sees the first question, he or she cannot back out. Up to that point the student can decide without penalty not to take the test.

With the questions and the system parameters finalized, the next step is to determine the data that will be necessary.

Of the several possible starting points, the most obvious is to begin with the student information you will need. First make a list of the elements. It will look something like this:

First name
Middle initial
Last name
Student PIN number
Exam 1 date
Exam 1 score
Exam 1 name
Exam 1 start time
Exam 1 end time
Sex (M/F)
Age
Proficiency level (freshman, sophomore, etc.)
Question 1 exam 1
Student answer question 1 exam 1
Correct answer question 1 exam 1
Exam 1 author
Exam 1 create date

Looking at this list, we can identify the student; the date, time, and name of the exam; the exact questions; the student's answers; and the correct answers. We also know the age, sex, and proficiency level of the student. And we will have a complete record of every exam that the student takes. What could be better?

Take another look. There are a couple of obvious problems. If we build the table so that it can contain, say, 30 questions for each exam, and we have enough tables for 10 exams, what will happen when someone decides to have 35 or 50 questions on an exam? What if your program becomes so popular that it grows to 100 exams? Obviously we cannot constantly be modifying our tables, so we have to take another look.

Other Uses

Another use for this program would be a kiosk at a department store that would help people make decisions. For example, if a customer were looking for a washing machine, and there were 200 possible models on the floor, you could modify this program to ask the customer a series of questions: what the desired price range is; what features the customer wants; how many loads the customer expects to do each week; whether any heavy loads, such as horse blankets, will need to be done; and whether front or top loading is desired. Your program would then produce a list of in-stock and on-order models meeting the criteria, thereby helping the customer narrow down the choices.

Looking again at the list of elements needed, it is clear that there are a few major sections.

- **Student information:** name, age, and so forth.
- **Test information:** questions, answers, author, and so forth.
- **History:** the questions that the student actually had on a given day and the answers the student gave.

In other words, for a given student you must be able to show the exam, the questions on that exam, the student, and the correct answers. Then you might want to know who wrote the exam, when it was written, and perhaps how many students have taken it and what their scores were. So there are really three logical groups: student, test, and history.

What we have just done is the beginning of what's called **data normalization.** Yes, I've snuck normalization in on you, and you're still alive! To be completely honest, what we're doing right now is working to create the **First Normal Form,** which has the simple rule of identifying and splitting out any repeating groups. Bear with me; I think this will become clear as we go through the next couple of steps.

Now back to our example. We have taken a look at our one big record and identified and split out any repeating groups, such as the test and the test questions. The result is one table with student information and one table with test number information:

STUDENTS Table	**TEST TAKEN Table**
Student ID	Test Number
Student Name	Student ID
	Date Taken
	Start Time
	End Time
	Question 1
	Student Answer 1
	Correct Answer 1
	and so on.

The two tables are linked by Student ID. If the student takes another test, it is added to the TEST TAKEN table.

Following the same reasoning, we have to split out another repeating group, the questions, into its own table. Questions are not dependent on test number because the same questions may appear on more than one test. We do not want to have all the repeated questions listed over and over for each test a student takes. Instead, we will add a QUESTIONS table that has the detailed questions, and each question will have a test number linking it to the TEST TAKEN table. From there, we can follow Student ID back to the STUDENTS table:

STUDENTS Table	**TEST TAKEN Table**	**QUESTIONS Table**
Student ID	Student ID	Test Number
Student Name	Test Number	Question 1
Student Age	Date Taken	Answer 1
	Start Time	Answer 2
	End Time	Answer 3
	Score	Answer 4
		Correct Answer

Does this make sense?

There's an immediate problem here. We have created another set of repeating data! The problem is that the questions and answers will have to be repeated for every test. We need another table to link the tests and the questions. The First Normal Form continues!

STUDENTS Table	TEST TAKEN Table	TESTS Table	QUESTIONS Table
Student ID	Student ID	Test Number	Question ID
Student Name	Test Number	Created by	Question
Student Age	Date Taken	Date Created	Answer 1
State	Start Time	Question ID 1	Answer 2
	End Time	Question ID 2	Answer 3
	Score	Question ID 3	Answer 4
		Question ID 4	Correct Answer

Now we can link everything. The QUESTIONS table has each question identified by Question ID. Question ID links to the TESTS table, which has a list of the question IDs associated with each test. We can now link to the test that the student took, and then to the student information. Student ID gives us data on the student and links us to the TEST TAKEN table, which in turn links us to the TESTS table. From there we can get the detailed questions and answers from the QUESTIONS table.

What we've done is move the test number out of the QUESTIONS table into another table. Because the questions had nothing to do with Test Number, we've taken care of the **Second Normal Form**, removing a multivalued key. Look at it this way. The original keys in the QUESTIONS table were Test Number and Question. However, the questions and answers do not depend at all on Test Number, so the table was changed to separate the two.

In practice, you will do the First Normal and Second Normal forms over and over until you have eliminated repeating information from your tables and have made sure that all the data in each column depends entirely on the primary key. Notice below that we have made another change: We have put the answers into their own table. Why? Follow this thinking: If we design a table that has four answers to each question, we will have a problem when someone wants to have five answers.

Sketching Table Design

Do your table design as a series of simple sketches, such as the one shown here. It will be easier to see the relationships and duplicate data. And as many of you know, some of your best ideas will be your notes on a napkin over lunch:

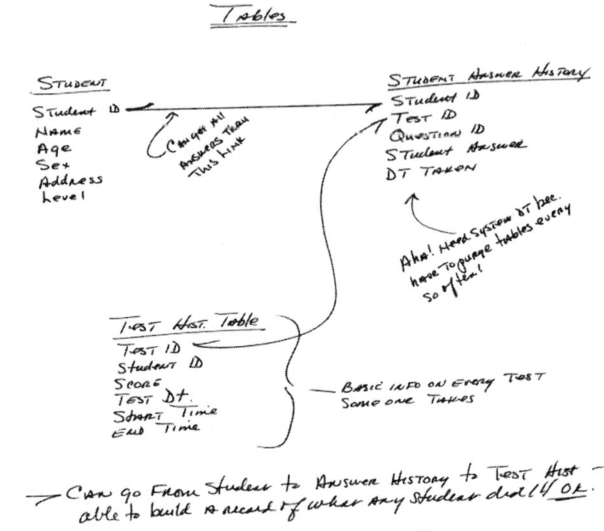

Here's what the tables for the waiver exam look like after several passes with First and Second Normal Forms:

STUDENTS Table
Student ID
Student Name
Student Age
Sex
Address
Student Level

TEST ID Table
Test ID
Test Name
Date Created
Author
Comments
Type ID
Type Description

TEST QUESTIONS LINK Table
Link Test ID
Link Question ID

QUESTIONS Table	ANSWERS Table
Question ID	Question ID
Question	Answer ID (answer #1 for the question)
Correct Answer	Answer (the actual answer for question #1)
	.
	.
	.
	(These rows repeat for all the answers for all the questions.)

STUDENT ANSWER HISTORY Table	TEST HISTORY Table
Student ID	Test ID
Test ID	Student ID
Question ID	Score
Student Answer	Date Taken
Date Taken	Start Time
	End Time

The final step, or **Third Normal Form**, is to go back to the TEST ID table. Type does *not* depend directly on the primary key, and if left in as is, it would cause an update nightmare. The student might take several tests of the same type, such as several SQL tests, and if the type description were changed, you would have to find every occurrence and change it. Instead, we build another table for Type that contains two columns:

TYPE	Table
Type	Code
Type	Description

There are many books on normalization, but they often scare people away. As a summation of the several favorite standards that are taught in universities, here's the gist of the first three normal forms:

1. **The First Normal Form** splits repeating groups. Failure to do so results in extremely large tables, update problems, and constant table modification.
2. **The Second Normal Form** states that each column in the table must depend entirely on the primary key. If this requirement is not enforced, there will be redundant data and problems with modification of the table.

3. **The Third Normal Form** is the rule that each column must depend directly on the primary key. A street address in the TEST TAKEN table, for example, would cause problems if the student moved. If the student had taken, say, 50 exams, moved, and asked that the results of all 50 tests be mailed to her, you would have to find and modify each of the 50 rows where there was an address for each test she took.

Normalization is done for several reasons, as you must have guessed by now:

1. We want to make logical arrangements of the data so that each group or table handles a homogeneous part of the entire database. Each table takes one section of data where the data logically go together.
2. One of the major goals of any relational database management system is to reduce data redundancy, and we have done that in the examples given. We could have included all the questions and answers over and over for each person taking the test, couldn't we? Instead, we devised a table schema and links that will give us the same information without having to repeat it.
3. The table should be built so that when it has to be modified, the change must be made in only one place. The QUESTIONS, ANSWERS, and TYPE tables are good examples.
4. Normalization helps ensure that we can easily access and manipulate the data without risking data integrity.

Tip

Here's a tip on building the tables, the next step. Use nonmeaningful primary keys. A simple sequential number is probably the easiest and best. If, for example, you create a student key that starts with C for computer courses, and your system then becomes expanded into other areas, the C prefix may become meaningless, and it may actually be a hindrance. As with every rule, however, there are logical exceptions. If you're building a system that already has a meaningful identifier, such as UPC code, then by all means use it!

To review, we have covered the first three steps of normalization. There are actually two more steps, but in practice, usually only the first three are used. The reason is that in many database designs, the first three steps will result in a good, practical, working schema. Going into the fourth and fifth normal forms just is usually not necessary.

In doing the first three forms, we have had to take a very close look at the data, the relationships between the data, and how we could build our tables in a logical and structured way.

Some of what you have to be familiar with before we move on to tables, the server, client, and programming are the concepts behind tables, such as rows and columns, relationships such as one to many, many to many, and many to one. These concepts were covered briefly in Chapter 3. For a much more complete discussion, I refer you to the many, many books on data normalization.

Chapter 5

Finalizing the Tables for the Waiver Exam

So far we've had a look at some of the basic SQL, SQL*Plus, and PL/SQL commands, and we've walked through some programming examples. And we've done all this using some basic business specs for a hypothetical waiver exam. Now it's time to start using the conceptual framework I've given you and come up with the actual table design, table relationships, and rules for our real objective, which is a useful, viable, and hopefully marketable waiver exam. From what you've been shown so far, you should be able to follow the steps as we get down to the nuts and bolts of these tasks.

We will be filling in the details of the tables we developed in Chapter 4, using the concepts of keys and relationships discussed in Chapter 3. We're also going to use several other Oracle constructs to build in data integrity that will help protect your database, so get ready to move into the world of constraints, foreign keys, and other such constructs that will ultimately make your life as an Oracle expert a little easier.

Once the tables are complete, we'll move away from them for a bit in the following three chapters while we build the server and establish our security schema. Then in Chapter 9 we'll be ready to take what we've done here and actually create the database tables. What we do here in Chapter 5 is the foundation for everything that follows. We must give a lot of care to our tables because they determine the success or failure of every other activity we do from this point forward.

Refining the Tables

When we left off in Chapter 4, we had defined eight tables (soon to be ten!) that we would need for our waiver exam database. Now our first step is to make sure we have all the items we will need for each table. Remember, these items are the *columns* of the tables; although we can add columns later, modify columns, and actually *drop* columns, it is really bad practice to have to make changes. Let's start with the STUDENTS table.

Chapter 4 defined just enough data elements so that we could do the data normalization necessary. However, suppose that you show your table design to some of the instructors, as a good database designer would, and their suggestion is to add a couple more items. The instructors want to know what department each student is in or, at a university level, what the student's major is. They believe that they'll be able to get some interesting demographic information once they have an operational database. This is the kind of thing researchers and marketing types are always looking for, and your proposed database is a natural. The instructors also mention that the TEST_HISTORY table should include the place where the test was taken, primarily for the sake of completeness.

As if this were not enough, the instructors tell you that they need to store the passing grade for each test. "Ah," you think, "simple." But then they say that sometimes the questions will have different weights. "Enough!" you think, as you take out another pencil to replace the one you just snapped. However, they show you the formula to use, and it becomes clear that all you have to do is add another column to each question on a particular test that will store the weight (with a default value of 1, since most exams are not weighted). As you're getting up to leave, another instructor stops you and asks the simple question: "When your system is done, can I get a list of all the questions by topic? Can I get all the ones for software or hardware or networking on a report? You know, things keep changing in the industry, and I want to make sure that what we ask is accurate and not outdated."

You go back to your office thinking that you now have a couple of important changes to make: You need to be able to give them the report by type of question, and you have to store information on place, passing grade, and weight. The last three are easy, so you sit at your terminal and make some changes, and the tables now look like this:

STUDENTS Table	TEST_HISTORY Table
Student_ID	Test_ID
F_Name	Student_ID
M_I	Score
L_Name	Date_Taken
SSNum	Start_Time
B_Date	End_Time
Sex	Location
Street1	
Street2	
Town	
State	
Country	
Zip	
Level	
Date_Created	
Created_By	
Department_Major	
Email	

You have to add the Passing Grade and Weight columns to two tables: TEST_ID and TEST_QUESTIONS_LINK. Fine; that's easy:

TEST_ID Table	TEST_QUESTIONS_LINK Table
Test_ID	
Test_Name	
Date_Created	Link_Test_ID
Author	Link_Question_ID
Comments	Weight
Type_ID	
Passing_Grade	
Time_Limit	

What about the type of question? What did the instructor mean when she asked for "a list of all the questions by topic"? Let's see; she wanted a report by type of question—that is, all the questions on a certain topic. So we need a way to mark each question with its "type" as well as to get a description of that type. Think back to normalization in Chapter 4. We automatically want to put Type and the Type_Desc with each question, right? Well, let's just add two columns: Question_Type and Type_Desc.

But wait a minute! Think about the nightmare that will be created when you want to change the description. You will have to go into every row in the QUESTIONS table and make the change! Instead, we do two things: (1) create a small table that has two columns—Question_Type and Question_Type_Desc—and then (2) add the Question_Type column to the QUESTIONS table. Anytime you need to report on the types of questions, you will just read the QUESTIONS table and link to the QUESTION_TYPE_DESC table. Because no other changes are necessary to handle question type, grade, location, and weight, all other tables stay as they are:

TEST_TYPE_DESC Table
Type_ID
Type_Desc

QUESTIONS Table
Question_ID
Question
Correct_Answer
Question_Type
Date_Created
Author_ID

ANSWERS Table
Answer_Question ID
Answer_ID (answer #1 for the question)
Answer (actual answer for question #1)
.
.
.
(These rows repeat for all the answers for each question.)

QUESTIONS_TYPE_DESC Table
Question_Type
Question_Type_Desc

STUDENT_ANSWER_HISTORY Table
Student_ID
Test_ID
Question_ID
Student_Answer

At the beginning of this chapter I told you that our eight tables would soon be ten. So now that we've added table nine, the QUESTION_TYPE_DESC table, what is the tenth one? If any of you caught the problem, congratulations!

It is a simple oversight, and I purposely waited until now to correct it. My thought was that it would make more sense to you at this point, where we've already covered normalization and preliminary table column definitions. What was missed in Chapter 4 was the fact that *one person can author more than one test*. See the break in normalization? We do not want to repeat the person's name over and over. Instead, we need a small AUTHORS table with just two entries—an identifier and the author's name:

AUTHORS Table
Author_ID
Author

The significance is that this will become one of the base tables that another table is dependent on.

Note

By leaving out the AUTHORS table until now, I hope to have taught you to be very aware that table design and data normalization are difficult. In almost every case, these processes mean going over and over the tables and matching them against the real application. And even after you start building your tables, you may suddenly realize that something is missing—be it a column, table, or link. Now is the time to make the change!

Data and Relationships

With the inclusion of our tenth table, we can be sure we have now taken care of all the information that our customers will need from the system. The next big step is to do a little abstract analysis on the logical way the tables will work in the real world. There are two things to consider: (1) what kind of data we want in the tables and (2) how the tables are related. In other words, it's OK to define ten tables according to established normalization principles, and you may get looks of admiration for doing so, but what does that mean in the real world?

On the second point, can we just start throwing data into the tables, or is there a natural rhyme and reason to the structure? Should some data exist before other data is entered, or don't we care? On the first point (the type of data), do we care if any data is entered anywhere, or are we expecting numbers in some places, letters in others? Is some data mandatory? Does it make any difference how long the columns are? These are the two major issues we will be addressing in this chapter.

Data

For those of you with programming background, or anyone with any kind of analytical experience—whether with respect to handling foreign currency, working on the Human Genome Project, or cataloging books in a library—you know that data has to be classified in some way for it to be useful, and for you to be able to find it when necessary. If data is left undefined, it may or may not behave the way you expect it to when you run it through your database programs.

In relational databases we can use certain standard definitions to classify data. These classifications are defined for the columns, and all rows of data entered for the columns must adhere to the definitions or there will be an automatic error. This means that we can use the built-in integrity features to help edit our data, thus eliminating much of the tedious editing that would have to be done.

Several standard data formats are commonly used. Others exist, but for our purposes the following will be more than adequate:

- **CHAR.** Used for fixed-length character strings (maximum length 255).
- **VARCHAR2.** Used for variable-length character strings (maximum length 2,000).
- **NUMBER.** Self-explanatory (maximum 38 digits).
- **DATE.** Self-explanatory (4712 B.C. to A.D. 4712).
- **TIME.** Self-explanatory. The default is "HH24:MI".

What's a **string**? It is any group of things, such as an address, a phone number, all the letters in this chapter, and so forth. For a mixture of letters and numbers, always use CHAR and VARCHAR2. For pure numeric strings, such as Social Security number, including any signs (plus, minus, etc.), use the NUMBER format. We'll cover more about strings later in the book.

DATE provides information about a date. The default format is *DD-MON-YY*. Dates are usually enclosed in single quotes—'09-Aug-01'—and the default is the system date.

Note

As a quick refresher, go back to Chapter 3 and study up on keys and constraints. We will be using them in the steps outlined here.

Let's define the data we want to capture, starting with the two question tables:

QUESTIONS Table	QUESTIONS_TYPE_DESC Table
Question_ID	Question_Type
Question	Questions_Type_Desc
Correct_Answer	
Question_Type	
Date_Created	
Author_ID	

Note

Here's a quick refresher. Remember that Chapter 4 talked about keeping things simple and clear? We use the Question_Type column instead of trying to put everything into the Question_ID column because this makes it much easier to find a group of like questions, and we do not run the risk of running out of positions to use. Making every position mean something is a good idea for table names, but not for keys. So don't try to cram too much information into your columns. Keep your major columns simple, and if at all possible, use ascending numerics. We will use a simple numeric ID, and we'll use another numeric column for the question type.

We know that in the QUESTIONS table, Question_ID must be unique or we'll have chaos. The Question and Correct_Answer columns will contain alphanumerics, and Question_Type will contain a numeric. In the QUESTIONS_ TYPE_DESC table, Question_Type must be unique because we want only one entry per type, and the Questions_Type_Desc field will contain free-form alphanumerics.

Our first pass at defining the tables looks like this:

QUESTIONS Table		QUESTIONS_TYPE_DESC Table	
Question_ID	NUMBER(6)	Question_Type	NUMBER(6)
Question	VARCHAR2(40)	Questions_Type_Desc	VARCHAR2(40)
Correct_Answer	VARCHAR2(2)		
Question_Type	NUMBER(6)		
Date_Created	DATE		
Author_ID	NUMBER(9)		

In our second pass, let's make the two important columns unique, and let's make the system check whether data is entered. What we'll do is use the null constraint and the uniqueness constraint. `NOT NULL` means that data has to be entered or there will be an error; `UNIQUE` means that we cannot have duplicate entries for either Question_ID or Question_Type. The system will do all this editing for us!

Using the same concepts of uniqueness and not null, we can define the columns for the remaining tables:

TEST_ID Table

Test_ID	NUMBER(6)	NOT NULL, UNIQUE
Test_Name	VARCHAR2(40)	NOT NULL
Date_Created	DATE	NOT NULL
Author	NUMBER(6)	
Comments	VARCHAR2(30)	
Type_ID	NUMBER(6)	NOT NULL
Passing_Grade	NUMBER(2)	NOT NULL
Time_Limit	NUMBER(4,2)	NOT NULL

TEST_QUESTIONS_LINK Table

Link_Test_ID	NUMBER(6)	
Link_Question_ID	NUMBER(6)	
Weight	NUMBER(2,1)	DEFAULT 1
UNIQUE(Test_ID, Question_ID)[a]		

AUTHORS Table

Author_ID	NUMBER(6)
Author	VARCHAR2(40)

TEST_TYPE_DESC Table

Type_ID	NUMBER(6)	UNIQUE, NOT NULL
Type_Desc	VARCHAR2(30)	NOT NULL

ANSWERS Table

Answer_Question_ID	NUMBER(6)	UNIQUE
Answer_ID	VARCHAR2(2)	NOT NULL
Answer	VARCHAR2(30)	NOT NULL

STUDENTS Table

Student_ID	NUMBER(9)	UNIQUE, NOT NULL
F_Name	VARCHAR2(15)	NOT NULL
M_I	VARCHAR2(1)	
L_Name	VARCHAR2(15)	NOT NULL
SSNum	NUMBER(9)	NOT NULL
B_Date	DATE	
Sex	VARCHAR2(1)	
Street1	VARCHAR2(15)	
Street2	VARCHAR2(15)	
Town	VARCHAR2(20)	
State	VARCHAR2(2)	
Country	VARCHAR2(2)	
Zip	NUMBER(5)	
Student_Level	NUMBER(6)	NOT NULL
Date_Created	DATE	
Created_By	VARCHAR2(20)	
Department_Major	VARCHAR2(10)	NOT NULL
Email	VARCHAR2(60)	

TEST_HISTORY Table

Test_ID	NUMBER(6)	NOT NULL
Student_ID	NUMBER(9)	NOT NULL
Score	NUMBER(3)	NOT NULL
Date_Taken	DATE	NOT NULL
Start_Time	VARCHAR2(8)	NOT NULL
End_Time	VARCHAR2(8)	NOT NULL
Location	VARCHAR2(15)	NOT NULL

STUDENT_ANSWER_HISTORY Table

Student_ID	NUMBER(9)	NOT NULL
Test_ID	NUMBER(6)	NOT NULL
Question_ID	NUMBER(6)	NOT NULL
Student_Answer	VARCHAR2(2)	default 0[b]

a. Notice how we made a unique key out of two columns. In this table it makes sense because the same test should not have the same question more than once. This ensures the integrity of the table.
b. Be aware that we have to program for those students who skip questions or don't finish the test. If we made the default `NOT NULL`, the record could not be saved if the student skipped a question, so we just set the answer to "0", which is invalid because by design, all answers have to be in the range of 1 to 4.

Let's keep going with our constraints. We want to introduce the concepts of a primary key and the check constraint. Further, the check constraint will let us talk about logical operators. And believe me, all these things will ultimately make your life easier!

A **primary key** is a column or columns that will be unique for each row in a table. (By definition, a primary key cannot be null, so you do not have to specify `NOT NULL` for the primary key columns.) Think of the primary key as the best way to identify a table, as that thing that makes the table easy to identify. In many, if not most, cases the primary key will be the column called "Something ID." Tables do *not* have to have a primary key. A history table, for example, is a repository of transactions, and we can simply make the transaction number or another column unique. In almost all cases, you will want your primary keys to be unique and not null.

One way to make the primary keys unique and also speed up processing is to use an **index**. An index operates in the same way as the index in this book: It helps find data quickly. Otherwise, Oracle would have to search every column when doing a query. (Yes, you can create an index for any column, up to 16 columns per table—and there may be times when this is good practice. In the history table mentioned in the preceding paragraph, you might want to create an index for the transaction date, as well as the transaction number, because both will be used extensively for data retrieval. More on this later.)

An index is an *optional feature* you set for a column(s) *after* the table has been created. There are two types of indexes: unique and nonunique. When you use the `CREATE INDEX` command, you can specify whether the index is unique. In the absence of that specification, a nonunique index is created.

OK, what have we learned so far? Remember back in the discussion of normalization in Chapter 4, where we worked through the Third Normal Form and made sure that all the columns in a table were directly dependent on a primary key? Well, a primary key is not just a concept. We can actually make columns into a primary key and, using various constraints, make it unique and not null. Further, we can create a unique index for the primary key column, speeding up processing and preventing duplicates.

Now let's take a look at **logical operators**. A logical operator is a way of asking Oracle to determine whether a particular piece of data fits a certain criterion. For example, we can say

```
salary number(9,2) check (salary between 50000 and 1000000)
```

and the system will automatically edit any inserts or updates and make sure that any salary entered is between $50,000 and $1 million.

Table 5.1 lists the logical operators.

Table 5.1 Logical Operators

Operator	Meaning
=	Equal to
!= or ^= or < >	Not equal to
>	Greater than
>=	Greater than or equal to
<	Less than
<=	Less than or equal to
(NOT) BETWEEN a and b	(Self-explanatory)
IS (NOT) NULL	(Self-explanatory)
(NOT) LIKE	(Self-explanatory); for example, `LIKE %abc%` returns anything with *abc* in it
IN	Usually used for a list—for example, IN ('CT', 'MA')

Another feature that is not a constraint, but may be helpful, is that we can add a default attribute to a column. For example, when the student logs on to the system and is asked to enter identifying information, the Location field can default to something like "Main Computer Lab" if this is where most, if not all, of the testing will take place. If we had a field such as `Veteran`? and the U.S. Navy bought this system, we could change the `Veteran`? default to "Yes". Got the idea?

Now we're going to go through the tables once again, adding the constraints we just talked about. We want to add primary keys and logical operators where applicable. Let's take a look at the STUDENTS table. This will set the example for the other tables. The key, naturally, is Student_ID. We want it to be unique and not null. However, later we will create an index for this column, so all we have to say now is that it is the primary key and not null.

We can qualify the Sex field by using the `check` constraint and saying:

```
Sex VARCHAR2(1) check (sex IN 'M', 'F', 'm', 'f')
```

We can get around having to specify both upper- and lowercase through programming, but this is a good example of the `IN` operator with the `check` constraint.

Here's how the modified STUDENTS and TEST_HISTORY tables now look:

STUDENTS Table

Student_ID	NUMBER(9)	PRIMARY KEY[a]
F_Name	VARCHAR2(15)	NOT NULL
M_I	VARCHAR2(1)	
L_Name	VARCHAR2(15)	NOT NULL
SSNum	NUMBER(9)	NOT NULL
B_Date	DATE	
Sex	VARCHAR2(1)	check (sex IN 'M', 'F', 'm', 'f')
Street1	VARCHAR2(15)	
Street2	VARCHAR2(15)	
Town	VARCHAR2(20)	
State	VARCHAR2(2)	
Country	VARCHAR2(2)	
Zip	NUMBER(5)	
Student_Level	NUMBER(6)	NOT NULL
Date_Created	DATE	
Created_By	VARCHAR2(20)	
Department_Major	VARCHAR2(10)	NOT NULL
Email	VARCHAR2(60)	

TEST_HISTORY Table

Test_ID	NUMBER(6)	NOT NULL
Student_ID	NUMBER(9)	NOT NULL
Score	NUMBER(3)	NOT NULL
Date_Taken	DATE	NOT NULL
Start_Time	VARCHAR2(8)	NOT NULL
End_Time	VARCHAR2(8)	NOT NULL
Location	VARCHAR2(15)	NOT NULL

a. In Oracle, a primary key is always assumed to be NOT NULL.

Note

Later, when we show you how to create a table, you will see that Oracle has certain rules. If you use only one column for a primary key, then you can say "primary key" in the column attributes, as in the STUDENTS table above. When you use more than one column, the primary key becomes a table constraint and must be defined at the end of the CREATE TABLE command. You'll see this in a couple of chapters when your tables come to life.

Here are the rest of our tables after we've added the latest round of constraints:

QUESTIONS Table

Question_ID	NUMBER(6)	PRIMARY KEY
Question	VARCHAR2(40)	NOT NULL
Correct_Answer	VARCHAR2(2)	NOT NULL
Question_Type	NUMBER(6)	NOT NULL
Date_Created	DATE	
Author_ID	NUMBER(9)	NOT NULL

QUESTIONS_TYPE_DESC Table

Question_Type	NUMBER(6)	PRIMARY KEY
Questions_Type_Desc	VARCHAR2(40)	NOT NULL

TEST_ID Table

Test_ID	NUMBER(6)	PRIMARY KEY
Test_Name	VARCHAR2(40)	NOT NULL
Date_Created	DATE	NOT NULL
Author	NUMBER(9)	
Comments	VARCHAR2(30)	
Type_ID	NUMBER(6)	NOT NULL
Passing_Grade	NUMBER(2)	NOT NULL
Time_Limit	NUMBER(4,2)	NOT NULL

TEST_QUESTIONS_LINK Table

Link_Test_ID	NUMBER(6)	
Link_Question_ID	NUMBER(6)	
UNIQUE (Test-ID, Question_ID)		
Weight	NUMBER(2,1)	default 1
PRIMARY KEY (Test_ID, Question_ID)		

AUTHORS Table

Author_ID	NUMBER(9)
Author	VARCHAR2(60)

TEST_TYPE_DESC Table

Type_ID	NUMBER(6)	PRIMARY KEY
Type_Desc	VARCHAR2(30)	NOT NULL

ANSWERS Table

Answer_Question_ID	NUMBER(6)	PRIMARY KEY
Answer_ID	VARCHAR2(2)	NOT NULL
Answer	VARCHAR2(30)	NOT NULL

STUDENT_ANSWER_HISTORY Table

Student ID	NUMBER(9)	NOT NULL
Test ID	NUMBER(6)	NOT NULL
Questions ID	NUMBER(6)	NOT NULL
Student Answer	VARCHAR2(2)	NOT NULL

So far, is everything clear? Notice that not every table has a key. But, as you will see later, we will be creating indexes for some tables to make data retrieval faster and to enforce uniqueness among the keys. Now let's move on to the last constraint that we will use with our tables—one that, like the ones we have just built, will save us a lot of grief later. This constraint is called **referential integrity** and is built on the relationships that naturally exist among the tables.

Relationships

Look at the ten tables at the end of the preceding section. Do you see a logical progression among them? That is, should we build the STUDENTS table first, or the TEST_HISTORY table, or is there a better way to do this? What really comes first—students, test, questions, or history? If you guessed questions, take yourself a well-deserved five-minute break. Doesn't the entire database really depend on having questions defined, along with their answers? It makes no difference if we have nice tests or really good students; without the questions, nothing will work.

This means that anything dependent on the QUESTIONS table is in a direct relationship with the QUESTIONS table. Take a look at the ten tables. See? The TEST_HISTORY, STUDENT_ANSWER_HISTORY, and TEST_QUESTIONS_LINK tables all depend on having real questions in the QUESTIONS table. Got the idea? Those tables *reference* the QUESTIONS table, and we will later build this reference into the tables.

Why? Well, if we don't, then we can add anything to the other tables, or, we'd have to do a lot of programming to catch errors. For example, if you were logging the information for a student and entered that the student had answered #4 on question 123, and there *was* no question 123, the system would let you create a bad record for that student. Of course, this would be the student who *would* call, and now how would you explain that he or she got a wrong answer on a question that does not exist?

With referential integrity, the system would catch the error and tell you that question ID 123 is invalid, and it would *not* let you update the student record. See? Referential integrity does error checking for you. Of course, as already mentioned, you could write code to edit the answer, but why bother when it can be done for you?

If the fields are tied together, the database will automatically alert you if you or your program tries to do something illegal. So if the fields had been tied together in our example, when the program or the data entry person tried to enter question ID 123 for the student, the database would have stopped the process immediately and prevented you from future embarrassment. Clearly this referential integrity stuff is a good idea!

So we can see that the first set of tables we have to build will be the QUESTIONS_TYPE_DESC table and the QUESTIONS table. We can't enter anything for Question_Type unless that type is already defined in the QUESTIONS_TYPE_DESC table, right? What next? Logically, the next step would be the ANSWERS table. Questions and answers go together like peanut butter and jelly.

Next? Look at the TEST_ID table? Oh, you're already there? Great—you've got the idea. And now, before we can add any test descriptions, we have to have entries in the TEST_TYPE_DESC table, right? So this table would be the next one to load with data.

After that, the next table to load would be what? STUDENTS? If you chose STUDENTS, skip lunch. Students will enter their own data when they take the test! Of course, you may have some historical data you want to test, but that doesn't count. Your next table would be the TEST_ID table—all those tests that you have in your development folder.

What tests, you ask? Why, the ones you developed with the instructional and teaching staff while you were also doing all this! (We're going to give you some real questions to use, but remember that in practice, such things are really defined by the users, not the technical staff. You will translate their ideas into the relational database, but the definitions come from them. Unless of course you are also a professor or instructor, in which case you can talk to yourself, in private, and get the job done quickly.)

See? The QUESTIONS, ANSWERS, TEST_TYPE_DESC, and TEST_ID tables are your foundation tables. Once those are in place, any student will be able to take the tests anytime, instructors will be able to create new tests, the history tables will start to be filled, you will be able to write reports and queries, and your customers will be writing glowing articles about you, and next thing you know, you'll be at the White House getting a medal. All because you thought out the relationships between your tables!

Now that you have the idea that some data is inherently dependent on other data, the question is how to program the relationships. Remember our discussion of constraints and keys in Chapter 3? We mentioned **foreign keys**, columns that refer to another column in another (or foreign) table. The power of the foreign key is that it ensures that you do not end up with unconnected data. In the previous example we talked about a student requesting his or her answers to a test, and it turned out that somehow his test history had an invalid question, with ID 123. As I explained, one way to prevent such a thing from happening is to use the referential integrity constraint, where one column in a table refers to another column in a different table.

Here's the theory. Table A has the names of all employees, including yours; Table B has the names of all employees and all the rewards they received. When you were testing these tables, you added, just to test, "Moby Dick" to the awards table and gave him the Golden Harpoon award. Then you forgot about it because the tables were done, and off they went into production.

Now comes the annual awards banquet, and just before your name is called, the VP of your company or university, reading from a list that was created from Table B, says, "Would Moby Dick please stand and be recognized?" After a few seconds, and some stifled laughter, you try to sneak out of the room. Of course, the VP, being the consummate professional, makes some kind of joke about this, while whispering that she wants to see you first thing tomorrow morning.

One way to avoid such embarrassment is to link the tables using referential integrity. Doing so would ensure that no names are allowed in Table B that are not in Table A. So if Moby Dick were not a valid employee listed in Table A, the system would stop you from adding it to Table B. (If there is a real employee named Moby Dick, you better hope he earned the reward you entered in Table B!)

To create the referential integrity we need, we add the constraint `references TABLE(column)` command. In our example, Table B would have a name field set up as follows:

Table B		
Name	VARCHAR2(30)	references TABLE_A(Name)
Reward	VARCHAR2(30)	
Dollar_Amount	NUMBER(6,2)	
and so forth . . .		

This would prevent anyone from entering a name in Table B that did not exist in Table A.

Got the idea? If we look at our tables, there are several places where we can use referential integrity. As I already mentioned, we should not allow a test type to be entered on the TEST_ID table unless the type already exists in the TEST_TYPE_DESC table. Hence we would add a `references` statement to make the link. We would do the same with the ANSWERS table. Because all answers are tied to questions, we will link the ANSWERS table to the Question_ID column of the QUESTIONS table. See how it all works? We don't want any disconnected data out there that could cause havoc, so we purposely tie the important fields together with the threads of referential integrity.

Now let's see what our tables look like with the addition of referential integrity constraints where necessary.

Note

Remember, for our purposes there are several foundation or base tables that the rest of the system depends on. These are the descriptor tables, and they question, answer, test, and link tables.

We start our table definition with the TEST_TYPE_DESC table and the AUTHORS table. Remember that without these tables, we cannot build the TEST_ID table, so these are the logical starting points:

TEST_TYPE_DESC Table

Type_ID	NUMBER(6)	PRIMARY KEY	
Type_Desc		VARCHAR2(30)	NOT NULL

Once the TEST_TYPE_DESC table has been created, the next one is the AUTHORS table because the TEST_ID table also depends on the author's being defined:

AUTHORS Table

Author_ID	NUMBER(9)	PRIMARY KEY
Author	VARCHAR2(60)	default 'Waiver Administration'

Next we make the changes to the TEST_ID table:

TEST_ID Table

Test_ID	NUMBER(6)	PRIMARY KEY
Test_Name	VARCHAR2(40)	NOT NULL
Date_Created	DATE	NOT NULL
Author	NUMBER(9)	references AUTHORS(Author_ID)
Comments	VARCHAR2(30)	
Type_ID	NUMBER(6)	references TEST_TYPE_DESC(Type_ID)
Passing_Grade	NUMBER(2)	NOT NULL
Time_Limit	NUMBER(4,2)	NOT NULL

Let's take a close look at what we just did. For Author, we added a referential integrity link back to the AUTHORS table, and we also created a default name just in case someone left it blank. For Type_ID, we added another referential integrity link, this one back to the TEST_TYPE_DESC table. Why? This way no one can enter an invalid test type description when creating a table entry in the TEST_ID table. Whatever someone enters in the Type_ID field of the TEST_ID table *will automatically be checked* against Type_ID in the TEST_TYPE_DESC table. Type_ID in the TEST_ID table is a *foreign key* that references Type_ID in the TEST_TYPE_DESC table. The same logic holds true for the Author column.

This philosophy should now be making sense, and you should be able to follow how the other tables are going to be tied together. We follow the same logic for the QUESTIONS_TYPE_DESC and QUESTIONS tables. First the descriptor table for questions:

QUESTIONS_TYPE_DESC Table		
Question_Type	NUMBER(6)	PRIMARY KEY
Questions_Type_Desc	VARCHAR2(40)	NOT NULL

Next the actual QUESTIONS table:

QUESTIONS Table		
Question_ID	NUMBER(6)	PRIMARY KEY
Question	VARCHAR2(40)	NOT NULL
Correct_Answer	VARCHAR2(2)	NOT NULL
Question_Type	NUMBER(6)	references QUESTIONS_TYPE_DESC (Question_Type)
Date_Created	DATE	
Author_ID	NUMBER(9)	NOT NULL references AUTHORS (Author_ID)

Notice that again, a column in one table *references* a column in another table, so we let Oracle do the editing for us. Also observe how often we use the `NOT NULL` phrase. In general, we want to avoid nulls. They can cause unpredictable results in queries, among other things.

As you undoubtedly expected, next we link the QUESTIONS and TEST_HISTORY tables by using the following linking table:

TEST_QUESTIONS_LINK Table

Link_Test_ID	NUMBER(6)	references TEST_ID(Test_ID)
Link_Question_ID	NUMBER(6)	references QUESTIONS(Question_ID)
Weight	NUMBER(2,1)	default 1
PRIMARY KEY (Link_Test_ID, Link_Question_ID)		

Look what we've done here! By using the `references` clause, we've really tied this table up so that no bad data can get in. Also notice that we have two columns for the primary key. We've done this to make queries and views go faster in case we ever want to get all the questions for a test, which we know we will have to be doing over and over as students take the tests.

Now let's create the last base table, ANSWERS:

ANSWERS Table

Answer_Question_ID	NUMBER(6)	PRIMARY KEY references QUESTIONS(Question_ID)
Answer_ID	VARCHAR2(2)	NOT NULL
Answer	VARCHAR2(30)	NOT NULL

Notice that the primary key of this table refers back to the QUESTIONS table. We don't want any answers out there unless they are tied to a valid question, right?

Once these base tables have been defined, we move on to the STUDENT and HISTORY tables. First look at the STUDENTS table; notice that nothing has changed. You could put in ranges for state, or have a STATE table with all the abbreviations, or a table for the departments or majors, and then use referential integrity. For our purposes we have kept this table as simple as possible. However, feel free to add additional tables and referential statements!

STUDENTS Table		
Student_ID	NUMBER(9)	PRIMARY KEY
F_Name	VARCHAR2(15)	NOT NULL
M_I	VARCHAR2(1)	
L_Name	VARCHAR2(20)	NOT NULL
SSNum	NUMBER(9)	NOT NULL, UNIQUE
B_Date	DATE	
Sex	VARCHAR2(1)	check (SEX IN ('M', 'F', 'm', 'f')
Street1	VARCHAR2(15)	
Street2	VARCHAR2(15)	
Town	VARCHAR2(20)	
State	VARCHAR2(2)	
Country	VARCHAR2(15)	default 'United States'
Zip	NUMBER(5)	NOT NULL
Student_Level	NUMBER(6)	NOT NULL
Date_Created	DATE	
Created_By	VARCHAR2(20)	
Department_Major	VARCHAR2(10)	NOT NULL
Email	VARCHAR2(60)	

Only two more to go! Now finish defining the TEST_HISTORY table:

TEST_HISTORY Table		
Test_ID	NUMBER(6)	references TEST_ID(Test_ID)
Student_ID	NUMBER(9)	references STUDENTS(Student_ID)
Score	NUMBER(3)	NOT NULL
Date_Taken	DATE	NOT NULL
Start_Time	VARCHAR2(8)	NOT NULL
End_Time	VARCHAR2(8)	NOT NULL
Location	VARCHAR2(15)	NOT NULL
PRIMARY KEY (Test_ID, Student_ID)		

With TEST_HISTORY we have added two referential clauses—one for Test_ID and one for Student_ID. This will make the system look at the TEST_ID table and the STUDENTS table anytime these fields are modified. We have also used these fields as a compound primary key.

Finally we come to the STUDENT_ANSWER_HISTORY table:

STUDENT_ANSWER_HISTORY Table		
Student_ID	NUMBER(9)	references STUDENTS(Student_ID)
Test_ID	NUMBER(6)	references TEST_ID(Test_ID)
Question_ID	NUMBER(6)	references QUESTIONS(Question_ID)
Student_Answer	VARCHAR2(2)	NOT NULL

Notice here that three of the four columns are defined by the use of referential integrity. This approach will really protect the data in this history file.

Here's a diagram of how the tables now link together:

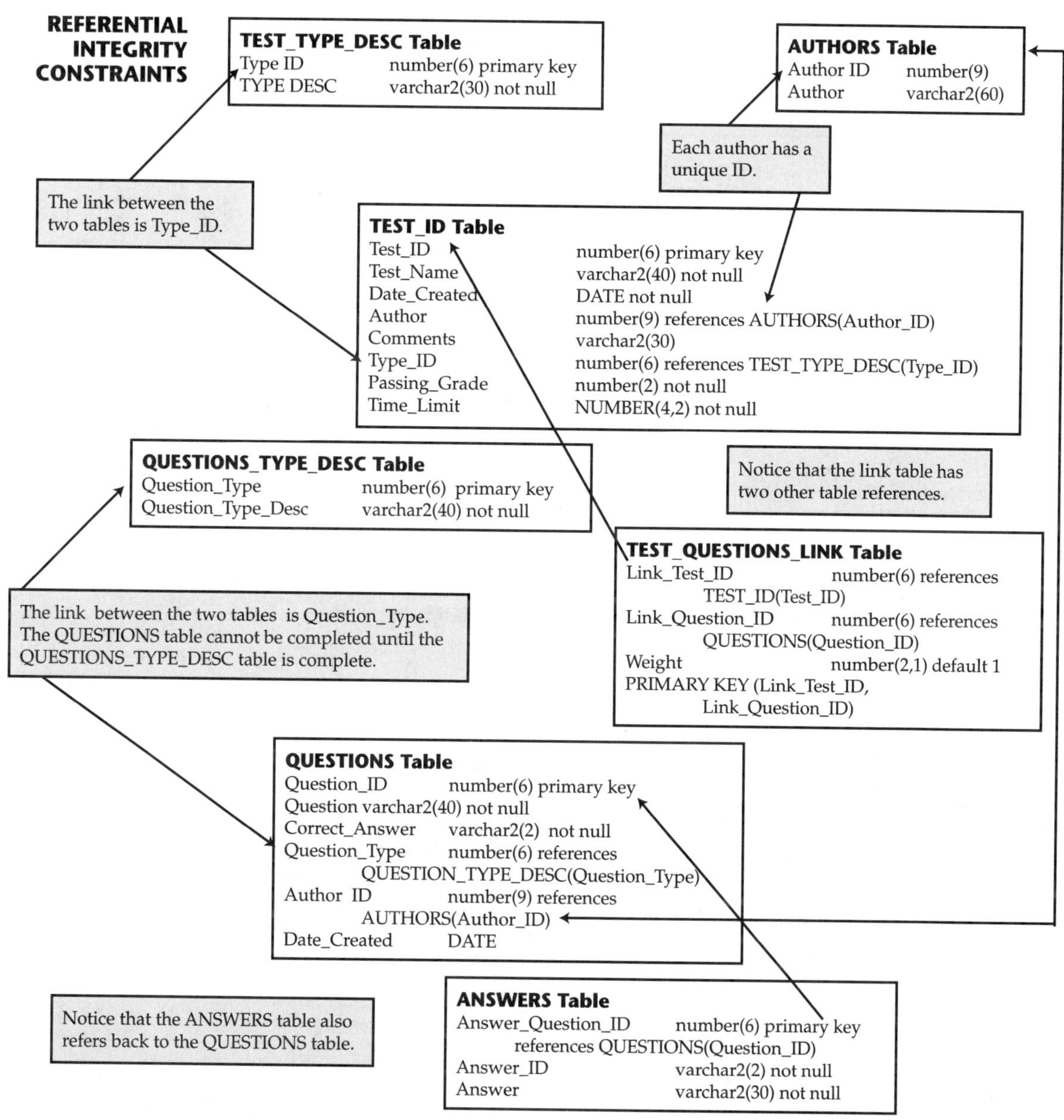

REFERENTIAL INTEGRITY CONSTRAINTS *(Continued)*

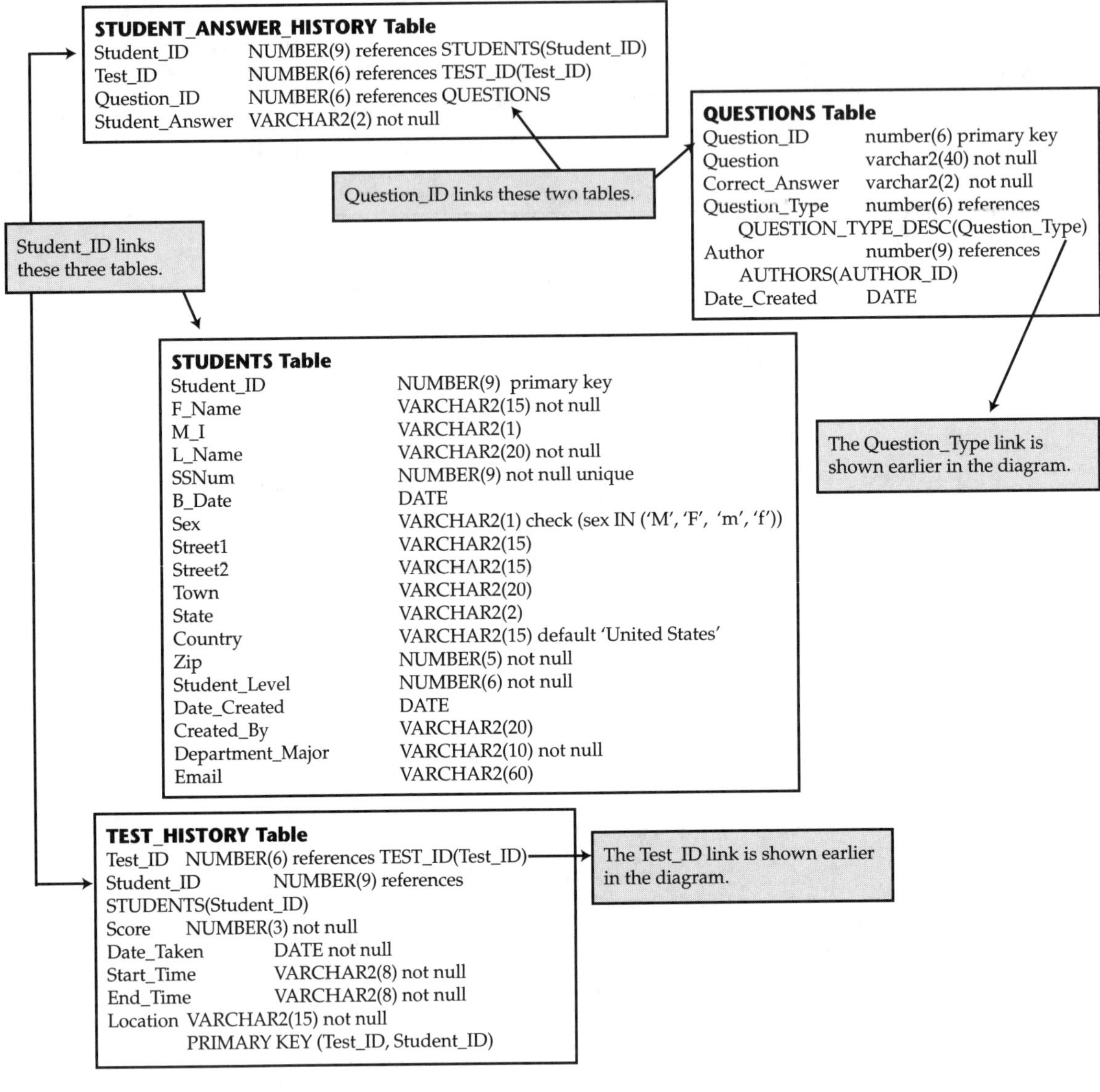
STUDENT_ANSWER_HISTORY Table
Student_ID NUMBER(9) references STUDENTS(Student_ID)
Test_ID NUMBER(6) references TEST_ID(Test_ID)
Question_ID NUMBER(6) references QUESTIONS
Student_Answer VARCHAR2(2) not null
QUESTIONS Table
Question_ID number(6) primary key
Question varchar2(40) not null
Correct_Answer varchar2(2) not null
Question_Type number(6) references QUESTION_TYPE_DESC(Question_Type)
Author number(9) references AUTHORS(AUTHOR_ID)
Date_Created DATE
Question_ID links these two tables.
Student_ID links these three tables.
The Question_Type link is shown earlier in the diagram.
STUDENTS Table
Student_ID NUMBER(9) primary key
F_Name VARCHAR2(15) not null
M_I VARCHAR2(1)
L_Name VARCHAR2(20) not null
SSNum NUMBER(9) not null unique
B_Date DATE
Sex VARCHAR2(1) check (sex IN ('M', 'F', 'm', 'f'))
Street1 VARCHAR2(15)
Street2 VARCHAR2(15)
Town VARCHAR2(20)
State VARCHAR2(2)
Country VARCHAR2(15) default 'United States'
Zip NUMBER(5) not null
Student_Level NUMBER(6) not null
Date_Created DATE
Created_By VARCHAR2(20)
Department_Major VARCHAR2(10) not null
Email VARCHAR2(60)
TEST_HISTORY Table
Test_ID NUMBER(6) references TEST_ID(Test_ID)
Student_ID NUMBER(9) references STUDENTS(Student_ID)
Score NUMBER(3) not null
Date_Taken DATE not null
Start_Time VARCHAR2(8) not null
End_Time VARCHAR2(8) not null
Location VARCHAR2(15) not null
PRIMARY KEY (Test_ID, Student_ID)
The Test_ID link is shown earlier in the diagram.

Guidelines for Using the `references` Clause

The foreign key that you refer back to must be unique and not null. It can be a primary key or not. So if you refer back to a nonprimary key, make sure that the column is defined as not null. This is very important, or you run the risk of duplicates, especially with nulls, and you will have problems.

Note

Referential integrity in which you can use a foreign key to reference a column in another table is an Oracle feature, and it works only in an Oracle environment. Although it is very powerful, it is not a recognized construct in other SQL databases. So if your environment includes databases other than Oracle, you cannot use the references statement when migrating tables and data.

We have now completed the table design for our system. We're ready to go to the server and start creating our Oracle server, database, and users. Then we will build the client PCs, connect them to the server, load the tables, and start programming!

Chapter 6

The Major Parts of an Oracle Windows Installation

As you gain experience with Oracle in the Windows NT and Windows 2000 (also known as W2K) world, you'll begin to appreciate the complexity and depth of both the Windows operating system and the Oracle database environment. However, becoming proficient in both is not an overnight process. In fact it will take years of handling the unexpected before you really understand the nuances of these systems.

In the meantime you can master certain fundamental parts, and doing so will allow you to create a functioning Oracle environment on a Windows NT and

2000 server and clients. These parts are what we will discuss in this chapter as preparation for actually building the parts on your server and client machines and maintaining your database.

Let's look at the basic parts of the Oracle Windows installation process. First there is creating the detailed database design, which includes business analysis, table normalization, and table design, which we have already done. Next comes building the Oracle server, in our case a Windows NT or 2000 server. Third comes creating the Oracle database, followed by building the tables, loading initial data, and addressing security considerations, then creating users, loading the clients, and some of the standard DBA (database administrator) tasks. In other words, now is when all the theory we covered in the first five chapters helps us develop a concrete, functioning database.

We have to figure out how much room we will need for our tables, determine who will be able to do what to the tables, actually build the tables and load them with some data, and then, finally, make the client PCs database smart. Once all that is done, we'll be in the perfect position to start using SQL, SQL*Plus, PL/SQL, Oracle Forms and Reports, and the Web to produce the well-designed and well-built system your customers have asked for. Ultimately, you will need to go through all of these steps to turn your normalized table design into a real, solid database.

Warning

To begin, you must know what you want to name your database (don't laugh), and you must have the necessary hardware and licenses. If you don't, get them now.

To move forward in this discussion we're going to have to get into some more terminology. Yes, learning more terms is necessary because they are what all Oracle designers, DBAs, and developers use. So let's start with the concepts and then move into the other major parts of the full installation and programming.

Concepts

An Oracle Instance

An **instance** is a running database. As soon as you start your database on your server, and Oracle allocates memory to something called the system global area

(SGA) and starts some of the database processes, you have an **Oracle instance**. It contains all the parts you need to make an Oracle database operational, such as the system monitor, process monitor, database writer, checkpoint and log writer, the data files that contain the tables, the control files that contain configuration information, the redo log files and archive files, other configuration files, and security information.

This goes beyond your local server installation because the term *instance* can refer to an Oracle system that is a node on a network that shares files. Also be aware that there is only one database per instance. And here's some interesting trivia: An Oracle database is limited, in 8*i*, to 4 petabytes (PB). The number of files per database varies by block size. A 2K block size supports up to 20,000 files, a 16K block size up to 65,536 files. If you're interested, I suggest you take a look at some of the more detailed technical information from Oracle, where system blocks, data blocks, extents, and segments are all discussed.

Tablespaces

A **tablespace** is an area of storage that has one or more **data files** that hold the data for tables, indexes, and all other database structures. Each Oracle instance usually has multiple tablespaces. For example, with every Oracle database, there is a tablespace called *SYSTEM*, and normally the DBA creates other tablespaces for applications, programming, and so forth. The SYSTEM tablespace is automatically created and holds the data dictionary and the location information for all the tables, indexes, other tablespaces, and so forth that make up this particular database.

One good practice is to create a temporary tablespace for **sorts**. Sorts are used by actions such as joins, the `ORDER BY` clause, the `GROUP BY` clause, and the `ANALYZE` function, and sometimes performance can be improved immensely if a temporary tablespace for sorts is available. We will use this feature later, when we are creating users for our database.

You can simply put everything (tables, user spaces, work areas, etc.) into the SYSTEM tablespace, but for practical reasons you will be creating many tablespaces. Usually there is a TEMP tablespace for tables that are not permanent. And in many cases it makes sense to assign individual tablespaces to each user or group of users. This is a way of controlling disk use, simplifying backup and restore operations, and protecting and balancing your system.

Just be aware that the term *tablespace* refers to a physical amount of storage space, and you will be slicing it up to meet your needs. Look at it this way:

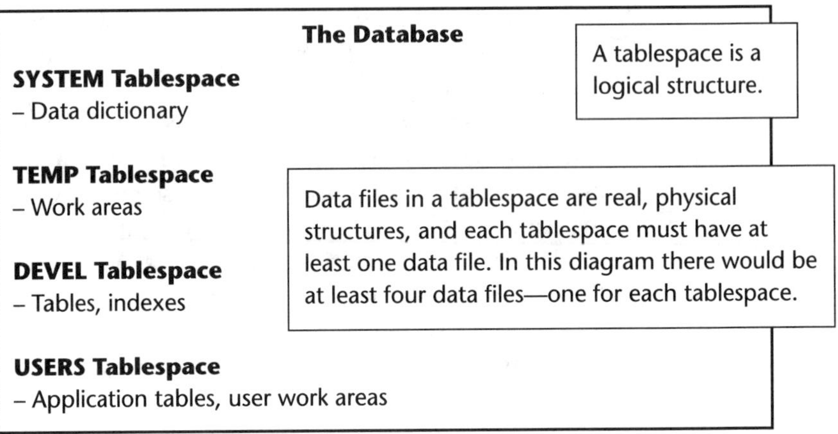

Now you can see why it is important to spend a bit of time calculating table sizes, the number of users, and so forth. There is a limit to how much storage space each system has, and you must plan carefully so that your customers don't get error messages.

To sum up, a tablespace is a physical storage space, and each table in the tablespace is assigned a piece of that space called a **segment**. Further, each segment starts out with a certain size, called the **initial extent**, and grows according to what has been defined in the **NEXT EXTENT** clause. Yes, you can run out of room if the tablespace gets full. At that point you will have to increase the overall tablespace size, or if only one file in the tablespace has reached the maximum size, you can increase the space allocated to that one file.

Schemas

Within every Oracle instance are **schemas** that contain all the database objects, such as views, tables, indexes, sequences, and so forth. Now, and this is important, each schema in a database belongs to a user. By default, when you create a user, that user gets his or her own schema, and *the schema has the user's name.* Everything the user creates will reside in his or her own schema.

Here's what you have to know: Database objects that are created in a schema can be accessed only by the user who owns them, or by users who have permission to access them. The syntax for accessing tables in a schema other than your own (except for the SYSTEM schema), is `schema_name.table_name`—for example, `Guerrilla_Schema.Test_Questions`.

As you can see, a schema is another way to protect tables, views, and other objects from unauthorized access.

Synonyms

A **synonym** is another name for a table or view. All tables and views belong to a schema, and they must be identified by that schema unless it is the SYSTEM schema, remember? Always having to identify tables and views by their schemas can become unwieldy, so synonyms are created. Usually the DBA creates **public synonyms** for tables and views that everyone will use, and if you have access to someone else's tables and views, you can also create synonyms for yourself for those objects.

Oracle Home

An **Oracle home** is where all the software will reside. You can have multiple Oracle homes, each one containing a release of the same Oracle products. In other words, you could have both a test version of release 8.x.x or 9.x.x, and a production version of 8.x.x or 9.x.x, on the same server. Or you might have an Oracle 7.x database already installed on your server. Each release will have its own Oracle home. You will have to know the paths to the various Oracle homes when you have multiple Oracle installations on your server so that you can connect to the database you want. Otherwise you will be connected to the most recently installed database.

Transaction Processing

Transaction processing is important because Oracle has developed techniques to prevent half-completed transactions in case of a system or program failure. The transaction is written to a series of files, buffers, and logs, and if anything problematic happens along the way, the system rolls back the activity to prevent incomplete updates from occurring. In other words, if you moved $100,000 from your savings account to your checking account, and the money was deposited in your checking account before it could be debited from your savings, and the system went down, Oracle would back out the transaction as soon as the system came back up. Otherwise you would have an extra $100,000 that you would have to return. Oracle works on the "all or none" idea. If either of the two transactions fails—the deposit or the withdrawal—then the entire process is backed out.

System Identifier

Each Oracle instance must have a unique name, and this name is called the **system identifier**, or SID.

Major Parts of the Installation

Installing the Server

To support the Oracle server and database, at least 10GB of disk space and least 128MB of RAM—preferably much more—must be available.

As with most server environments, the server itself should be kept dedicated to the database function and maintained free from other applications. Being a server, it should not also be treated as a client. That is, applications such as MS Office, audio, and video should not be installed. The existence of multiple applications on a server makes support and troubleshooting quite difficult, and the last thing you want is to have your server go down unexpectedly late Friday afternoon just when the president asks for the month-end report to bring to the shareholders meeting that evening.

Note

Protect your server and your server will protect you.

Your Windows NT or 2000 server will support the two main Oracle systems: the server and the database. Operating together, the Oracle server and database will provide your programmers, users, customers, and students with the ability to program in SQL*Plus and to access the developed applications.

Oracle Server is the foundation for the entire Oracle installation. Whether you are installing Oracle 8.x, 8*i*, or 9*i*, your entire Oracle shop starts with installing Oracle Server. To do this, we use the installation CD and follow the online instructions. The step-by-step procedure will be presented in detail in Chapter 7.

Creating the Database

Once you have configured the Oracle server, the next step is to create a database. In fact, the first steps of creating the database will take place in a series of meetings with your users and customers, when you will define the data; the data relationships; the kinds of reporting and inquiring necessary; daily, monthly, weekly, and yearly cycles; and so on. We will go into more detail when we talk more about security in Chapter 8, where you will have to determine the parameters of your database, the users who will need to access it, and what those users will need to do with it.

Like the Oracle server, the database is created through the Oracle installation process. In fact, because the installation has become so automated, you have very few steps to perform. No matter how easy the process seems, however, you must know what you're doing because it is very difficult to make changes to the base parameters of the database once it has been created. This is the reason for giving you detailed, step-by-step instructions.

For now, however, just realize that behind the scenes Oracle is performing something just short of magic. Within a few minutes, using the installation guide, you will create the shell for what will eventually become, in your hands, a fully operational Oracle database. Totally transparently to you, Oracle creates the data dictionary, a host of system files and tables, and other operating system functions that stand ready to support the tables, views, and scripts that will eventually become your Oracle system.

Here's a summation of the system files and tables that will be created automatically. First a successful database installation will create seven tablespaces, each with its own data file, as Table 6.1 shows. In addition, an initialization parameter file called `INIT.ORA` will be created in your `ORACLE_HOME/ADMIN/DB_NAME/PFILE` directory. This file will contain all the default parameters that Oracle needs to create an instance. Although you can tweak these parameters, it is not the intent of this book to cover them. But once you have your system running, I encourage you to take a look at other reference books and see what `INIT.ORA` is all about.

Table 6.1 Tablespaces Created During Oracle Database Creation

Tablespace	Data File	Contents
SYSTEM	SYSTEM01.DBF	Data dictionary, definitions of tables, views
USERS	USER01.DBF	Data for applications
TEMP	TEMP01.DBF	Space for sorts
RBS	RBS01.DBF	Rolled-back transactions that did not complete normally
INDX	INDX01.DBF	Indexes tied to the data in the USERS tablespace
DRSYS	DR01.DBF	Objects tied to Oracle *inter*Media
TOOLS	TOOLS01.DBF	Initially empty, used for third-party software

Later we will be talking about backup and recovery. For now it will suffice just to point out that the installer creates three of the most important files: the **redo logs**. These are REDO01.LOG, REDO02.LOG, and REDO03.LOG.

Along with INIT.ORA and the redo logs, the installer creates three **control files**: CONTROL01.CTL, CONTROL02.CTL, and CONTROL03.CTL. These are necessary for the database to start and run, and they contain information on the physical parameters of the database, as well as the names and locations of other database files. In addition, other necessary parts of backup and recovery are the 18 **rollback segments**: SYSTEM, RB_TEMP, and RB1 through RB16.

Finally, the **data dictionary** is also created. This is a special collection of tables and views that provide reference information about the database, users, and relationships. The data dictionary is something you must become familiar with, and it will be discussed in its own chapter (Chapter 10). Do not leave home without your data dictionary. This is the only place you'll be able to find the information that will save your neck in a crisis.

Creating Tables

With the database now created, your next major step is to create the tables. I will show you how to use scripts to turn the tables you built in Chapters 4 and 5 into live tables, where the referential integrity constraints you worked so hard to build start to pay off. I will also show you how to load data from scripts, and I'll introduce you to SQL*Loader.

Adding Users

After you have defined the database and tables on your Windows NT or 2000 server, the next step is to add users. This is the logical step after the Oracle security step, in which you will create the profiles, roles, and individual users on the basis of what you have determined they need. You will control each user's read, write, and delete powers, how much space each user has to create tables, timeout parameters, and so forth. Without a valid user account for the database, your customers simply will not be able to access the data. (Many Oracle-based applications have their own security system built in along with the native Oracle security. They complement each other.)

As you might expect, your programmers will have very powerful accounts, and your users will have limited accounts. The DBA and backup DBA will have the most powerful IDs.

Installing Clients and Net8

Now that you have a database and a group of active user accounts, the next step is to provide your programmers, customers, and students with access to your database. Access is provided through Oracle Net8 (formerly SQL*Net), the Oracle method of connecting a client site (local or remote) to the database. Net8 allows you to log in directly to the Oracle database and then perform the functions defined in your security setup. We will take you through the steps necessary to install the client PC to make it Oracle "smart."

DBA Tasks and Programming

When your server, database, and security are complete, you will need to make sure your backup and other DBA functions are under control. Once you have your daily and weekly operations planned, the next step is to start using the tables, creating views, and then putting the two together in user-friendly applications. This is the SQL*Plus/PL/SQL step, in which you will use Oracle's extensions to SQL to create user access modules; write the programs to update, delete, and report on the data; create views; and so forth. You will be given a solid fundamental introduction to SQL*Plus.

Web Enabling

Finally, to bring your now vibrant application into the contemporary technological and business world, you will enhance what you've created by extending it to the World Wide Web. Using Oracle's own features in 8*i* and 9*i*, you will be adding HTML to provide Web access to your applications and data. Using other techniques, you will open your database to other, non-Oracle applications, giving your application additional value. As you will see, your model waiver exam will then have an appealing Web presence with e-commerce functionality.

Interfacing

As discussed in Chapter 14, it is very common to move data from another system into an Oracle database, as well as from Oracle into something such as Excel. Although there are several ways to do this, the most common way to migrate table information into Oracle is to use Oracle SQL*Loader. We will discuss this program in some detail in Chapter 9.

In addition, there are ways to link other databases, such as Access databases, directly to Oracle. There is a lot of documentation on how to do this, and I encourage you to do some research and then try linking a small Access database to your Oracle database, using native Access or a Visual Basic program. Here's a hint. In Windows, go to **Settings | Control Panel | Data Sources (ODBC)**, click on **Add**, select **Microsoft ODBC for Oracle Setup**, and configure the setup:

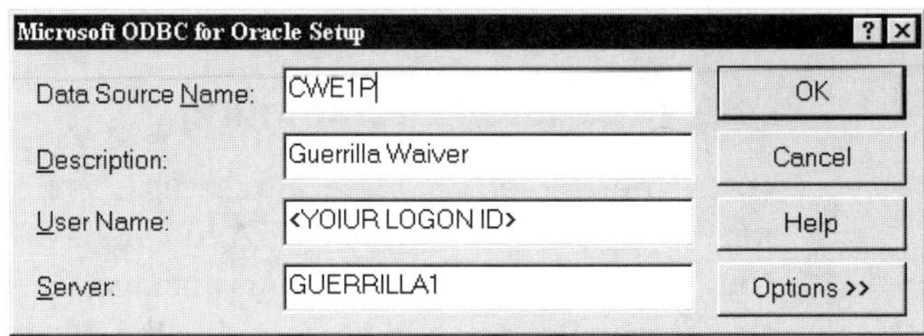

This example shows the setup for someone who wants to reach the Oracle database named CWE1P, on a server named GUERRILLA1. When your Access program requires information from the database, this ODBC driver will make the connection to Oracle.

These major steps will be covered in as much detail as necessary in the chapters that follow. If you are responsible for the entire Oracle operation at your location, by all means go through every step. Even if your job description says "Programmer" or "DBA," you can learn a lot from at least trying the steps for each of these functions. At the least, you will learn to appreciate what your coworker does.

Chapter 7

Installing the Oracle 8*i* and 9*i* Database Server

Oracle has done an amazing job with the 8*i* and 9*i* Install wizards. As you will see, in a matter of about 20 to 30 minutes, you will have your Oracle 8*i* or 9*i* server and a database operational. The wizard will guide you through all the necessary steps.

Before you start, make sure you have all your licenses, your database name (we'll be calling ours *CWE1P*), and enough room on your server—2GB. With these requirements met, you're ready to go!

Warning

The installation process is *memory intensive*! A low-memory server—128MB, for example—will be excruciatingly s-l-o-w. Be prepared to spend at least an hour. And if you are using a low-memory server, maximize your paging file to something like 600 to 1000MB! With W2K, you can change the paging-file size on the fly, so set it very high and change it after the installation. I do *not* advise using a server with less than 128MB of memory. Not only is the installation more complicated, but it will be so slow that you might as well plan on spending the better part of a day watching your memory manager show "FULL" and listening to your disk drive churn. Then when your users log on, be prepared for so many complaints that you'll wish you had decided to grow roses for a career!

The Installation

Load the 8*i* or 9*i* Server CD (or if you have the software on a network drive, go to the folder and run the `setup.exe` program.) The only difference between the 8*i* and 9*i* wizards is the background image. I'll show you an example of both for a couple of screens; then I'll show just the 8*i* screens. The first screen is the welcome screen:

Oracle 8*i* Opening Screen

Oracle 9*i* Opening Screen

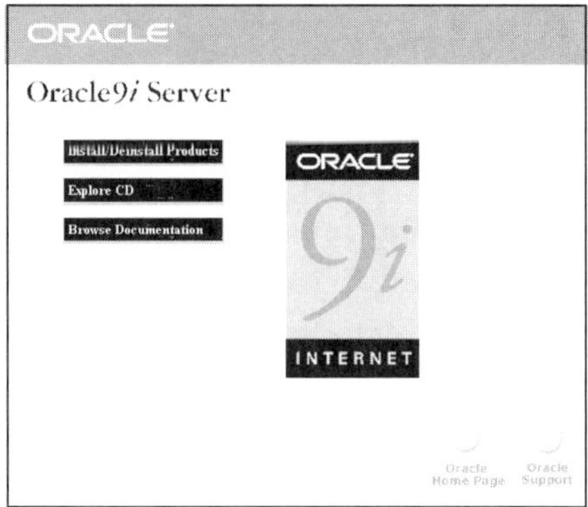

Click on **Install/Deinstall Products** to launch Oracle's new Universal Installer:

Oracle Universal Installer Title Screen

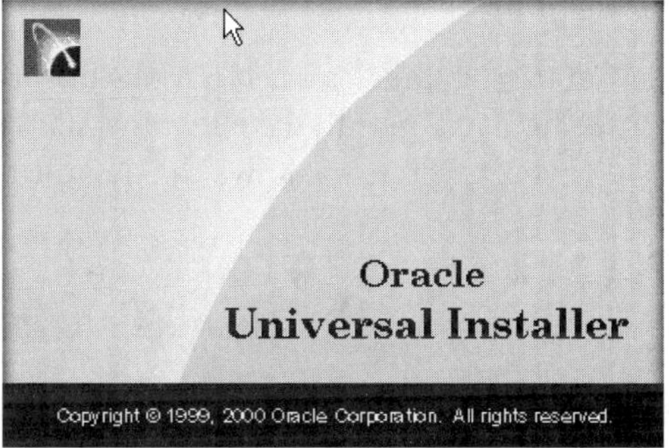

8*i* Universal Installer Welcome Screen

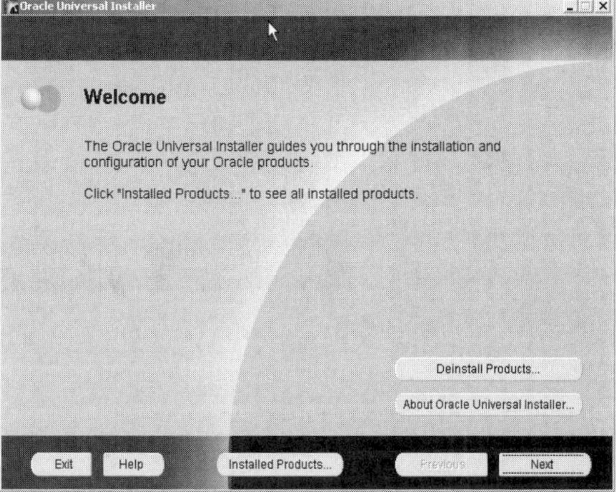

9*i* Universal Installer Welcome Screen

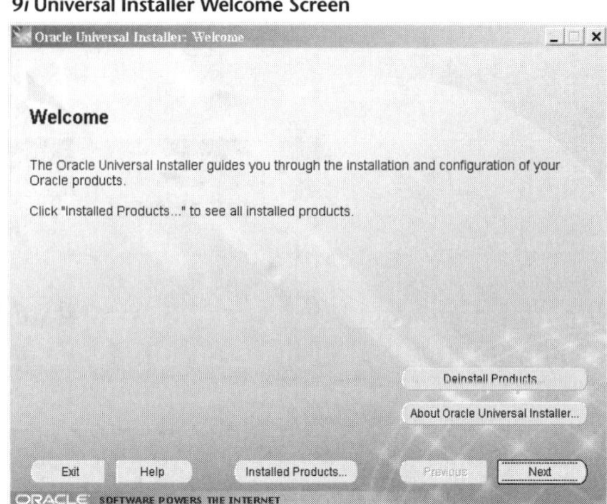

Get used to this installer; it looks like it will be around for a long time. You'll be seeing it again with the client installation.

The next screen shows the default directories:

8*i* File Locations Screen

9*i* File Locations Screen

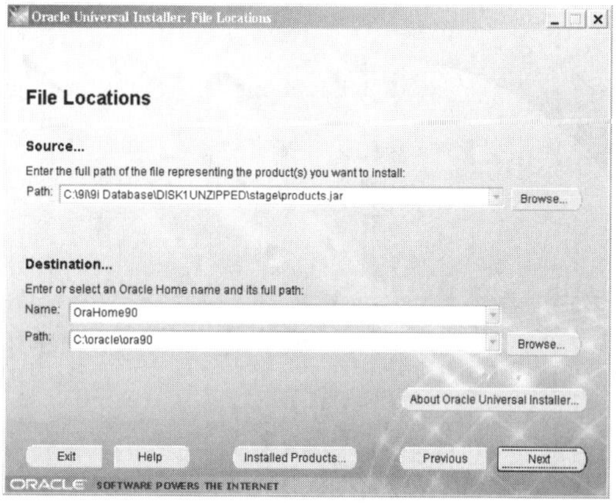

You will see the standard status bar while products are being loaded:

8*i* File Locations Screen with Status Bar

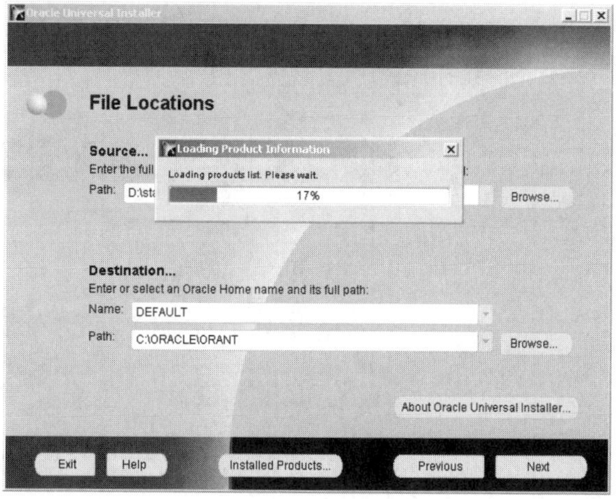

9*i* File Locations Screen with Status Bar

Loading products list. Please wait.
10%
File Locations
Source...
Enter the full path of the file representing the product(s) you want to install:
Path: C:\9i\9i Database\DISK1 UNZIPPED\stage\products.jar
Browse...
Destination...
Enter or select an Oracle Home name and its full path:
Name: OraHome90
Path: C:\oracle\ora90
Browse...
About Oracle Universal Installer...
Exit
Help
Installed Products...
Previous
Next
ORACLE SOFTWARE POWERS THE INTERNET

Oracle 9*i* has an extra screen asking for the character set. Just take the default.

The next screen gives you choices. Select the database product:

8*i* Product Selection Screen

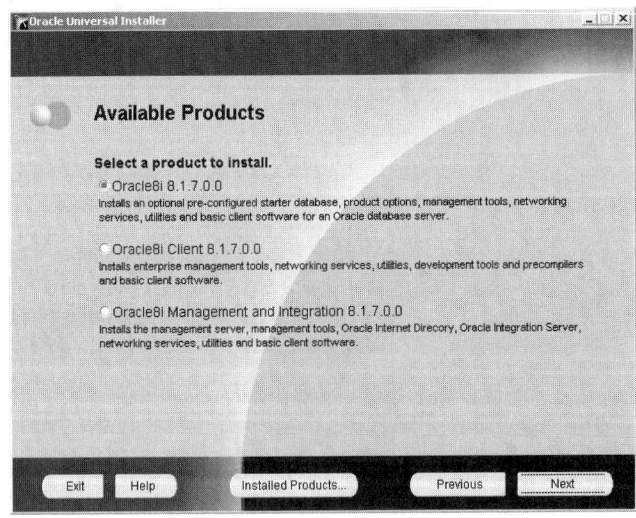

9*i* Product Selection Screen

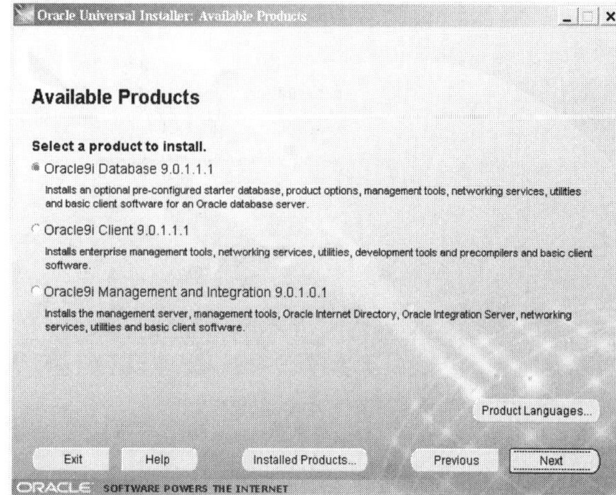

Next you can choose the type of installation you want. Select **Typical** for 8*i* and **Enterprise Edition** for 9*i*:

8*i* Installation Types Screen

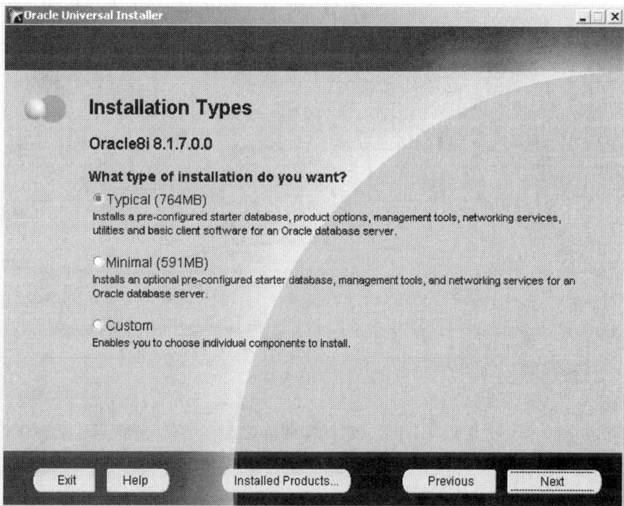

9*i* Installation Types Screen

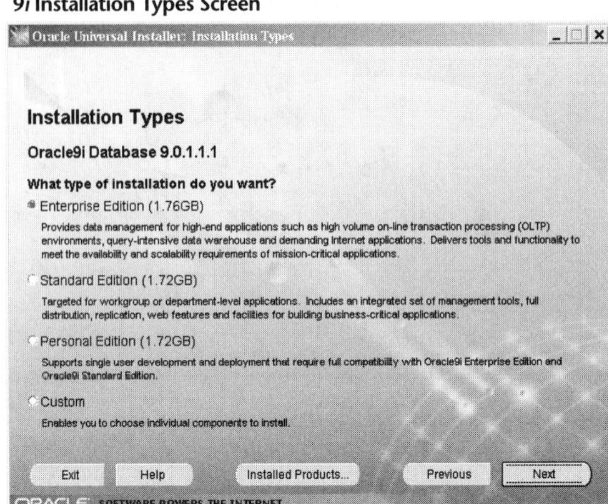

It may be a couple of minutes before anything happens. Be patient! Notice the blue status bar in the upper right-hand corner:

9*i* Installation Types Screen with Status Bar

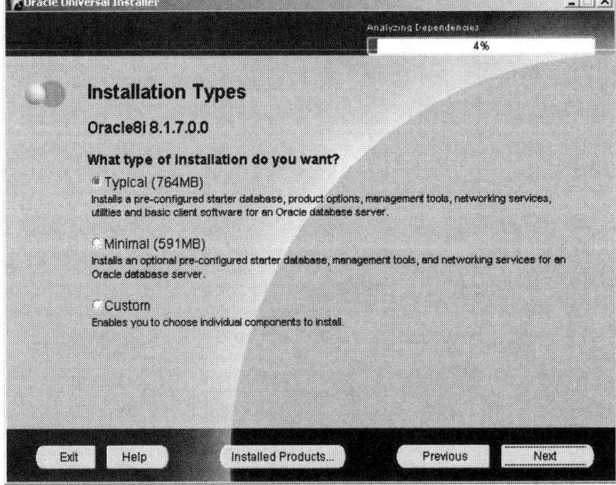

Notice that the 9*i* Enterprise Edition gives you several more choices, including **Transaction Processing** and **Data Warehouse**. If you're installing 9*i*, select **General Purpose**:

9*i* Database Configuration Screen

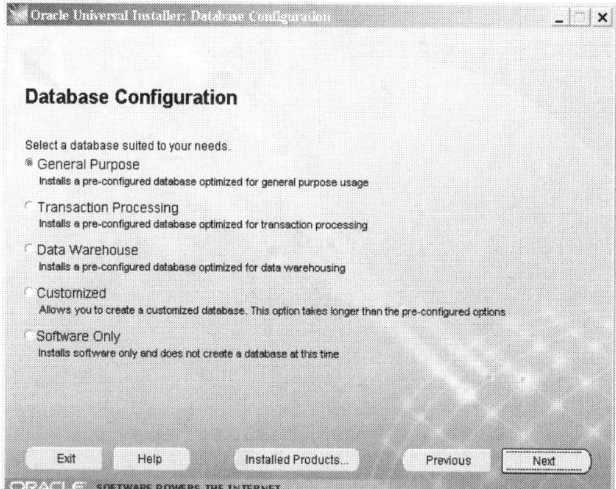

While the program is loading, the installer will prompt for the database name:

9*i* Database Identification (Name) Screen

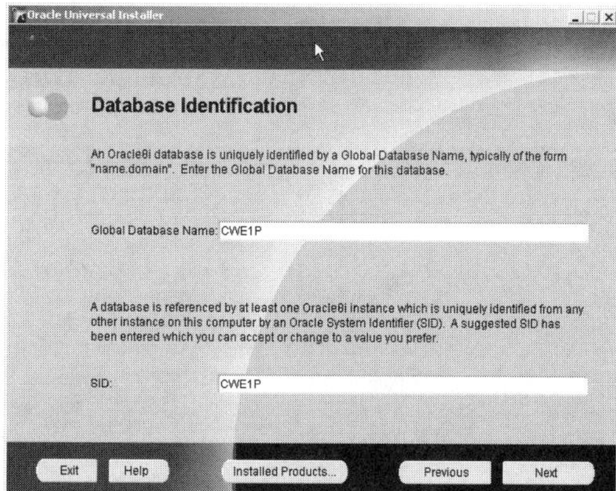

The installation continues; check the blue bar at upper right for the status:

Database Identification Screen with Status Bar

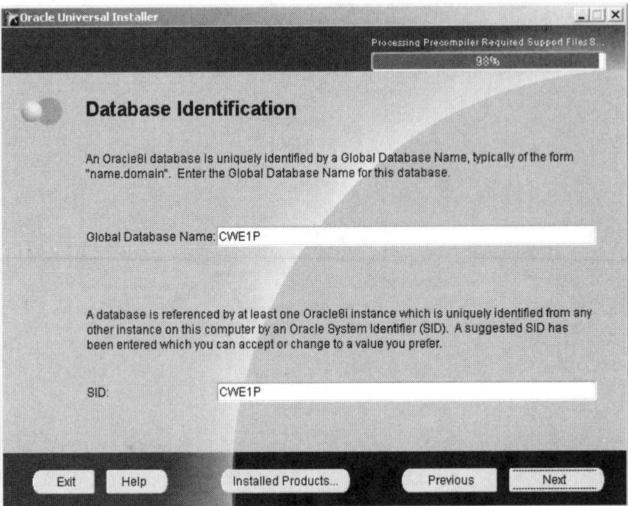

Now the installer shows you the products and their storage requirements:

Summary of Products Installed

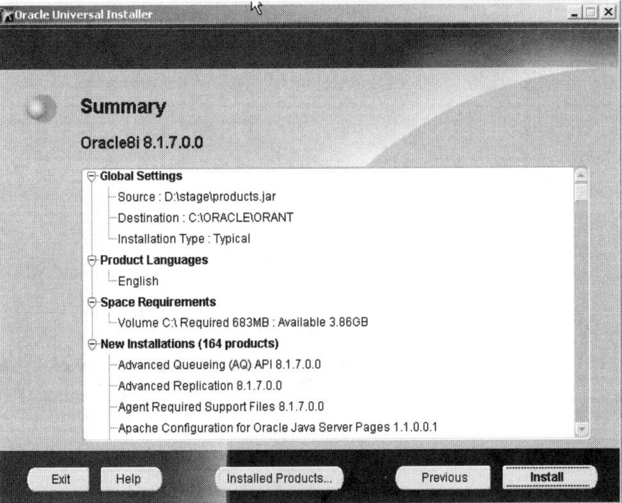

You can scroll through the products to get a good idea of all the programs that will be installed. One interesting feature is that if you pause on an item, you will see a brief explanation of what that item does:

Installed Products List with Explanation of Product Function

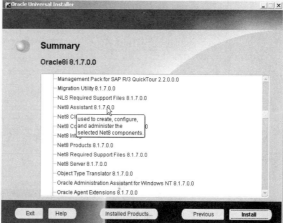

At this point select **Install**, and the process will start, showing the familiar status bar. The next screen mentions that a log of the install session is automatically created at `C:\Program Files\Oracle\Inventory\logs\InstallActions.log`:

Install Screen with Status Bar

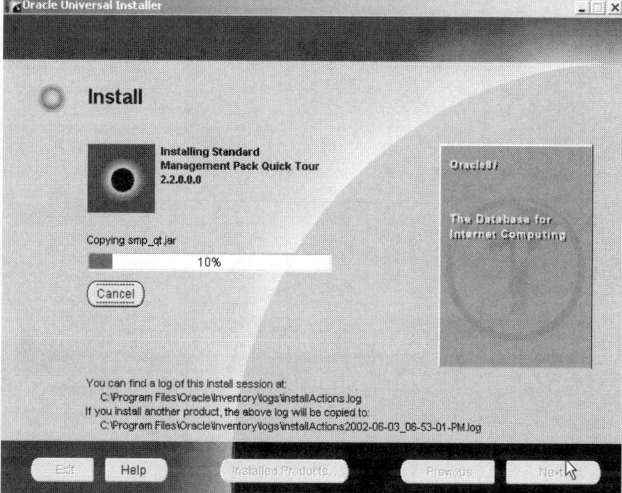

This step will take several minutes, so be patient.

Next comes a screen showing the various configuration tools being installed:

Configuration Tools Summary

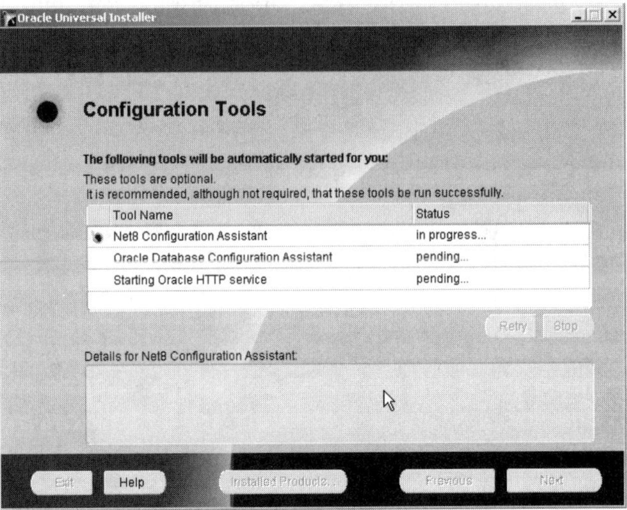

At the end, a completion message appears. Note that 9*i* gives you a chance to *change the system passwords*!

8*i* Completion Screen

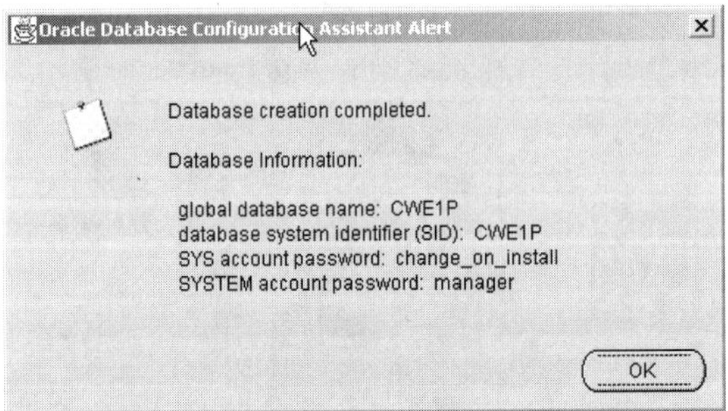

9*i* Completion Screen

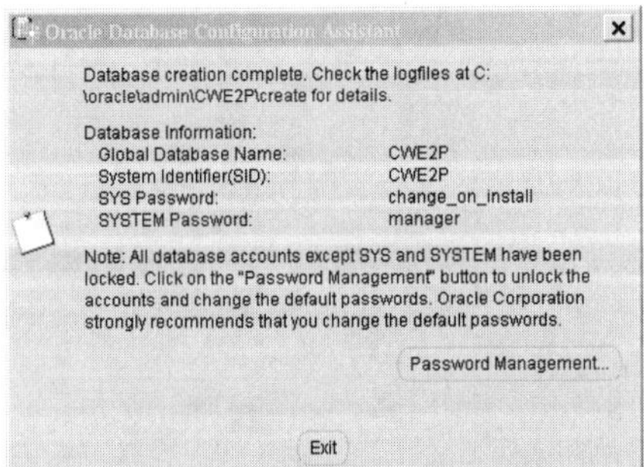

The completion screen is followed by the **End of Installation** screen:

8*i* End of Installation Screen

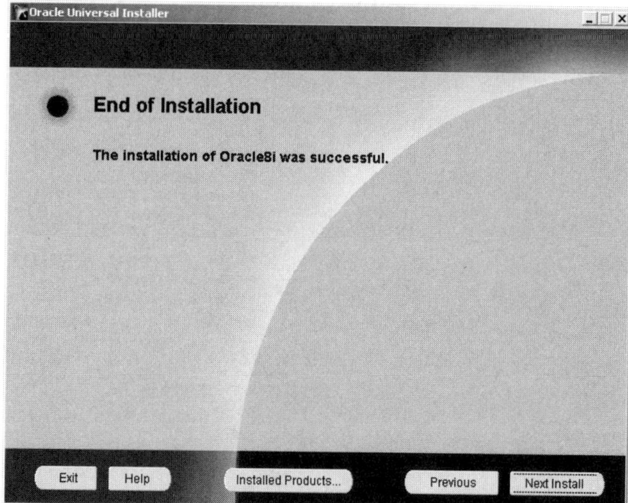

9*i* End of Installation Screen

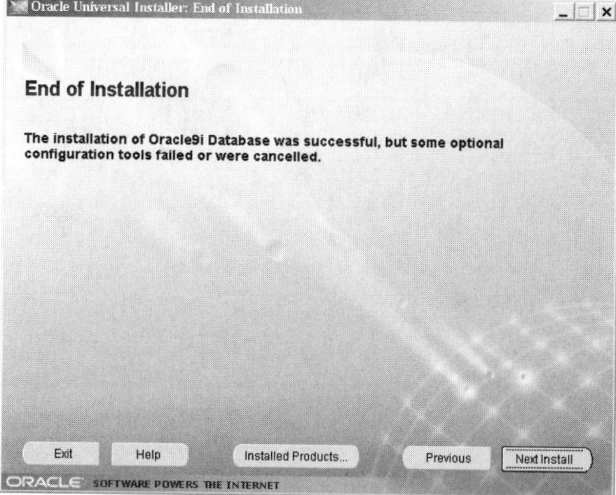

The installer automatically starts up the HTTP server.

You can now take a look at what has been installed by clicking on the **Installed Products...** button:

Inventory of Installed Products

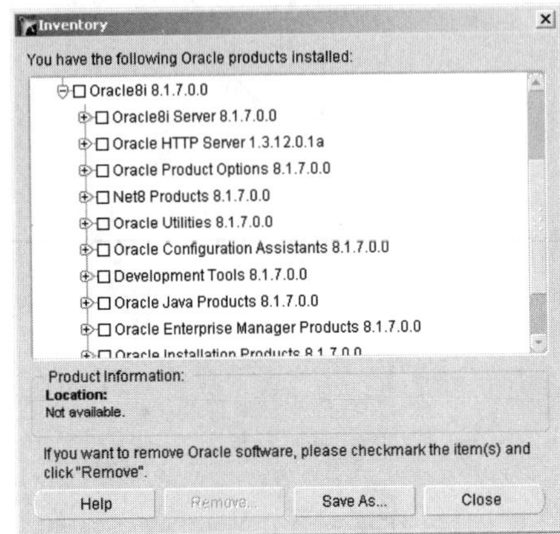

Now that the server and database have been created, select **Close**. You will get the usual confirmation screen:

Exit Confirmation Screen

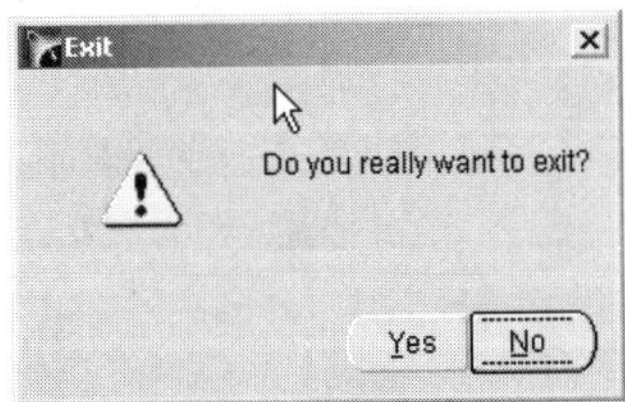

Now in Windows go to **Start | Programs**, and you will see two new major entries—**Oracle - DEFAULT** and **Oracle Installation Products**:

Oracle Products Installed Screen

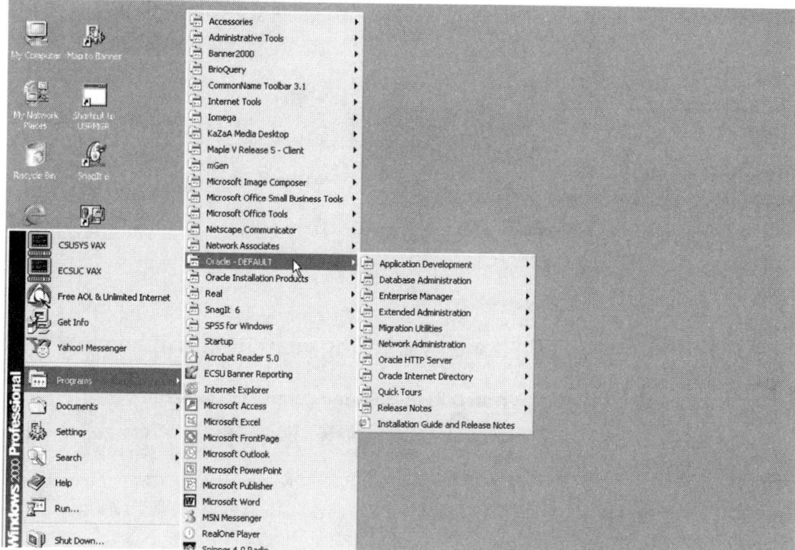

Also in Windows go to **Control Panel | Admin Tools | Services**, and you will see which Oracle services are running:

Oracle Products Started

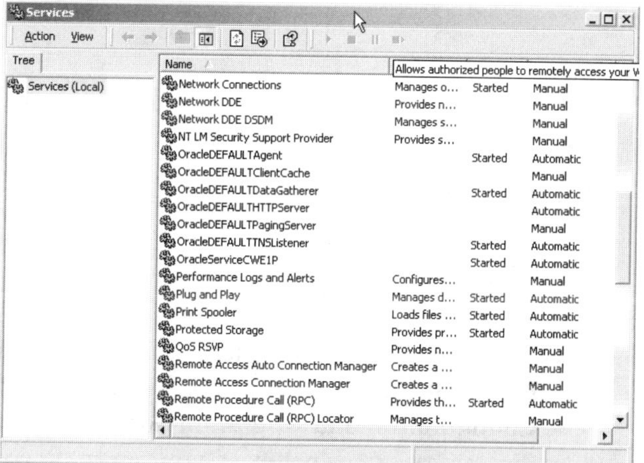

The last step for all you skeptics out there is to run SQL*Plus and try to attach to the new database, CWE1P (in W2K, you would select **Start | Programs | Oracle Home | Application Development | SQL Plus**):

Attaching SQL*Plus to Database

Log On

User Name: system

Password: *******

Host String: cwe1p

OK Cancel

If you've done everything right, this will be your reward:

System Output, Showing Connection Message

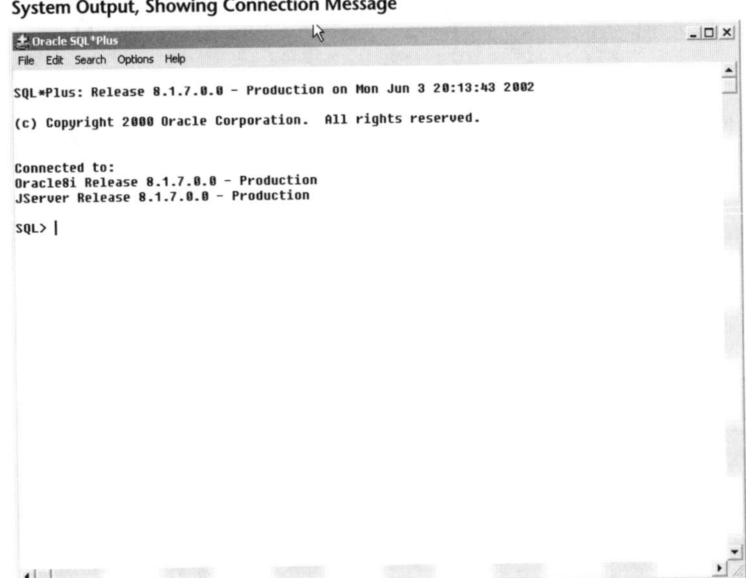

If you get a message like "Can't resolve name," use the database assistant to see if the database exists. (In W2K, select **Start | Programs | Oracle Home | Configuration and Migration Tools | Database Configuration Assistant**.) If the database does not exist, you can try to create one, or you can do things the hard way—that is, go back to the Universal Installer, deinstall everything, and do a reinstall. Sometimes you have to do it the hard way.

Note

With 9*i*, sometimes one of the options won't work. Instead of completely deinstalling, just start it up again and do another installation. It will automatically deinstall Oracle, or so it says, and reinstall it, without wiping out any database that you may have already created.

So you've installed the Oracle 8*i* or 9*i* server and created a database. Impressive, yes? What you've done is created the system foundation for your Guerrilla Oracle system. Once you have the tables created, the client PCs installed and configured with SQL*Plus, and Net8 installed, you will be ready to really move ahead with your new system. These are the ideas that will be discussed in the next chapters.

Chapter 8

Security

In this chapter I will discuss the concept of security. First I'll give you a conceptual framework for your own security policy. If your Oracle installation is new, the following pages will be very important. If your shop is already an Oracle site, what follows will be a good overview. After the introduction, we'll get right to work and build all the parts that will go into your security schema.

Security. What are we trying to protect? First, of course, is your database, or what can be thought of as your system. Second is the data itself. What do we need to protect from? Primarily your users. In almost all cases, users are not malicious; in fact, any problems that arise are usually much less dramatic. When bad things happen to your data, the cause is almost always purely accidental, a result of insufficient security. Very, very few users have the time to invest or interest in breaking security, and most users really don't care if you're using an RDBMS or a pile of bricks. What you have to do is protect both your data and your users, including both programming staff and business users.

There are two threats: (1) user mistakes made with no ill intent and (2) deliberate attempts to damage your system. Your security schema, then, has two major tasks: (1) to prevent as well as possible any damage and (2) to recover quickly and accurately when necessary. We will be talking about the first of these—the steps you can take to reduce things such as unauthorized (or inadvertent) access, unauthorized (or inadvertent) update, and fraudulent and/or malicious update. In Chapter 12 we will discuss backup and recovery.

In addition, there must be an overall policy to control passwords, auditing, and the like. This policy must be well thought out to strike the balance between just enough security and ease of work flow for your users. In other words, you could force a password change every seven days, but you will run into some very, very strong opposition.

The preceding is the outline for this chapter. We'll be talking about overall system security, data security, user security, and finally passwords and auditing. Each topic will include the background information you will need in Chapter 9, when you will actually go back to your Oracle server and start creating roles, profiles, and users.

System Security

When you are thinking about the overall protection for your Oracle RDBMS, here are some of the major considerations:

- Who will create and alter tables?
- Who will create and manage users?
- Who will administer passwords?
- Who do users go to when the database has a problem?
- What will your users—business and technical—need in order to do their jobs?

In smaller shops, one person may be the technical generalist and do all these things, along with database design, table design, programming, and documentation. In larger shops, these functions may be split among several trusted individuals. And in very large shops, there may be separate departments to control user security, table creation, and so forth.

Now think what your users will have to do. For example, sometimes you will want your programming staff to control certain tables; at other times you will want table creation strictly controlled by a DBA or operations person.

Data Security

The type of data security policy you establish depends on how important the data is. Private data, such as personal information in Human Resources, will need very tight security. Test tables probably will need very little security. Another way to look at this is: What is the impact if the data is lost? If the data is used by many areas in a production environment, you will have to take the necessary steps to protect it. If it is used by one individual only as a "sandbox," then your security doesn't have to be so tight.

As you will see, there are a couple of standard ways of implementing data security: privileges and roles. We'll discuss privileges and roles later in this chapter.

User Security

The most common methods used to implement user security are *passwords* and *roles*. It is advised that each user be required to enter an ID and a password when accessing the database. This ID and password can and should be in addition to any network (for example, NT) ID and password. In addition, many shops have a change schedule for passwords, usually about 60 days. Regular changes of passwords are also thought to help reduce the risk of unauthorized access. Just be aware that both internal and external auditors are now taking a very close look at computer security, and this will be one of your major responsibilities for the foreseeable future.

Roles are a very common way of handling security. Think of a role as a cloak or special coat. Here's an example: To handle the payroll process at one particular company, 8 database programs are involved. There are 14 payroll staff. You can either take the time and give all 14 staff members the rights to each of the 8 programs, or you can create a role that has rights to the 8 programs and then assign the 14 payroll staff members that role.

Note

Let me push the analogy a bit and tell you that a user can have many roles, so you can think of a role as a hat, with users having many hats to go with their many cloaks. (I hear your groans . . .)

What's the advantage of using roles? Well, if you suddenly needed 9 programs for payroll, you would just change the role instead of each staff member's security. Conversely if your payroll system dropped to 6 programs, again you would just change the role instead of performing an emergency change to 14 accounts.

Special consideration must be given to the very sensitive administration accounts. These are accounts with the IDs *SYS* and *SYSTEM*, and their passwords should be changed as soon as the system is installed. In addition, roles are usually created for all DBAs. These roles contain the various administrative privileges that a DBA has. The same scheme that I described for the preceding payroll example is followed.

Then we have the programmers, or application developers. Perhaps the best way to protect the system is to allow the developers much freedom in a test environment, and then completely restrict them in the production environment. In many cases, there will be several test databases that various development groups will use, and within their own database the developers will have a fairly free hand.

Password Management Policy

To many people, passwords are a necessary evil; to others, they are just a waste of time. No matter what camp you're in, over time the technical world has developed several basic processes that seem to work very well. These are password aging, account locking, password complexity, and password history.

Password Aging

The **password aging** parameter is set in the user's profile. (We'll be discussing profiles shortly.) It refers to the length of time before a password expires.

Account Locking

Account locking consists of two parameters that are set in the user's profile:

1. How many failed login attempts will be allowed before the account is locked
2. How long the account will remain locked when it is locked

Password Complexity

Although Oracle provides a minimum set of criteria, some shops create their own scripts to force things like upper- and lowercase, a minimum number of numerics, or a special character. Such customized routines are included in `CREATE/ALTER PROFILE` statements. All of the nuances in the criteria that are developed for passwords are referred to collectively as **password complexity**.

Password History

Another profile parameter—**password history**—specifies how many times a password must be changed before a particular password can be used again.

Auditing

Auditing is normally done for system tuning and performance reasons. However, there are tools that allow you to track the following if you suspect a security problem:

- **SQL statements**. You can refine the auditing process to track the statements of just one user.
- **Privileges**. An example is the ability to create tables.
- **Schemas**. Here the focus is a particular user and all the objects in that user's schema.

These types of auditing actions are usually initiated when a real or potential security breach is suspected. More details can be found in the Oracle documentation. This short section is just meant to let you know that security auditing does exist.

Building Your Security Schema

How does all this fit together? I've just given you a plateful of concepts, haven't I? Don't worry. Security is really not that complicated, and in the following pages I will take all the concepts just mentioned and walk you through the activities necessary to turn the concepts into realities. When we're done, you will have put a system security policy in place, created users, and protected your data.

A security system consists of three main parts: profiles, roles, and users. Each of these concepts carries with it some complexity, as the discussion that follows will illustrate.

A **profile** controls system resources, such as how many concurrent logons a user may have, idle time, and so forth. Users get a **default profile** automatically, but in the default profile all parameters are set to "unlimited". Although you can change the default profile, you are better off creating your own profiles. In most cases you need to set only a couple of parameters, so creating and managing profiles is not complex.

Roles were defined earlier in the chapter, and the **user account** is the unique account that you create for each user of your database.

With this quick overview, let's try to make connections to our waiver database. After that, we can march boldly into building the profiles, roles, and users.

Profiles

As already mentioned, profiles control the system resources that users need. For the waiver database, we have three user groups: developers, business users, and students. Let's look at some of the characteristics of each group, using a simple chart:

PROFILE

Profile Group	Multiple Logons	Idle Time	CPU Usage Control
Developers	Yes	High	Yes
Business users	No	Low	No
Students	No	No	No

Here's what we need to consider for the three groups:

1. **Developers** want more than one session, and we may want to limit their CPU usage to prevent runaway programs. You've all experienced this phenomenon, when you get a call from Operations about your program eating CPU time because of an infinite loop or something similar.
2. **Business users** need one logon session, and because they can be called away from their desks or sidetracked by phone calls, they should have a timeout parameter to protect the system.
3. **Students** will log on on only at certain workstations, and because the tests have a limited time span, we can let the testing program keep track of the time. The tests will be taken in a monitored room, so there is no risk if a student gives up and walks away from the screen.

Roles

Now that we have our three profiles, let's look at the roles that go with these profiles: Developer, Business, and Student. The Developer role is easy: full access. The Student role is also easy: just the ability to run certain programs. The Business role, however, is more complex, because we have those who can create and alter tests and questions, those who can enter only new authors, and those who will be doing queries and reports and *not* updating any tables.

For business users, then, we must have three subroles: one to manage tests, one to manage authors, and one to create queries and reports. So really we have five roles altogether.

Now bear with me here. Ultimately we want to control access to all the database objects, including forms, reports, and scripts. However, we have not yet written the forms, reports, and scripts, so we cannot grant any security privileges to these objects right now. Instead, we're going to start with our ten tables (which are listed in Table 8.1). After we have completed the programs, you should go back and modify the roles.

Table 8.1 shows how important roles really are. They clearly offer us a way to secure our system and data while letting our users do their jobs. Going through the preceding exercise is basically the way that you establish your system security policy.

Table 8.1 Defining Security Policies for Different Roles

		Business			
Tables	**Developer**	**B1**	**B2**	**B3**	**Student**
AUTHORS	C	C	C	R	R
QUESTIONS	C	C	R	R	R
ANSWERS	C	C	R	R	R
STUDENTS	C	R	R	R	C[a]
STUDENT_HISTORY	C	R	R	R	C[a]
TEST_ID	C	C	R	R	R
QUESTION_TYPE_DESC	C	C	R	R	R
TEST_QUESTIONS_LINK	C	C	R	R	R
TEST_HISTORY	C	R	R	R	R
TEST_TYPE_DESC	C	C	R	R	R

Note: B1 = create tests; B2 = add authors; B3 = run queries; R = read; W = write; C = create (includes R and W).

a. Since we have given the students complete rights to these tables, isn't there a potential problem? Well, most systems give the rights to change the data in tables to the programs they run to take the test, not to the students. That is, the student can run the program, but the program has the power to change the tables. The problem with giving students these rights is that a student who by chance is able to get to the SQL> prompt could change the records. If we give them the rights to the program, any students going to the SQL> prompt will not be able to change their records because Oracle security will recognize that they do not have the right to change any data. Some of you have guessed that the students really don't need access to the tables, and that's right. All they need is a valid logon to run the test programs! I am keeping it simple here, however, just to show you the steps you have to go through to determine your security scheme. In Chapter 13 (Forms 6*i*), I will talk about how to give security rights to the programs instead of the users.

Users

Now that you have defined your profiles and roles, the next step is to take a look at the individual user accounts. There are a few things you will want to consider. Remember back in Chapter 6 we mentioned tablespaces? Well, they're back.

Each user will default to the SYSTEM tablespace unless you specify another tablespace. This is the area where the user can create tables and so forth. However, keep in mind two things here: We don't want the users doing too much in the SYSTEM tablespace because that activity will (1) slow the system and (2) open up important system tables, such as the data dictionary, to potential harm. Those who really need their own tablespaces will get them, but otherwise similar workers will share a particular tablespace.

We also need a TEMP tablespace. As described in Chapter 6, the TEMP tablespace is where sorts and the like take place. Again, we do not want everyone to default to the SYSTEM tablespace, so we will specify a particular TEMP tablespace for our users.

Let's start with an example before we look at our waiver database. We'll begin by creating a profile called WILD_HORSES, with a limit of two concurrent logons and 30 minutes of idle timeout and a maximum connect time of 8 hours. Here's the syntax:

❶ Note the keyword LIMIT.

❷ Two logons maximum.

❸ Log off after 30 minutes.

❹ Log off after 8 hours.

❺ End with a semicolon.

```
CREATE PROFILE WILD_HORSES LIMIT ❶
SESSIONS_PER_CPU 2 ❷
CPU_P_SESSION UNLIMITED
IDLE_TIME 30 ❸
CONNECT_TIME 480; ❹ ❺
```

Suppose that the staff now starts spending half the day in the corrals with the horses. To limit the connect time, you can just use the ALTER statement:

```
ALTER PROFILE WILD_HORSES LIMIT
CONNECT_TIME 240;
```

To delete a profile that is no longer needed, use the DROP command:

```
DROP PROFILE WILD_HORSES CASCADE;
```

CASCADE means that all users who have this profile defined in their security will now default to the default profile.

Let's jump ahead a bit, and I'll show you how you can find out which profile an individual has by looking at all the profiles. We have mentioned one of the database's most powerful tool, the *data dictionary*. Here's a quick glimpse of the kind of information we can get from the data dictionary. These are data dictionary *views* that you can access right from the SQL*Plus prompt:

View	Description
USER_USERS	Shows user name, profile, and account status for the user
DBA_PROFILES	Shows all profiles and their limits

To run the DBA_PROFILES view, for example, just type in SQL> `Select * from DBA_PROFILES;` and you will get a listing of all existing profiles. You will find these data dictionary views very helpful later, when you can't find your documentation and have forgotten who has which profile and what the profiles mean.

Privileges

Now let's look at **privileges**. Roles define privileges, and these privileges can be SYSTEM privileges, such as the ability to update any table on the data dictionary, program privileges, or even column privileges, such as the ability to insert only certain columns in a particular table. You get the idea. Privileges are the core of a role, and you have to be very careful with them. Fortunately, creating roles is easy. First you define the role:

```
SQL > CREATE ROLE WILD_HORSES_ROLE;
Role created.
```

Now comes the fun part. You have to *grant* certain privileges to the role. There are some standard privileges, such as creating a session, without which the user would not be able to log on. Be aware that there are well over a hundred privileges that can be granted, including the abilities to create roles and alter roles.

Let's look at the privileges that the WILD_HORSES folks will need:

```
GRANT    CREATE SESSION to WILD_HORSES_ROLE;
GRANT    CREATE VIEW    to WILD_HORSES_ROLE;
GRANT    INSERT (horse-type) on WILD_HORSES to
WILD_HORSES_ROLE;
GRANT    SELECT on WILD_HORSES to WILD_HORSES_ROLE;
```

These GRANT statements let users do the following:

- Open a database session
- Create a view
- Update the one field in the WILD_HORSES table
- Look at anything in the WILD_HORSES table

I hope that this small example has shown you what you can do with roles. Given the complexity of our waiver database, you must be aware by now that you're going to have to be very careful with what you let people do. Within the role commands, as you've just seen, are enough tools to protect your data while allowing your customers to do what they have to.

Now we're ready to move ahead and start building the security schema for our waiver database.

Note

You can assign more than one role to a user. In fact, this is usually the case, and it makes user account support much easier than if we tried to keep everything in one role or a couple of roles.

Waiver Database Security

We are going to accomplish the major task of creating security for our waiver database by separately creating the four key elements of the security system:

1. Tablespaces
2. Profiles
3. Roles
4. Users

Tablespaces

We'll create two tablespaces: USERS and TEMP. Here's the first one:

```
CREATE TABLESPACE USERS
  DATAFILE 'D:\USERS.DAT' SIZE 300M REUSE ❶
  AUTOEXTEND ON NEXT 1M MAXSIZE 500M
  ONLINE;
```

❶ Use single quotes around the data file name.

This is pretty clear. We use the CREATE TABLESPACE command, give the tablespace a name, and give the data file a name and a start size. In this case we assigned the data file 300MB to support about 20 users, told it to grow if it had to (up to 500MB), and stated that this tablespace was to be online.

Now we do the same thing for the TEMP tablespace:

❶ Use single quotes around the data file name.
❷ Notice TEMPORARY.

```
CREATE TABLESPACE TEMP
  DATAFILE 'D:\TEMP.DAT' SIZE 300M REUSE ❶
  AUTOEXTEND ON NEXT 1M MAXSIZE 500M
  TEMPORARY; ❷
```

Profiles

Moving on to profiles, first we'll create the Developer profile:

```
CREATE PROFILE WAIVER_DEV_PROFILE
  LIMIT SESSIONS_PER_USER UNLIMITED
        CPU_PER_CALL      3000
        CONNECT_TIME      UNLIMITED
        IDLE_TIME         45;
```

Then the Business profile:

```
CREATE PROFILE WAIVER_BUS_PROFILE
  LIMIT SESSIONS_PER_USER 1
        CPU_PER_CALL      UNLIMITED
        CONNECT_TIME      UNLIMITED
        IDLE_TIME         15;
```

And finally, the Student profile:

```
CREATE PROFILE WAIVER_STUDENT_PROFILE
  LIMIT SESSIONS_PER_USER 1
        CPU_PER_CALL      UNLIMITED
        CONNECT_TIME      UNLIMITED
        IDLE_TIME         UNLIMITED;
```

One interesting thing is that in a profile you can have quite a bit of control over logins. Let's say you want to limit the number of failed login attempts, and then lock the user account for one hour when the maximum number of attempts is reached. To do this, add the following lines to the profile:

```
FAILED_LOGIN_ATTEMPTS     5
PASSWORD_LOCK_TIME       60;
```

You can go much further and control when passwords have to be changed, how long before a user can reuse a password, whether there is a grace period for changing a password before the account is locked, and so forth. Consult the Oracle documentation for details. There's enough power here to satisfy even the most demanding auditor.

Roles

Moving on to roles, we use the following command to create the Developer role:

```
CREATE ROLE WAIVER_DEV_ROLE;
```

Then we issue the GRANT statements to the role:

```
GRANT  CREATE SESSION      TO WAIVER_DEV_ROLE;
GRANT  CREATE SYNONYM      TO WAIVER_DEV_ROLE;
GRANT  CREATE TABLE        TO WAIVER_DEV_ROLE;
GRANT  CREATE VIEW         TO WAIVER_DEV_ROLE;
GRANT  CREATE PROCEDURE    TO WAIVER_DEV_ROLE;
GRANT  CREATE TRIGGER      TO WAIVER_DEV_ROLE;
GRANT  SELECT ANY TABLE    TO WAIVER_DEV_ROLE;
```

Note the following:

- **ANY** means that this role can perform the named function in the schema(s) to which it has rights, not just its own. Hence, we want to be careful *not* to grant blanket rights such as UPDATE ANY TABLE because then everything would be opened up to the developers. What we do want to give them, however, is the right to *look* at any table, as the SELECT ANY TABLE statement indicates. In other words, in the test database you would give the developers UPDATE and CREATE rights, but not in the production database.
- **SESSION** means the ability to start a database session.
- **SYNONYM** means creating synonyms for objects.
- **TABLE** and **VIEW** are self-explanatory.
- **Procedures** are programs.
- **Triggers** are pieces of code that are fired off under certain conditions.

Moving on to the Business users, we have to create three roles:

```
CREATE ROLE WAIVER_BUS_ROLE1;
CREATE ROLE WAIVER_BUS_ROLE2;
CREATE ROLE WAIVER_BUS_ROLE3;
```

and then assign the grants to each one. Here are the GRANT statements for the first role:

❶ This role can update the QUESTIONS, ANSWERS, AUTHORS, AND TEST_ID tables. Hence it needs rights to add, modify, and delete entries in those tables, along with all the description tables.

```
GRANT CREATE SESSION TO WAIVER_BUS_ROLE1; ❶

GRANT INSERT ON QUESTIONS TO WAIVER_BUS_ROLE1;
GRANT UPDATE ON QUESTIONS TO WAIVER_BUS_ROLE1;
GRANT DELETE ON QUESTIONS TO WAIVER_BUS_ROLE1;

GRANT INSERT ON ANSWERS TO WAIVER_BUS_ROLE1;
GRANT UPDATE ON ANSWERS TO WAIVER_BUS_ROLE1;
GRANT DELETE ON ANSWERS TO WAIVER_BUS_ROLE1;

GRANT INSERT ON AUTHORS TO WAIVER_BUS_ROLE1;
GRANT UPDATE ON AUTHORS TO WAIVER_BUS_ROLE1;
GRANT DELETE ON AUTHORS TO WAIVER_BUS_ROLE1;

GRANT INSERT ON TEST_ID TO WAIVER_BUS_ROLE1;
GRANT UPDATE ON TEST_ID TO WAIVER_BUS_ROLE1;
GRANT DELETE ON TEST_ID TO WAIVER_BUS_ROLE1;

GRANT INSERT ON TEST_TYPE_DESCRIPTION TO WAIVER_BUS_ROLE1;
GRANT UPDATE ON TEST_TYPE_DESCRIPTION TO WAIVER_BUS_ROLE1;
GRANT DELETE ON TEST_TYPE_DESCRIPTION TO WAIVER_BUS_ROLE1;

GRANT INSERT ON TEST_QUESTIONS_LINK TO WAIVER_BUS_ROLE1;
GRANT UPDATE ON TEST_QUESTIONS_LINK TO WAIVER_BUS_ROLE1;
GRANT DELETE ON TEST_QUESTIONS_LINK TO WAIVER_BUS_ROLE1;

GRANT INSERT ON QUESTION_TYPE_DESCRIPTION TO WAIVER_BUS_ROLE1;
GRANT UPDATE ON QUESTION_TYPE_DESCRIPTION TO WAIVER_BUS_ROLE1;
GRANT DELETE ON QUESTION_TYPE_DESCRIPTION TO WAIVER_BUS_ROLE1;
```

```
GRANT CREATE VIEW TO WAIVER_BUS_ROLE1;
GRANT SELECT TABLE TO WAIVER_BUS_ROLE1;
```

Here are the GRANT statements for the second role:

❶ This role can update only the AUTHORS table.

```
GRANT CREATE SESSION TO WAIVER_BUS_ROLE2; ❶

GRANT INSERT ON AUTHORS TO WAIVER_BUS_ROLE2;
GRANT UPDATE ON AUTHORS TO WAIVER_BUS_ROLE2;
GRANT DELETE ON AUTHORS TO WAIVER_BUS_ROLE2;

GRANT CREATE VIEW TO WAIVER_BUS_ROLE2;
GRANT SELECT TABLE TO WAIVER_BUS_ROLE2;
```

And finally, here are the GRANT statements for the third role:

❷ This role can run reports and views only, on any table.

```
GRANT CREATE SESSION TO WAIVER_BUS_ROLE3; ❷

GRANT CREATE VIEW TO WAIVER_BUS_ROLE3;
GRANT SELECT TABLE TO WAIVER_BUS_ROLE3;
```

Note

IMPORTANT: Again, when we create forms, procedures, and so forth later, the users will have rights to run those programs. We will modify the roles as necessary!!!

The last role is the Student role. We create it like this:

```
CREATE ROLE WAIVER_STUDENT_ROLE;
```

And here are the GRANT statements to go along with the Student role:

❸ This role can add a record to the STUDENTS table. The programs will have rights to update all the other tables such as TEST_HISTORY.

```
GRANT CREATE SESSION TO WAIVER_STUDENT_ROLE; ❸

GRANT INSERT ON STUDENTS TO WAIVER_STUDENT_ROLE;

GRANT SELECT TABLE TO WAIVER_STUDENT_ROLE;
```

Users

The fourth step is to create the user accounts. We're almost done. By now you're probably starting to understand how logical the process is. We're going to create accounts for ten developers, ten business users, and ten students. The ten student accounts are to control the test process. As you've seen, we could alter STUDENT_ROLE to allow ten concurrent logons, but we'd prefer not to.

Creating a user involves only two steps: (1) using the CREATE USER command and (2) assigning it any role(s). Here's the syntax:

```
CREATE USER <USER_NAME>
  IDENTIFIED BY <PASSWORD>
  DEFAULT TABLESPACE <TABLESPACE NAME>
  TEMPORARY TABLESPACE <TABLESPACE NAME>
  QUOTA <XX> ON <TABLESPACE NAME>
  QUOTA <XX> ON <TEMPORARY TABLESPACE NAME>
  PROFILE <PROFILE NAME>;
```

After the user is created, issue the GRANT statement:

```
GRANT <ROLE> TO <USER_NAME>;
```

Now let's put the pieces together:

```
CREATE USER WAIVER_DEV1
  IDENTIFIED BY WAIVER_DEV_PW1 ❶
  DEFAULT TABLESPACE USERS
  TEMPORARY TABLESPACE TEMP ❷
  QUOTA 25M ON USERS
  QUOTA 25M ON TEMP
  PROFILE WAIVER_DEV_PROFILE ❸

GRANT WAIVER_DEV_ROLE TO WAIVER_DEV1; ❹
```

❶ We have included the password WAIVER_DEV_PW1, ❷ then assigned this user to the two tablespaces we created, ❸ and last, tied the user to the Developer Profile.

❹ The last step is to tie the user to the Developer role.

Repeat these steps for users WAIVER_DEV2 through WAIVER_DEV10.

Now do the same for the Business users, being careful about which profile goes to whom.

```
CREATE USER WAIVER_BUS1
  IDENTIFIED BY WAIVER_BUS_PW1
  DEFAULT TABLESPACE USERS
  TEMPORARY TABLESPACE TEMP
  QUOTA 25M ON USERS
  QUOTA 25M ON TEMP
  PROFILE WAIVER_BUS_PROFILE;

GRANT WAIVER_BUS_ROLE1 to WAIVER_BUS1;
```

After creating the first Business user, create user accounts for WAIVER_BUS2 through WAIVER_BUS4 just as you did for BUS1. Then create the BUS5 user account like this:

```
CREATE USER WAIVER_BUS5
  IDENTIFIED BY WAIVER_BUS_PW5
  DEFAULT TABLESPACE USERS
  TEMPORARY TABLESPACE TEMP
  QUOTA 25M ON USERS
  QUOTA 25M ON TEMP
  PROFILE WAIVER_BUS_PROFILE;

GRANT WAIVER_BUS_ROLE2 to WAIVER_BUS5;
```

Now create two more Business users—BUS6 and BUS7—exactly as you created BUS5.

Create the eighth Business user like this:

```
CREATE USER WAIVER_BUS8
  IDENTIFIED BY WAIVER_BUS_PW8
  DEFAULT TABLESPACE USERS
  TEMPORARY TABLESPACE TEMP
  QUOTA 25M ON USERS
  QUOTA 25M ON TEMP
  PROFILE WAIVER_BUS_PROFILE;

GRANT WAIVER_BUS_ROLE3 to WAIVER_BUS8;
```

And finally, create BUS9 and BUS10 just as you created BUS8.

Moving on to the students, create Student users 1 through 10 like this:

```
CREATE USER WAIVER_STU1
  IDENTIFIED BY WAIVER_STU_PW1
  DEFAULT TABLESPACE USERS
  TEMPORARY TABLESPACE TEMP
  QUOTA 25M ON USERS
  QUOTA 25M ON TEMP
  PROFILE WAIVER_STUDENT_PROFILE;

GRANT WAIVER_STUDENT_ROLE TO WAIVER_STU1;
```

Here's a quick synopsis of the entire process:

❶ Create the default tablespace.

❷ Create the default TEMP tablespace.

❸ Create the profile.

❹ Create the role.

❺ Grant privileges to the role.

```
1. CREATE TABLESPACE USERS ❶
     DATAFILE  'D:\USERS.DAT' SIZE 300M REUSE
     AUTOEXTEND ON NEXT 1M MAXSIZE 500M
     ONLINE;
2. CREATE TABLESPACE TEMP ❷
     DATAFILE  'D:\TEMP.DAT' SIZE 300M REUSE
     AUTOEXTEND ON NEXT 1M MAXSIZE 500M
     ONLINE;
3. CREATE PROFILE WAIVER_DEV_PROFILE ❸
     LIMIT SESSIONS_PER_USER      5
           CPU_PER_SESSION      UNLIMITED
           CPU_PER_CALL         UNLIMITED
           CONNECT_TIME         UNLIMITED
           IDLE_TIME            UNLIMITED;
4. CREATE ROLE WAIVER_DEV_ROLE; ❹
5. GRANT CREATE SESSION TO WAIVER_DEV_ROLE; ❺
   GRANT CREATE SYNONYM TO WAIVER_DEV_ROLE;
   GRANT CREATE TABLE TO WAIVER_DEV_ROLE;
   GRANT CREATE VIEW TO WAIVER_DEV_ROLE;
   GRANT CREATE PROCEDURE TO WAIVER_DEV_ROLE;
   GRANT CREATE TRIGGER TO WAIVER_DEV_ROLE;
   GRANT SELECT ANY TABLE TO WAIVER_DEV_ROLE;
```

❻ Create user account.

```
6. CREATE USER WAIVER_DEV1 ❻
     IDENTIFIED BY WAIVER_DEV1_PW1
     DEFAULT TABLESPACE USERS
     TEMPORARY TABLESPACE TEMP
     QUOTA 25M ON USERS
     QUOTA 25M ON TEMP
     PROFILE WAIVER_DEV_PROFILE;
7. GRANT WAIVER_DEV_ROLE TO WAIVER_DEV1; ❼
```

❼ Give the user a role.

Note

Here's an important point: Users cannot see tables that are owned by another user unless they have rights to those tables. (That is, the tables are in another schema.) Sometimes users find another user's table name when using ALL_TABLES, but they get an "ORA-0403" or similar error message saying that the table does not exist. The owner knows the table exists because he or she is the one who created it.

Users who have rights to a table that they do not own can see the table in two ways: using either a synonym or the format "schema name.table name". After creating a synonym, an owner can either specifically give other users the rights to use that synonym or make the synonym public. Here's how we create public synonyms for tables:

```
CREATE public synonym STUDENTS for STUDENTS;
```

As you probably guessed, because it is a public synonym, anyone can now access the table. As mentioned, a user who has been given rights to the table can always put the schema name in front of the table name—for example:

```
SELECT * from SYSTEM.STUDENTS;
```

However, this command is unwieldy, so most sites create synonyms for tables.

Also be aware that the owner of the schema has to create these synonyms for tables. So if you find that your users cannot access the tables that you created with the system ID or another ID, then create public synonyms for all of the tables, and you should be all set. Use the same name as the original table.

Help from the Data Dictionary

Earlier in this chapter I showed you how to look at profiles using the data dictionary. Although I will discuss the data dictionary in more detail in

Chapter 10, I want to include in this chapter other data dictionary views that are helpful when you're looking for information on tablespaces, roles, and password limits. Table 8.2 lists these views.

Table 8.2 Data Dictionary Views Relevant to Tablespaces, Roles, and Password Limits

View	Description
DBA_TS_QUOTAS	Shows the tablespace quotas for *all* users.
USER_TS_QUOTAS	Shows the tablespace quotas for the current user only.
USER_PASSWORD_LIMITS	Shows any password restrictions in the user's profile.
USER_RESOURCE_LIMITS	Shows any resource limits for the current user.
USER_COL_PRIVS	Shows any particular columns in tables that the user has special rights to and what the user can do to those columns.
ALL_COL_PRIVS	Shows all columns in all tables for all users that have special column privileges.
USER_TAB_PRIVS	Shows all object privileges for a particular user.
SESSION_PRIVS	Lists all the system privileges for a particular user.
DBA_SYS_PRIVS	Shows all system privilege grants made to roles and users.
DBA_ROLE_PRIVS	Shows all roles that have been granted both to users and to other roles.
DBA_ROLES	Lists all the roles for a database administrator.

The Entire Waiver Database Security Script

Often the security setup is done from a script. At the end of the script I'll give you a tip on how to have it prompt you for user name and so forth. Most security folks use such scripts to make their lives easier as staff roles change. For now, though, here is the complete script to create all the profiles, roles, and user accounts mentioned in this chapter:

```
--  Script to build profiles, roles, and user accounts
--
--          Guerrilla Oracle
--
--        Run this script from the SQL> prompt:
--              SQL>@SECURITY_LOAD.SQL
--                   where @ = path to the script
--
```

```
--     When you make changes, remember to save the file as:
--             TYPE = 'all files'
--             and put double quotes around the name:
--                  "SECURITY_LOAD.SQL"
--------------------------------------------------------------

CREATE PROFILE    WAIVER_DEV_PROFILE  LIMIT
   SESSIONS_PER_USER          UNLIMITED
   CPU_PER_CALL               4000
   CONNECT_TIME               UNLIMITED
   IDLE_TIME                  45;

CREATE PROFILE    WAIVER_BUS_PROFILE  LIMIT
   SESSIONS_PER_USER          1
   CPU_PER_CALL               UNLIMITED
   CONNECT_TIME               UNLIMITED
   IDLE_TIME                  15;

CREATE PROFILE    WAIVER_STUDENT_PROFILE  LIMIT
   SESSIONS_PER_USER          1
   CPU_PER_CALL               UNLIMITED
   CONNECT_TIME               UNLIMITED
   IDLE_TIME                  UNLIMITED;

ALTER PROFILE    WAIVER_BUS_PROFILE   LIMIT
   FAILED_LOGIN_ATTEMPTS          5
   PASSWORD_LOCK_TIME            15;

ALTER PROFILE    WAIVER_DEV_PROFILE   LIMIT
   FAILED_LOGIN_ATTEMPTS          3
   PASSWORD_LOCK_TIME             5;

CREATE ROLE      WAIVER_DEV_ROLE;


GRANT   CREATE SESSION      TO WAIVER_DEV_ROLE;
GRANT   CREATE SYNONYM      TO WAIVER_DEV_ROLE;
GRANT   CREATE TABLE        TO WAIVER_DEV_ROLE;
GRANT   CREATE VIEW         TO WAIVER_DEV_ROLE;
```

```
GRANT   CREATE PROCEDURE   TO WAIVER_DEV_ROLE;
GRANT   CREATE TRIGGER     TO WAIVER_DEV_ROLE;
GRANT   SELECT ANY TABLE   TO WAIVER_DEV_ROLE;


CREATE ROLE  WAIVER_BUS_ROLE1;
CREATE ROLE  WAIVER_BUS_ROLE2;
CREATE ROLE  WAIVER_BUS_ROLE3;
--
--
--  Grants to the WAIVER_BUS_ROLE1:
--
GRANT CREATE SESSION TO WAIVER_BUS_ROLE1;

GRANT INSERT ON QUESTIONS TO WAIVER_BUS_ROLE1;
GRANT UPDATE ON QUESTIONS TO WAIVER_BUS_ROLE1;
GRANT DELETE ON QUESTIONS TO WAIVER_BUS_ROLE1;

GRANT INSERT ON ANSWERS TO WAIVER_BUS_ROLE1;
GRANT UPDATE ON ANSWERS TO WAIVER_BUS_ROLE1;
GRANT DELETE ON ANSWERS TO WAIVER_BUS_ROLE1;

GRANT INSERT ON AUTHORS TO WAIVER_BUS_ROLE1;
GRANT UPDATE ON AUTHORS TO WAIVER_BUS_ROLE1;
GRANT DELETE ON AUTHORS TO WAIVER_BUS_ROLE1;

GRANT INSERT ON TEST_ID TO WAIVER_BUS_ROLE1;
GRANT UPDATE ON TEST_ID TO WAIVER_BUS_ROLE1;
GRANT DELETE ON TEST_ID TO WAIVER_BUS_ROLE1;

GRANT INSERT ON TEST_TYPE_DESC TO WAIVER_BUS_ROLE1;
GRANT UPDATE ON TEST_TYPE_DESC TO WAIVER_BUS_ROLE1;
GRANT DELETE ON TEST_TYPE_DESC TO WAIVER_BUS_ROLE1;

GRANT INSERT ON TEST_QUESTIONS_LINK TO WAIVER_BUS_ROLE1;
GRANT UPDATE ON TEST_QUESTIONS_LINK TO WAIVER_BUS_ROLE1;
GRANT DELETE ON TEST_QUESTIONS_LINK TO WAIVER_BUS_ROLE1;
```

```
GRANT INSERT ON QUESTIONS_TYPE_DESC TO WAIVER_BUS_ROLE1;
GRANT UPDATE ON QUESTIONS_TYPE_DESC TO WAIVER_BUS_ROLE1;
GRANT DELETE ON QUESTIONS_TYPE_DESC TO WAIVER_BUS_ROLE1;

GRANT CREATE VIEW TO WAIVER_BUS_ROLE1;
--
--
-- Grants to the WAIVER_BUS_ROLE2:
--
GRANT CREATE SESSION TO WAIVER_BUS_ROLE2;

GRANT INSERT ON AUTHORS TO WAIVER_BUS_ROLE2;
GRANT UPDATE ON AUTHORS TO WAIVER_BUS_ROLE2;
GRANT DELETE ON AUTHORS TO WAIVER_BUS_ROLE2;

GRANT CREATE VIEW TO WAIVER_BUS_ROLE2;
--
--
-- Grants to the WAIVER_BUS_ROLE3:
--
GRANT CREATE SESSION TO WAIVER_BUS_ROLE3;

GRANT CREATE VIEW TO WAIVER_BUS_ROLE3;


----          Student role and grants     -----
--
CREATE ROLE WAIVER_STUDENT_ROLE;

GRANT CREATE SESSION         TO WAIVER_STUDENT_ROLE;

GRANT INSERT ON STUDENTS     TO WAIVER_STUDENT_ROLE;

--
--
--       Create users and assign roles
--
--
```

```
--  First build ten Developer accounts:
CREATE USER    WAIVER_DEV1
   IDENTIFIED BY WAIVER_DEV_PW1
   DEFAULT TABLESPACE   USERS
   TEMPORARY TABLESPACE  TEMP
   QUOTA 25M ON USERS
   QUOTA 25M ON TEMP
   PROFILE   WAIVER_DEV_PROFILE;
GRANT  WAIVER_DEV_ROLE TO WAIVER_DEV1;

CREATE USER    WAIVER_DEV2
   IDENTIFIED BY WAIVER_DEV_PW2
   DEFAULT TABLESPACE   USERS
   TEMPORARY TABLESPACE  TEMP
   QUOTA 25M ON USERS
   QUOTA 25M ON TEMP
   PROFILE   WAIVER_DEV_PROFILE;
GRANT  WAIVER_DEV_ROLE TO WAIVER_DEV2;

CREATE USER    WAIVER_DEV3
   IDENTIFIED BY WAIVER_DEV_PW3
   DEFAULT TABLESPACE   USERS
   TEMPORARY TABLESPACE  TEMP
   QUOTA 25M ON USERS
   QUOTA 25M ON TEMP
   PROFILE   WAIVER_DEV_PROFILE;
GRANT  WAIVER_DEV_ROLE TO WAIVER_DEV3;

CREATE USER    WAIVER_DEV4
   IDENTIFIED BY WAIVER_DEV_PW4
   DEFAULT TABLESPACE   USERS
   TEMPORARY TABLESPACE  TEMP
   QUOTA 25M ON USERS
   QUOTA 25M ON TEMP
   PROFILE   WAIVER_DEV_PROFILE;

GRANT  WAIVER_DEV_ROLE TO WAIVER_DEV4;
```

```
CREATE USER    WAIVER_DEV5
   IDENTIFIED BY WAIVER_DEV_PW5
   DEFAULT TABLESPACE   USERS
   TEMPORARY TABLESPACE  TEMP
   QUOTA 25M ON USERS
   QUOTA 25M ON TEMP
   PROFILE   WAIVER_DEV_PROFILE;
GRANT  WAIVER_DEV_ROLE TO WAIVER_DEV5;

CREATE USER    WAIVER_DEV6
   IDENTIFIED BY WAIVER_DEV_PW6
   DEFAULT TABLESPACE   USERS
   TEMPORARY TABLESPACE  TEMP
   QUOTA 25M ON USERS
   QUOTA 25M ON TEMP
   PROFILE   WAIVER_DEV_PROFILE;
GRANT  WAIVER_DEV_ROLE TO WAIVER_DEV6;

CREATE USER    WAIVER_DEV7
   IDENTIFIED BY WAIVER_DEV_PW7
   DEFAULT TABLESPACE   USERS
   TEMPORARY TABLESPACE  TEMP
   QUOTA 25M ON USERS
   QUOTA 25M ON TEMP
   PROFILE   WAIVER_DEV_PROFILE;
GRANT  WAIVER_DEV_ROLE TO WAIVER_DEV7;

CREATE USER    WAIVER_DEV8
   IDENTIFIED BY WAIVER_DEV_PW8
   DEFAULT TABLESPACE   USERS
   TEMPORARY TABLESPACE  TEMP
   QUOTA 25M ON USERS
   QUOTA 25M ON TEMP
   PROFILE   WAIVER_DEV_PROFILE;
GRANT  WAIVER_DEV_ROLE TO WAIVER_DEV8;

CREATE USER    WAIVER_DEV9
   IDENTIFIED BY WAIVER_DEV_PW9
   DEFAULT TABLESPACE   USERS
   TEMPORARY TABLESPACE  TEMP
```

```
   QUOTA 25M ON USERS
   QUOTA 25M ON TEMP
   PROFILE  WAIVER_DEV_PROFILE;
GRANT  WAIVER_DEV_ROLE TO WAIVER_DEV9;

CREATE USER    WAIVER_DEV10
   IDENTIFIED BY WAIVER_DEV_PW10
   DEFAULT TABLESPACE   USERS
   TEMPORARY TABLESPACE  TEMP
   QUOTA 25M ON USERS
   QUOTA 25M ON TEMP
   PROFILE  WAIVER_DEV_PROFILE;
GRANT  WAIVER_DEV_ROLE TO WAIVER_DEV10;

--  Next build four business users for BUS1_ROLE:

CREATE USER    WAIVER_BUS1
   IDENTIFIED BY WAIVER_BUS_PW1
   DEFAULT TABLESPACE   USERS
   TEMPORARY TABLESPACE  TEMP
   QUOTA 25M ON USERS
   QUOTA 25M ON TEMP
   PROFILE  WAIVER_BUS_PROFILE;
GRANT  WAIVER_BUS_ROLE1 TO WAIVER_BUS1;

CREATE USER    WAIVER_BUS2
   IDENTIFIED BY WAIVER_BUS_PW2
   DEFAULT TABLESPACE   USERS
   TEMPORARY TABLESPACE  TEMP
   QUOTA 25M ON USERS
   QUOTA 25M ON TEMP
   PROFILE  WAIVER_BUS_PROFILE;
GRANT  WAIVER_BUS_ROLE1 TO WAIVER_BUS2;

CREATE USER    WAIVER_BUS3
   IDENTIFIED BY WAIVER_BUS_PW3
   DEFAULT TABLESPACE   USERS
   TEMPORARY TABLESPACE  TEMP
   QUOTA 25M ON USERS
```

```
    QUOTA 25M ON TEMP
    PROFILE   WAIVER_BUS_PROFILE;
GRANT  WAIVER_BUS_ROLE1 TO WAIVER_BUS3;

CREATE USER    WAIVER_BUS4
    IDENTIFIED BY WAIVER_BUS_PW4
    DEFAULT TABLESPACE   USERS
    TEMPORARY TABLESPACE  TEMP
    QUOTA 25M ON USERS
    QUOTA 25M ON TEMP
    PROFILE   WAIVER_BUS_PROFILE;
GRANT  WAIVER_BUS_ROLE1 TO WAIVER_BUS4;

CREATE USER    WAIVER_BUS6
    IDENTIFIED BY WAIVER_BUS_PW6
    DEFAULT TABLESPACE   USERS
    TEMPORARY TABLESPACE  TEMP
    QUOTA 25M ON USERS
    QUOTA 25M ON TEMP
    PROFILE   WAIVER_BUS_PROFILE;
GRANT  WAIVER_BUS_ROLE2 TO WAIVER_BUS6;

CREATE USER    WAIVER_BUS7
    IDENTIFIED BY WAIVER_BUS_PW7
    DEFAULT TABLESPACE   USERS
    TEMPORARY TABLESPACE  TEMP
    QUOTA 25M ON USERS
    QUOTA 25M ON TEMP
    PROFILE   WAIVER_BUS_PROFILE;
GRANT  WAIVER_BUS_ROLE2 TO WAIVER_BUS7;

CREATE USER    WAIVER_BUS8
    IDENTIFIED BY WAIVER_BUS_PW8
    DEFAULT TABLESPACE   USERS
    TEMPORARY TABLESPACE  TEMP
    QUOTA 25M ON USERS
    QUOTA 25M ON TEMP
    PROFILE   WAIVER_BUS_PROFILE;
GRANT  WAIVER_BUS_ROLE3 TO WAIVER_BUS8;
```

```
CREATE USER    WAIVER_BUS9
   IDENTIFIED BY WAIVER_BUS_PW9
   DEFAULT TABLESPACE   USERS
   TEMPORARY TABLESPACE  TEMP
   QUOTA 25M ON USERS
   QUOTA 25M ON TEMP
   PROFILE   WAIVER_BUS_PROFILE;
GRANT  WAIVER_BUS_ROLE3 TO WAIVER_BUS9;

CREATE USER    WAIVER_BUS10
   IDENTIFIED BY WAIVER_BUS_PW10
   DEFAULT TABLESPACE   USERS
   TEMPORARY TABLESPACE  TEMP
   QUOTA 25M ON USERS
   QUOTA 25M ON TEMP
   PROFILE   WAIVER_BUS_PROFILE;
GRANT  WAIVER_BUS_ROLE3 TO WAIVER_BUS10;

--
--
--            Now create the Student accounts
--

CREATE USER    WAIVER_STU1
   IDENTIFIED BY WAIVER_STU_PW1
   DEFAULT TABLESPACE   USERS
   TEMPORARY TABLESPACE  TEMP
   QUOTA 25M ON USERS
   QUOTA 25M ON TEMP
   PROFILE   WAIVER_STUDENT_PROFILE;
GRANT  WAIVER_STUDENT_ROLE TO WAIVER_STU1;


CREATE USER    WAIVER_STU2
   IDENTIFIED BY WAIVER_STU_PW2
   DEFAULT TABLESPACE   USERS
   TEMPORARY TABLESPACE  TEMP
   QUOTA 25M ON USERS
```

```
  QUOTA 25M ON TEMP
  PROFILE   WAIVER_STUDENT_PROFILE;
GRANT  WAIVER_STUDENT_ROLE TO WAIVER_STU2;

CREATE USER    WAIVER_STU3
  IDENTIFIED BY WAIVER_STU_PW3
  DEFAULT TABLESPACE   USERS
  TEMPORARY TABLESPACE  TEMP
  QUOTA 25M ON USERS
  QUOTA 25M ON TEMP
  PROFILE   WAIVER_STUDENT_PROFILE;
GRANT  WAIVER_STUDENT_ROLE TO WAIVER_STU3;

CREATE USER    WAIVER_STU4
  IDENTIFIED BY WAIVER_STU_PW4
  DEFAULT TABLESPACE   USERS
  TEMPORARY TABLESPACE  TEMP
  QUOTA 25M ON USERS
  QUOTA 25M ON TEMP
  PROFILE   WAIVER_STUDENT_PROFILE;
GRANT  WAIVER_STUDENT_ROLE TO WAIVER_STU4;

CREATE USER    WAIVER_STU5
  IDENTIFIED BY WAIVER_STU_PW5
  DEFAULT TABLESPACE   USERS
  TEMPORARY TABLESPACE  TEMP
  QUOTA 25M ON USERS
  QUOTA 25M ON TEMP
  PROFILE   WAIVER_STUDENT_PROFILE;
GRANT  WAIVER_STUDENT_ROLE TO WAIVER_STU5;

CREATE USER    WAIVER_STU6
  IDENTIFIED BY WAIVER_STU_PW6
  DEFAULT TABLESPACE   USERS
  TEMPORARY TABLESPACE  TEMP
  QUOTA 25M ON USERS
  QUOTA 25M ON TEMP
  PROFILE   WAIVER_STUDENT_PROFILE;
GRANT  WAIVER_STUDENT_ROLE TO WAIVER_STU6;
```

```
CREATE USER    WAIVER_STU7
   IDENTIFIED BY WAIVER_STU_PW7
   DEFAULT TABLESPACE   USERS
   TEMPORARY TABLESPACE  TEMP
   QUOTA 25M ON USERS
   QUOTA 25M ON TEMP
   PROFILE   WAIVER_STUDENT_PROFILE;
GRANT  WAIVER_STUDENT_ROLE TO WAIVER_STU7;

CREATE USER    WAIVER_STU8
   IDENTIFIED BY WAIVER_STU_PW8
   DEFAULT TABLESPACE   USERS
   TEMPORARY TABLESPACE  TEMP
   QUOTA 25M ON USERS
   QUOTA 25M ON TEMP
   PROFILE   WAIVER_STUDENT_PROFILE;
GRANT  WAIVER_STUDENT_ROLE TO WAIVER_STU8;

CREATE USER    WAIVER_STU9
   IDENTIFIED BY WAIVER_STU_PW9
   DEFAULT TABLESPACE   USERS
   TEMPORARY TABLESPACE  TEMP
   QUOTA 25M ON USERS
   QUOTA 25M ON TEMP
   PROFILE   WAIVER_STUDENT_PROFILE;
GRANT  WAIVER_STUDENT_ROLE TO WAIVER_STU9;

CREATE USER    WAIVER_STU10
   IDENTIFIED BY WAIVER_STU_PW10
   DEFAULT TABLESPACE   USERS
   TEMPORARY TABLESPACE  TEMP
   QUOTA 25M ON USERS
   QUOTA 25M ON TEMP
   PROFILE   WAIVER_STUDENT_PROFILE;
GRANT  WAIVER_STUDENT_ROLE TO WAIVER_STU10;
```

Here are some examples of what you will see if you run each of the commands from the SQL> prompt:

```
SQL> CREATE TABLESPACE USERS
  2  DATAFILE 'D:\USERS.DAT'  SIZE 300M  REUSE
  3  AUTOEXTEND ON NEXT 1M MAXSIZE 500M
  4  ONLINE;

Tablespace created.
```

```
SQL> CREATE PROFILE   WAIVER_DEV_PROFILE
  2    LIMIT  SESSIONS_PER_USER   UNLIMITED
  3           CPU_PER_CALL        3000
  4           CONNECT_TIME        UNLIMITED
  5*          IDLE_TIME           45

Profile created.
```

```
SQL> ALTER PROFILE WAIVER_BUS_PROFILE
  2  LIMIT
  3  SESSIONS_PER_USER 10;

Profile altered.
```

```
SQL> CREATE ROLE WAIVER_DEV_ROLE;

Role created.
```

```
SQL> GRANT CREATE SESSION    TO WAIVER_DEV_ROLE;

Grant succeeded.
```

```
SQL> CREATE USER    WAIVER_DEV11
       IDENTIFIED BY WAIVER_DEV_PW11
       DEFAULT TABLESPACE   USERS
       TEMPORARY TABLESPACE  TEMP
       QUOTA 25M ON USERS
       QUOTA 25M ON TEMP
       PROFILE   WAIVER_DEV_PROFILE;

User created.
```

As I mentioned earlier, you can have the script prompt you for the variables. This is the more common approach, and in time you will have a folder of such scripts so that you can easily add new users, delete users, change roles, and so forth. The command you use is very simple. In your script just write the following:

```
ACCEPT  '&USER ID'
ACCEPT '&PASSWORD'
ACCEPT '&ROLE'
```

and so on. When you run the script, you'll be prompted for the variables, and once they have been entered, the script will take off all by itself. In Chapter 14 I will show you how to use the same technique with reports.

Chapter 9

Creating the Tables

Now that the server is running, the database has been created, and users have been defined, we can go ahead and create our tables. As you saw in Chapters 4 and 5, a lot of work went into determining the business needs and translating them into a solid table design. After all the coffee cups were cleared away and the final diagrams were drawn on the whiteboard, we ended up with ten tables. Remember that there is a real dependency among the tables because of the referential integrity constraints that we built into them.

This means that certain core tables are the foundation for the entire system. These are the question, answer, and test tables (QUESTIONS, ANSWERS, and TEST_ID); the question and test descriptor tables (QUESTIONS_TYPE_DESC and TEST_TYPE_DESC); the AUTHORS table; and the table linking questions and test (TEST_QUESTIONS_LINK). These tables must be defined first, and the order in which you create them is important, as you will see.

Overview

How are we going to create and load the tables? First off, we'll use straight **SQL*Plus** right on the Oracle server. In the coming chapters you will learn how to install Net8 on the local client, as well as on remote devices, but for our purposes we are going to stay right on the Oracle server and build those tables.

Our user will be the highly privileged user that we discussed in Chapter 8 when we played with the IDs that were automatically created when we installed the Oracle database back in Chapter 7. Soon you will learn how to create other users, including a "superuser" that will be your main administration account. For now, let's stick with the superuser ID that Oracle gave us: SYSTEM/MANAGER.

Second, we'll create the table manually so that I can explain the steps, showing you a script that you can modify for your site. This script will show you the basic table commands, and I'll also include the SQL listing to show you the system messages. Refer back to Chapter 6 for a refresher on the terminology if you have to.

Finally, once the tables have been created, I'll show you how to load data. Often legacy data has to be ported to the new Oracle database. One way to do this is to use the Oracle tool SQL Loader, another is to write a script that contains all the data, and a third is to create a quick-and-dirty graphical user interface (GUI) form to enter the data. We'll take a look at all three methods.

Table Creation Syntax

For the creation of tables, the SQL commands DROP/CREATE TABLE and ALTER/DROP/CREATE TABLESPACE are a very important part of the syntax:

```
CREATE TABLE    table name         (
  Column-name1          datatype1  column1 constraint,
  Column-name2          datatype2,
   .                           .
   .                           .
   .                           .
  any primary key combinations...❶
                        )
  TABLESPACE    tablespace-name ❷
                          ;
```

❶ Note that the last column definition does *not* end in a comma.

❷ Note that the TABLESPACE line comes *after* the right parenthesis.

We will use these commands extensively in this chapter. Here's a concrete example:

```
CREATE TABLE MY_TABLE   (
FIRST_NAME  VARCHAR2(20),
LAST_NAME VARCHAR2(20),
PRIMARY KEY FIRST_NAME, LAST_NAME
                       )
TABLESPACE  MY_NAME_TABLESPACE
```

Syntax Rules

Here are the specific syntax rules for creating tables:

- Column definitions are contained in parentheses. Start the column definition with a left parenthesis; put a comma after each column definition line *except* the last one; end the column definitions with the right parenthesis.
- Place the TABLESPACE line after you close out the column definitions.
- Wrap the whole thing up with a semicolon.

You need to be very careful with special characters such as the parenthesis, comma, and semicolon. After you get syntax errors a couple of times, you'll catch on. I have tried to make these characters clear by highlighting them in the example at the beginning of this section. You do not need to put them on their own lines, as this example shows:

```
CREATE TABLE NAMES (FIRST_NAME VARCHAR2(20))
TABLESPACE   NAMES_SPACE;
```

Remember that constraints include making a column a primary key, making it "not null", and adding referential integrity. Quite a few other variables can be used with table creation, but the ones I have described here will suffice for our purposes.

Remember tablespaces? We will be putting all our tables into the tablespace that was created when the Oracle database was built: the CW1 tablespace.

Tablespaces

Remember that a tablespace is just a slice of storage. We separate tables for performance, backup, and other reasons. In a multidisk system, you can balance the input/output load by separating the system tables and the data tables into their own tablespaces on their own disks.

Here's the general process:

1. Make sure that the tablespace is deleted if it already exists. Unlike the process with tables, this is done in two steps:
    1) Alter the tablespace to put it offline in normal mode.
    2) Drop the tablespace.
2. Create the tablespace.

And here's the syntax:

```
ALTER TABLESPACE MY_NAMES
   OFFLINE NORMAL
            ;
DROP TABLESPACE MY_NAMES
   INCLUDING CONTENTS
            ;
CREATE TABLESPACE MY_NAMES
   DATAFILE  'D:\TABLESPACES\DATA\MY_NAMES'  SIZE 500M
   ONLINE
   PERMANENT
            ;
```

Note the following about the syntax with tablespace creation:

- Everything ends with a semicolon.
- NORMAL in the ALTER statement means wait until all users are out of the tablespace before taking it offline. In our case there is no activity, so this statement has the effect of taking the tablespace offline *immediately*.
- In the DROP command, INCLUDING CONTENTS means delete the tablespace even if it contains tables.
- The CREATE statement also stipulates that we want the tablespace to be online and permanent. (We will create a temporary tablespace later that will be used for sorts and other temporary tables and files.) Put the data file name in single quotes. (There are many other ways to refine the CREATE command, but this is enough to get us going. You will learn more as you gain experience.)

- Finally, if you don't specify the path and directory for the data file, Oracle will put it in the `\oracle\oraXX\database` folder.

Note

Now that you're familiar with the syntax for tablespace and table creation, I want to make you aware that tablespaces can be refined further to significantly improve performance. The refinement is to define the tablespaces as *locally managed*. We do this by adding `EXTENT MANAGEMENT LOCAL` to the `CREATE TABLESPACE` syntax. This command gives the tablespace control over space allocation and deallocation as blocks are used and released.

I refer you to more technical documentation for an in-depth discussion of locally managed tablespaces and the advantages.

Creating the Tables

OK, ready to go? Start SQL*Plus and log on to the database using the SYSTEM/MANAGER ID. You should see the `SQL>` prompt.

I will walk you through the script lines, pointing out various important processing steps. The script commands and system messages will be shown in **bold**. At the end, I'll give you the complete script and the output listing showing what the system generated, along with comments to help you follow the flow. For those of you who are wondering whether there's an easier way, the answer is yes. In practice, all of us have a medicine bag of various tools, tricks, and scripts that we create in a text editor and save as a `.sql` type. Here's an example of saving a script in Notepad. Notice that the file name is in quotes, and it is saved as type "All Files":

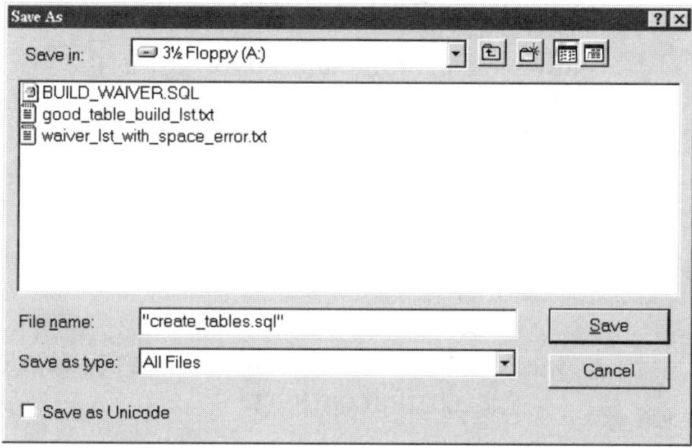

These files can then be run from the SQL> prompt: @A:\CREATE_TABLES.SQL. For your own learning, however, I advise you to type the commands manually, get the normal syntax errors, struggle with cleaning them up, and in general become very good at creating SQL*Plus commands. (This exercise will be frustrating at times, but believe me, it will be worth it.)

Getting Started

The first step is to tell Oracle to create an output listing of all commands and system messages. We do this by using two SQL commands—SPOOL and SET ECHO:

1. SPOOL tells Oracle to create a file that will contain every command and system message that is generated when you create the tables.

> **Note**
>
> Note that SPOOL cannot create a folder, so if you want to use something like C:\SPOOL_FILES as a folder, you must create the folder first.

2. SET ECHO ON means that you want to see every system message that appears when you run your commands, including all errors.

So here are the first couple of lines to type in:

```
SQL> SET ECHO ON;
SQL>SPOOL C:\SPOOL_FILES\WAIVER.LST;
```

Creating the Tablespace

Now we create the tablespace, using the ALTER, DROP, CREATE commands we just talked about. Type in the following:

```
ALTER TABLESPACE TABLESPACE_FOR_WAIVERS
OFFLINE
NORMAL
      ;

DROP TABLESPACE TABLESPACE_FOR_WAIVERS
  INCLUDING CONTENTS
      ;
```

```
CREATE TABLESPACE  TABLE_SPACE_FOR_WAIVERS
  DATAFILE   'D:\TABLESPACES\DATA\TABLESPACE_FOR_WAIVERS'
  SIZE 1000M
  OFFLUNE
  PERMANENT
      ;
```

"Whoa," you say? Just got a nasty error:

```
SQL> ALTER TABLESPACE TABLESPACE_FOR_WAIVERS
  2  OFFLUNE;
OFFLUNE
*
ERROR at line 2:
ORA-02142: missing or invalid ALTER TABLESPACE option
```

You've discovered by now (unless you're a perfect typist) that *you cannot backspace* when working from the SQL command line. Do you have to retype the entire command? No. SQL*Plus comes with a default editor (you can change it, but we're not going to discuss that right now). If you are running straight SQL commands, you can type them in on the command line and then easily edit them by typing EDIT at the SQL> prompt. This command takes you right to the editor, and the editor (in this example Notepad) shows you your latest SQL command:

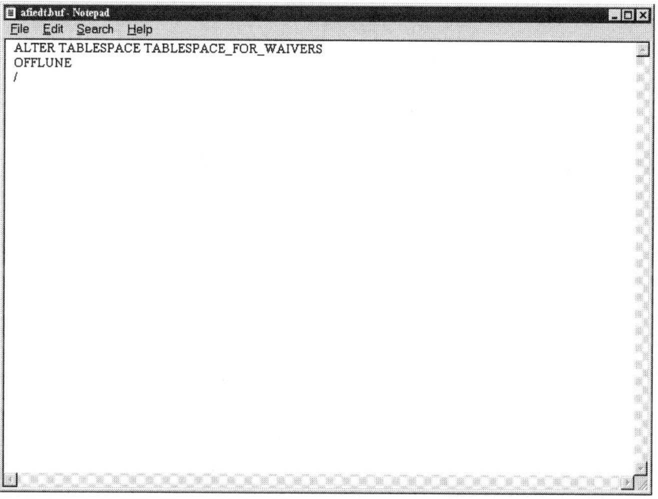

Now you can correct the error. In this example OFFLUNE should be OFFLINE. After you correct the error, select **File | Save**, and at the SQL> prompt, just type "RUN", and the ALTER command will fire off:

❶ Note that this is the error you want to see.

```
SQL>RUN
SQL> ALTER TABLESPACE TABLESPACE_FOR_WAIVERS  ❶
  2  OFFLINE;
  ALTER TABLESPACE TABLESPACE_FOR_WAIVERS
*
ERROR at line 1:
ORA-00959: tablespace 'TABLESPACE_FOR_WAIVERS' does not exist
```

Now type in the other two commands—DROP and CREATE—and you should see these messages:

❷ This is what you want to see.

```
SQL> DROP TABLESPACE TABLESPACE_FOR_WAIVERS  ❷
  2  INCLUDING CONTENTS;

  Tablespace does not exist.

++++++++++++++++++++++++++++++++++++++++++

  SQL> RUN
  1 CREATE TABLESPACE TABLESPACE_FOR_WAIVERS
  2 DATAFILE 'D:\TABLESPACES\DATA\TABLESPACE_FOR_WAIVERS'
  3 SIZE 1000M
  3 ONLINE
  4 PERMANENT

Tablespace created.  ❸
```

❸ This is the message that you want.

Note

When you drop a tablespace, unfortunately *the data file is not deleted.* The tablespace name is gone, but if you try to re-create it using the same data file, you will get the following error:

```
            *
            ERROR at line 1:
            ORA-01119: error in creating database file
'TABLESPACE_FOR_WAIVERS'
            ORA-07399: sfccf: file exists.
```

This means that the file named TABLESPACE_FOR_WAIVERS already exists, so you cannot use it to create another tablespace. However, you can use something like TABLESPACE2_FOR_WAIVERS:

```
SQL>RUN
        CREATE TABLESPACE TABLESPACE_FOR_WAIVERS
        DATAFILE

'D:\TABLESPACES\DATA\TABLESPACE2_FOR_WAIVERS'
        SIZE 1M
        ONLINE
        PERMANENT

Tablespace created.
```

Or you can delete the file (that is, go to the D:\TABLESPACES\DATA folder and delete the file called TABLESPACE_FOR_WAIVERS) and then reuse the name.

Note

The editor is fine for straight SQL commands, but not for PL/SQL commands such as loops and procedures. To run PL/SQL, you have to run a script. How do you run a script from the command line? Easy—just type in "@<path> & script name.SQL". For example, to run the script New_Names that is on your C: drive in your SQL_SCRIPTS folder, type in "@C:\SQL_SCRIPTS\NEW_NAMES.SQL" at the SQL> prompt, and SQL will then execute the script. We'll talk about this more in the context of other programming examples throughout the book, but for those of you who are curious, go ahead and write a couple of the commands we're using here, save them as a .sql file, and run them from the SQL command line.

Creating Tables

Now we're ready to create our tables. Remember that because we have constraints in the form of referential integrity built in, the tables must be created in a certain sequence. The error in the preceding section was included to try to make this clear.

First we need the TEST_TYPE_DESC table. To drop and create this table, type in the following commands. Once SQL senses the semicolon, it will run the command:

```
DROP TABLE TEST_TYPE_DESC  CASCADE CONSTRAINTS;

CREATE TABLE TEST_TYPE_DESC    (
TYPE_ID     NUMBER(6) PRIMARY KEY,
TYPE_DESC   VARCHAR2(30) NOT NULL
                                 )
TABLESPACE TABLESPACE_FOR_WAIVERS
                                 ;
```

Note

CASCADE CONSTRAINTS means that Oracle will "drop" any referential integrity constraints associated with this table. So be very careful with this command. It is normally used when tables are first being created just in case they already exist, most likely from earlier testing. The DROP...CASCADE construction is also often used when we're working with a test database, where the tables are constantly changing.

Next we need the AUTHORS table:

```
DROP TABLE AUTHORS    CASCADE CONSTRAINTS;

CREATE TABLE  AUTHORS              (
AUTHOR_ID          NUMBER(9) PRIMARY KEY,
AUTHOR            VARCHAR2(60) DEFAULT 'WAIVER ADMINISTRATION'
                                                         )
      TABLESPACE TABLESPACE_FOR_WAIVERS
                                                         ;
```

Then we create the TEST_ID table:

```
DROP TABLE TEST_ID CASCADE CONSTRAINTS;

CREATE TABLE  TEST_ID          (
TEST_ID        NUMBER(6)     PRIMARY KEY,
TEST_NAME      VARCHAR2(40)  NOT NULL,
```

```
DATE_CREATED   DATE          NOT NULL,
AUTHOR         NUMBER(9)     REFERENCES AUTHORS(AUTHOR_ID),
COMMENTS       VARCHAR2(30),
TYPE_ID        NUMBER(6)     REFERENCES TEST_TYPE_DESC(TYPE_ID),
PASSING_GRADE  NUMBER(2)     NOT NULL,
TIME_LIMIT     NUMBER(4,2)   NOT NULL
                              )
TABLESPACE TABLESPACE_FOR_WAIVERS
                              ;
```

Notice that if you try to create a table that references a table that has not been built yet, you get this error:

```
SQL> CREATE TABLE TEST_QUESTIONS_LINK   (
  2  LINK_TEST_ID       NUMBER(6) REFERENCES TEST_ID(TEST_ID),
  3  LINK_QUESTION_ID   NUMBER(6) REFERENCES QUESTIONS(QUESTION_ID),
  4  PRIMARY KEY (LINK_TEST_ID, LINK_QUESTION_ID)
  5               );
LINK_QUESTION_ID        NUMBER(6) REFERENCES QUESTIONS(QUESTION_ID),
                        *
ERROR at line 3:
ORA-00904: invalid column name
```

In other words, the QUESTIONS table does not exist yet, and Oracle is already enforcing referential integrity!

Now work on the questions by starting with the QUESTIONS_TYPE_DESC table:

```
DROP TABLE QUESTIONS_TYPE_DESC   CASCADE CONSTRAINTS;

CREATE TABLE      QUESTIONS_TYPE_DESC             (
QUESTION_TYPE     NUMBER(6) PRIMARY KEY,
QUESTION_TYPE_DESC VARCHAR2(40) NOT NULL
                                                  )
TABLESPACE TABLESPACE_FOR_WAIVERS
                                                   ;
```

And next create the QUESTIONS table itself:

```
DROP TABLE QUESTIONS  CASCADE CONSTRAINTS;

CREATE TABLE      QUESTIONS      (
QUESTION_ID       NUMBER(6) PRIMARY KEY,
QUESTION          VARCHAR2(500) NOT NULL,
CORRECT_ANSWER    VARCHAR2(2) NOT NULL,
QUESTION_TYPE     NUMBER(6) REFERENCES
QUESTIONS_TYPE_DESC(QUESTION_TYPE)
                              )
TABLESPACE TABLESPACE_FOR_WAIVERS
                              ;
```

Next link the QUESTIONS and TEST_ID tables by creating the linking table TEST_QUESTIONS_LINK:

```
DROP TABLE TEST_QUESTIONS_LINK  CASCADE CONSTRAINTS;

CREATE TABLE      TEST_QUESTIONS_LINK   (
LINK_TEST_ID      NUMBER(6) REFERENCES TEST_ID(TEST_ID),
LINK_QUESTION_ID NUMBER(6) REFERENCES QUESTIONS(QUESTION_ID),
WEIGHT            NUMBER(2,1) DEFAULT 1,
PRIMARY KEY (LINK_TEST_ID, LINK_QUESTION_ID)
                                        )
TABLESPACE TABLESPACE_FOR_WAIVERS
                                        ;
```

Now create the last core table, ANSWERS:

```
DROP TABLE ANSWERS  CASCADE CONSTRAINTS;

CREATE TABLE ANSWERS                   (

ANSWER_QUESTION_ID  NUMBER(6) PRIMARY KEY REFERENCES
  QUESTIONS(QUESTION_ID),
ANSWER_ID           VARCHAR2(2) NOT NULL,
ANSWER              VARCHAR2(30) NOT NULL
                                      )
TABLESPACE TABLESPACE_FOR_WAIVERS

                                      ;
```

Once these base tables have been defined, we can move on to the student and history tables. First create the STUDENTS table:

```
DROP TABLE     STUDENTS   CASCADE CONSTRAINTS;

CREATE TABLE   STUDENTS                    (
STUDENT_ID     NUMBER(9) PRIMARY KEY,
F_NAME         ARCHAR2(15) NOT NULL,
M_I            VARCHAR2(1),
L_NAME         VARCHAR2(20) NOT NULL,
SSNUM          NUMBER(9) NOT NULL UNIQUE,
B_DATE         DATE,
SEX            VARCHAR2(1) CHECK (SEX IN ('M', 'F', 'm', 'f')),
STREET1        VARCHAR2(15),
STREET2        VARCHAR2(15),
TOWN           VARCHAR2(20),
STATE          VARCHAR2(2),
COUNTRY        VARCHAR2(15) DEFAULT 'UNITED STATES',
ZIP            NUMBER(5) NOT NULL,
STUDENT_LEVEL  NUMBER(6) NOT NULL,
DATE_CREATED   DATE,
CREATED_BY     VARCHAR2(20),
DEPARTMENT_MAJOR VARCHAR2(10) NOT NULL,
EMAIL          VARCHAR2(60)
                                           )
TABLESPACE TABLESPACE_FOR_WAIVERS
                                           ;
```

Only two more to go! First create the TEST_HISTORY table:

```
DROP TABLE  TEST_HISTORY   CASCADE CONSTRAINTS;

CREATE TABLE   TEST_HISTORY       (
TEST_ID        NUMBER(6) REFERENCES TEST_ID(TEST_ID),
STUDENT_ID     NUMBER(9) REFERENCES STUDENTS(STUDENT_ID),
SCORE          NUMBER(3) NOT NULL,
DATE_TAKEN     DATE NOT NULL,
START_TIME     VARCHAR2(8) NOT NULL,
END_TIME       VARCHAR2(8) NOT NULL,
```

```
LOCATION       VARCHAR2(15) NOT NULL,
  PRIMARY KEY (TEST_ID, STUDENT_ID)
                                  )
TABLESPACE TABLESPACE_FOR_WAIVERS


                                  ;
```

And finally, the last table is STUDENT_ANSWERS_HISTORY:

```
DROP TABLE STUDENT_ANSWER_HISTORY  CASCADE CONSTRAINTS;

CREATE TABLE  STUDENT_ANSWER_HISTORY     (
  STUDENT_ID      NUMBER(9) REFERENCES STUDENTS(STUDENT_ID),
  TEST_ID         NUMBER(6) REFERENCES TEST_ID(TEST_ID),
  QUESTION_ID     NUMBER(6) REFERENCES QUESTIONS,
  STUDENT_ANSWER  VARCHAR2(2) NOT NULL
                                       )
TABLESPACE TABLESPACE_FOR_WAIVERS
                                       ;
```

The Entire Table Creation Script

As promised, here's the entire script for creating tables:

```
/* Script to drop and then create the tables for the waiver
database  */

SET ECHO ON;
SPOOL C:\SPOOL_FILES\WAIVER.LST;

/* Start with the TABLESPACE commands     */

ALTER TABLESPACE  TABLESPACE_FOR_WAIVERS
  OFFLINE   NORMAL;

DROP TABLESPACE TABLESPACE_FOR_WAIVERS
  INCLUDING CONTENTS;

CREATE TABLESPACE  TABLESPACE_FOR_WAIVERS
```

```
  DATAFILE   'D:\TABLESPACES\DATA\TABLESPACE_FOR_WAIVERS' SIZE
1000M
  ONLINE
  PERMANENT;

/*  Table creation steps  */

/*                                                      */
 DROP TABLE  TEST_TYPE_DESC  CASCADE CONSTRAINTS;

 CREATE TABLE TEST_TYPE_DESC (
   TYPE_ID        NUMBER(6)  PRIMARY KEY,
   TYPE_DESC      VARCHAR2(30)  NOT NULL
          )
   TABLESPACE TABLESPACE_FOR_WAIVERS
          ;
/*                        */

 DROP TABLE  TEST_ID   CASCADE CONSTRAINTS;

 CREATE TABLE TEST_ID  (
   TEST_ID        NUMBER(6) PRIMARY KEY,
   TEST_NAME      VARCHAR2(40) NOT NULL,
   DATE_CREATED   DATE NOT NULL,
   AUTHOR         VARCHAR2(30) DEFAULT 'WAIVER ADMINISTRATION',
   COMMENTS       VARCHAR2(30),
   TYPE_ID        NUMBER(6) REFERENCES TEST_TYPE_DESC(TYPE_ID),
   PASSING_GRADE  NUMBER(2) NOT NULL,
   TIME_LIMT      NUMBER(4,2) NOT NULL
          )
   TABLESPACE TABLESPACE_FOR_WAIVERS
              ;

/*                        */
 DROP TABLE   QUESTIONS_TYPE_DESC   CASCADE CONSTRAINTS;

 CREATE  TABLE   QUESTIONS_TYPE_DESC    (
   QUESTION_TYPE            NUMBER(6)  PRIMARY KEY,
   QUESTIONS_TYPE_DESC      VARCHAR2(50)  NOT NULL
```

```
                )
  TABLESPACE    TABLESPACE_FOR_WAIVERS
                ;


/*                              */
 DROP TABLE  QUESTIONS    CASCADE CONSTRAINTS;

 CREATE TABLE  QUESTIONS      (
   QUESTION_ID     NUMBER(6) PRIMARY KEY,
   QUESTION        VARCHAR2(500) NOT NULL,
   CORRECT_ANSWER VARCHAR2(2) NOT NULL,
   QUESTION_TYPE   NUMBER(6) REFERENCES
               QUESTIONS_TYPE_DESC(QUESTION_TYPE),
   DATE_CREATED    DATE,
   AUTHOR_ID       NUMBER(9)   REFERENCES AUTHORS(AUTHOR_ID)
            )
   TABLESPACE TABLESPACE_FOR_WAIVERS
            ;

/*                              */
  DROP TABLE AUTHORS   CASCADE CONSTRAINTS;

  CREATE TABLE AUTHORS   (
    AUTHOR_ID  NUMBER(9) PRIMARY KEY,
    AUTHOR     VARCHAR2(75) DEFAULT 'WAIVER ADMINISTRATION'
           )
    TABLESPACE  TABLESPACE_FOR_WAIVERS
           ;

/*                              */
 DROP TABLE  QUESTIONS    CASCADE CONSTRAINTS;

 CREATE TABLE  QUESTIONS      (
   QUESTION_ID                 NUMBER(6)  PRIMARY KEY,
   QUESTION                    VARCHAR2(500) NOT NULL,
   CORRECT_ANSWER              VARCHAR2(2) NOT NULL,
   QUESTION_TYPE                NUMBER(6) REFERENCES
                  QUESTIONS_TYPE_DESC(QUESTION_TYPE),
   DATE_CREATED                DATE,
```

```
   AUTHOR_ID                  NUMBER(9) REFERENCES
AUTHORS(AUTHOR_ID)
              )
   TABLESPACE TABLESPACE_FOR_WAIVERS
              ;

/*                          */
 DROP TABLE  TEST_QUESTIONS_LINK  CASCADE CONSTRAINTS;

 CREATE table TEST_QUESTIONS_LINK   (
   LINK_TEST_ID      NUMBER(6)  REFERENCES TEST_ID(TEST_ID),
   LINK_QUESTION_ID  NUMBER(6)  REFERENCES
QUESTIONS(QUESTION_ID),
   PRIMARY KEY (LINK_TEST_ID, LINK_QUESTION_ID)
                )
   TABLESPACE TABLESPACE_FOR_WAIVERS
                ;


/*                          */
 DROP TABLE  ANSWERS CASCADE CONSTRAINTS;

 CREATE TABLE  ANSWERS    (
   ANSWER_QUESTION_ID    NUMBER(6)  PRIMARY KEY REFERENCES
                         QUESTIONS(QUESTION_ID),
   ANSWER_ID             VARCHAR2(2) NOT NULL,
   ANSWER                VARCHAR2(30) NOT NULL
                )
   TABLESPACE TABLESPACE_FOR_WAIVERS
                ;

/*                          */
 DROP TABLE  STUDENTS    CASCADE CONSTRAINTS;

 CREATE TABLE    STUDENTS   (
   STUDENT_ID        NUMBER(9) PRIMARY KEY,
   F_NAME            VARCHAR2(15) NOT NULL,
   M_I               VARCHAR2(1),
   L_NAME            VARCHAR2(20) NOT NULL,
```

```
  SSNUM             NUMBER(9) NOT NULL UNIQUE,
  B_DATE            DATE,
  SEX               VARCHAR2(1) CHECK (SEX IN ('M', 'F', 'm',
                      'f')),
  STREET1           VARCHAR2(15),
  STREET2           VARCHAR2(15),
  TOWN              VARCHAR2(20),
  STATE             VARCHAR2(2),
  COUNTRY           VARCHAR2(15) DEFAULT 'UNITED STATES',
  ZIP               NUMBER(5) NOT NULL,
  STUDENT_LEVEL     NUMBER(6) NOT NULL,
  DATE_CREATED      DATE,
  CREATED_BY        VARCHAR2(20),
  DEPARTMENT_MAJOR  VARCHAR2(10) NOT NULL,
  EMAIL             VARCHAR2(60)
          )
  TABLESPACE TABLESPACE_FOR_WAIVERS
          ;


/*                          */
 DROP TABLE  TEST_HISTORY CASCADE CONSTRAINTS;

 CREATE  TABLE      TEST_HISTORY   (
  TEST_ID           NUMBER(6)  REFERENCES TEST_ID(TEST_ID),
  STUDENT_ID        NUMBER(9)  REFERENCES STUDENTS(STUDENT_ID),
  SCORE             NUMBER(3)  NOT NULL,
  DATE_TAKEN        DATE NOT NULL,
  START_TIME        VARCHAR2(8) NOT NULL,
  END_TIME          VARCHAR2(8) NOT NULL,
  LOCATION          VARCHAR2(15) NOT NULL,
  PRIMARY KEY (TEST_ID, STUDENT_ID)
                )
  TABLESPACE TABLESPACE_FOR_WAIVERS
                ;

/*                          */
 DROP TABLE  STUDENT_ANSWER_HISTORY CASCADE CONSTRAINTS;
```

```
 CREATE TABLE  STUDENT_ANSWER_HISTORY    (
   STUDENT_ID        NUMBER(9) REFERENCES STUDENTS(STUDENT_ID),
   TEST_ID           NUMBER(6) REFERENCES TEST_ID(TEST_ID),
   QUESTION_ID       NUMBER(6) REFERENCES
QUESTIONS(QUESTION_ID),
   STUDENT_ANSWER VARCHAR2(2) NOT NULL
              )
   TABLESPACE TABLESPACE_FOR_WAIVERS
              ;

 SPOOL OFF;
```

The Output Spool File

Here's the output spool file with our notes from creation of the tables. Your spool file should look similar:

❶ Start by turning spooling and echo on.

❷ First create a special tablespace for the data files.

❸ Since the tablespace doesn't exist, this message is OK.

```
SQL>SET ECHO ON; ❶
SQL>SPOOL C:\SPOOL_FILES\WAIVER.LST

SQL>
SQL> ALTER TABLESPACE  TABLESPACE_FOR_WAIVERS ❷
  2        OFFLINE   NORMAL;
ALTER TABLESPACE  TABLESPACE_FOR_WAIVERS
*
ERROR at line 1:
ORA-00959: tablespace 'TABLESPACE_FOR_WAIVERS' does not exist 3


SQL>
SQL> DROP TABLESPACE TABLESPACE_FOR_WAIVERS
  2         INCLUDING CONTENTS;
DROP TABLESPACE TABLESPACE_FOR_WAIVERS
*
ERROR at line 1:
ORA-00959: tablespace 'TABLESPACE_FOR_WAIVERS' does not exist
```

```
SQL>
SQL>
SQL> CREATE TABLESPACE   TABLESPACE_FOR_WAIVERS
  2    DATAFILE   'TABLESPACE_FOR_WAIVERS' SIZE 500M
  3    ONLINE
  4    PERMANENT;
```

❹ This is the message you want to see!

```
Tablespace created. ❹
```

```
SQL>
SQL>
SQL> /*                                          */
SQL>  DROP TABLE  TEST_TYPE_DESC  CASCADE CONSTRAINTS;
 DROP TABLE  TEST_TYPE_DESC  CASCADE CONSTRAINTS
             *
```

❺ Since the file doesn't exist, this message is OK.

```
ERROR at line 1:
ORA-00942: table or view does not exist  ❺
```

```
SQL>
SQL>  CREATE TABLE TEST_TYPE_DESC (
  2    TYPE_ID        NUMBER(6) PRIMARY KEY,
  3    TYPE_DESC        VARCHAR2(30) NOT NULL
  4                                   )
  5    TABLESPACE TABLESPACE_FOR_WAIVERS
  6                                    ;
```

❻ This is the message you want to see!

```
Table created. ❻
```

Now continue with the rest of the tables.

```
SQL> /*                                        */
SQL>
SQL>  DROP TABLE  TEST_ID   CASCADE CONSTRAINTS;
 DROP TABLE  TEST_ID   CASCADE CONSTRAINTS
             *
ERROR at line 1:
ORA-00942: table or view does not exist
```

```
SQL>
SQL>  CREATE TABLE TEST_ID  (
  2    TEST_ID      NUMBER(6) PRIMARY KEY,
  3    TEST_NAME    VARCHAR2(40) NOT NULL,
  4    DATE_CREATED DATE NOT NULL,
  5    AUTHOR       VARCHAR(30) DEFAULT 'WAIVER ADMINISTRATION',
  6    COMMENTS     VARCHAR2(30),
  7    TYPE_ID      NUMBER(6) REFERENCES
TEST_TYPE_DESC(TYPE_ID),
  8    PASSING_GRADE  NUMBER(2) NOT NULL,
  9    TIME_LIMIT     NUMBER(4,2) NOT NULL
 10                               )
 11    TABLESPACE TABLESPACE_FOR_WAIVERS
 12                                         ;

Table created.

SQL>
SQL> /*                                    */
SQL>   DROP TABLE  QUESTIONS_TYPE_DESC CASCADE CONSTRAINTS;
  DROP TABLE  QUESTIONS_TYPE_DESC   CASCADE CONSTRAINTS
       *
ERROR at line 1:
ORA-00942: table or view does not exist


SQL>
SQL>   CREATE TABLE QUESTIONS  QUESTIONS_TYPE_DESC   (
  2    QUESTION_TYPE       NUMBER(6) PRIMARY KEY,
  3    QUESTION_TYPE_DESC  VARCHAR2(40) NOT NULL
  4                                     )
  5    TABLESPACE TABLESPACE_FOR_WAIVERS
  6                                     ;
  CREATE TABLE QUESTIONS  QUESTIONS_TYPE_DESC   (
             *
ERROR at line 1:
ORA-00922: missing or invalid option
```

Note

Here's something you may come across if you use MS Word, Notepad, or another text editor. Every so often a command simply doesn't work, and you cannot find the problem.

The preceding code is an example: Even though the command is perfectly constructed, it generates an error. In these cases, all you can do is retype the command or copy the script into another text editor. Strange but true.

In this case, then, we try retyping the commands and it works! The original error was probably caused by simple, poor typing that resulted in an unprintable character or escape sequence being entered.

```
SQL>  DROP TABLE  QUESTIONS_TYPE_DESC  CASCADE CONSTRAINTS;
 DROP TABLE  QUESTIONS_TYPE_DESC  CASCADE CONSTRAINTS
             *
ERROR at line 1:
ORA-00942: table or view does not exist


SQL>
SQL>      CREATE TABLE  QUESTIONS_TYPE_DESC      (
  2        QUESTION_TYPE           NUMBER(6) PRIMARY KEY,
  3        QUESTIONS_TYPE_DESC      VARCHAR2(50) NOT NULL
  4                                   )
  5        TABLESPACE   TABLESPACE_FOR_WAIVERS
  6                                   ;

Table created.

SQL> /*                                     */
SQL>  DROP TABLE  QUESTIONS    CASCADE CONSTRAINTS;
 DROP TABLE  QUESTIONS    CASCADE CONSTRAINTS
             *
ERROR at line 1:
ORA-00942: table or view does not exist
```

```
SQL>
SQL>   create table  QUESTIONS      (
  2        QUESTION_ID     NUMBER(6) PRIMARY KEY,
  3        QUESTION        VARCHAR2(500) NOT NULL,
  4        CORRECT_ANSWER  VARCHAR2(2)  NOT NULL,
  5        QUESTION_TYPE   NUMBER(6) REFERENCES
QUESTIONS_TYPE_DESC(QUESTION_TYPE),
  6        DATE_CREATED    DATE,
  7        AUTHOR_ID       NUMBER(9) REFERENCES
AUTHORS(AUTHOR_ID)
  8                                  )
  9        TABLESPACE TABLESPACE_FOR_WAIVERS
 10                                     ;
   AUTHOR_ID           NUMBER(9) REFERENCES AUTHORS(AUTHOR_ID)
                                              *
ERROR at line 7:
ORA-00942: table or view does not exist


SQL> /* Following is a retype of the CREATE TABLE statement
because what's shown above keeps producing an error */
SQL>
SQL>   CREATE TABLE QUESTIONS       (
  2        QUESTION_ID     NUMBER(6) PRIMARY KEY,
  3        QUESTION        VARCHAR2(500) NOT NULL,
  4        CORRECT_ANSWER  VARCHAR2(2) NOT NULL,
  5        QUESTION_TYPE   NUMBER(6) REFERENCES
QUESTIONS_TYPE_DESC(QUESTION_TYPE),
  6        DATE_CREATED    DATE,
  7        AUTHOR_ID       NUMBER(9) REFERENCES
AUTHORS(AUTHOR_ID)
  8                                   )
  9        TABLESPACE   TABLESPACE_FOR_WAIVERS
 10                                   ;
    AUTHOR_ID       NUMBER(9) REFERENCES AUTHORS(AUTHOR_ID)
                                              *
ERROR at line 7:
ORA-00942: table or view does not exist
```

```
SQL>
SQL>
SQL> /*                                                    */
SQL>   DROP TABLE AUTHORS   CASCADE CONSTRAINTS;
  DROP TABLE AUTHORS   CASCADE CONSTRAINTS
             *
ERROR at line 1:
ORA-00942: table or view does not exist


SQL>
SQL>   CREATE TABLE AUTHORS   (
  2                          AUTHOR_ID   NUMBER(9) PRIMARY KEY,
  3                          AUTHOR      VARCHAR2(75) DEFAULT
'WAIVER ADMINISTRATION'
  4                             )
  5                          TABLESPACE  TABLESPACE_FOR_WAIVERS
  6                             ;

Table created.

SQL>
SQL> /*                                                   */
SQL>   DROP TABLE  QUESTIONS    CASCADE CONSTRAINTS;
  DROP TABLE  QUESTIONS    CASCADE CONSTRAINTS
              *
ERROR at line 1:
ORA-00942: table or view does not exist


SQL>
SQL>   create table  QUESTIONS      (
  2         QUESTION_ID     NUMBER(6) PRIMARY KEY,
  3         QUESTION        VARCHAR2(500) NOT NULL,
  4         CORRECT_ANSWER  VARCHAR2(2) NOT NULL,
  5         QUESTION_TYPE NUMBER(6) REFERENCES
QUESTIONS_TYPE_DESC(QUESTION_TYPE),
  6         DATE_CREATED    DATE,
  7         AUTHOR_ID       NUMBER(9) REFERENCES
AUTHORS(AUTHOR_ID)
```

```
  8                                    )
  9         TABLESPACE TABLESPACE_FOR_WAIVERS
 10                                    ;

Table created.

SQL>
SQL>
SQL> /*                                          */
SQL>   DROP TABLE  TEST_QUESTIONS_LINK CASCADE CONSTRAINTS;
  DROP TABLE  TEST_QUESTIONS_LINK  CASCADE CONSTRAINTS
              *
ERROR at line 1:
ORA-00942: table or view does not exist


SQL>
SQL>   CREATE table TEST_QUESTIONS_LINK   (
  2         LINK_TEST_ID      NUMBER(6) REFERENCES
TEST_ID(TEST_ID),
  3         LINK_QUESTION_ID  NUMBER(6) REFERENCES
QUESTIONS(QUESTION_ID),
  4         PRIMARY KEY (LINK_TEST_ID, LINK_QUESTION_ID)
  5                                    )
  6         TABLESPACE TABLESPACE_FOR_WAIVERS
  7                                    ;

Table created.

SQL>
SQL>
SQL> /*                                          */
SQL>   DROP TABLE  ANSWERS CASCADE CONSTRAINTS;
  DROP TABLE  ANSWERS CASCADE CONSTRAINTS
              *
ERROR at line 1:
ORA-00942: table or view does not exist
```

```
SQL>
SQL>   CREATE TABLE  ANSWERS    (
           ANSWER_QUESTION_ID   NUMBER(6) PRIMARY KEY REFERENCES
QUESTIONS(QUESTION_ID),
           ANSWER_ID           VARCHAR2(2) NOT NULL,
           ANSWER              VARCHAR2(30) NOT NULL
                               )
           TABLESPACE TABLESPACE_FOR_WAIVERS
                               ;

Table created.

SQL>
SQL> /*                                         */
SQL>   DROP TABLE  STUDENTS    CASCADE CONSTRAINTS;
  DROP TABLE  STUDENTS    CASCADE CONSTRAINTS
              *
ERROR at line 1:
ORA-00942: table or view does not exist


SQL>
SQL>   CREATE TABLE       STUDENTS      (
           STUDENT_ID      NUMBER(9)  PRIMARY KEY,
           F_NAME          VARCHAR2(15) NOT NULL,
           M_I             VARCHAR2(1),
           L_NAME          VARCHAR2(20) NOT NULL,
           SSNUM           NUMBER(9) NOT NULL UNIQUE,
           B_DATE          DATE,
           SEX             VARCHAR2(1) CHECK (SEX IN ('M', 'F',
                             'm', 'f')),
           STREET1         VARCHAR2(15),
           STREET2         VARCHAR2(15),
           TOWN            VARCHAR2(20),
           STATE           VARCHAR2(2),
           COUNTRY         VARCHAR2(15) DEFAULT 'UNITED STATES',
           ZIP             NUMBER(5) NOT NULL,
           STUDENT_LEVEL   NUMBER(6) NOT NULL,
```

```
 16         DATE_CREATED      DATE,
 17         CREATED_BY        VARCHAR2(20),
 18         DEPARTMENT_MAJOR VARCHAR2(10) NOT NULL,
 19         EMAIL             VARCHAR2(60)
 20                                      )
 21         TABLESPACE TABLESPACE_FOR_WAIVERS
 22                                      ;

Table created.

SQL>
SQL>
SQL> /*                                                         */
SQL>   DROP TABLE  TEST_HISTORY CASCADE CONSTRAINTS;
  DROP TABLE  TEST_HISTORY CASCADE CONSTRAINTS
             *
ERROR at line 1:
ORA-00942: table or view does not exist


SQL>
SQL>   CREATE TABLE    TEST_HISTORY       (
  2        TEST_ID            NUMBER(6) REFERENCES
TEST_ID(TEST_ID),
  3         STUDENT_ID   NUMBER(9) REFERENCES
STUDENTS(STUDENT_ID),
  4        SCORE              NUMBER(3) NOT NULL,
  5        DATE_TAKEN         DATE NOT NULL,
  6        START_TIME         VARCHAR2(8) NOT NULL,
  7        END_TIME           VARCHAR2(8) NOT NULL,
  8        LOCATION           ARCHAR2(15) NOT NULL,
  9        PRIMARY KEY (TEST_ID, STUDENT_ID)
 10                                          )
 11         TABLESPACE TABLESPACE_FOR_WAIVERS
 12                                          ;

Table created.
```

```
SQL>
SQL> /*                                                              */
SQL>   DROP TABLE  STUDENT_ANSWER_HISTORY CASCADE CONSTRAINTS;
  DROP TABLE  STUDENT_ANSWER_HISTORY CASCADE CONSTRAINTS
              *
ERROR at line 1:
ORA-00942: table or view does not exist


SQL>
SQL>   CREATE TABLE  STUDENT_ANSWER_HISTORY   (
                         STUDENT_ID     NUMBER(9) REFERENCES
STUDENTS(STUDENT_ID),
                         TEST_ID        NUMBER(6) REFERENCES
TEST_ID(TEST_ID),
                         QUESTION_ID    NUMBER(6) REFERENCES
QUESTIONS(QUESTION_ID),
                         STUDENT_ANSWER   VARCHAR2(2)     NOT NULL
                                                )
                         TABLESPACE TABLESPACE_FOR_WAIVERS
                                                ;

Table created.

SQL>
SQL>   SPOOL OFF; ❼
```

❼ Finish by turning spooling off. If you don't do this, your spool file will be empty until you either exit SQL or turn spooling off.

Loading the Tables

Method 1: SQL*Loader

SQL*Loader is a nifty little utility from Oracle that you use to load external data, such as spreadsheets and flat files, into your tables. As with all such powerful utilities, you have to do a little work. Fortunately, there are only two steps and only one command for using SQL*Loader. The two steps are:

1. Create a control (`.ctl`) file.
2. Create the data file itself.

Then, at the command prompt (DOS prompt), type in "SQLLDR" *followed by parameters*. (Yes, in the Windows [NT and W2K] world, you run SQL*Loader from the DOS prompt! All you DOS types, this is your chance to cheer.)

Oracle also throws in two other files automatically: a log and a file containing any bad records. You can also get a discard file if you specify it. (**Bad** records are ones that could not be loaded, **discard** records are those that were blank or did not meet the `WHEN` clause condition.):

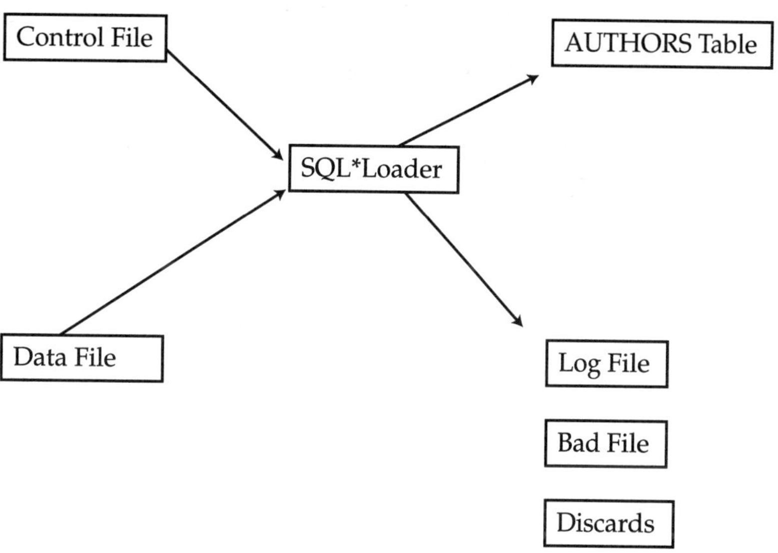

Note

Just a little note before you get too excited: SQL*Loader *cannot* create tables; they must already be present in the database.

This section is going to give you a look at two of the most common SQL*Loader activities: (1) loading a comma-delimited file, such as from a spreadsheet, into the AUTHORS table; and (2) doing the same thing with a fixed-format flat file, in which the columns are a fixed length. After we discuss these processes, I'll give you some examples of more complicated scenarios. You will soon be so good at using plain old SQL*Loader that you'll be looking for more complex challenges.

Housekeeping

Before you start handling any data or writing any SQL*Loader commands, do a little housekeeping. Although SQL*Loader doesn't care what you name your files, there are some conventions that I *strongly recommend* you follow. Believe me, you will be lost a couple of months from now if you start using your literary talents to come up with creative, though oblique, names.

The first recommendation is to use the suffix `.ctl` for control files, `.dat` for data, `.dsc` for the discard file, `.bad` for the bad records, and `.log` for all log files. Second, create a folder called `SQLLOAD`, with subfolders named `BAD`, `CTL`, `DATA`, `DISCARD`, and `LOG`:

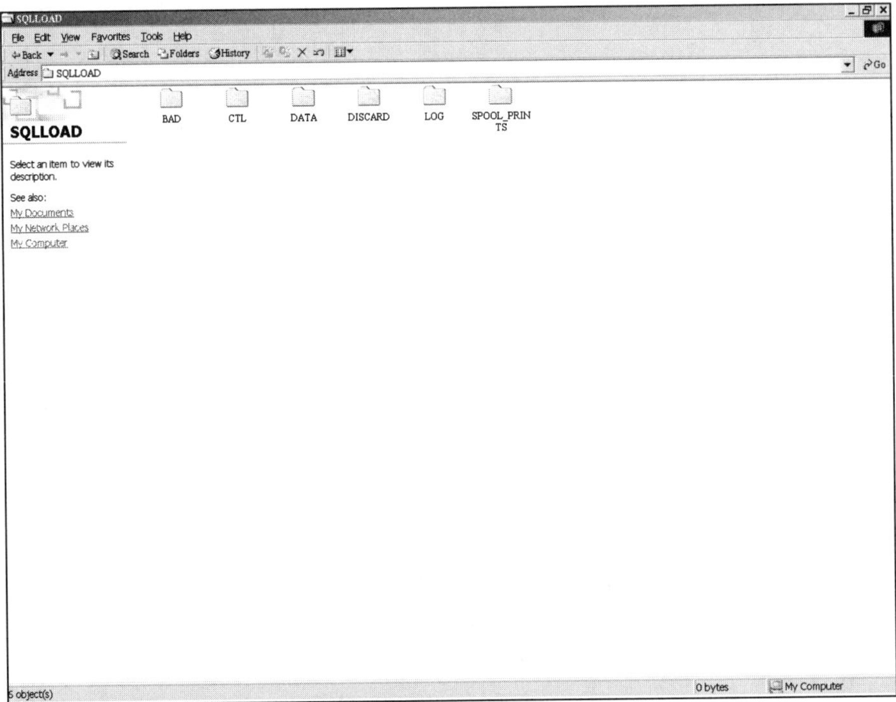

In the subfolders you can create additional folders for each table or group of tables. For your first couple of attempts, I suggest keeping the files in folders named after the tables you're loading. That is, in the `LOG` folder have another folder for AUTHORS_LOG, and move the log file into it after you have loaded the AUTHORS table. These little folders will eventually become part of your personal bag of tricks because they will contain examples of successful file loads, as well as errors and problems. (Yes, errors. We learn much from our mistakes!)

The Data File

Now you're ready to get your data file. For our purposes, let's say it's a spreadsheet with all the author data in it that the training area has been keeping for several years. By now, hundreds of authors are defined, and it would be a serious task to have to rekey the data. The data entry unit manager has given you his "Don't even ask" look, so you know you had better find an easier way. It dawns on you that if the data entry folks won't key in the data for a small table such as AUTHORS, you better not approach them for the larger tables! So you agree to automate the transfer, and I'll show you how. Just remember that the exact same steps will be used for any data that you want to load into your Oracle database tables.

Maybe, if you're very good and very lucky, once or twice in your life you will get a data file that has everything you need. Unfortunately, usually the raw data that you get will be missing some information, or additional calculations on existing fields may be needed. So let me warn you that in real life you will most likely have to write a program to reformat the data *before* you can run SQL*Loader. (Of course, if the data is coming from another system, and you have friends on that project, a little groveling might be advisable to get them to send you the file in the format you need. Just remember that they may come back to you at some point for a favor.)

The fields in your data file do *not* have to be in the same sequence as the columns in your table if our input file is a certain type. In the second example that I will present shortly, I'll show you how to take fields from any place in the data file and match them to a column. That said, for the first example I'm going to give you one of those rarities: a file with fields that are perfect. Just take this as one of your lucky days.

Here's the author data as it appears in a spreadsheet:

ID	Name	Phone	Department	Date Added	Comments
118765443	John Smith	X34342	Advanced Computers	06/4/95	Excellent teacher
227653089	Harry Wellins	X55543	Intro Courses	04/18/96	New to staff
337640276	Eleanor Satkowski	X66543	Office Apps	05/12/96	Transferred from Research
442876009	George Drum	X99876	Office Apps	05/12/96	New to staff
554118332	Judy Farr	X32112	Data Base Design	05/30/96	Database expert
660034285	Whitney Jacobucci	X98443	Help Desk	05/31/96	Generalist
775439112	Amy Elias	X66432	Supervisor	07/14/96	Full office apps expert
886549054	Dan Green	X43445	Research	11/14/96	Data base theory
994230655	Alan White	X55432	Research	01/14/97	Super computer technology
105439768	Daniel Sobiern	X98445	Networking	02/12/97	Documentation
679982154	Sally Hobbs	X66543	Networking	09/24/97	Ethernet
690753214	Jason Hodings	X88724	Infrastructure	12/16/97	Wiring expert
987578843	Michael Starr	X55432	Security	08/30/98	Firewalls
155427666	Philip Rodder	X65224	Security	09/23/98	User definitions
876509876	Damian Zachary	X55421	Databases	11/24/98	Oracle expert

Now the question is how to put this information into a file format that Oracle can use. In this case, here's what we'll do:

1. Delete the header line.
2. Then simply save the information as a comma-delimited, or `.csv`, file:

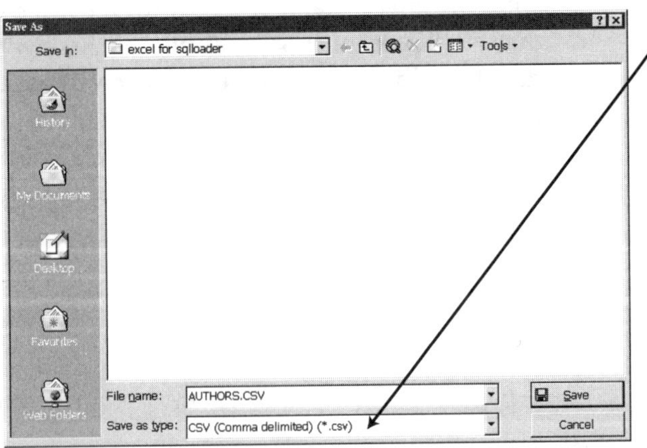

That's it for this file. It is now ready to become your input file for the AUTHORS table. Of course, if the columns were in a different sequence, you would have to do some moving or copying.

The Control File

This is going to be a bit complicated, but if you follow along through the examples, you will get the main points of SQL*Loader.

Let's start with a few *syntax rules*:

- Two dashes (--) together indicate comments until the end of the line. It is good practice to put a comment paragraph at the start of the control file. You can also specify the data file, log file, and bad file in the control file. If you include your data file in the control file, do not use comments (text delineated by the two dashes) in the data.
- SQL*Loader is *not* case-sensitive, but there are reserved words, and if you happen to have used some of them as data object names, you'll have to put single or double quotes around them.
- Most of the time SQL*Loader is run from another program or script, and the various file names are used in the argument strings, as we'll show you shortly.
- Do *not* use commas after the commands in the control file. You must still use them when you define each column in the table (except for the last one), but not after commands such as `LOAD DATA` or `INTO TABLE XXXXX`. I don't know why, but this is the way it is. (Actually SQL*Loader uses DDL [Data Definition Language] statements, but we haven't talked about that yet.)
- There are three verbs: `INSERT`, `APPEND`, and `REPLACE`. `INSERT` is used only on *empty* tables. It will bomb if you try to use it otherwise. `REPLACE` really does replace *everything* in the table; that is, the entire content of the table is deleted. `APPEND` just adds rows to the table; it is the most often used of the three verbs. Be careful which verb you use.

There are many refinements that you will eventually learn to use with SQL*Loader, but for now let's just look at a real example. Here's the control file for the `.csv` data file:

```
------------------------------------------------------------
--          C O M M E N T S   A R E A                    --
--            Authors_CSV.CTL                            --
--                                                       --
--            Guerrilla Oracle                           --
--                                                       --
```

```
-- data file is D:\SQLLOAD\DATA\AUTHORS_CSV.DAT   --
-- log is D:\SQLLOAD\LOG.AUTHORS.LOG              --
-- bad is D:\SQLLOAD\BAD\AUTHORS.BAD              --
-- discard is D:\SQLLOAD\DSC\AUTHORS.DSC          --
----------------------------------------------------------
--  First command  --



LOAD DATA
-- Use APPEND

APPEND

 INTO TABLE AUTHORS
 FIELDS TERMINATED BY ','
 OPTIONALLY ENCLOSED BY " "
 TRAILING NULLCOLS

--  Now list the columns in the table  ---


 (
AUTHOR_ID,
AUTHOR_NAME
)
```

We start with `LOAD DATA`, followed by `INTO TABLE` *`table name`*. Then we tell SQL*Loader that the fields are separated by a comma or a double quotation mark, and we add `TRAILING NULLCOLS` as a safety measure. Then we start defining the columns to be loaded.

Now save your file in the appropriate directory, something like

```
D:\SQLLOAD\CTL\AUTHORS_CSV.CTL
```

That's it! You have completed your control file for loading the AUTHORS table with a comma-delimited file.

Running SQL*Loader

You now have a data file, D:\SQLLOAD\DATA\AUTHORS_CSV.DAT, and your control file, D:\SQLLOAD\CTL\AUTHORS_CSV.CTL, so you're ready to run SQL*Loader. Just go to the DOS prompt—D:>, for example—and type the following:

```
SQLLDR  USERID=SYSTEM/MANAGER@CWE1P
     CONTROL=D:\SQLLOAD\CONTROL\AUTHORS_CSV.CTL
     DATA=D:\SQLLOAD\DATA\AUTHORS_CSV.DAT
     LOG=D:\SQLLOAD\LOG\AUTHORS.LOG
     BAD=D:\SQLLOAD\BAD\AUTHORS.BAD
```

Now go to your LOG, DISCARD, and BAD folders and check your work. If the load was successful, you will see this in the LOG file:

```
SQL*Loader: Release 8.1.7.0.0 - Production on Sat Sep 22
16:51:16 2001

(c) Copyright 2000 Oracle Corporation.  All rights reserved.

Control File:   D:\SQLLOAD\CTL\AUTHORS_CSV.CTL
Data File:      D:\SQLLOAD\DATA\AUTHORS_COMMA.DAT
  Bad File:     D:\SQLLOAD\BAD\AUTHORS.BAD
  Discard File:  none specified

 (Allow all discards)

Number to load: ALL
Number to skip: 0
Errors allowed: 50
Bind array:     64 rows, maximum of 65536 bytes
Continuation:    none specified
Path used:      Conventional


Table AUTHORS, loaded from every logical record. ❶
Insert option in effect for this table: APPEND
TRAILING NULLCOLS option in effect
```

```
   Column Name                  Position   Len  Term Encl Datatype
------------------------------ ---------- ----- ---- ---- ---------
AUTHOR_ID                       FIRST       *    ,   O(") CHARACTER
AUTHOR                          NEXT        *    ,   O(") CHARACTER


Table AUTHORS:
  15 Rows successfully loaded. ❷
  0 Rows not loaded due to data errors.
  0 Rows not loaded because all WHEN clauses were failed.
  0 Rows not loaded because all fields were null.

Space allocated for bind array:            33024 bytes(64 rows) ❸
Space allocated for memory besides bind array:        0 bytes


Total logical records skipped:          0
Total logical records read:            15
Total logical records rejected:         0
Total logical records discarded:        0

Run began on Sat Sep 22 16:51:16 2001
Run ended on Sat Sep 22 16:51:22 2001

Elapsed time was:     00:00:05.16
CPU time was:         00:00:00.03
```

❷ All 15 records from the spreadsheet were successfully loaded.

❸ This is what you want to see!

A little earlier I told you about SQL*Loader's three verbs: APPEND, INSERT, and REPLACE. Let's look at some samples of logs from these commands. Here's the log from the INSERT command on a file that already has records:

```
SQL*Loader: Release 8.1.7.0.0 - Production on Sat Sep 22
16:52:17 2001

(c) Copyright 2000 Oracle Corporation.  All rights reserved.
```

```
Control File:   D:\SQLLOAD\CTL\AUTHORS_CSV.CTL
Data File:      D:\SQLLOAD\DATA\AUTHORS_COMMA.DAT
  Bad File:     D:\SQLLOAD\BAD\AUTHORS.BAD
  Discard File:  none specified

 (Allow all discards)

Number to load: ALL
Number to skip: 0
Errors allowed: 50
Bind array:     64 rows, maximum of 65536 bytes
Continuation:    none specified
Path used:      Conventional

Table AUTHORS, loaded from every logical record.
Insert option in effect for this table: INSERT
TRAILING NULLCOLS option in effect

   Column Name                  Position   Len  Term Encl Datatype
------------------------------ ---------- ----- ---- ---- ---------
AUTHOR_ID                       FIRST      *    ,    O(") CHARACTER
AUTHOR                          NEXT       *    ,    O(") CHARACTER
ERROR!!


SQL*Loader-601: For INSERT option, table must be empty.
Error on table AUTHORS
```

If you have a constraint built in, Oracle will reject any records that violate that constraint. The `.bad` file that follows this paragraph shows what happens if we run the file twice, using `APPEND`. In this case the table has a `UNIQUE` constraint on the key field, so when `INSERT` tries to add a duplicate key, it is rejected. See the value of using constraints and keys?

```
SQL*Loader: Release 8.1.7.0.0 - Production on Sat Sep 22
16:48:25 2001

(c) Copyright 2000 Oracle Corporation.  All rights reserved.
```

```
Control File:   D:\SQLLOAD\CTL\AUTHORS_CSV.CTL
Data File:      D:\SQLLOAD\DATA\AUTHORS_COMMA.DAT
  Bad File:     D:\SQLLOAD\BAD\AUTHORS.BAD
  Discard File:  none specified

 (Allow all discards)

Number to load: ALL
Number to skip: 0
Errors allowed: 50
Bind array:     64 rows, maximum of 65536 bytes
Continuation:    none specified
Path used:      Conventional

Table AUTHORS, loaded from every logical record.
Insert option in effect for this table: APPEND


TRAILING NULLCOLS option in effect

   Column Name                  Position   Len  Term Encl Datatype
------------------------------ ---------- ----- ---- ---- ---------
AUTHOR_ID                      FIRST       *    ,    O(") CHARACTER
AUTHOR                         NEXT        *    ,    O(") CHARACTER

Record 1: Rejected - Error on table AUTHORS.
ORA-00001: unique constraint (SYSTEM.SYS_C001376) violated

Record 2: Rejected - Error on table AUTHORS.
ORA-00001: unique constraint (SYSTEM.SYS_C001376) violated

Record 3: Rejected - Error on table AUTHORS.
ORA-00001: unique constraint (SYSTEM.SYS_C001376) violated

Record 4: Rejected - Error on table AUTHORS.
ORA-00001: unique constraint (SYSTEM.SYS_C001376) violated
```

```
Record 5: Rejected - Error on table AUTHORS.
ORA-00001: unique constraint (SYSTEM.SYS_C001376) violated
.
.
.
Record 14: Rejected - Error on table AUTHORS.
ORA-00001: unique constraint (SYSTEM.SYS_C001376) violated

Record 15: Rejected - Error on table AUTHORS.
ORA-00001: unique constraint (SYSTEM.SYS_C001376) violated


Table AUTHORS:
  0 Rows successfully loaded.
  15 Rows not loaded due to data errors.
  0 Rows not loaded because all WHEN clauses were failed.
  0 Rows not loaded because all fields were null.


Space allocated for bind array:                33024 bytes(64 rows)
Space allocated for memory besides bind array:         0 bytes

Total logical records skipped:          0
Total logical records read:            15
Total logical records rejected:        15
Total logical records discarded:        0

Run began on Sat Sep 22 16:48:25 2001
```

Here's the log from a REPLACE command. Notice that it is the same as the INSERT log:

```
SQL*Loader: Release 8.1.7.0.0 - Production on Sat Sep 22
16:53:14 2001

(c) Copyright 2000 Oracle Corporation.  All rights reserved.
```

```
Control File:   D:\SQLLOAD\CTL\AUTHORS_CSV.CTL
Data File:      D:\SQLLOAD\DATA\AUTHORS_COMMA.DAT
  Bad File:     D:\SQLLOAD\BAD\AUTHORS.BAD
  Discard File:  none specified

 (Allow all discards)

Number to load: ALL
Number to skip: 0
Errors allowed: 50
Bind array:     64 rows, maximum of 65536 bytes
Continuation:    none specified
Path used:      Conventional

REPLACE Command

Table AUTHORS, loaded from every logical record.
Insert option in effect for this table: REPLACE
TRAILING NULLCOLS option in effect

   Column Name                  Position   Len  Term Encl Datatype
------------------------------ ---------- ----- ---- ---- ---------
AUTHOR_ID                       FIRST      *    ,    O(") CHARACTER
AUTHOR                          NEXT       *    ,    O(") CHARACTER


Table AUTHORS:
  15 Rows successfully loaded. ❶
  0 Rows not loaded due to data errors.
  0 Rows not loaded because all WHEN clauses were failed.
  0 Rows not loaded because all fields were null.


Space allocated for bind array:                  33024 bytes(64
rows)
Space allocated for memory besides bind array:        0 bytes
```

❶ **All 15 records loaded successfully—they REPLACED the existing records.**

```
Total logical records skipped:          0
Total logical records read:            15
Total logical records rejected:         0
Total logical records discarded:        0

Run began on Sat Sep 22 16:53:14 2001
Run ended on Sat Sep 22 16:53:19 2001

Elapsed time was:     00:00:05.11
CPU time was:         00:00:00.04
```

What have you learned from these examples? Well, you have now successfully used SQL*Loader to load an Oracle table in your new database with 15 author records, using the APPEND command. You know the logs and files involved and have developed a logical structure to keep track of all the files as you load your tables. And you have taken one of the most common types of input data, the comma-delimited file, and loaded it.

Now for our second example, let's take a look at another file type that you will also come across quite often, the fixed-format record (that is, a record with fixed-length fields). Here's a sample:

```
123456789012345678901234567890123456789012345678901234567890123456789012345678901234567890
         1         2         3         4         5         6         7         8         9
John Smith          X34342118765443     Advanced Computers  06/04/95  excellent teacher
Harry Wellins       X55543227653089     Intro Courses       04/18/96  new to staff
Eleanor Satkowski   X66543337640276     Office Apps         05/12/96  transferred from Research
George Drum         X99876442876009     Office Apps         05/12/96  new to staff
Judy Farr           X32112554118332     Data Base Design    05/30/96  database expert
Whitney Jacobucci   X98443660034285     Help Desk           05/31/96  generalist
Amy Elias           X66432775439112     Supervisor          07/14/96  Full office apps expert
Dan Green           X43445886549054     Research            1/14/96   Data Base Theory
Alan White          X55432994230655     Research            01/14/97  super computer technology
Daniel Sobiern      X98445105439768     Networking          02/12/97  Documentation
Sally Hobbs         X66534679982154     Networking          09/24/97  Ethernet
Jason Hodings       X88724690753214     Infrastructure      12/16/97  Wiring expert
Michael Starr       X55432987578843     Security            08/30/98  Firewalls
Philip  Rodder      X65224155427666     Security            09/23/98  User Definitions
Damian Zachary      X55421876509876     Databases           11/24/98  Oracle expert
```

Notice that this is another type of flat file, in which the fields are fixed lengths. The first field is Name, the second Phone Extension, the third ID, the fourth Department, the fifth Date, and the sixth Comments. For our purposes, we care about only two fields: Author and Author ID.

The numbers at the top of the record are *not* part of the file. I included them only to make it easy to map the columns.

First map out the record layout:

Columns	Field
1–23	Name
24–29	Phone Extension
30–38	ID
39–56	Department
57–64	Date
65–90	Comments

Second, to get only the two fields we want, just change the control file:

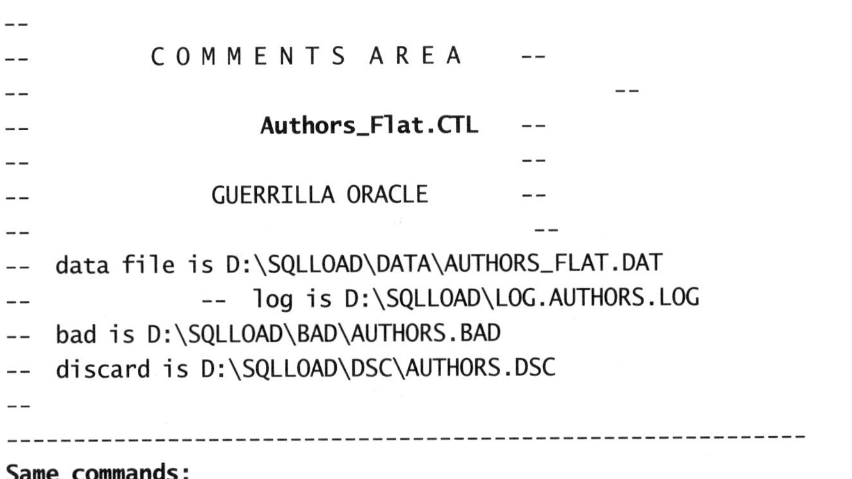

```
----------------------------------------------------------------
--
--          C O M M E N T S   A R E A      --
--                                                  --
--                    Authors_Flat.CTL     --
--                                         --
--              GUERRILLA ORACLE           --
--                                          --
--  data file is D:\SQLLOAD\DATA\AUTHORS_FLAT.DAT
--             --  log is D:\SQLLOAD\LOG.AUTHORS.LOG
--  bad is D:\SQLLOAD\BAD\AUTHORS.BAD
--  discard is D:\SQLLOAD\DSC\AUTHORS.DSC
--
------------------------------------------------------------
Same commands:
```

```
LOAD DATA
APPEND

 INTO TABLE AUTHORS
```

Now list the columns in the table and the corresponding positions in the input file:

```
 (
AUTHOR_ID   POSITION(30:38) NUMERIC EXTERNAL,
AUTHOR      POSITION(1:23)  CHAR
)
```

Note

Although SQL*Loader can load data in either binary or character format, we normally use

- **CHAR** for alphanumerics
- **NUMERIC EXTERNAL** for whole numbers
- **DECIMAL INTEGER** for numerics with decimal places

When we use the POSITION statement, we tell SQL*Loader the starting and ending position of the data that will go into each column. (It makes no difference where the data is positioned in the flat file.) For the AUTHORS table, then, we must specify where the Author_ID and Author fields start and stop. Notice that in the preceding example, Author ID is the first column for the AUTHORS table, but it is the third field in the record. We also tell SQL*Loader that the fields are normal, CHAR type. SQL*Loader can handle many data formats. In fact, 14 data types can be defined when you use the POSITION statement, each telling SQL*Loader the kind of data that is being pulled, as well as the size of each data type. You cannot override these sizes.

We run SQL*Loader on the flat file just as we did on the comma-delimited file; all we have to do is change the data file name. We will also get the same log, discard, and bad files. Here's what the DOS command looks like:

```
C:\WINNT\System32\cmd.exe
C:\>
C:\>
C:\>
C:\>
C:\>
C:\>
C:\>
C:\>
C:\>
C:\>
C:\>SQLLDR  USERID=SYSTEM/MANAGER@CWE1P
      CONTROL=C:\SQLLOAD\CTL\AUTHORS_CSV.CTL
        DATA=C:\SQLLOAD\DATA\AUTHORS_CSV.DAT
         LOG=C:\SQLLOAD\LOG\AUTHORS.LOG
         BAD=C:\SQLLOAD\BAD\AUTHORS.BAD

SQL*Loader: Release 9.0.1.1.1 - Production on Sat Jun 8 15:34:12 2002

(c) Copyright 2001 Oracle Corporation.  All rights reserved.

Commit point reached - logical record count 14

C:\>
```

The Last Step

The last step is always to check your tables. Go to SQL*Plus and take a look. You should see all the data that the logs said was loaded.

Note

If you use something like Notepad or WordPad or another such utility, it is very important that you *save the file using double quotes around the name*. For example, if someone creates a list file that you want to call `Authors.Dat`, save it as `"AUTHORS.DAT"`, and the file type should be "all files". If you don't use the double quotes, sometimes editing characters are automatically added to the file, and SQL*Loader will *not* be able to open the file. (You will get a SQL*Loader 500 error.) This is usually not a problem with a comma-delimited file created from a spreadsheet utility.

I have looked for deep, technical problems with input files that SQL*Loader just would not take, only to discover that the problem was simply that the file needed to be saved with quotes around the name! I'm just trying to save you hours of futile troubleshooting.

Some Advanced SQL*Loader

During this discussion I imagine you've had a few things on your mind: (1) How do we skip fields in a file that is comma-delimited? (2) How do we add fields such as date, user ID, and so forth? And (3) can we use conditional logic? I'm glad you asked, because these are the features that make SQL*Loader such a helpful tool. And now is the time for the answers.

In answer to the first question—skipping fields in a comma-delimited file—unfortunately the only two ways are to rebuild the input file or to load all the data into a temporary table and then write a script to pull just the data you want. You would then either use more commas or create a file with fixed-length columns.

Note

Here's the rule: You must specify something for every column in the table that you're loading.

For example, let's take the following fictitious table and input file:

WILD_HORSES Table	Input File

SEQ_NUM
TYPE_OF_HORSE
AGE
UNIQUE CHARACTERISTICS
DATE CAUGHT
CAUGHT BY
CURRENT LOCATION
SPECIAL DIET
BRAND MARK
M_F
WEIGHT
COMMENTS
	`001,Palamino,14 hands,gentle,10,black,10/10/97,GHR,...`
	`002,Paint,12 hands,wild,7,brown&white,06/04/96,BWW,...`
	`003,Chestnut,13.5 hands, wild,4,chestnut/white,`
	`06/29/99,...`

The input file has a bit more information than we want. For example, it has the size (14, 12, 13.5 hands) and the disposition (gentle, wild). To load this information into the table, either we would first have to rewrite the file so that it is in the right sequence, and then drop some information:

Input File

```
001,Palamino,10,black,10/10/97,GHR,...
002,Paint,7,brown&white,06/04/96,BWW,...
003,Chestnut,4,chestnut/white,06/29/99,...
```

or we could write the information to a fixed-format file:

Input File

```
001  Palamino       10   black            10/10/97 GHR,...
002  Paint           7   brown&white      06/04/96 BWW,...
003  Chestnut        4   chestnut/white   06/29/99 ,...
```

Once we have the data in a usable format, we can easily load it using the techniques already shown.

Note

Another option is to load the entire file into a holding or temporary table. After loading the temporary table using SQL*Loader, write a script to pull just the data you want. This is actually one of the most common ways to handle input files that do not match your table layout.

Now for the second question—adding dates, user ID, and so forth. Here's the rule: Again, you must have an entry for every column in your table. The data can come from the input file, or you can use constants, system fields, and the like.

Let's take a look at our WILD_HORSES table. Suppose that you know that MMF is the only one who has ever caught a wild horse, and that all the horses ever caught were brown and white mustangs. Your control file would then look like this:

```
--                                                      --
--              WILD HORSE .CTL FILE                    --
--                                                      --

LOAD DATA
APPEND
INTO TABLE  WILD_HORSES
```

```
FIELDS TERMINATED BY ','
OPTIONALLY ENCLOSED BY '"'
TRAILING NULLCOLS
(
SEQ NUM,
TYPE_OF_HORSE,
AGE,
UNIQUE CHAR  CONSTANT 'BROWN&WHITE', ❶
DATE CAUGHT,
CAUGHT_BY   CONSTANT 'MMK',
...
)
```

❶ Note use of CONSTANT.

With regard to the third question—conditional logic—fortunately SQL*Loader does support the WHEN statement if you're using a fixed-format file. Why? You have to be able to specify the field you want to test:

```
-                                                      -
-               WILD HORSE  .CTL FILE                  -
-                                                      -

LOAD DATA
APPEND
INTO TABLE  WILD_HORSES

WHEN (27:2) = 10 ❷
(
SEQ NUM,
TYPE_OF_HORSE,
AGE,
UNIQUE CHAR  CONSTANT 'BROWN&WHITE',
DATE CAUGHT,
CAUGHT_BY   CONSTANT 'MMF',
...
)
```

❷ Note the use of WHEN to test the age of the horse.

In this example you could change the control file to say to test whatever is in positions 27 and 28 and see if it equals "10". (The idea is to test for the age of the horse, and to load records only for horses that are 10 years old.)

There are many other powerful SQL*Loader features, and I encourage you to investigate them. For example, you can load sequence numbers, pull data from reports, and so forth. However, the examples presented here will give you plenty to work with for the time being.

Note

There are two Oracle methods for loading data using SQL*Loader: **direct path** and **conventional path**. I have not mentioned direct path because there are some restrictions. For mass loads of thousands of records, however, direct path is faster because it bypasses most of the RDBMS processing during the loading of records. I recommend that you investigate direct load further if you have occasion for managing the loading of massive amounts of data.

Now I need to cover one more aspect of SQL*Loader: date handling. Remember we said that the normal Oracle date format is DD-MON-YYYY? Often your data will be input in the format DD-MM-YY. Can you load this data? Yes, because Oracle allows you to tell it what the incoming data format is, and then Oracle reformats it automatically into its preferred format of DD-MON-YYYY. Suppose that the date field, `IN_DATE`, in your input file has the format DD-MM-YY. All you do in your SQL*Loader control file is tell it the format: `IN_DATE  DATE(8)  "MM-DD-YY"`. That's it! Here's a simple example in which the data is in the `.CTL` file:

```
-- Test script to load date in nonstandard format--
LOAD DATA
  INFILE *
APPEND
INTO TABLE TEST_DATE
FIELDS TERMINATED BY ","   OPTIONALLY ENCLOSED BY '"'
(NAME1, DATE1  DATE(8) "MM-DD-YY")
BEGINDATA
"Michael", 01-25-98
"Mark", 02-25-99
"Philip", 03-25-99
```

And here's the output:

NAME1	DATE1
Richard1	25-JAN-98
Damian1	25-FEB-99
Philip1	25-MAR-99

Method 2: Using a Script

Instead of using SQL*Loader, you can create a SQL*Plus script to load the records. As you will shortly see, this will be a long series of INSERT commands. This method is useful when you're testing a database and the tables are periodically destroyed, or when you're creating databases for training purposes.

Here's an example of a SQL*Plus load script:

❶ Note that numeric fields do *not* need quotes, but character fields do need them.

❷ As you can see, this is the hard way to enter data!

```
/*
GUERRILLA ORACLE
*/

INSERT INTO AUTHORS
     VALUES ( 118765443,  ❶
              'John Smith'
              );
INSERT INTO AUTHORS
     VALUES ( 227653089,
              'Harry Wellins'
              );

INSERT INTO AUTHORS
     VALUES ( 337640276,
              'Eleanor Satkowski'
              );

INSERT INTO AUTHORS  ❷
     VALUES ( 442876009,
              'George Drum'
              );
```

and so forth.

You can create your script using a text editor, making sure you follow the syntax shown here. For larger tables, of course you would have more entries in the VALUES clause.

To run the scripts, go the SQL> prompt and type the following:

```
@D:\SCRIPTS\TABLE_LOAD\LOAD_AUTHORS_SCRIPT.SQL
```

Warning

Just as we told you with the data and control files, when you create a SQL script in a text editor, remember to save it with double quotes. For example you would save the file name shown here as "LOAD_AUTHORS_SCRIPT.SQL".

Variation on Using a Script

In some cases, when you're retrieving data from another system you can load that data into a spreadsheet, where you can manipulate it and add the LOAD commands. That is, you can rearrange your columns in the spreadsheet so that the items are in the right sequence, and then create a couple other columns with the commands, commas, and so forth. Here's a fictitious spreadsheet with data that should go into your system:

My List of All Instructors for Computer Training Classes
George Stuctured, Ph.D

ID	Fname	Lname	Dt Hired	Specialty
110011	Harry	Smith	01-NOV-1990	Databases
220022	Jane	Ernest	17-FEB-1990	PL/SQL
330033	Laura	Werner	17-MAY-1993	SQL*Plus
440044	Sam	Wreston	09-DEC-1988	Networks
550055	Mary	Greening	22-SEP-1989	Programming

In this example we will start with five columns of data and end up with ten after adding the correct syntax to change the spreadsheet into a SQL script. First, we delete the headers:

110011	Harry	Smith	01-NOV-1990	Databases
220022	Jane	Ernest	17-FEB-1990	PL/SQL
330033	Laura	Werner	17-MAY-1993	SQL*Plus
440044	Sam	Wreston	09-DEC-1988	Networks
550055	Mary	Greening	22-SEP-1989	Programming

Second, we add columns containing the syntax necessary for an INSERT statement:

INSERT into TEST_TABLE values (	110011	,'	Harry	','	Smith	','	01-NOV-1990	','	Databases	');
	220022		Jane		Ernest		17-FEB-1998		PL/SQL	
	330033		Laura		Werner		17-MAY-1993		SQL*Plus	
	440044		Sam		Wreston		09-DEC-1988		Networks	
	550055		Mary		Greening		22-SEP-1989		Programming	

Third, we copy the new columns:

INSERT into TEST_TABLE values (	110011	,'	Harry	','	Smith	','	01-NOV-1990	','	Databases	');
INSERT into TEST_TABLE values (	220022	,'	Jane	','	Ernest	','	17-FEB-1998	','	PL/SQL	');
INSERT into TEST_TABLE values (	330033	,'	Laura	','	Werner	','	27-MAY-1993	','	SQL*Plus	');
INSERT into TEST_TABLE values (	440044	,'	Sam	','	Wreston	','	09-DEC-1988	','	Networks	');
INSERT into TEST_TABLE values (	550055	,'	Mary	','	Greening	','	22-SEP-1989	','	Programming	');

Finally, we save the data as a `.sql` file (note the quotes around the name), and we have a script that we can run at the SQL> prompt:

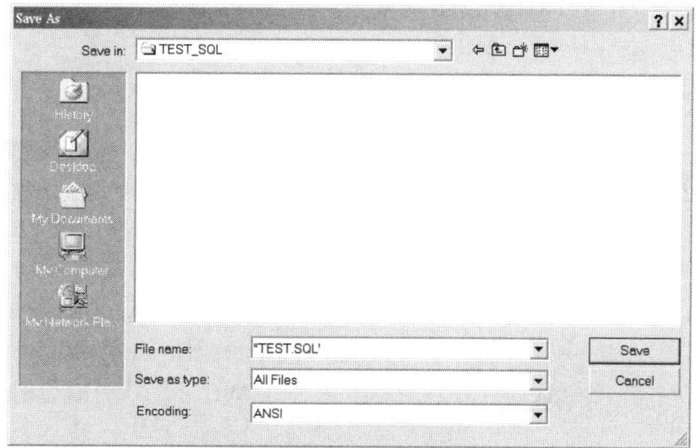

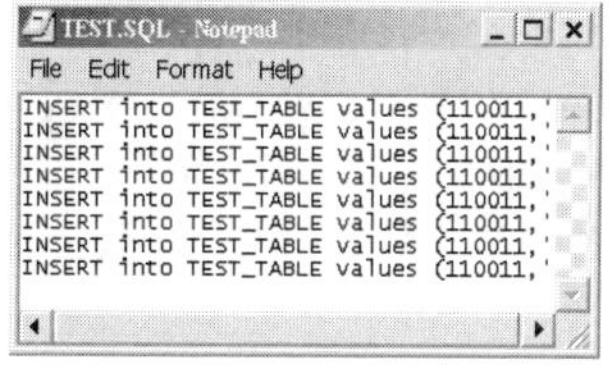

Sometimes using a script to load data can be a quick and dirty way to move relatively small files. Other times, getting the syntax correct can be so time-consuming that it is much better to use SQL*Loader. But notice that you *can* manipulate the spreadsheet data to make your life easier.

As with SQL*Loader, you're probably asking the question, What if the dates are in nonstandard format? The answer is the same: Use Oracle's date features to define the format mask, and then let Oracle do the rest. (We will talk a lot more about dates in Chapter 14.)

Here's an example of what you would have to add to your spreadsheet to specify the input format:

```
insert into TEST_DATE values
 ('jon2', TO_DATE('01-11-90',  'DD-MM-YY')) ❶
```

❶ **Notice the use of TO_DATE and then the format mask of DD_MM_YY.**

And here's what TEST_TABLE now looks like:

NAME1	DATE1
Richard1	25-JAN-98
Damian1	25-FEB-99
Philip1	25-MAR-99
Jon2	01-NOV-90

Method 3: Using a GUI Form

Another fairly good way to add data to your tables, if you have good data entry staff available, is to use Forms 6*i* and build yourself a simple GUI form. Here are the steps to quickly crank out such a form. (We call this the quick and dirty method of form generation—that is, doing just enough to get the job done.)

First open Forms 6*i* Form Builder, and, using the Data Block Wizard, select the type of data block you would like to create.

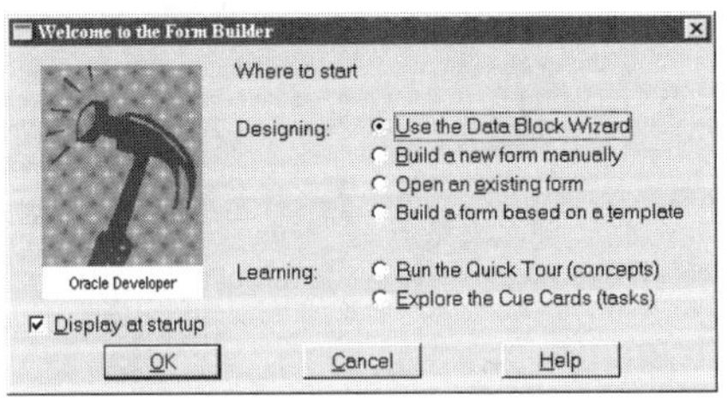

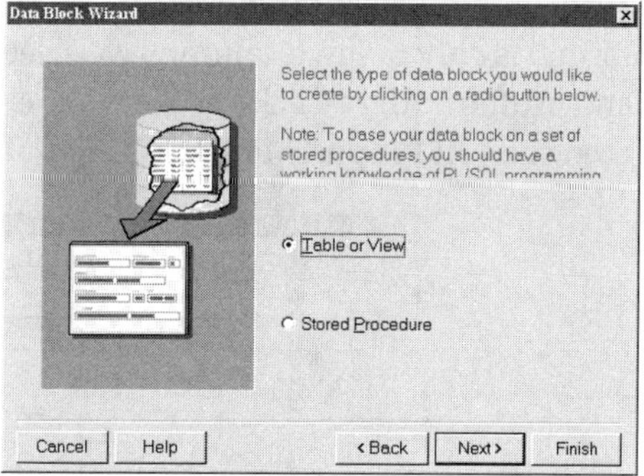

Now select the table (in this case AUTHORS) and the two columns: Author_ID and Author. Note that it is *very important* to check the **Enforce data integrity** box:

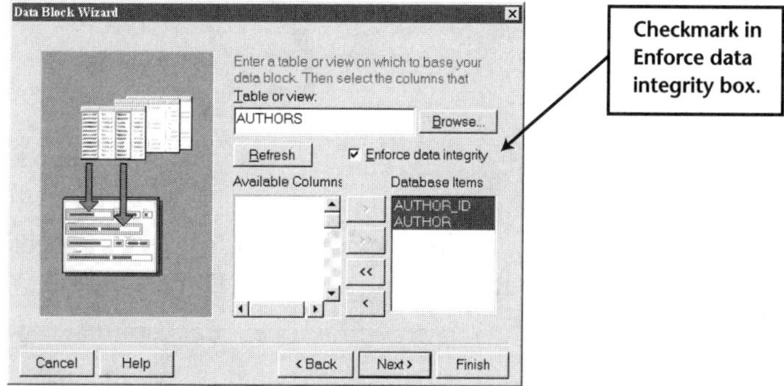

Use the Layout Wizard:

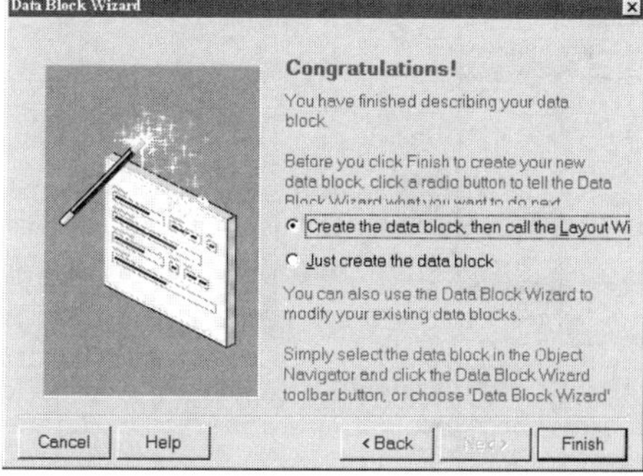

Forms 6*i* will then automatically give you the following form. Notice that this form has only the two columns we selected from the AUTHORS table: Author_ID and Author. Right-click on the data entry block that says "AUTHOR_ID" and then click on **Property Palette**:

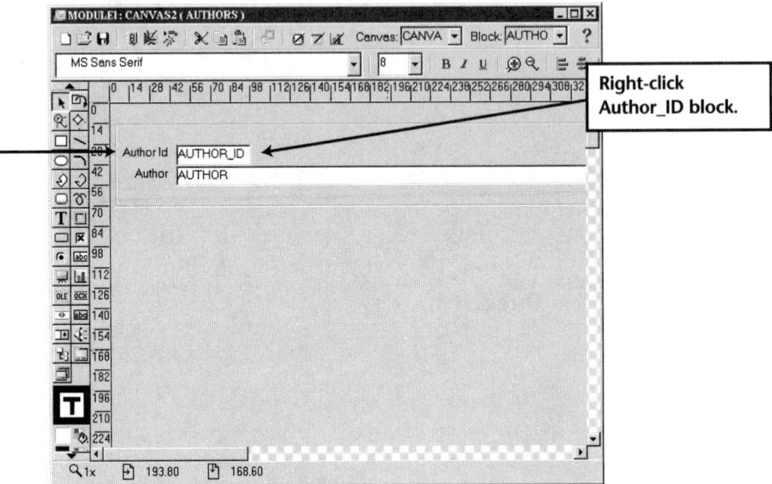

Now scroll down to the **Data** section and change **Maximum Length** to 9, also making sure that **Data Type** says "Number" and **Fixed Length** says "Yes":

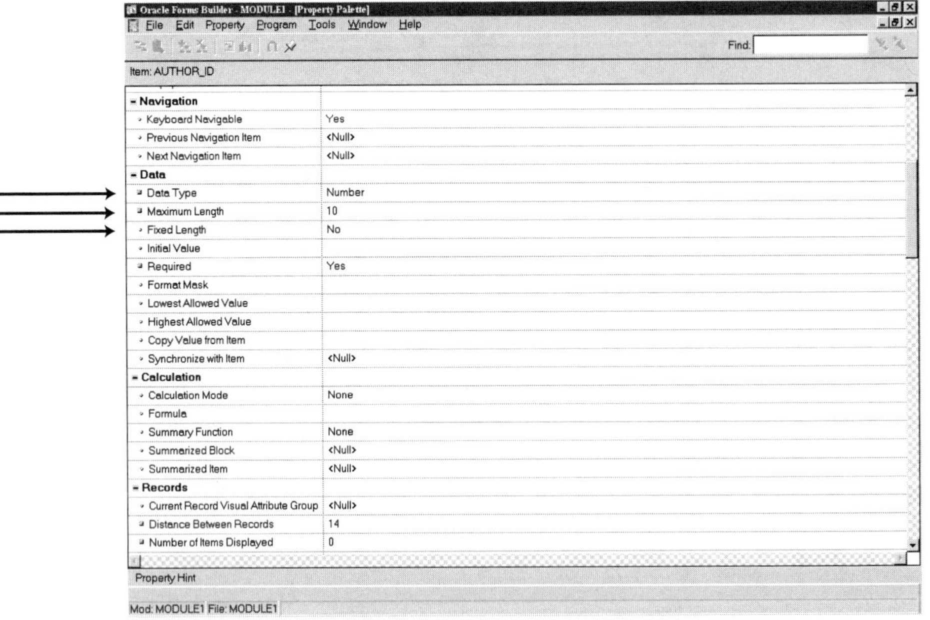

- Navigation	
Keyboard Navigable	Yes
Previous Navigation Item	<Null>
Next Navigation Item	<Null>
- Data	
Data Type	Number
Maximum Length	10
Fixed Length	No
Initial Value	
Required	Yes
Format Mask	
Lowest Allowed Value	
Highest Allowed Value	
Copy Value from Item	
Synchronize with Item	<Null>
- Calculation	
Calculation Mode	None
Formula	
Summary Function	None
Summarized Block	<Null>
Summarized Item	<Null>
- Records	
Current Record Visual Attribute Group	<Null>
Distance Between Records	14
Number of Items Displayed	0

Click the X in the upper-right corner to exit from the Author_ID Property Palette. Now right-click on the data entry block that says Author and then click on Property Palette. In the Data section, check to make sure that Maximum Length is 75:

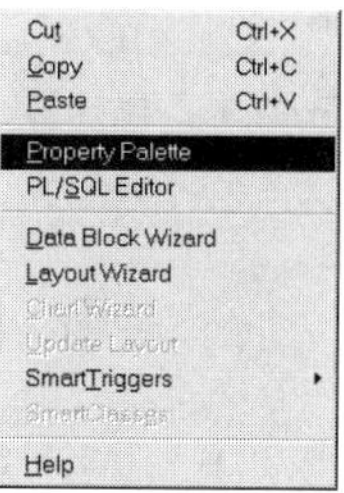

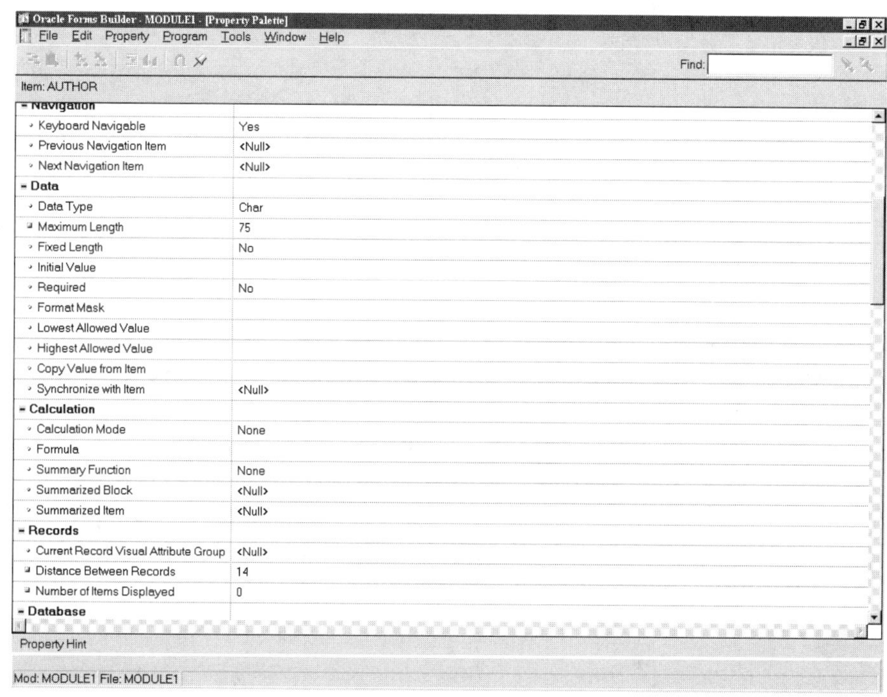

Again, click on the upper right X to exit. Now you can run the form. Click on the green traffic light:

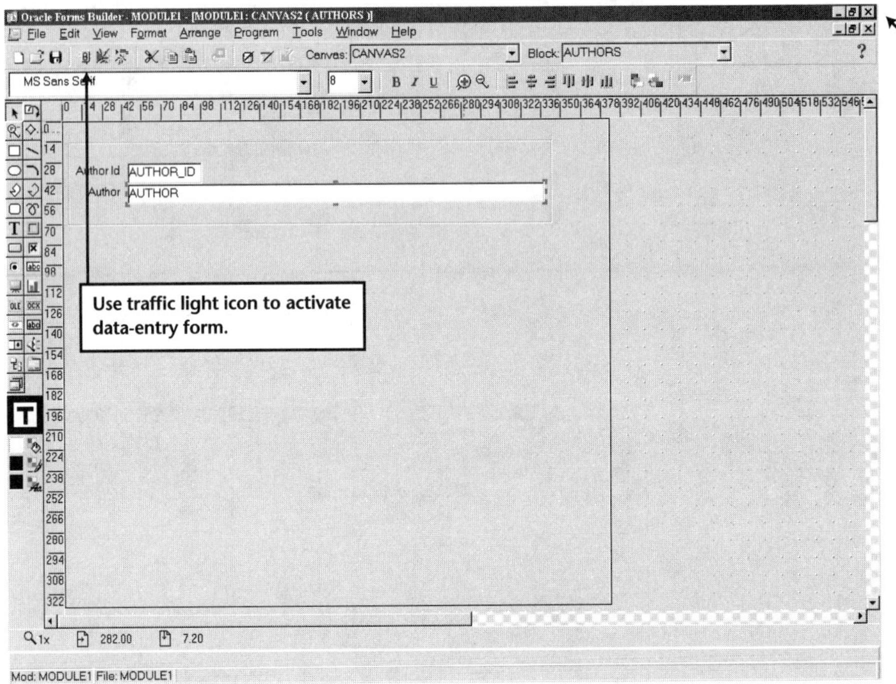

Almost by magic, you now have a running, functioning, simple data entry form. Notice that at the bottom is says "Record: 1/1". The reason is that at this time the AUTHORS table is empty.

Also notice the blue arrows, the green plus sign, and the red X at the top, in the toolbar. As you might guess, the green plus sign is used to add a record, the red X to delete a record, and the arrows to navigate through the table. Pretty straightforward, no?

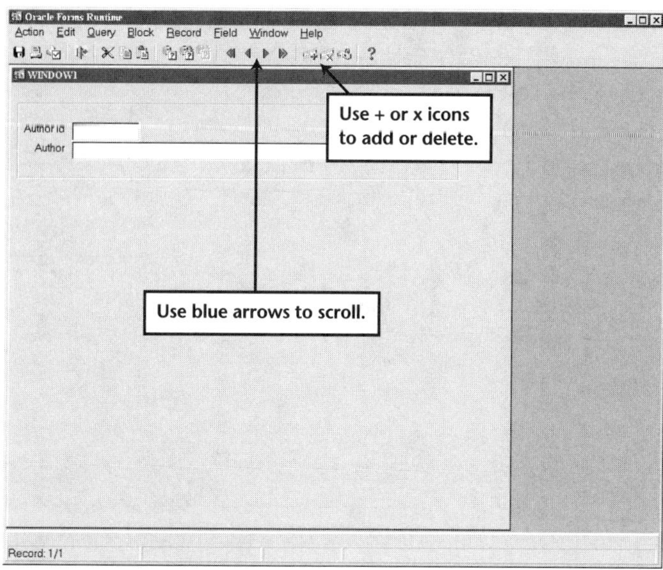

To add a record, do the following:

1. Click on the green plus sign.
2. Type in the data, with the Forms 6*i* editor, making sure that the proper formats are followed and that the mandatory field is filled in.

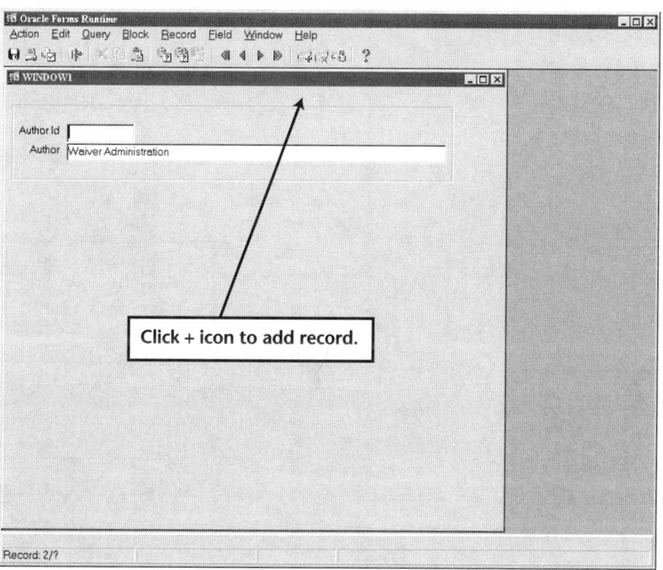

3. Click on the diskette icon to save the information:

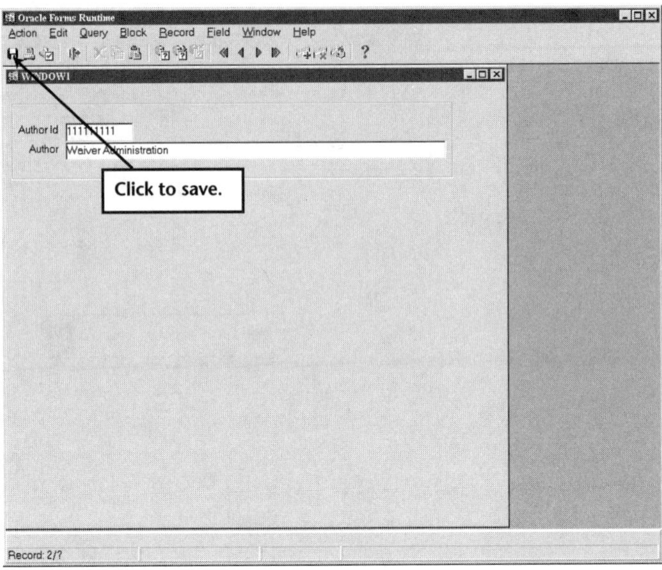

Repeat these steps until all records have been entered and saved.

Note that you will get errors if you try to save a record without enough data, or you enter a duplicate key:

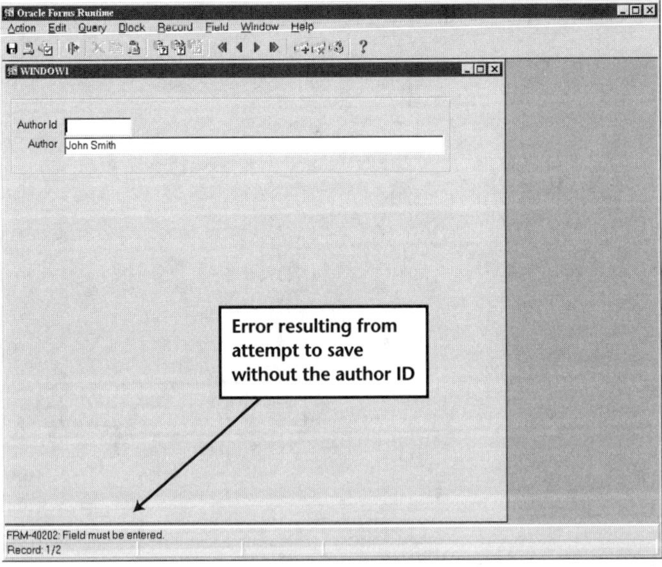

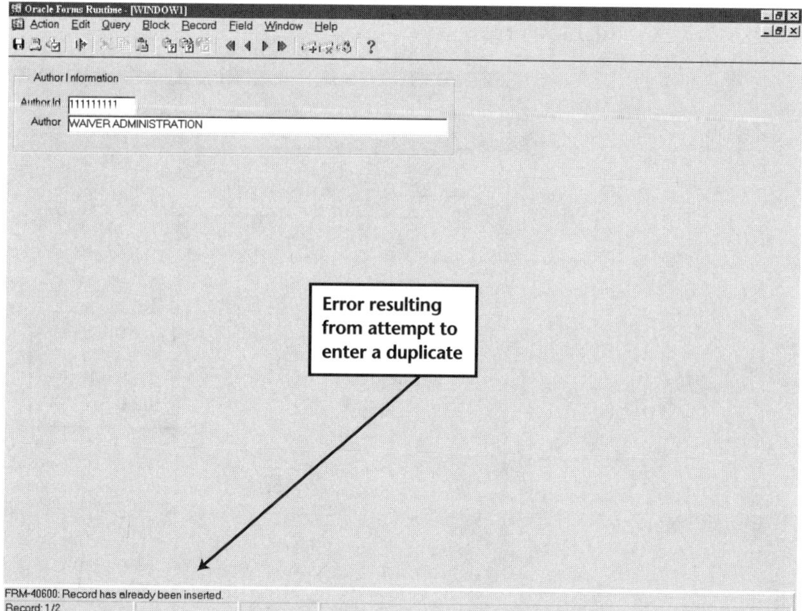

As you add records, notice that the counter at the bottom increments:

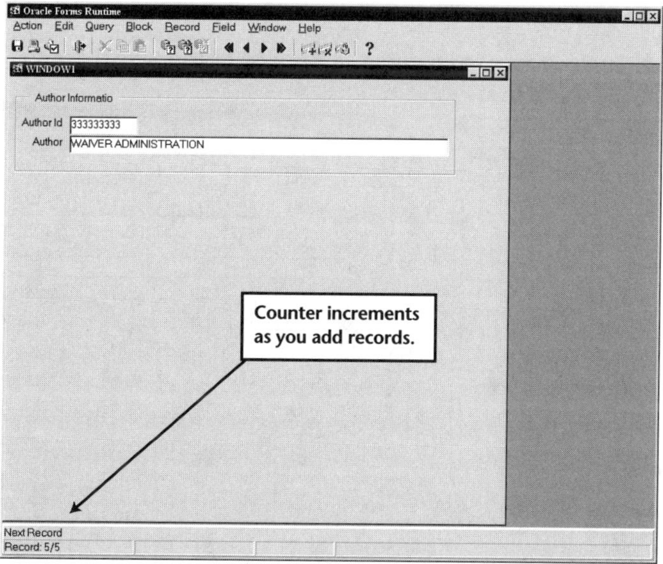

Don't forget that you can scroll back and forth through the table by using the blue arrows:

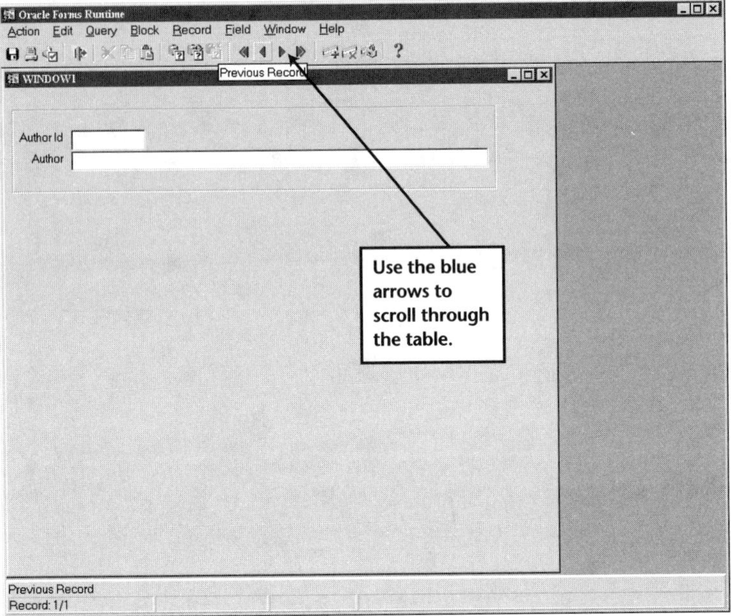

You can change the form to hold more than one record:

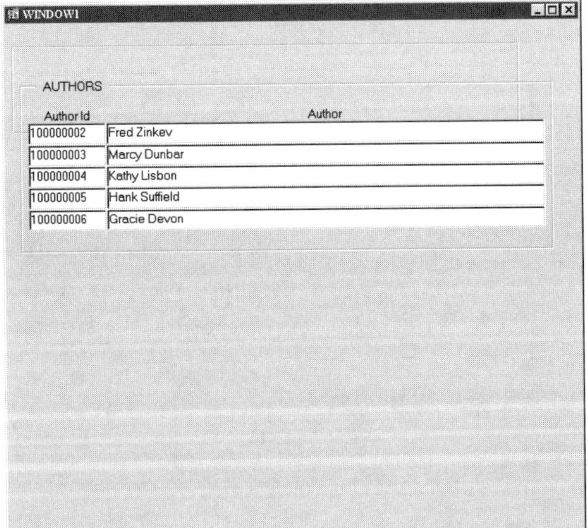

The same rules apply: Click on the green + icon to add the records, then the diskette icon to save. The only remaining trick is to select **Action | Clear All** when you have saved all the records. Doing this refreshes the entire screen so that you can enter more records.

That's it for using forms. Don't forget, this is a very quick and dirty way to build a simple data entry screen.

To review, in this chapter I have shown you how to load data into your tables in three different ways: using SQL*Loader, using a script, and making a simple GUI form using Forms 6*i*. Most programmers prefer SQL*Loader as the simplest and fastest way to move large amounts of information into a table or series of tables. Users, however, normally do not have rights to run SQL, so a GUI interface is more appropriate if your users will be loading the data.

Chapter 10

The Data Dictionary

If you have a photographic memory or keep perfect records or just don't ever create more than ten tables, you can skip this chapter. For the rest of us, however, the data dictionary is the one Oracle tool that consistently saves us from disaster and from wasting time.

For example, suppose that six months from now you have to go into the waiver database and revisit some of the constraints or take a look at all the users you created. You can't remember all the tables you created, and besides, you did such a fine job on the waiver project that they gave you two more and you've been buried with those. The waiver project is now just one of those happy memories of success. Nor do you remember all the waiver users you created, though you have a hunch that it's something like 100 or so.

Well, you *could* start hunting and pecking through your old documentation, reports, scripts, and views, and hopefully find what you need. Or you could whip out your data dictionary "cheat sheet" and quickly find the information you need and look like a hero, again.

You will learn that *the data dictionary is your friend*. You will soon know that the data dictionary can turn your hunches into facts because it is loaded with views of tables, users, constraints, rights, privileges, and so forth. Learning how the data dictionary works will pay you back a hundredfold, so pay attention.

What Is the Data Dictionary?

Think of the data dictionary as a gift. Without our having to do anything, Oracle provides a tool that automatically creates views and tables of the database, all its users, and its various structures. The data dictionary contains:

- Information about integrity constraints
- All the privileges and roles that each user has
- The names of all users
- All the names and definitions, as well as the space allocated and used, for all the schemas in the database

How Does the Data Dictionary Work?

Each database has its own data dictionary that is stored in the SYSTEM tablespace and consists of two major parts:

1. The system-maintained group of **base tables**. The base tables are not normally accessed by users because the data is in a cryptic format.
2. The assorted collection of views that Oracle creates from the base tables. These are the views that users normally access.

Warning

Do *not* fiddle with the data dictionary tables. These tables are owned by the user SYS, and no one should *alter* them in any way. The database most likely will no longer work if they are changed, because Oracle uses the data dictionary to manage the database. (Oracle does provide a safe way to *add* tables and views, but we will not be discussing it here.)

Oracle uses the dictionary in this general fashion: Every time you ask for something—whether a table, view, or row—Oracle checks with the data dictionary to see if what you want exists and if you have rights to it. Then if you create, modify, or delete a table or view, Oracle updates the data dictionary with the new information. The data dictionary is a great *reference tool.*

The Data Dictionary Views

There are four major groups of data dictionary views. The easiest way to identify them is by the prefix: *USER, ALL, DBA,* or *V$*. In general, the USER, ALL, and DBA views have pretty much the same information. USER views can be seen as a subset of ALL views, and ALL views as a subset of DBA views. V$ views contain dynamically changing information, such as system usage, and they are usually of interest only to DBAs.

To be perfectly clear, the DBA views provide information about the entire database: all users, all tables. ALL views return information about all the objects that a particular user can access in all schemas in the entire database—but they are still user-oriented. And USER views provide information on only the particular schema that each user owns.

For example, if you requested a list of all the objects for a typical user—`SQL> SELECT OBJECT_NAME FROM USER_OBJECTS`—maybe only a couple or a dozen or two dozen objects would be returned. If the user were a developer, however, you might get hundreds or thousands. Make the same request for `ALL_OBJECTS`, and Oracle will return thousands of objects, reflecting all the data dictionary views, system tables and indexes, and so forth that a user automatically can access. Log on as a DBA, and even more objects will be returned if you make the same request for `DBA_OBJECTS`. Is this clear? Good. It's just a hierarchical way of looking at the data.

Table 10.1 summarizes the different groups of data dictionary views.

Table 10.1 The Four Major Groups of Data Dictionary Views

Prefix	Explanation
USER	These are the user's views—only what is in the *user's* schema.
ALL	Again, these are the user's views, but they show whatever the user has rights to in *all* schemas.
DBA	These are the high-level, DBA views that show *everything* about a database.
V$	These are dynamic "performance tables" maintained by Oracle that record what is currently going on with the database. Usually only DBAs access V$ views.

Although thousands of views are available, you will use just a small set of them most frequently. Let's cover these commonly used views first. What follows is a collection of the most frequently asked questions, along with answers that reveal the views in this category. You may want to consider starting your own list of such questions as the beginning of your own data dictionary cheat sheet:

Q: How do I find all the tables and views in the data dictionary?
A: `SQL>SELECT * FROM DICTIONARY;`

Note

A nickname for *dictionary* is *dict*—for example: `select * from DICT;`

Q: How do I show *all* tables in a database?
A: `SQL>SELECT * FROM DBA_TABLES;`

Q: How do I show all the tables that a user *owns*?
A: `SQL>SELECT * FROM USER_TABLES;`

Q: How do I show all tables in a database that a user can *access*?
A: `SQL>SELECT * FROM ALL_TABLES;`

Note

There is a nickname (actually, it's a public synonym) for USER tables. Just use *TABS*, as in

```
SQL>SELECT * FROM TABS
```

(Another nickname, *TAB*, returns only three columns of information about a table, unlike the 26 columns that TABS returns.)

Q: How do I check whether an account is locked?
A: `SQL>SELECT * FROM USER_USERS WHERE USER = <username>;`

What's in USER_USERS? There are eight columns of information:

1. **Username**. Self-explanatory
2. **User_ID**. A system-generated number
3. **Default_Tablespace**. What you gave the user when you created the account
4. **Temporary_Tablespace**. Same as Default_Tablespace
5. **Created**. Date the account was created
6. **Account_Status**. Locked, unlocked, or expired
7. **Lock_Date**. Date the account was locked
8. **Expiry_Date**. Date the account will expire

Note

Let's review what synonyms, or public synonyms, are. (We talked about these in Chapter 8, but the idea is worth repeating.) We can create alternate names for objects, either to hide the underlying name, especially for a table, or to make the name easier for users to handle. Such a name is called a **synonym**. It just makes life easier to use the nicknames. If you're a purist, go ahead and use the full, original names. The SELECT commands will work no matter which name you use! (As long as you have the security rights. That is, if you have rights to the synonym but not the real table name, you cannot do a SELECT using the real table name. You'll get the "Object *xxx* DOES NOT EXIST" error message.)

Q: How do I show all columns in all tables?
A: `SQL>SELECT * FROM ALL_TAB_COLUMNS;` or
`SQL>SELECT * FROM USER_TAB_COLUMNS;`

Q: How do I find the columns in the data dictionary views and tables?
A: `SQL>SELECT * FROM DICT_COLUMNS;`

Tip

Given that the data dictionary will have the data for well over 10,000 tables and views—more likely close to 20,000—it is strongly advised that you qualify any SELECT * statement. Otherwise, you should have spooling turned on and be prepared to spend hours searching a large file to find what you need.

Instead, use qualifiers or exact names to reduce the number of rows returned—for example,

```
SQL>SELECT * FROM ALL_TABLES
WHERE TABLE_NAME LIKE " WAIVER%";
```

Just be careful. The table names are *case-sensitive*, so put them in UPPERCASE or you won't get anything back.

Q: How do I find out which privileges the different roles have?
A: `SQL>SELECT * FROM ROLE_TAB_PRIVS;`

Q: How do I find out which roles a particular user has?
A: `SQL> SELECT * FROM USER_ROLE_PRIVS WHERE USERNAME = <username>;`

Q: How do I find out all the tables and views that a user owns?
A: `SQL> SELCT * FROM DBA_TABLES WHERE OWNER = <ownername>;`

Note

DBA tables can be seen only by users who have the "SELECT ANY TABLE" privilege.

Q: How do I find out which constraints a table has?
A: `SQL>SELECT * FROM ALL_CONSTRAINTS WHERE TABLE_NAME = <table-name>;`

Q: What's a quick way to list every user in the database?
A: `SQL>SELECT * FROM ALL_USERS;` (You will get only three columns—Username, User_ID, and Created—but if all you want is a list, this is the best command. You can then use USER_USERS to get more details.)

Q: How do I find out what the default tablespaces are for a user?
A: `SQL>SELECT * FROM USER_USERS WHERE USERNAME = <username>;` (Yes, I showed you USER_USERS a little earlier. It is one of the most widely used data dictionary views when one is working with a user account.)

Q: How do I find all the profiles in the database?
A: `SQL>SELECT * FROM DBA_PROFILES;`

In the preceding Q&A section, I have given you a quick list of the data dictionary views that you will use the most. As mentioned already, there are many, many more. Let's take a look at some of them. My approach to showing you more of the data dictionary is to follow what we have already done. We have:

1. Created tables
2. Added constraints
3. Created primary keys
4. Created profiles
5. Created roles
6. Created users
7. Added limits to users
8. Created tablespaces

The next steps will be to show you the the power of the data dictionary with respect to these tasks. When you need to see what you have done, or when a user complains about a security or space error, how can you track it down quickly? In other words, *how do you find this information after the fact?*

But wait, we're not done! We're also going to take a look at:

9. A little bit more on auditing
10. Dynamic tables—the V$ environment

1. Tables

Start with the basic view, ALL_TABLES. Quite a bit of information is returned from the command `SQL>DESC ALL_TABLES`:

ALL_TABLES View

Name	Type	Null?
Owner	VARCHAR2(30)	NOT NULL
Table_Name	VARCHAR2(30)	NOT NULL
Tablespace_Name	VARCHAR2(30)	NOT NULL
Cluster_Name	VARCHAR2(30)	
Pct_Free	NUMBER	
Pct_Used	NUMBER	NOT NULL
Ini_Trans	NUMBER	NOT NULL
Max_Trans	NUMBER	NOT NULL
Initial_Extent	NUMBER	
Next_Extent	NUMBER	
Min_Extents	NUMBER	
Max_Extents	NUMBER	
Pct_Increase	NUMBER	
Freelists	NUMBER	
Freelist_Groups	NUMBER	
Backed_up	VARCHAR2(1)	
Num_Rows	NUMBER	
Blocks	NUMBER	
Empty_Blocks	NUMBER	
Avg_Space	NUMBER	
Chain_Cnt	NUMBER	
Avg_Row_Len	NUMBER	
Degree	VARCHAR2(10)	
Instances	VARCHAR2(10)	
Cache	VARCHAR2(5)	
Table_Lock	VARCHAR2(8)	

2. Constraints

To find the constraints for a table, use the command SQL>DESC_ALL_CONSTRAINTS:

ALL_CONSTRAINTS View

Name	Type	Null?
Owner	VARCHAR2(30)	NOT NULL
Constraint_Name	VARCHAR2(30)	NOT NULL
Constraint_Type	VARCHAR2(1)	
Table_Name	VARCHAR2(30)	NOT NULL
Search_Condition	LONG	
R_Owner	VARCHAR2(30)	
R_Constraint_Name	VARCHAR2(30)	
Delete_Rule	VARCHAR2(9)	
Status	VARCHAR2(8)	

To look at any constraints on a particular column in a table, use the ALL_CONS_COLUMNS view:

ALL_CONS_COLUMNS View

Name	Type	Null?
Owner	VARCHAR2(30)	NOT NULL
Constraint_Name	VARCHAR2(30)	NOT NULL
Table_Name	VARCHAR2(30)	NOT NULL
Column_Name	VARCHAR2(30)	NOT NULL
Position	NUMBER	

3. Primary Keys

To find the primary key for a table, use the command SQL>DESC ALL_CONSTRAINTS to get the ALL_CONSTRAINTS view, and look at Constraint_Type. Here's an example:

ALL_CONSTRAINTS View

Table_Name	Constraint_Type	Constraint_Name
TEST_TABLE	P	SYS_C0021715

Notice that the type is P, for *primary key*. If this were a foreign key, which we have in our waiver tables, there would be something in the columns R_Owner and R_Constraint_Name (see the complete list of columns in the ALL_CONSTRAINTS view in the preceding section).

Now how would you find all the columns involved with a primary key if the primary key were made up of several columns? There are two steps: (1) run the ALL_CONSTRAINTS view (you've already done this); (2) take the information for Constraint_Name and run the view ALL_CONS_COLUMNS, using Constraint_Name:

```
Select COLUMN_NAME from USER_CONS_COLUMNS
Where
CONSTRAINT_NAME = 'SYS_C0021715';
```

This command will return any columns that are part of the primary key.

4. Profiles

To show the user's profile, you have to use a DBA view—DBA_USERS:

DBA_USERS View

Name	Type	Null?
Username	VARCHAR2(30)	NOT NULL
User_ID	NUMBER	NOT NULL
Password	VARCHAR2(30)	
Default_Tablespace	VARCHAR2(30)	NOT NULL
Temporary_Tablespace	VARCHAR2(30)	NOT NULL
Created	DATE	NOT NULL
Profile	VARCHAR2(30)	NOT NULL

Notice that this view gives you the profile name only. To see what the profile actually is, use the DBA_PROFILES view. The command is:

```
SQL> select resource_name, Limit from dba_profiles
  2  where profile = 'WAIVER_DEV_PROFILE';
```

DBA_PROFILES View

Resource_Name	Limit
Composite_Limit	DEFAULT
Sessions_Per_User	UNLIMITED
CPU_Per_Session	DEFAULT
CPU_Per_Call	3000
Logical_Reads_Per_Session	DEFAULT
Logical_Reads_Per_Call	DEFAULT
Idle_Time	45
Connect_Time	UNLIMITED
Private_SGA	DEFAULT

See how this view will show you all the limits for the particular profile?

Note

Remember that to see the DBA views, you must have the "SELECT ALL TABLES" privilege!

5. Roles

To find out what roles exist, use the DBA_ROLES view:

DBA_ROLES View

Role	Password
Connect	NO
Resource	NO
DBA	NO
Exp_Full_Database	NO
Imp_Full_Database	NO
Waiver_Dev_Role	NO
Waiver_Bus_Role	NO
Waiver_Student_Role	NO

Then use the view DBA_ROLE_PRIVS to get some more details about a particular role:

DBA_ROLE_PRIVS View

Name	Type	Null?
Grantee	VARCHAR2(30)	
Granted_Role	VARCHAR2(30)	NOT NULL
Admin_Option	VARCHAR2(3)	
Default_Role	VARCHAR2(3)	

Notice that this view tells you who granted the role, and whether it was granted with the powerful Admin_Option.

Well and good, you may be thinking, but the roles we created have lots of other information about things like number of sessions and so forth. Where do we find that information?

It's not easy. Unfortunately, no single view shows you every privilege for a role. But since you've gotten this far in the book, you're obviously stubborn enough to stick with me as I show you how to get the final details.

First understand that there are really three kinds of grants:

1. Grants given about tables and sometimes columns
2. Grants that give the role *system privileges*
3. Grants that give roles to other roles

Each of these grants has its own view, as you might have suspected. I told you this would be a little complicated!

Let's go. For grants about tables and columns, use the ROLE_TAB_PRIVS view:

ROLE_TAB_PRIVS View

Name	Type	Null?
Role	VARCHAR2(30)	NOT NULL
Owner	VARCHAR2(30)	NOT NULL
Table_Name	VARCHAR2(30)	NOT NULL
Column_Name	VARCHAR2(30)	
Privilege	VARCHAR2(40)	NOT NULL
Grantable	VARCHAR2(3)	

For grants about any system privileges, use the ROLE_SYS_PRIVS view:

ROLE_SYS_PRIVS View

Name	Type	Null?
Role	VARCHAR2(30)	NOT NULL
Privilege	VARCHAR2(40)	NOT NULL
Admin_Option	VARCHAR2(3)	

And for information about grants that give roles to other roles, use the ROLE_ROLE_PRIVS view:

ROLE_ROLE_PRIVS View

Name	Type	Null?
Role	VARCHAR2(30)	NOT NULL
Granted_Role	VARCHAR2(30)	NOT NULL
Admin_Option	VARCHAR2(3)	

Finally, to find out which roles a particular user has, use the USER_ROLE_PRIVS view:

USER_ROLE_PRIVS View

Name	Type	Null?
Username	VARCHAR2(30)	
Granted_Role	VARCHAR2(30)	
Admin_Option	VARCHAR2(3)	
Default_Role	VARCHAR2(3)	
OS_Granted	VARCHAR2(3)	

6. Users

Let's start with basic user information. The most basic data dictionary view for users is USER_USERS:

USER_USERS View

Name	**Type**	**Null?**
Username	VARCHAR2(30)	NOT NULL
User_ID	NUMBER	NOT NULL
Default_Tablespace	VARCHAR2(3)	NOT NULL
Temporary_Tablespace	VARCHAR2(3)	NOT NULL
Created	DATE	NOT NULL

Although this data dictionary view doesn't give much information, you can use it to:

- Quickly find a user
- Get the user's default tablespaces

To see which, if any, system privileges a user may have, use the USER_SYS_PRIVS view:

USER_SYS_PRIVS View

Name	**Type**	**Null?**
Username	VARCHAR2(30)	
Privilege	VARCHAR2(40)	NOT NULL
Admin_Option	VARCHAR2(3)	

And to find all the tables, views, and so forth that the user owns, use the USER_CATALOG view:

USER_CATALOG View

Name	**Type**	**Null?**
Table_Name	VARCHAR2(30)	NOT NULL
Table_Type	VARCHAR2(11)	

For user information, Table 10.2 gives a good synopsis of the available data dictionary views.

Table 10.2 USER Data Dictionary Views

View	Contents
USER_CATALOG	Tables, views, synonyms, and sequences that the user owns. There are only two columns of data: Table_Name and Table_Type.
USER_CONS_COLUMNS	The columns that are involved with the constraints. Use this with USER_CONSTRAINTS.
USER_CONSTRAINTS	Any constraints on any table that the user owns. Use ALL_CONSTRAINTS to see the constraints on all the tables that the user can access.
USER_OBJECTS	Information for all types of objects for the user.
USER_RESOURCE_LIMITS	Any limits, such as logons, that were given to the user's profile.
USER_SEQUENCES	All the sequences that the user owns. Use ALL_SEQUENCES to see all the sequences that the user can access.
USER_SYNONYMS	Synonyms that the user owns. Use ALL_SYNONYMS to see the entire list of synonyms that the user can access.
USER_TAB_COLS	All the columns for all the tables that the user owns. Use ALL_TAB_COLS to see all the tables and columns that the user can access.
USER_TABS	26 columns of information on tables that the user owns. Use the ALL_TABS view to see all the tables that the user can access.
USER_VIEWS	Views that the user owns. Use ALL_VIEWS to see the views that the user can access.

7. Limits

This one is also not simple. You have to look at various views to get all the limits that have been set for the user. Some of the more common data dictionary views to check the limits are SESSION_PRIVS and SESSION_ROLES. These views describe all the privileges and roles that are available to the current session.

8. Tablespaces

Finding the tablespaces is easy. Just use the USER_TABLESPACES view:

USER_TABLESPACES View

Name	Type	Null?
Tablespace_Name	VARCHAR2(30)	NOT NULL
Initial_Extent	NUMBER	
Next_Extent	NUMBER	
Min_Extents	NUMBER	NOT NULL
Max_Extents	NUMBER	NOT NULL
Pct_Increase	NUMBER	NOT NULL
Status	VARCHAR2(9)	
Contents	VARCHAR2(9)	

To find the quotas for a user's tablespaces, use the USER_TS_QUOTAS view:

USER_TS_QUOTAS View

Name	Type	Null?
Tablespace_Name	VARCHAR2(30)	NOT NULL
Bytes	NUMBER	
Max_Bytes	NUMBER	
Blocks	NUMBER	NOT NULL
Max_Blocks	NUMBER	

Note

Don't forget: Most of these views can be run as USER, ALL, or DBA views.

9. Auditing

Remember the short paragraph on auditing in Chapter 8? Well, as you have probably guessed, there is a plain, standard audit trail that anyone can look at, and three very complete views are available. Each of these views can be run as USER or DBA views.

To follow the audit trail, you must have the auditing feature turned on for your database. Normally auditing is done for three types of things, through three different views:

1. Objects (through the USER_AUDIT_OBJECT view)
2. Session information (through USER_AUDIT_SESSION)
3. Certain commands that the user might use, such as audit, no audit, grant, revoke, and others (through USER_AUDIT_STATEMENT)

Anyone can look at the USER_AUDIT_TRAIL view. This view has 30 columns that include information about all three types of auditing. Confused? I suggest that you consult the Oracle documentation when you need to use the auditing feature.

10. V$ Tables

The last stop on the Data Dictionary Express is to give you some information on the tables that are used to show how the system is performing and to provide a sundry list of statistics. As I mentioned earlier, V$ views are normally used by DBAs. Here are the most common V$ views:

- **V$SESSION** shows all current sessions.
- **V$SYSSTAT** gives statistics about the entire database.
- **V$BGPROCESS** shows any background processes that are active.
- **V$DATAFILE** shows data on the files in the database.

You get the idea. Along with information on users, tables, rights, roles, and so forth, Oracle keeps real-time information on system performance. Again I encourage you to search the Oracle documentation for more information. This short discussion on the V$ tables is meant simply to make you aware that they exist.

There are many more tables in the data dictionary. Some, such as USER_SOURCE, list any functions, packages, or procedures that you may create. Others show details on space usage, extents, and so forth. Don't be afraid to take a look at the "DICT" view and see what's out there.

My goal in covering the basics of the data dictionary was to make you aware of this very powerful reference tool. In the Q&A section of this chapter I tried to start you on your way to your own data dictionary "cheat sheet" by showing you some of the most common commands. You can use the Q&A section as a starting point and add to it as you need to.

You will find that your use of the data dictionary will change depending on what you're doing—working with user accounts, creating roles, programming, and so forth. Just remember that many of the commands come with a *USER_*, *ALL_*, or *DBA_* prefix, and you'll be in good shape. If you try one that doesn't seem to work, then run a DESCRIBE operation on it, and if that doesn't work, look for it in the data dictionary by using the following command:

```
SQL>SELECT * FROM DICT
WHERE TABLE_NAME LIKE '%what you're looking for%';
```

Good hunting!

One Last Thought

Now that you have worked a bit with the data dictionary, don't you think it makes sense to develop *naming standards*? For example, in our waiver database, our tables have plain English names—AUTHORS, QUESTIONS, and so forth. However, when you start developing systems with hundreds or thousands of tables, you will quickly run out of simple names. Hence I suggest that you develop a *seven-character naming schema* that will fit all the applications you develop. The first letter would stand for the general area—F for finance, E for education, P for payroll, and so forth. Then the remaining characters would be used to refine the name.

What does this gain for you? You immediately have a *shortcut* for the data dictionary. If you wanted to find all the tables associated with education, you could run your data dictionary query to find all tables that begin with *E*.

Here's an example of a fairly standard naming convention:

Position	**Explanation**
1	The system that owns the object (form, report, table)
2	The module within the system that owns the object
3	The type of object—form, query, report, view
4–7	Unique identifiers for the object

Here's how it would work. Let's take finance as an example because that's an easy area to understand. The database object *FAQBUDG* translates into:

F = Finance, the system that owns this object
A = Accounts Payable, the module within Finance that owns this object
Q = Query
BUDG = Identifies this object as a budget query

Continued

If you wanted all the objects that had to do with the Accounts Payable area, you could query the data dictionary by looking for tables beginning with *FA%*.

See how easy it becomes to navigate through the data dictionary when you have a solid naming convention? It will take time to develop, but it is well worth it in the long run.

OK, One More

I don't want to leave you with the idea that the data dictionary contains magic wands that will easily answer all your questions. Actually, quite the opposite. In many cases you will have to work to get all the answers you need. As I have discussed, it is somewhat difficult to get all the information you need for something as common as roles. And one real shortcoming is that Oracle has no way to provide you with your original statements creating the roles.

So let me leave you with a question: What is Oracle Designer, and what does *repository* mean? (Hint: Oracle Designer, one of the Oracle development tools, is a general-purpose modeling tool used to design and document databases. Although there is work to be done to maintain the information, the payback is having complete and accurate reference materials—more complete and organized than in the data dictionary. When you decide to create a database or are assigned to a project that must create a database, I strongly advise that you use either Oracle Designer or another such tool.)

Chapter 11

Installing the Oracle 8*i* and 9*i* Client

After you have configured the Oracle 8i or 9i server, and you have created at least one Oracle database and users, the next step in the process is to get a local PC operational, or "Oracle-smart." (As you will see, an 8*i* or 9*i* client can access any Oracle 8 database. In addition, an Oracle 8 client can access an 8*i* or 9*i* database. There is full compatibility between Oracle 8 and Oracle 8*i* and 9*i* databases.)

A client can be made Oracle-smart in two steps:

1. The Oracle Universal Wizard is used to install the Oracle client software with the proper modules.
2. The wizard automatically takes you to the necessary network configurations so that your client PC knows where the Oracle database is, what the

database name is, and what alias will be used. This will all become clear in the instructions that follow.

Warning

Starting with 8*i*, *you must use the wizards* to configure the network parameters, especially the `TNSNAMES.ORA` file. With Oracle 8, you could manually change `TNSNAMES.ORA`. With 8*i* and 9*i*, this is an absolute no-no. If you do change `TNSNAMES.ORA`, it will become invisible to the Net8 communications program, and you will receive Oracle error 12154: "Could not resolve service name." Later I'll show you how to add or modify your communications entries. Just do *not* do it manually!

The Installation

To install Oracle 8*i* or 9*i*, follow these instructions:

First check for space on the hard drive. You do not want to get an "out of space" message at the end of the installation! Oracle 8*i* needs about 300MB, and 9*i* needs 1GB. Note that it is customary, for performance reasons, to put the Oracle folder on a drive other than C:\\.

Note

In the following instructions, the Oracle folder will be installed on D:.

Oracle Universal Installer Screen

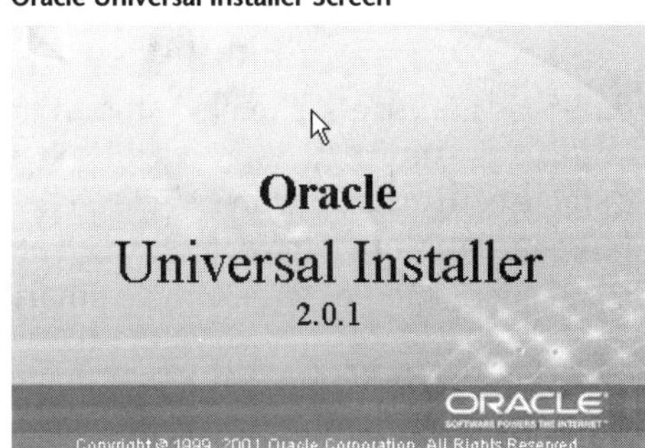

Load the Oracle 8*i* or 9*i* client CD. For 8*i*, you will immediately see the **Oracle Universal Installer** screen, followed by the **Oracle8*i* Client – Autorun** screen:

Oracle 8*i* Client-Autorun Screen

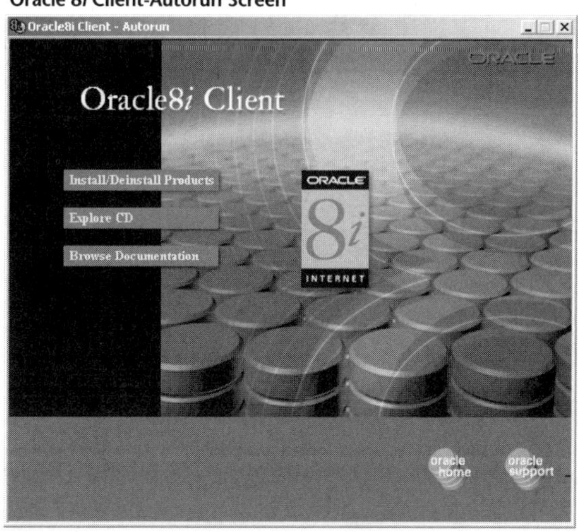

For 9*i*, you'll see the new, blue **Welcome** screen, where you can (1) deinstall if necessary, (2) look at the help files, and (3) review what has already been installed. Click **Next**:

Oracle Universal Installer Welcome Screen

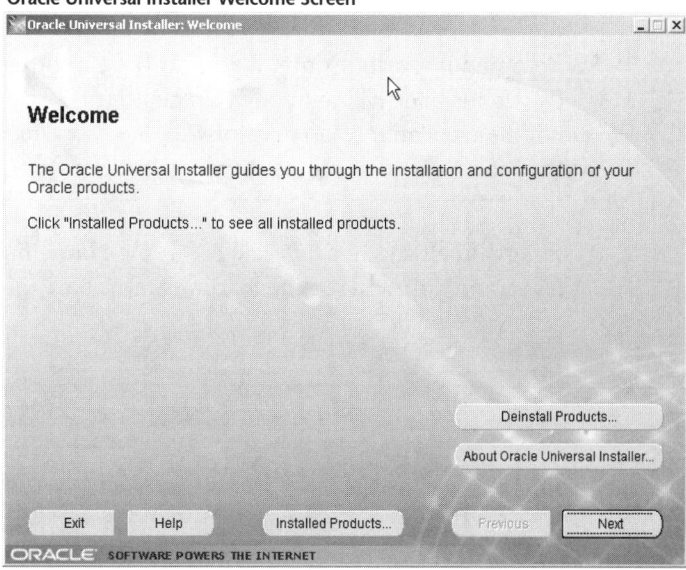

If you do not already have a version of Oracle installed on this PC, take the defaults for the source and destination locations:

Oracle 8*i* File Locations Screen

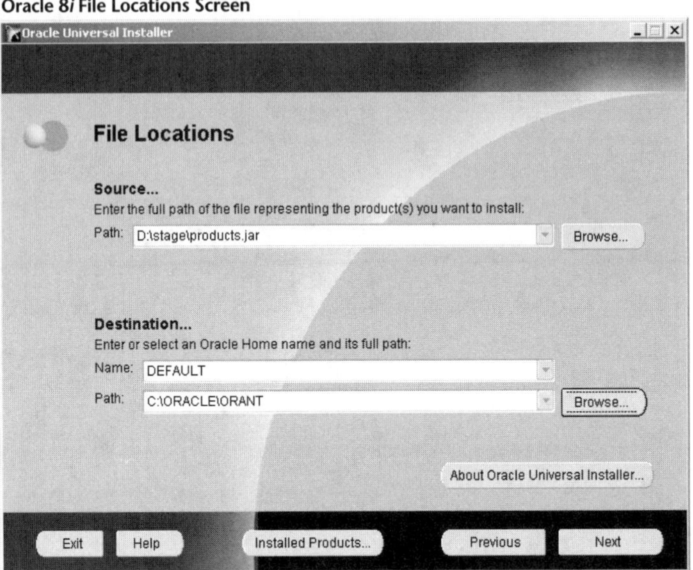

Note

Here's an important note: If you do have another version of Oracle on this PC, Oracle Installer will tell you, "Oracle 9*i* (or 8*i* if you're installing 8*i*) Client cannot be installed into an existing 7.*x*, 8.*x*, 9.*x* Oracle_Home." What this means is that you have to specify *another* destination (or Oracle home).

Enter something like "Oracle 8*i*" in the **Name** field under **Destination....** Click **Next**, and you will see the loading status bar:

Loading Status Bar

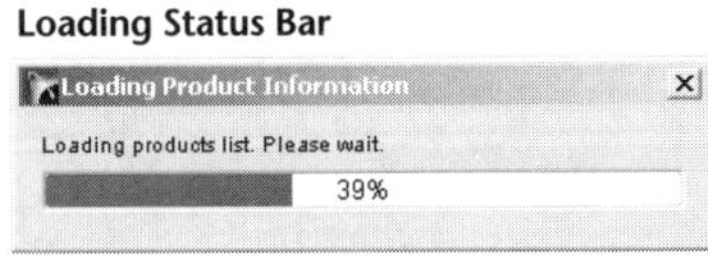

For 9*i*, it's pretty much the same, except the screen format is slightly different, with the status bar in the upper right-hand corner:

Oracle 9*i* File Locations Screen

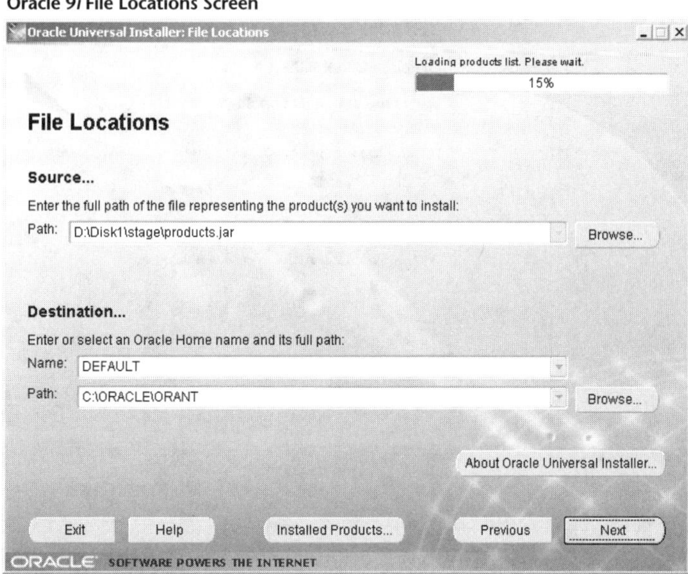

Now you will be given a choice of installation types:

Oracle 8*i* Installation Types Screen

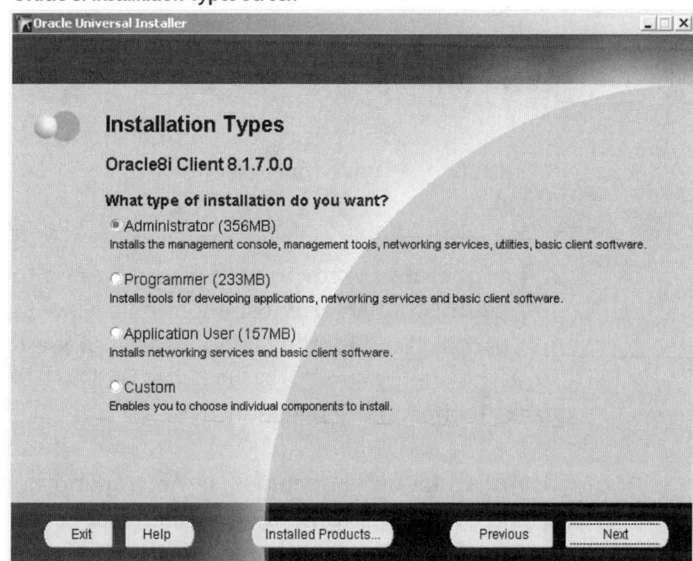

Oracle 9*i* Installation Types Screen

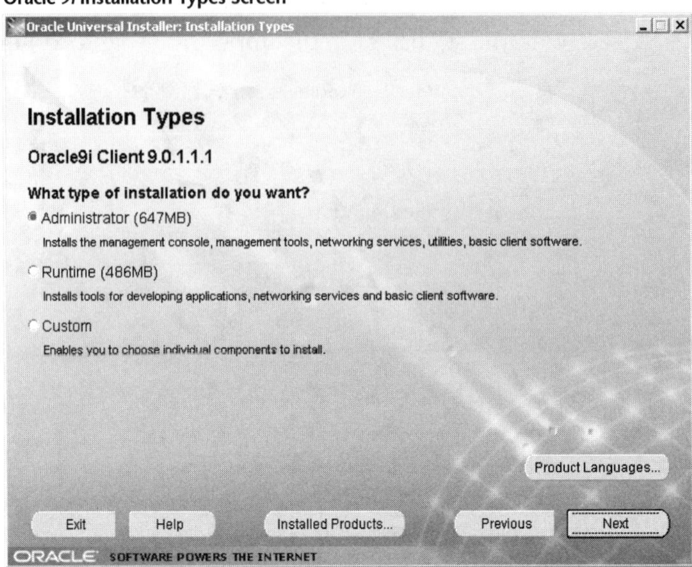

For 8*i*, if this is a client PC, select **Application User**; if it's a programmer's PC, select **Programmer**. And if this is your PC, I suggest that you select **Administrator**. For 9*i*, the selections are somewhat different, and I suggest that you select **Administrator** for all cases. Once you have an "Admin" PC configured, you can install the end-user PCs with the runtime version.

Client Installations

There are various types of client installations.

With 8*i*, you have four selections:

1. **Administrator** gives you the most power.
2. **Programmer** provides the programming tools.
3. **Application User** is just enough to allow connection to the database.
4. **Custom** is not for the faint of heart. I suggest staying away from this option.

Oracle 9*i* offers three selections:

1. **Administrator** includes all networking and client software, along with the Oracle Enterprise management tools.
2. **Runtime** gives you the networking and support files only.
3. **Custom**, as in 8*i*, is complicated. And again, I suggest staying away from it.

Click **Help** anytime for a brief explanation of the screen items:

Oracle Help Screen, Showing Client Installation Types

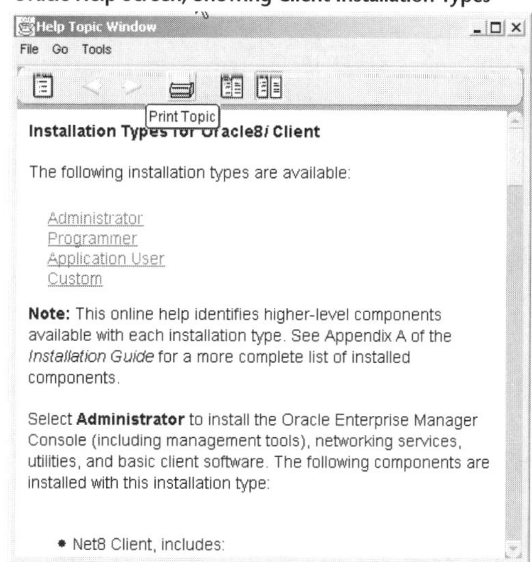

At this point the installer will determine which products to install. All you will see at this point is a status bar. When the installer has decided what to do, you will see the next screen, and if you scroll down, you'll be able to see the 70+ items that will be installed:

Oracle 8*i* Client Products Summary Screen

Oracle Universal Installer

Summary

Oracle8i Client 8.1.7.0.0

Global Settings
Source : D:\stage\products.jar
Destination : C:\ORACLE\ORANT
Installation Type : Administrator
Product Languages
English
Space Requirements
Volume C:\ Required 300MB : Available 251MB
New Installations (113 products)
Advanced Queueing (AQ) API 8.1.7.0.0
Agent Required Support Files 8.1.7.0.0
Assistant Common Files 8.1.7.0.0
Authentication and Encryption 8.1.7.0.0

Exit Help Installed Products... Previous Install

Oracle 9*i* Client Products Summary Screen

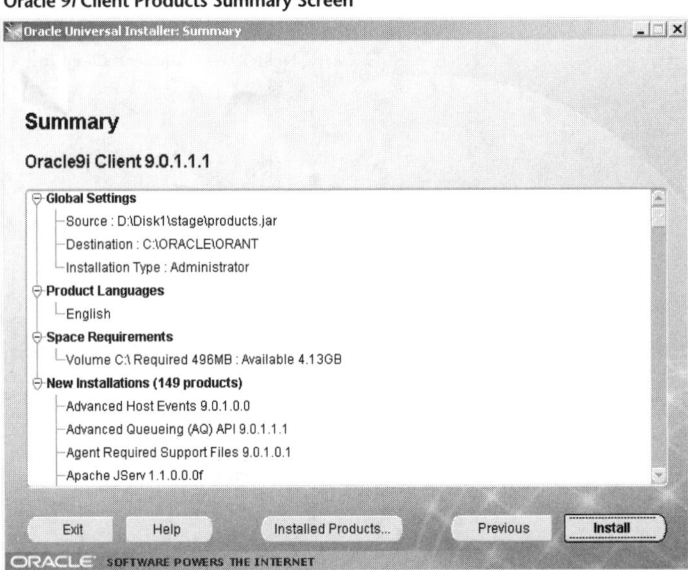

I suggest you take a look, and see how many of the Oracle products are Web oriented. Now, click **Install**, and the product installation will start. During the installation you can monitor progress on the following screen:

Oracle 8*i* Client Install Screen

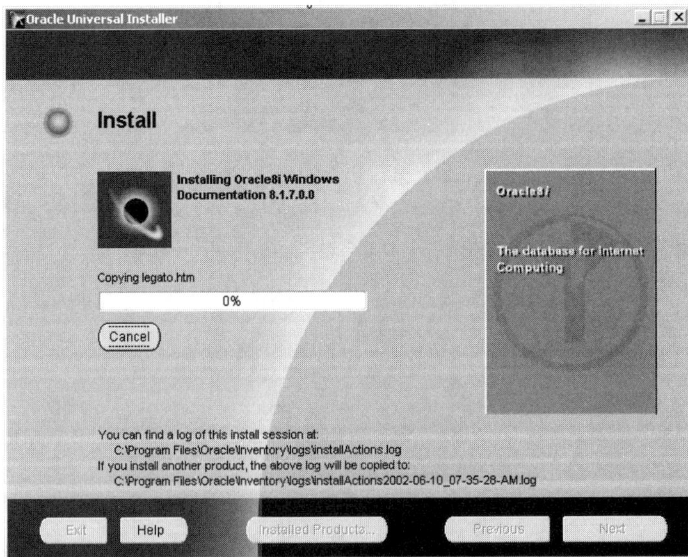

Oracle 9*i* Client Install Screen

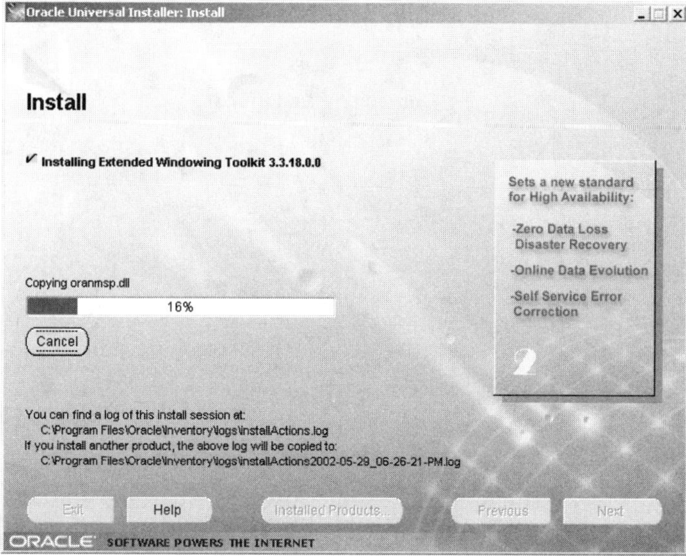

Once the installation is complete, this screen pops up:

Configuration Tools Screen

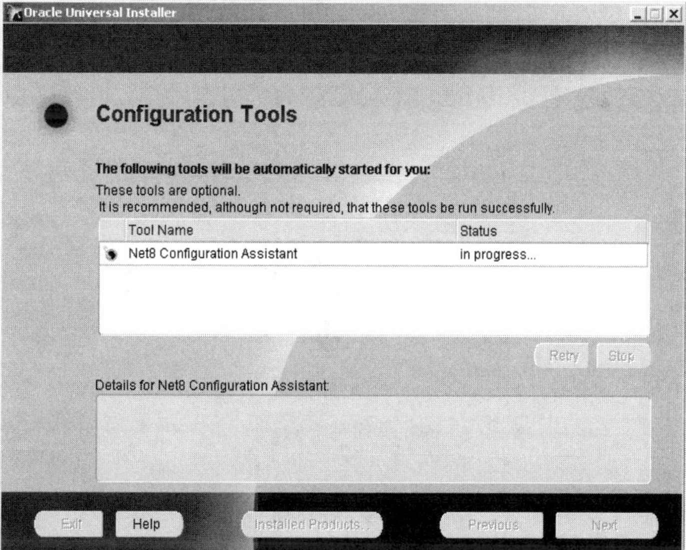

Oracle 9*i* Component Locations Screen

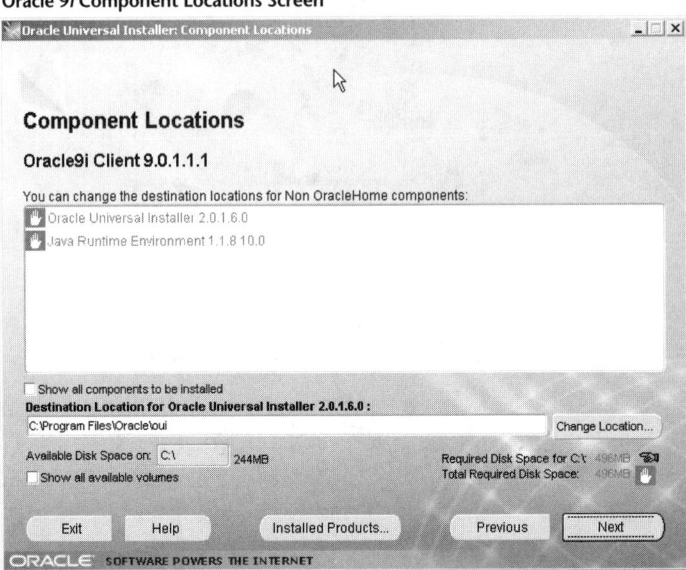

What's interesting is that *the installer goes directly to the next major component* that you need, Communications, which is now called Net8 (formerly known as SQL*Net.)

Do not be frightened by this screen; there's nothing you have to do. Notice in the 8*i* version that there is a **Status** column, and before you have a chance to really study the screen, the following screen appears (the 9*i* screen is the same):

Net8 Welcome Screen

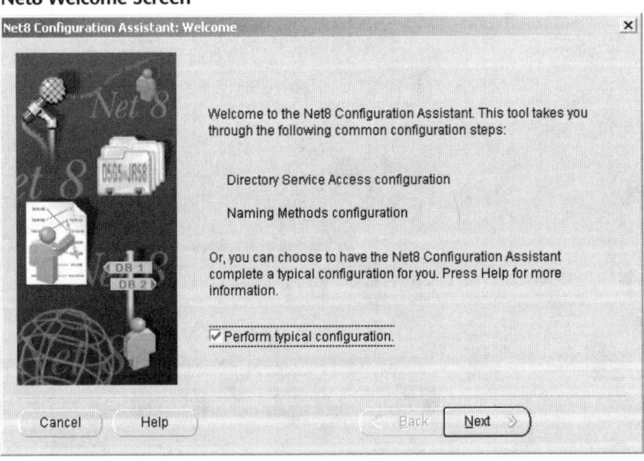

Let the installer complete a typical configuration.

On the next screen, select **No**, unless you really do have a directory service on your network:

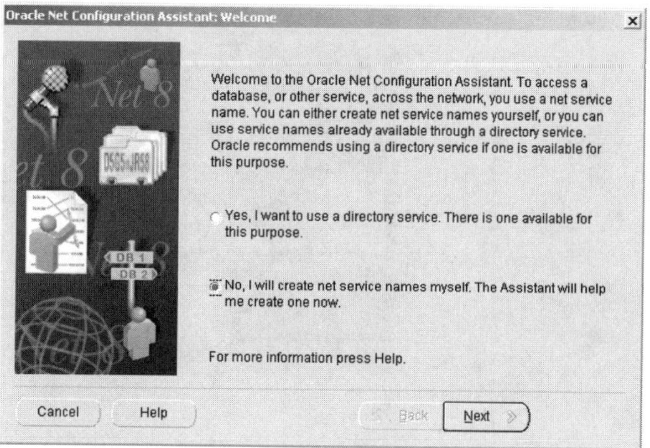

Note

It's time for a short discussion on what's happening. Remember back in Chapters 6 and 7 when I walked you through creating the database? We gave the database a name: CWE1P. In the next series of steps, you will be telling your client PC how to reach the database, along with another Oracle database that was developed earlier. You will also have a chance to test your setup, and I strongly advise that you do that when the appropriate screen pops up.

On the next screen you will be asked to identify the version of the Oracle database you will access. Note that you can add more later by running the Net8 Configuration Assistant. First point to the computer waiver exam database (CWE1P), which is an Oracle 8*i* database:

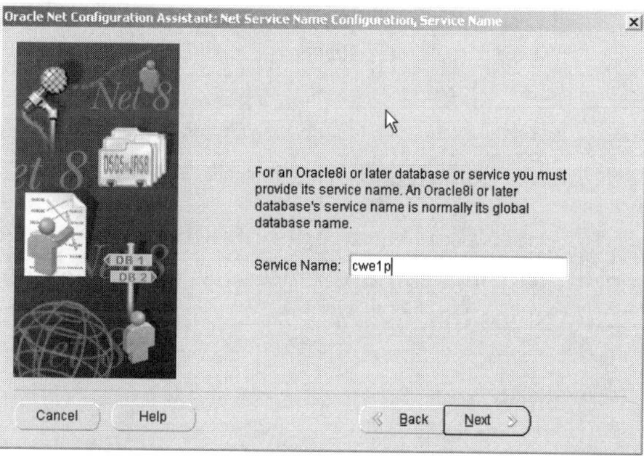

Next select the communications protocol:

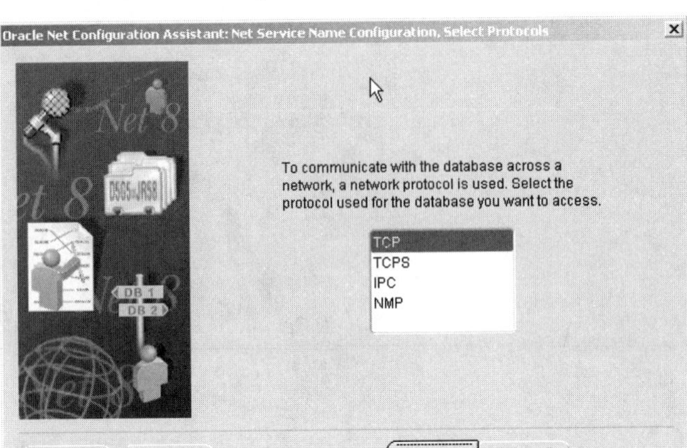

Now define the host computer. This gets interesting. If you are installing the client software on a PC connected to a local area network (LAN), type in the server name. Here's what the screen looks like for a PC on a LAN:

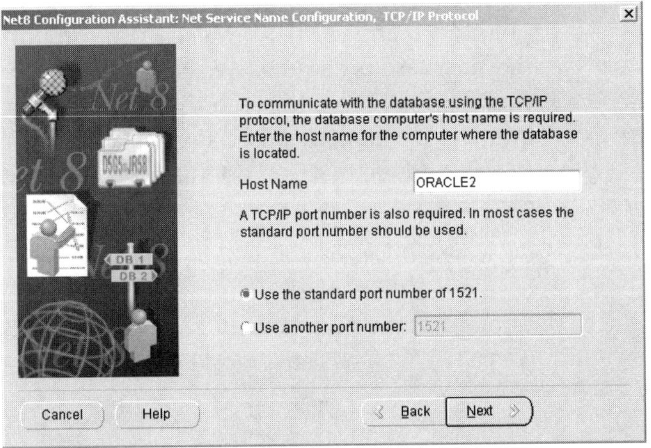

Note

Here's an important note: If you are configuring a PC that will be used to dial in to the database, enter the *IP address of the server with the database*. See the steps that follow!

Here's what the screen looks like for a dial-in configuration:

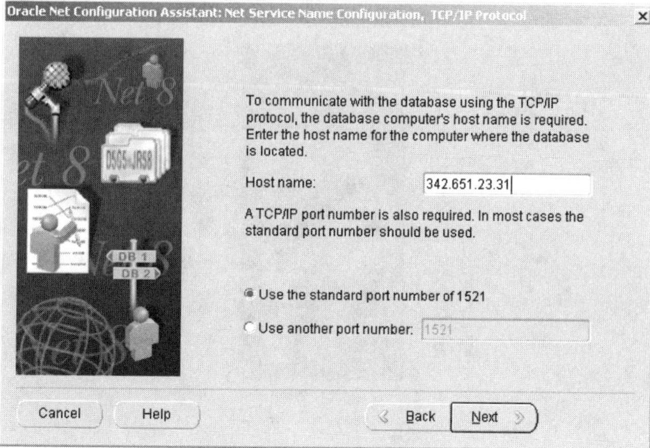

As I said already, when the next screen appears, run the test:

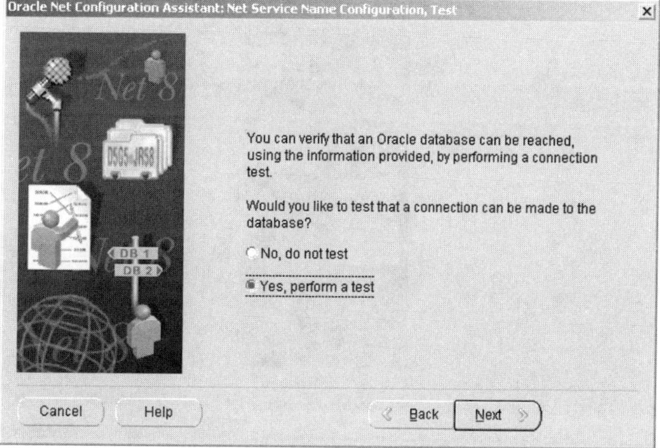

Soon you should see the following message:

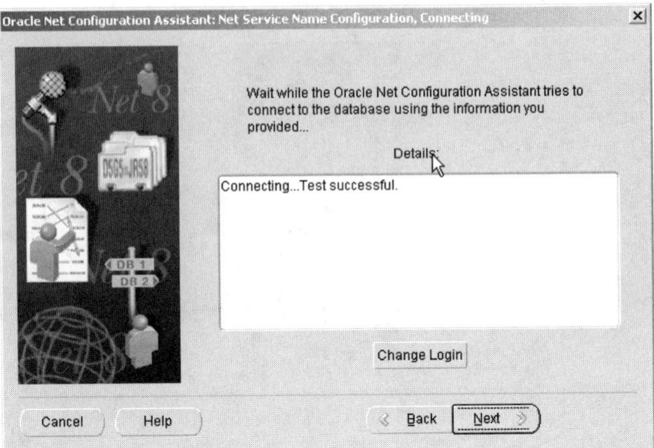

The next step is to give the host a name. This will be the name you will use when you log on. It can be any name:

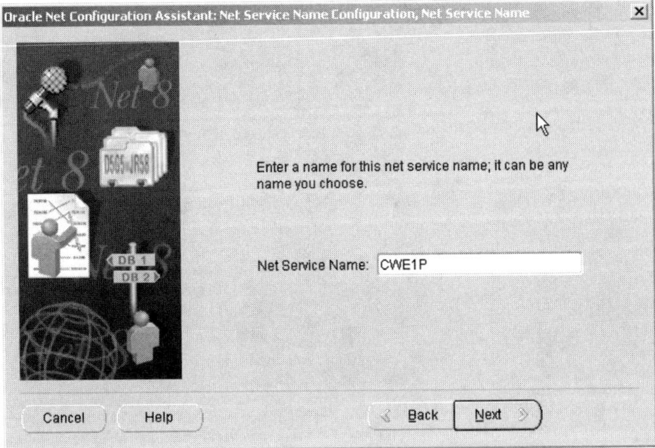

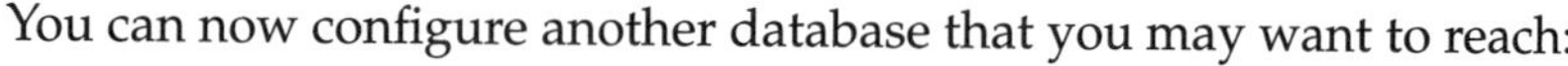

You can now configure another database that you may want to reach:

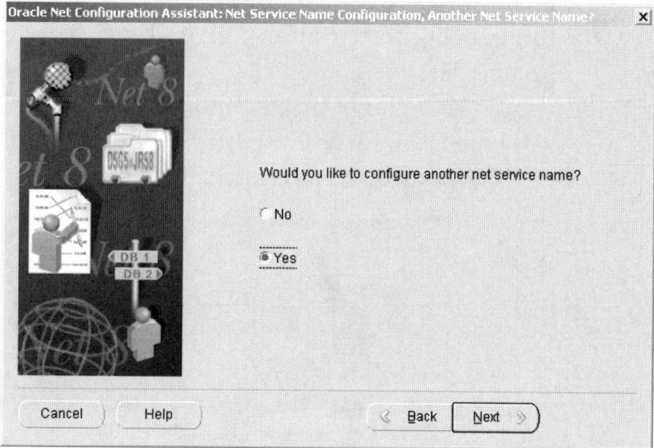

As an example of connecting to a second database, I will use an Oracle 8 database from my lab, with the system ID (SID) CWETEST:

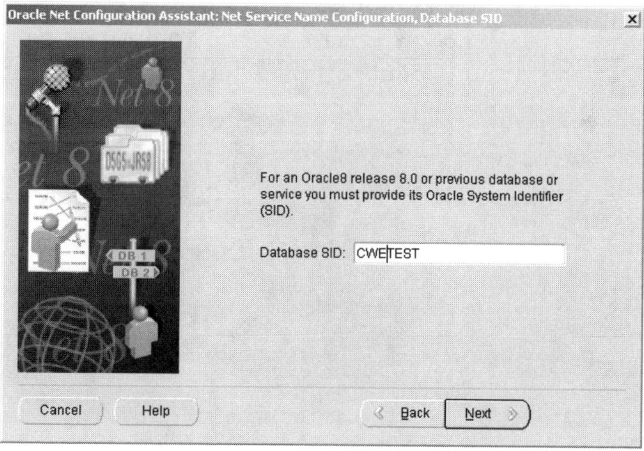

The name is generic because this Oracle database is used for testing, development, prototyping, and so forth. There may be many systems, programs, and forms being tested at any given time, so a neutral name is the best choice. Remember, this is the name we will use to log on to the database. We can always change it because no matter what we call it, behind the scenes the Net8 software knows it as CWETEST. I'll say more about this shortly.

Now select the communications protocol:

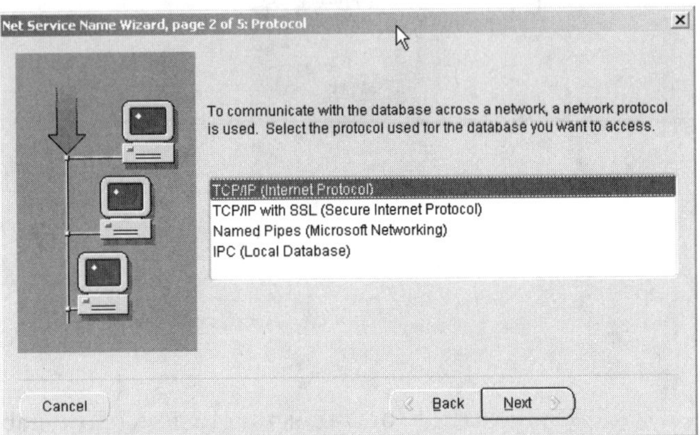

The host computer in this example is GUERRILLA2, with the IP address 344.321.34.56. Enter whatever your server name is in the **Host Name** field. I'll say more about ports and port numbers later; for now, take the default:

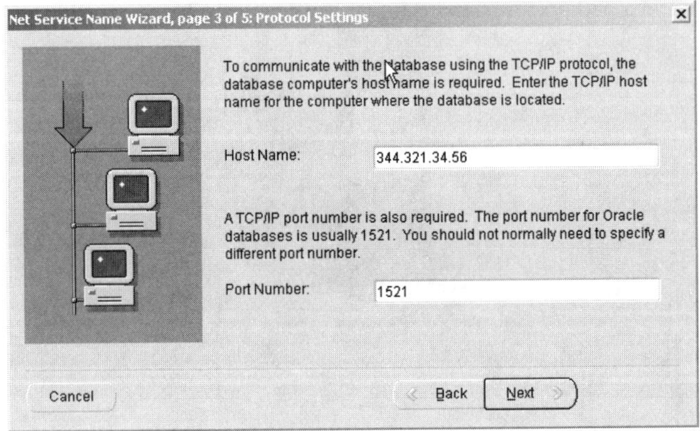

Run the test:

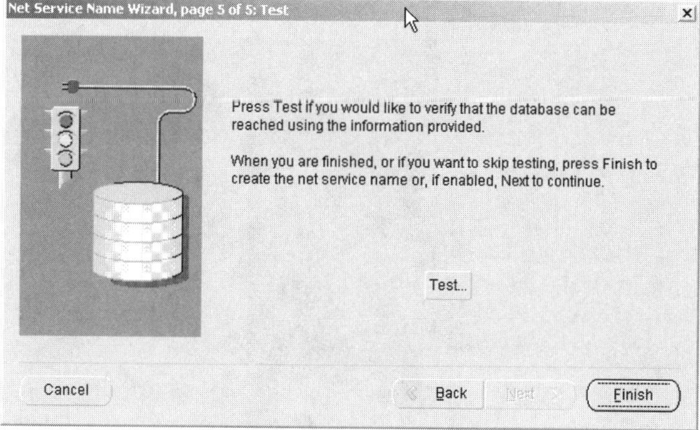

If the connection fails and you get an error message like this, go back and correct your spellings and other parameters:

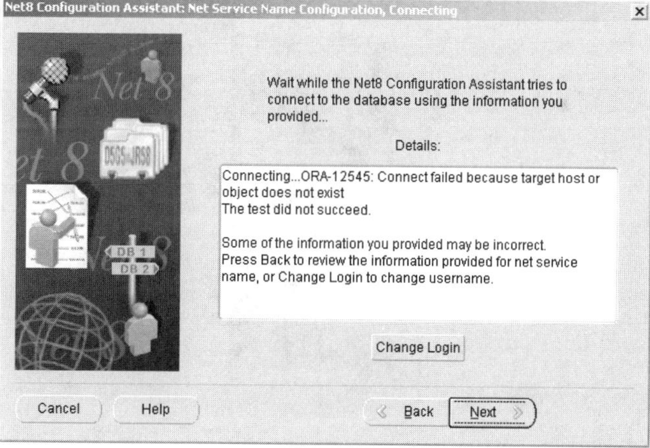

After you have successfully reached both databases, there are no more to connect to. Select **No**:

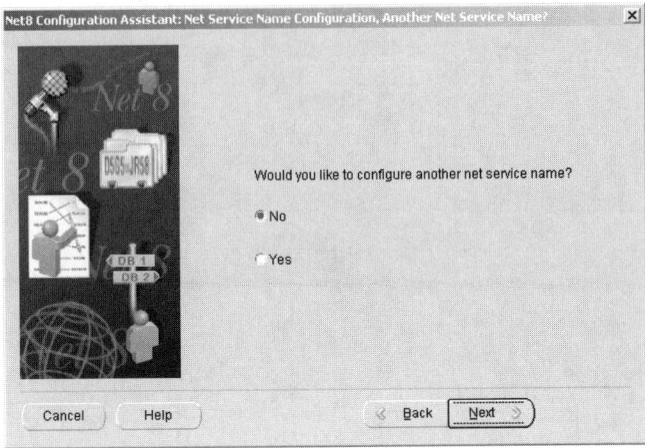

Here's the next message you will see:

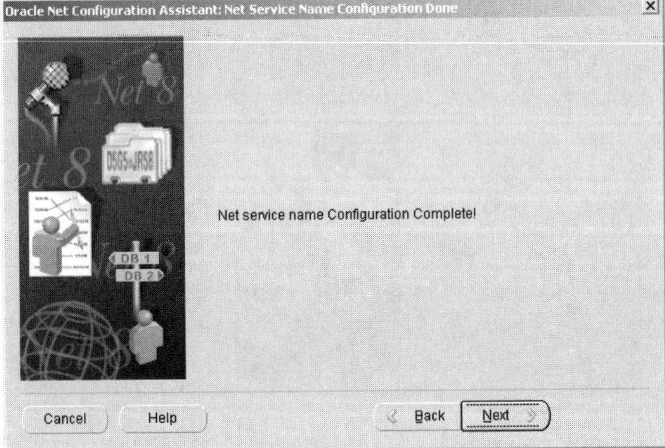

And this message will be followed by another:

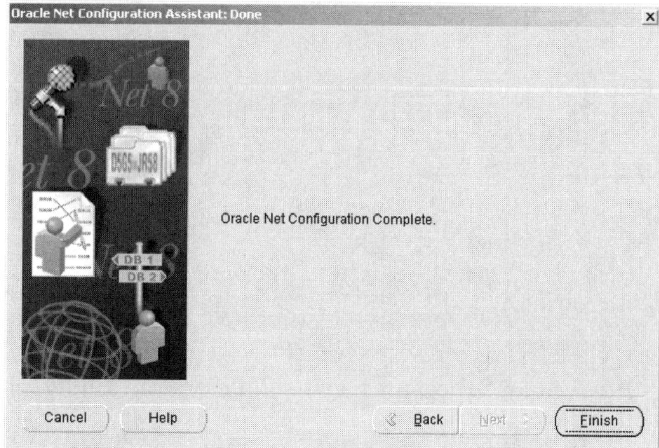

The final screen looks like this:

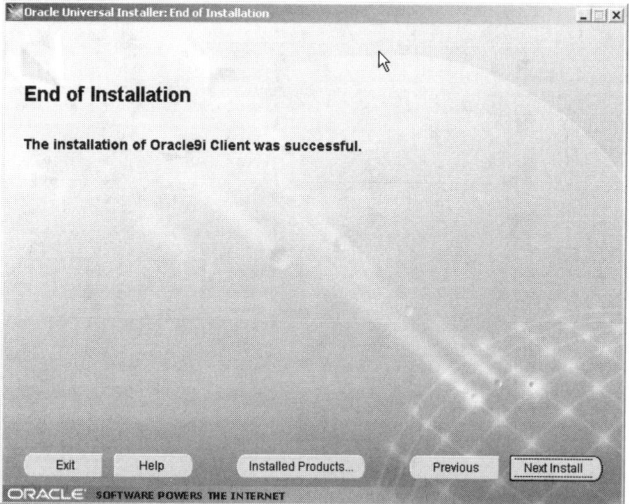

You get one more chance to change your mind before exiting:

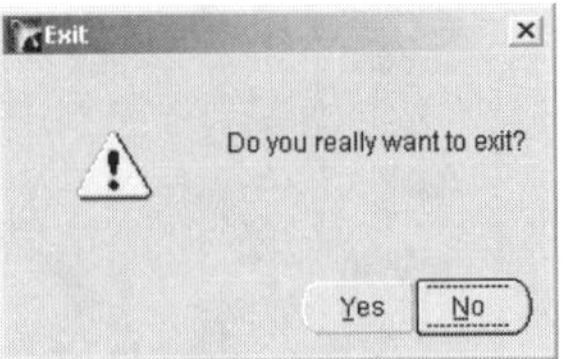

Congratulations! You have now defined two Oracle servers to your client PC. Now restart your PC to complete the installation. If you go to Windows **Start | Programs**, you should see the following new selections:

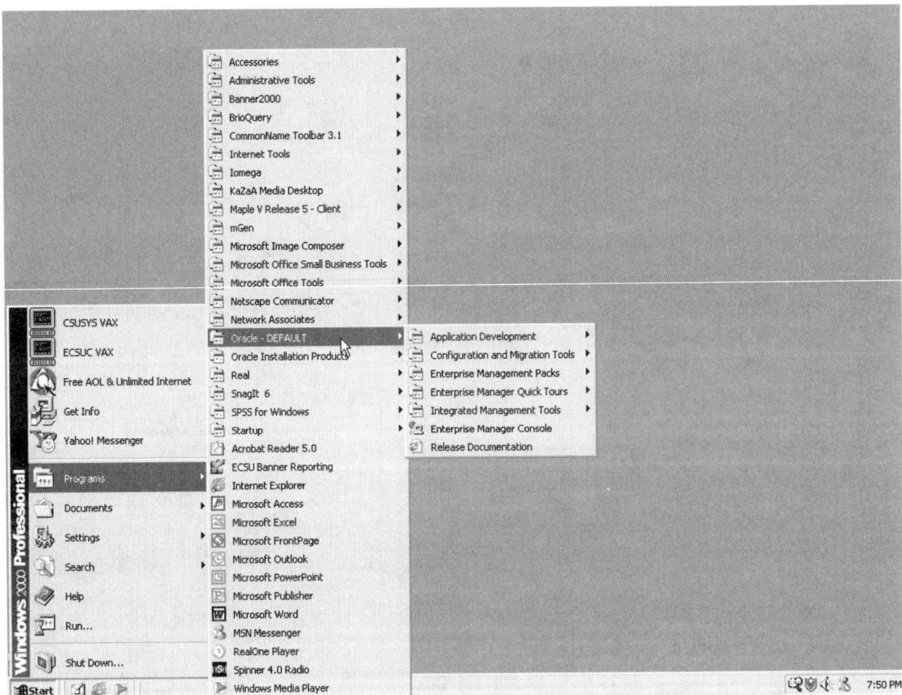

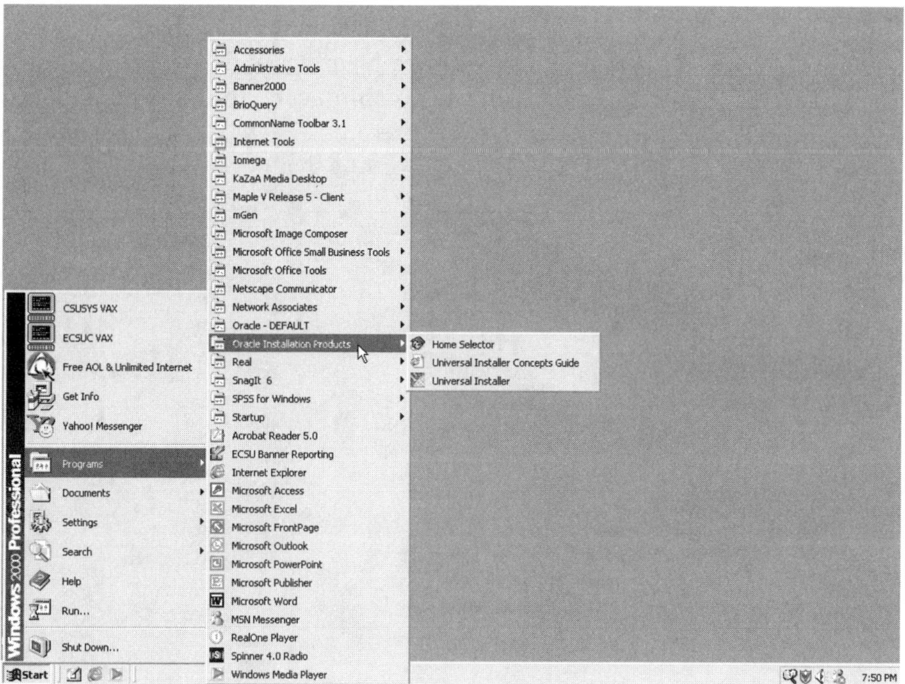

Adding Another Service

Suppose that you have just been given the OK to work from home on your database project. You need access to the database from your beach house, your cabin, and of course your office at home, and the only way is to dial in. To do this, you have to use the Net8 Configuration Assistant and add the new service. (Note: These steps are the same for 8*i* and 9*i*. The 8*i* and 9*i* Net8 Configuration Assistant screens are also virtually the same.)

First go to **Start | Programs** and look for **Oracle Net8 Assistant**. You'll find it under something like "Oracle for NT":

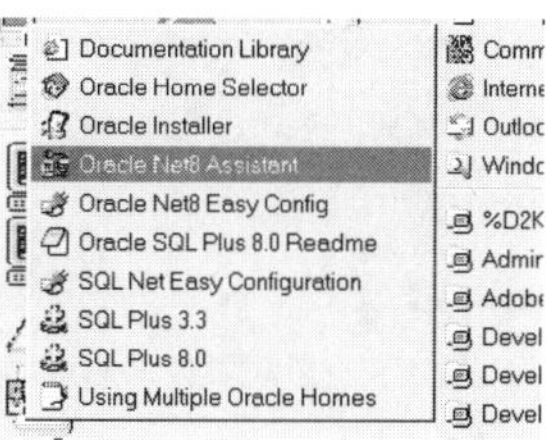

Clicking on **Oracle Net8 Assistant** will bring up the following screen. Click on **Local** and then **Service Naming**, and you will see all the current databases with which you can communicate. In our example you will see the two entries created in the preceding steps. These are really the entries in your `TNSNAMES.ORA` file. Make sure that **Service Naming** is highlighted:

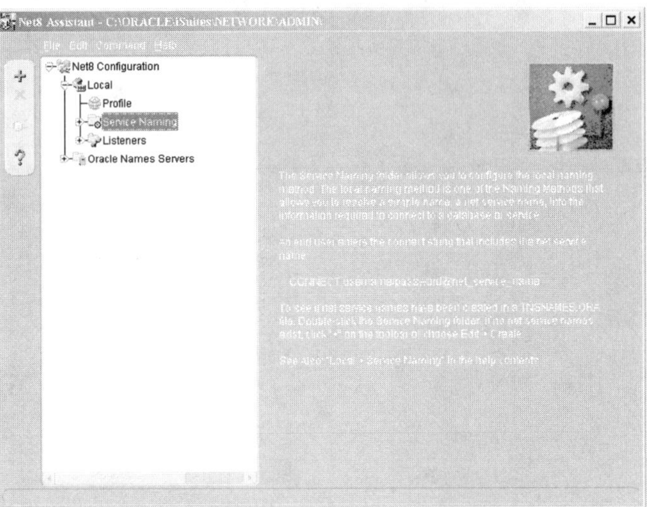

To add another service, click on the green plus sign in the upper left corner, or select **Edit | Create**:

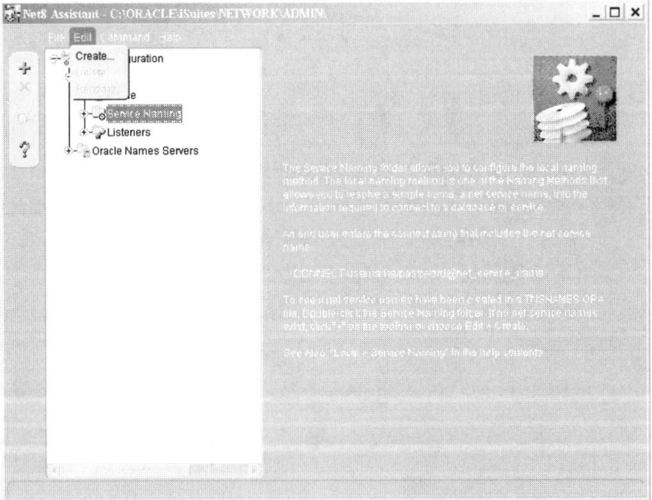

From here on, you will be using the exact same screens that you used when you first installed the Oracle 8*i* client. The important thing to remember is that you must use the IP address for the host name because you will be using an external network to reach it, not your internal network where server names are constantly available to all network devices.

Enter any name you want for this new service, using something that you can remember and that is meaningful, and then click **Next**.

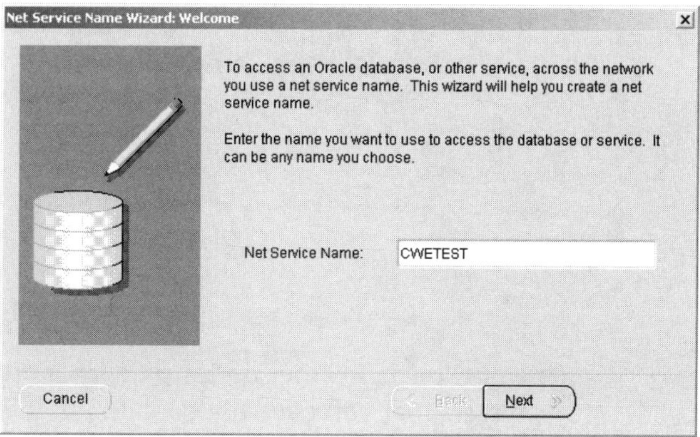

Select the communications protocol:

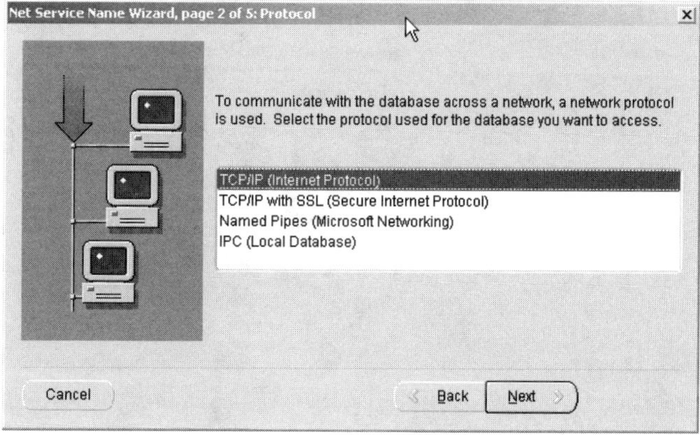

Again, enter the IP address in the **Host Name** field, and take the port default:

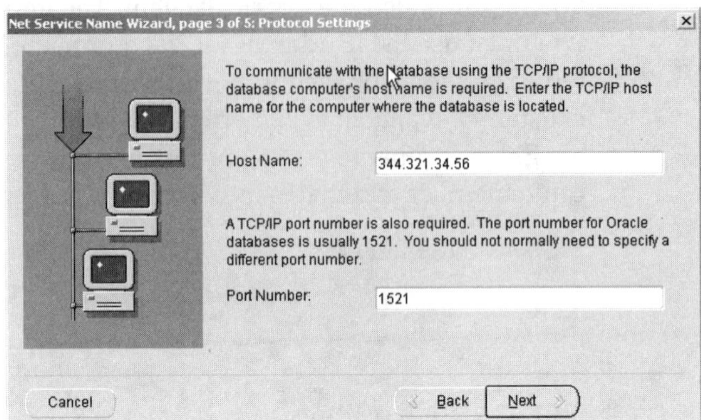

Note

Some networks use other ports for their various servers, so be careful when you add servers that you have not configured. In such cases, check with your network administrator. You will get an error when you test if the port number is not correct.

Type in the real database name:

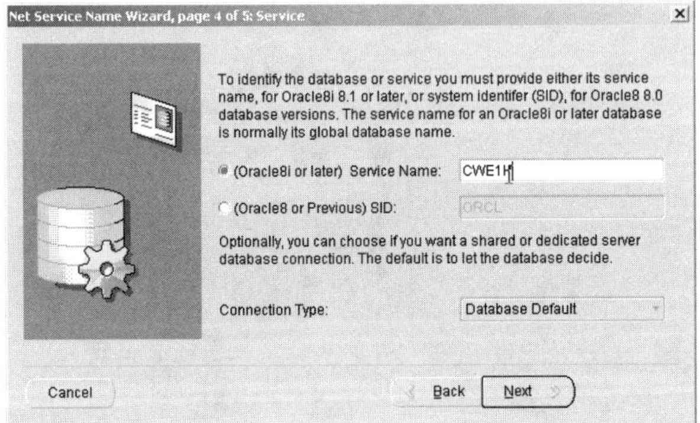

Now test:

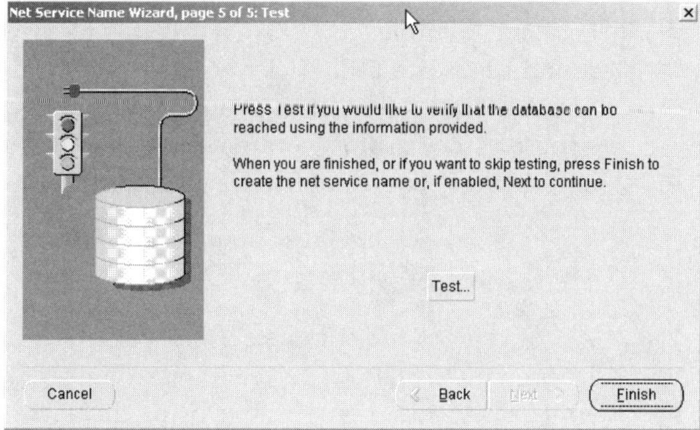

When the test is done, click **Finish**, and your **Service Naming** directory should now look like this:

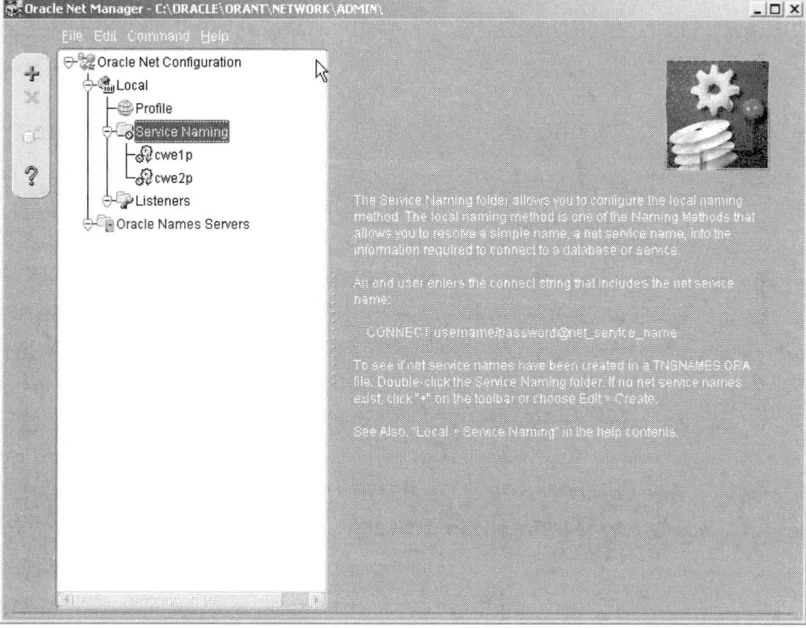

Note that before the new service can be used, it must be saved. (In other words, if you now go to your SQL*Plus screen and try to reach the new database, for example, you will get an error message saying that the name was not found.) This is a little tricky because the normal thing is just to exit and think you're all done. So I advise you to select **File | Save**, and if when you exit you get a message telling you that the network configuration has been modified and asking if you want to save or discard the changes, choose **Save**.

In Case of Failure

As convenient and complete as the wizards are, suppose that during the installation, your `TNSNAMES.ORA` file was damaged. What happened was that you could easily add more services using theNet8 Configuration Assistant, and test them successfully, but you could never save the changes.

What you have to do in a case like that is either restore the `TNSNAMES` file from your backup, or totally deinstall Oracle 8*i* or 9*i* Client and then reinstall it. This takes a bit of time, but it is fairly straightforward. Insert the client CD, select **Installation**, then select **Deinstall**. Now follow the directions and mark all the boxes, click **Deinstall**, and the wizard will take over. However, the original directory you used for 8*i* or 9*i* might not be removed, so double-check, and if it's still there, delete it. Then just reinstall the client.

Warning

If there is a radical failure during the installation, such as the PC shutting down, a memory error, or something that causes the installation not to complete, you will be faced with a tedious task of carefully removing entries in the registry, as well as the folders on your D: or C: drive. For this I refer you to the Oracle installation guide for 9*i* or 8*i*.

I have run into this situation only when the client PC was simply not robust enough because of a slow processor. Oracle advises that you use at least a 266MHz processor, but I strongly advise you to use nothing less than a 600MHz processor or you will most likely have problems. Some laptops, however, run fine with a slower processor.

Chapter 12

DBA Tasks

Congratulations! In the previous chapters you have actually performed some of the traditional DBA tasks. Activities such as creating the database and various tables, developing security, creating users, and creating tablespaces are all normally seen as DBA functions. You have done them, and they work!

Let's start our discussion of DBA tasks by listing some of the major functions that a DBA performs:

1. Installing Oracle Server
2. Creating the database
3. Creating users
4. Developing the security schema
5. Creating tables
6. Creating roles and profiles

7. Managing grants
8. Installing system upgrades
9. Enforcing Oracle licensing
10. Starting up and shutting down the database
11. Backing up and recovering data: import and export
12. Creating "instances" of the database for testing and development
13. Modifying the database and tuning the system

and any other tasks that your supervisor, or her supervisor, asks you to do! Since you've already mastered functions 1 through 7, we'll start here with 8.

System Upgrades

Oracle releases upgrades from time to time, and these always come with extensive instructions. Be aware that although some are easy, some take quite a bit of care. For your own sanity, keep meticulous track of what versions you have on your database. There are compatibility issues among versions and application software, and it is the DBA's responsibility to make sure all the parts fit. Yes, it is also the DBA who sometimes has to push the users and developers to test new releases. It's a tough job.

Caution

If you are using Internet Explorer to download files, be sure to read the note at the end of this chapter. It may save you some grief!

Oracle uses a five-digit numbering schema for its releases, as follows:

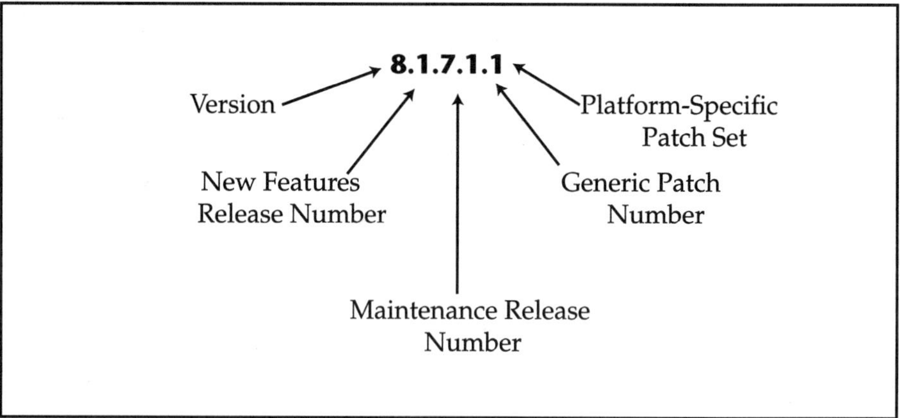

Now let's use something you learned about in Chapter 10: the data dictionary. To find the versions of what you have installed, run the data dictionary view PRODUCT_COMPONENT_VERSION, which will give you the following information about your Oracle components:

PRODUCT_COMPONENT_VERSION View

Name	Type	Null?
Product	VARCHAR2(64)	
Version	VARCHAR2(64)	
Status	VARCHAR2(64)	

Oracle Licensing

In many shops the DBA is not directly responsible for keeping licenses current. However, if something does expire unexpectedly, everyone will look to the DBA. Your task as the DBA might really mean keeping your supervisor informed about renewals so that fees are built into the budget process. In addition, the DBA has to make sure that the policy against pirating is well known and enforced by monitoring where the installation and patch software is kept.

Startup and Shutdown

Databases don't just appear by magic. You can go through all the steps of installing an Oracle server and building a database, but the database must be *running* or your customers will not be able to get to it.

Normally your database starts up automatically whenever you boot the server. In Chapter 7 we discussed how to find out which Oracle services, including databases, are running (**Start | Control Panel | Services**, or **Control Panel | Admin Tools | Services** for W2K). The following screen shot shows services on a Windows 2000 Oracle database server with four databases running. (The Services screen on an NT server is almost exactly the same.)

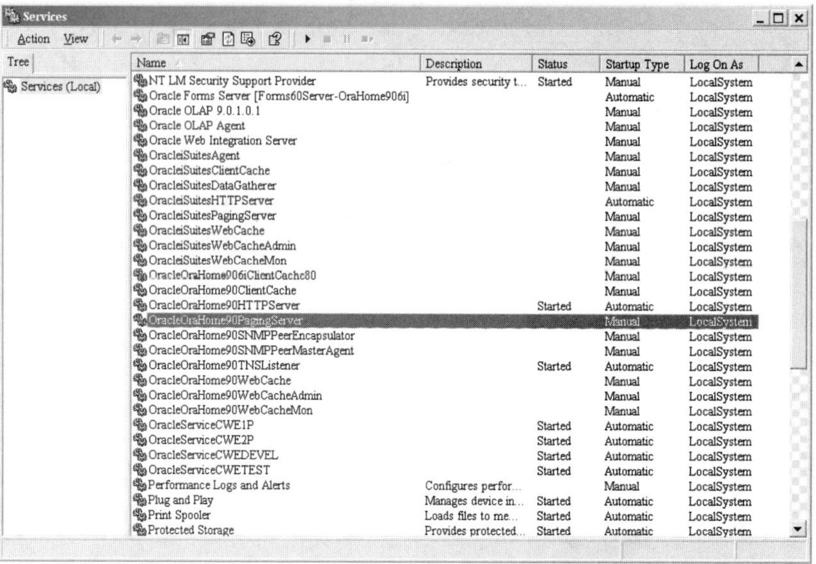

Now let's discuss how we go about starting up and shutting down the database (actually, starting up and shutting down the services) when we have to, and then how to bring it back up.

Why would we want to shut a database down? Here are the usual reasons:

- Upgrades or maintenance
- An emergency
- Backups
- Loading data, such as with SQL*Loader
- Import or export

Usually you will *not* want to shut the database down during normal business hours, but if you must, get the word to your customers as quickly as possible.

In the NT/W2K world, there are several ways to start and stop a database. I'll talk about two in detail, and then briefly mention a few others:

1. If you have the Enterprise version, you also have the Enterprise manager utilities, which include the instance manager. I refer you to the documentation if you are running the Enterprise version.

2. With the standard version, many DBAs prefer to use an Oracle program called SVRMGRL. There are a few tricks to using SVRMGRL:
   - You must go to the directory of the database you want to shut down and start. Do not try this at the root directory.
   - Be patient. Sometimes the shutdown or startup can take a few minutes.
   - This is *not* supported in 9*i*!
   - To get a good understanding of the process, take a look at this screen:

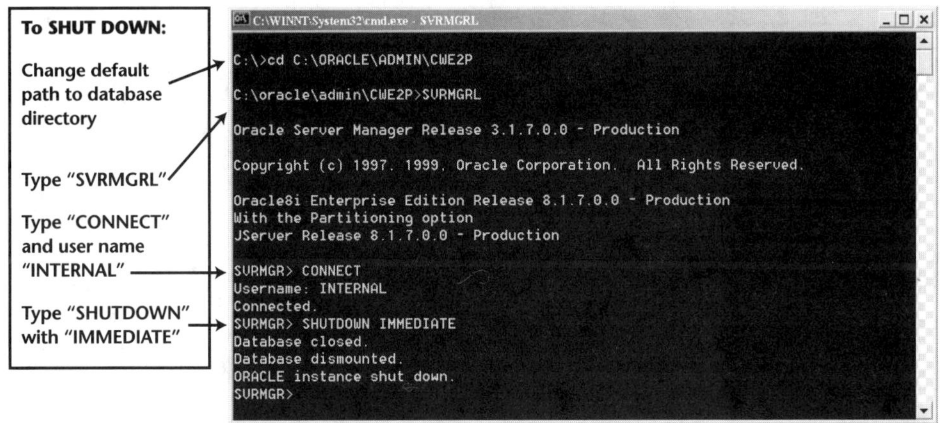

You must be at the directory of the database that is being shut down. So when you first go into DOS, use the `CD` command to change to that directory. Then just enter "SVRMGRL", use the ID "CONNECT", and then type "SHUTDOWN". This may take a couple of minutes, so just wait.

Note

If you go to **Services**, you will see it shows the database as active. This is confusing, but unfortunately for now, it's just the way it is, so accept it. The database is really shut down! Anyone trying to log on will get an error message.

To *start* the database, again make sure you are in the directory of the database you want to bring up, start SVRMGRL, and then just type "STARTUP".

Oracle's SVRMGRL will generate several system messages that will keep you occupied while the database comes back online:

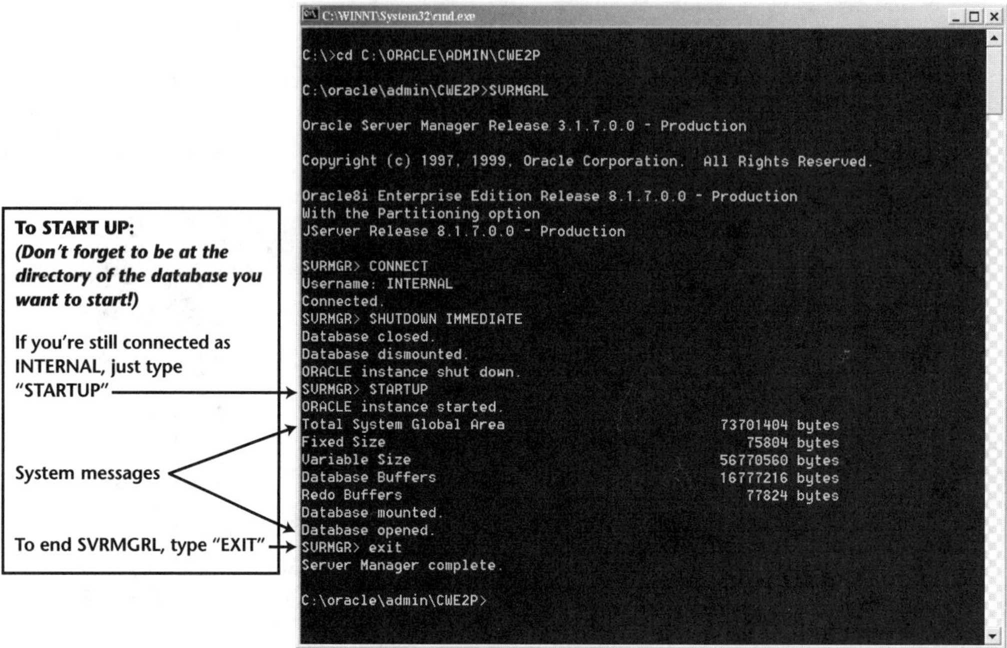

You're probably wondering about the `IMMEDIATE` parameter. There are actually three choices:

1. **NORMAL** means to wait until everyone is logged off. It also prevents anyone from starting a new session. This is the default.
2. **IMMEDIATE** is a full shutdown, with rollback of any active transactions.
3. **ABORT** is used only in emergencies. No rollback is done at this time; rather it is done the next time the database is started. Again, use this option only in emergencies. This kind of thing happens when your system is under attack, or there is a physical emergency such as a water main burst or something similar. (I have never yet run into this situation—fortunately!)

Usually you will use `IMMEDIATE`. But be sure that your users are logged off first! It is best to use `NORMAL`, but sometimes after you've sent out a dozen e-mail reminders, called users who are still logged on, and it's getting late, you have no choice but to send out one last reminder that the database is coming down in five minutes regardless, and then do an immediate shutdown.

The second way to start and stop a database is to get to the services mentioned earlier (this is why you have to be on the database server). To start the database in the W2K world, select the Oracle Services ID that you want, and click on **Action | Start**. And as you might have guessed, to shut the database down, click on **Action | Stop**.

For NT, highlight the service, and then click on the **Start** or **Stop** button. On a W2K server, highlight the service with the database name, then hit **Action | Stop**, and you will see the following status bar:

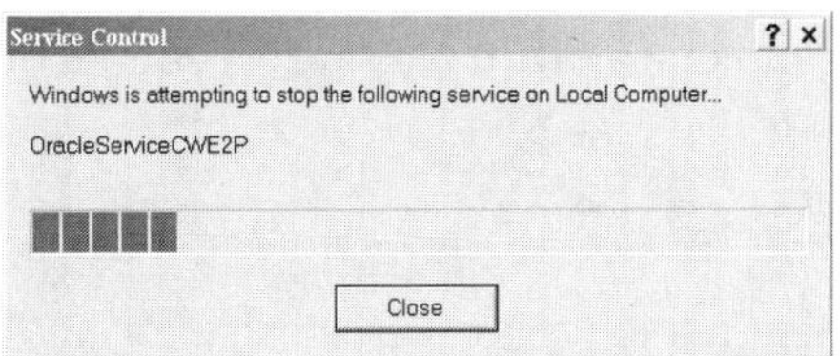

This shutdown goes very quickly. When it is done, the W2K **Services** screen looks like this:

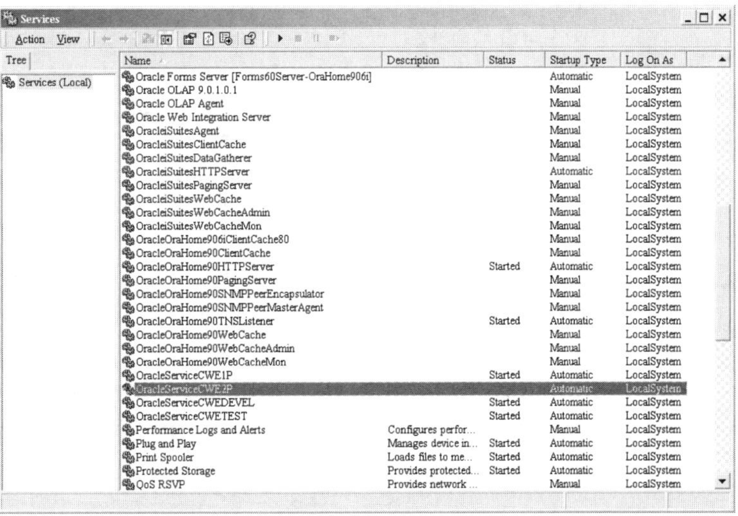

To start up a database in the W2K world, again click on **Action | Start**, and you'll see the following status bar:

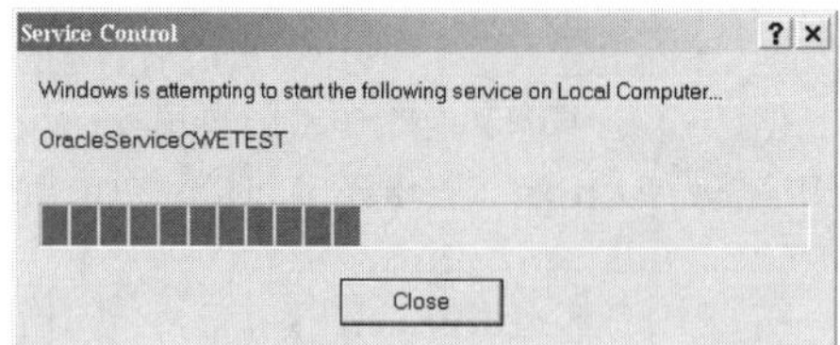

Note that startup may take a couple of minutes.

Note

Services looks to the registry for shutdown information. At installation, your registry has a default of `I` (for `IMMEDIATE`) for the shutdown; it will happen very, very quickly. You can change the setting to `N` (for `NORMAL`), send an e-mail warning to your users ahead of time, then follow up with e-mails every five minutes. You can then check to see who has a session open. Use the data dictionary view, give them a call, and tell them to wrap it up. You can also set the wait time before the database is shut down.

To change the registry settings, go to `HKEY_LOCAL_MACHINE\SOFTWARE\ORACLE`. Look for `ORA_<SID-ID>_SHUTDOWN_TYPE` and set it to `N` if you want. Then go to `ORA_<SID-ID>SHUTDOWN_TIMEOUT` and set the time to whatever you would like.

Get ready. We have three more ways to stop and start a database:

1. For NT, Oracle's Admin Assistant works very well: Go to `START/PROGRAMS/ORACLEHOME/DATABASE ADMINISTRATION/ADMIN ASSISTANT`. The first screen provides an overview of the Admin Assistant. Read it, then click on **Oracle Managed Objects**, and then keep clicking down the tree until you get to your database. You can now right-click on the database name and see selections for **Connect**, **Stop**, **Startup/Shutdown**, and so forth.

2. You can also use Oracle's NET STOP and NET START commands. These commands offer a quick and simple way to cycle the database, as the following screen shot shows:

```
C:\WINNT\System32\cmd.exe

C:\Documents and Settings\Administrator>net stop OracleServiceCWETEST
The OracleServiceCWETEST service is stopping..
The OracleServiceCWETEST service was stopped successfully.

C:\Documents and Settings\Administrator>net start OracleServiceCWETEST
The OracleServiceCWETEST service is starting............
The OracleServiceCWETEST service was started successfully.

C:\Documents and Settings\Administrator>
```

   The syntax is just NET STOP (or START) <*service name*>. What's interesting here is that if you go to **Services**, you will see "STARTING" under the **Status** column for the service.

3. Another method, and this is the last one I'll show you, is to go back to the DOS prompt and use the ORADIM commands. Run ORADIM (notice the spelling; everyone tries "oradMIN"!) from the DOS prompt, and use only the two commands with the database name as shown in this screen print:

```
C:\WINNT\System32\cmd.exe

C:\>ORADIM  -SHUTDOWN -SID CWETEST

C:\>ORADIM  -STARTUP -SID CWETEST
```

You do not get any messages while the processes are running; it either works or doesn't work! This is why many DBAs prefer to use SVRMGRL.

The following screen shot shows an example of an error from Services that illustrates why some DBAs prefer to use the command line instead of Services. If you use Services and there is a problem, all you get is a generic error. In this case, we were trying to start the database CWE2P:

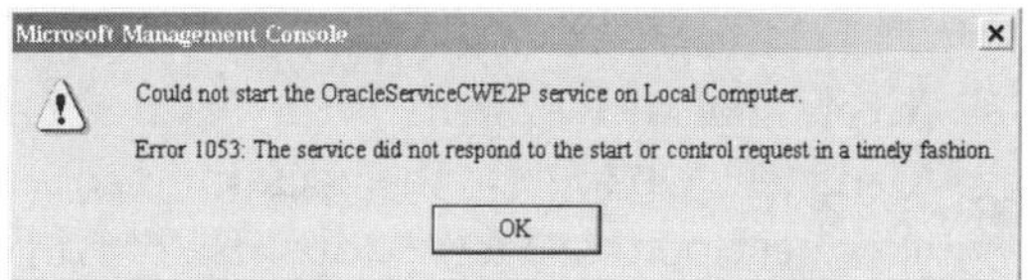

Unfortunately, this leaves the service between up and down, and it will show a status of "STARTING." At this point all you can do is (1) wait a couple of minutes; (2) stop and restart; or (3) as a last resort, reboot the server. Often either the service will eventually come up, or a stop and start will work.

Note

You will find your own preferred method for handling this task. Feel free to experiment, as there are other ways besides what I have shown you here. These seem to be the most popular and the easiest approaches, at least for now. Many DBAs like the messages that come with SVRMGRL; others like the speed of using Services. Try them both and then decide.

Backup and Recovery

Backing up and recovering data are perhaps the most unrecognized functions of a DBA. These tasks are done daily, quietly, with lots of shuffling of tapes, paper, logs, and so forth. But let the database take a hit, and suddenly the entire world wants to know how good the backup and recovery are: Do we have the latest copy? Can the database be restored? The moral here is never to skip doing your backups—*never, never, never*.

You can tackle this very necessary task in several different ways:

- **Oracle Enterprise Manager tools**, using the Backup and Recovery wizards. These are great tools.
- **Recovery Manager (RMAN)**—another very good tool, but without the graphical user interface.
- **Third-party products**, such as Legato, which is actually shipped with Oracle.
- **OCOPY**, another Oracle utility that is used when you have to quickly back up a tablespace. Oracle provides good documentation on OCOPY; I suggest you refer to it.

Let me give you the lowdown here. Oracle has just begun to ship a relatively decent backup system with 9*i*, the new and improved RMAN (Recovery Manager). Up to now, the backup/recovery function has not been one of Oracle's strongest points. Most shops use third-party products or develop an in-house guru who can run RMAN. However, fortunately Oracle products have been evolving. RMAN, for example, is a true command-line utility in 8 and 8*i*, but it has become much more streamlined in 9*i*. Given this constant flux, I'm going to severely limit our discussion of backup/recovery. My guess is that years from now, historians will call this confusing time the Period of Too Many Backups.

I will quickly cover only one of the major backup and recovery processes: import/export. I'll give you enough information to gain some familiarity with both of these, while not burying you with the incredible number of details that both utilities offer. As you get used to them, I encourage you to look through their manuals and refine your processes. It is amazing how much capability Oracle has built into these processes. And stay tuned—Oracle is constantly improving its backup and recovery offerings!

Import and Export

IMPORT and EXPORT are a nicely balanced, matched pair of Oracle utilities that let you scoop up an entire database, a table or two, or all objects belonging to a user, and then use what you have to restore objects or create an entirely new database. Hence, IMPORT and EXPORT are used to:

- Provide full backup and recovery capabilities
- Provide the capability to restore a table or other object that is accidentally deleted
- Create test databases
- Move objects from one environment to another
- Defragment tablespaces by exporting them and then importing them back

Just be aware up front that you have to use both of these utilities; the file created by EXPORT can be read only by IMPORT. Otherwise all you need to worry about is whether you have enough space to store the backup file from EXPORT and whether you know the syntax.

(To get a good idea of the size of the database you will be exporting, use the command `>select sum(bytes) from user_segments where segment_type = 'TABLE';` and then translate the number of bytes into megabytes to see how much space you'll need.)

The Export Step

As you have probably already guessed, the export step is pretty easy. You start it from your favorite place, the DOS command line. Yes, you can create a parameter file, and we suggest you do so, after you become familiar with the basic commands.

One neat thing about the EXPORT utility is that most of the time it prompts you for the variables if you don't enter them on the first line. The IMPORT utility is not this friendly, as you'll see.

To start, just type in "EXP *<user-id/password@database to be copied>*" at the C: prompt, as shown here:

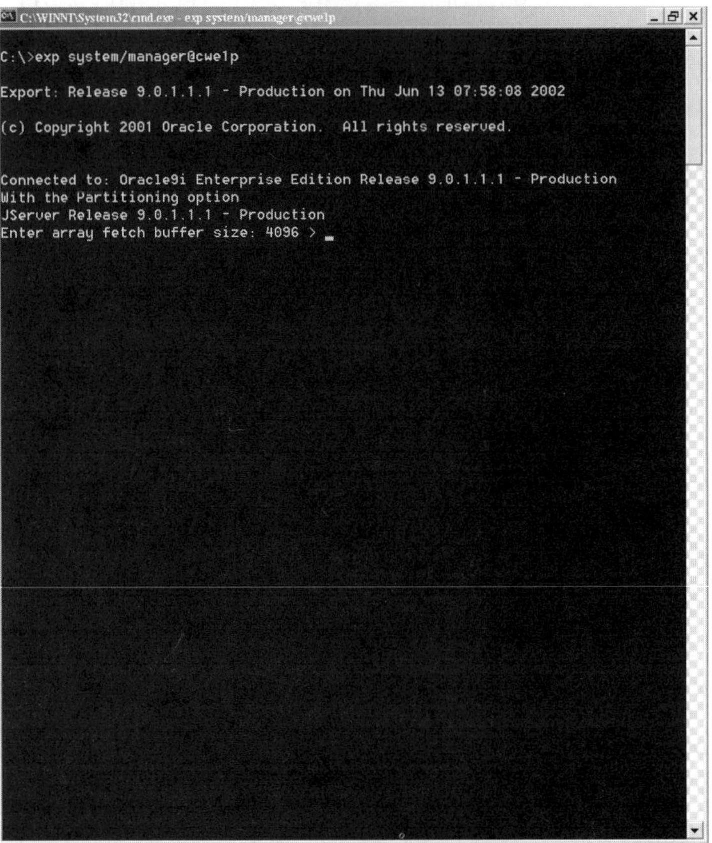

This command starts the process.

In the following screen I want to show you that EXPORT cannot create a folder; it must already exist. We told it to put the `.dmp` file in `C:\CWE1P_BACKUP\`, but the folder did not exist, so we had to create it and then come back. Again, I suggest that you be careful in naming your backup files, preferably putting them in separate folders. You also may want to add a date to the file name. In this example we are exporting the database CWE1P only, and we are creating an output file by the same name.

The next prompts are for the entire database, export grants, and export table data. Take the defaults:

```
C:\WINNT\System32\cmd.exe - exp system/manager@cwe1p

C:\>exp system/manager@cwe1p

Export: Release 9.0.1.1.1 - Production on Thu Jun 13 08:02:34 2002

(c) Copyright 2001 Oracle Corporation.  All rights reserved.


Connected to: Oracle9i Enterprise Edition Release 9.0.1.1.1 - Production
With the Partitioning option
JServer Release 9.0.1.1.1 - Production
Enter array fetch buffer size: 4096 >

Export file: EXPDAT.DMP > C:\CWE1P_BACKUP\CWE1P.DMP

EXP-00028: failed to open C:\CWE1P_BACKUP\CWE1P.DMP for write
Export file: EXPDAT.DMP > C:\CWE1P_BACKUP\CWE1P.DMP

(1)E(ntire database), (2)U(sers), or (3)T(ables): (2)U > 1

Export grants (yes/no): yes > n

Export table data (yes/no): yes > yes
```

Once the export starts, you will see screen after screen showing you the files, objects, and so forth that are being exported to the backup file:

```
C:\WINNT\System32\cmd.exe - exp system/manager@cwe1p

About to export the entire database ...
. exporting tablespace definitions
. exporting profiles
. exporting user definitions
. exporting roles
. exporting resource costs
. exporting rollback segment definitions
. exporting database links
. exporting sequence numbers
. exporting directory aliases
. exporting context namespaces
. exporting foreign function library names
. exporting object type definitions
. exporting system procedural objects and actions
. exporting pre-schema procedural objects and actions
. exporting cluster definitions
. about to export SYSTEM's tables via Conventional Path ...
. . exporting table                        ANSWERS         40 rows exported
. . exporting table            AQ$_INTERNET_AGENTS          0 rows exported
. . exporting table        AQ$_INTERNET_AGENT_PRIVS         0 rows exported
. . exporting table                    AUDIT_TABLE          0 rows exported
. . exporting table                        AUTHORS          5 rows exported
. . exporting table                   AUTHOR_AUDIT          2 rows exported
. . exporting table                   COURSE_TABLE         20 rows exported
. . exporting table                    DEF$_AQCALL          0 rows exported
. . exporting table                   DEF$_AQERROR          0 rows exported
. . exporting table                  DEF$_CALLDEST          0 rows exported
. . exporting table               DEF$_DEFAULTDEST          0 rows exported
. . exporting table               DEF$_DESTINATION          0 rows exported
. . exporting table                     DEF$_ERROR
```

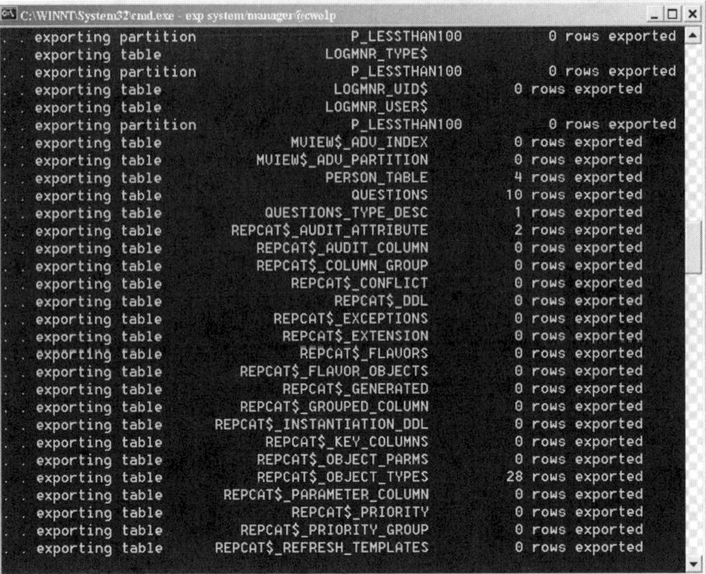
```
C:\WINNT\System32\cmd.exe - exp system/manager@cwelp
. . exporting partition                 P_LESSTHAN100          0 rows exported
. . exporting table                  LOGMNR_TYPE$
. . exporting partition                 P_LESSTHAN100          0 rows exported
. . exporting table                   LOGMNR_UID$          0 rows exported
. . exporting table                  LOGMNR_USER$
. . exporting partition                 P_LESSTHAN100          0 rows exported
. . exporting table              MVIEW$_ADV_INDEX          0 rows exported
. . exporting table          MVIEW$_ADV_PARTITION          0 rows exported
. . exporting table                  PERSON_TABLE          4 rows exported
. . exporting table                     QUESTIONS         10 rows exported
. . exporting table           QUESTIONS_TYPE_DESC          1 rows exported
. . exporting table        REPCAT$_AUDIT_ATTRIBUTE          2 rows exported
. . exporting table           REPCAT$_AUDIT_COLUMN          0 rows exported
. . exporting table           REPCAT$_COLUMN_GROUP          0 rows exported
. . exporting table               REPCAT$_CONFLICT          0 rows exported
. . exporting table                    REPCAT$_DDL          0 rows exported
. . exporting table             REPCAT$_EXCEPTIONS          0 rows exported
. . exporting table              REPCAT$_EXTENSION          0 rows exported
. . exporting table                REPCAT$_FLAVORS          0 rows exported
. . exporting table          REPCAT$_FLAVOR_OBJECTS          0 rows exported
. . exporting table              REPCAT$_GENERATED          0 rows exported
. . exporting table          REPCAT$_GROUPED_COLUMN          0 rows exported
. . exporting table       REPCAT$_INSTANTIATION_DDL          0 rows exported
. . exporting table            REPCAT$_KEY_COLUMNS          0 rows exported
. . exporting table           REPCAT$_OBJECT_PARMS          0 rows exported
. . exporting table           REPCAT$_OBJECT_TYPES         28 rows exported
. . exporting table        REPCAT$_PARAMETER_COLUMN          0 rows exported
. . exporting table               REPCAT$_PRIORITY          0 rows exported
. . exporting table          REPCAT$_PRIORITY_GROUP          0 rows exported
. . exporting table       REPCAT$_REFRESH_TEMPLATES          0 rows exported
```

Ultimately what you want to see is the success message at the end:

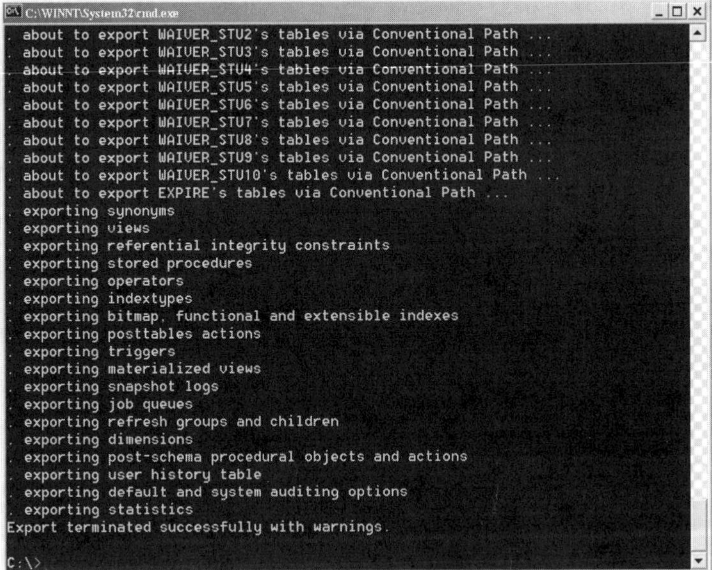
```
C:\WINNT\System32\cmd.exe
. about to export WAIVER_STU2's tables via Conventional Path ...
. about to export WAIVER_STU3's tables via Conventional Path ...
. about to export WAIVER_STU4's tables via Conventional Path ...
. about to export WAIVER_STU5's tables via Conventional Path ...
. about to export WAIVER_STU6's tables via Conventional Path ...
. about to export WAIVER_STU7's tables via Conventional Path ...
. about to export WAIVER_STU8's tables via Conventional Path ...
. about to export WAIVER_STU9's tables via Conventional Path ...
. about to export WAIVER_STU10's tables via Conventional Path ...
. about to export EXPIRE's tables via Conventional Path ...
. exporting synonyms
. exporting views
. exporting referential integrity constraints
. exporting stored procedures
. exporting operators
. exporting indextypes
. exporting bitmap, functional and extensible indexes
. exporting posttables actions
. exporting triggers
. exporting materialized views
. exporting snapshot logs
. exporting job queues
. exporting refresh groups and children
. exporting dimensions
. exporting post-schema procedural objects and actions
. exporting user history table
. exporting default and system auditing options
. exporting statistics
Export terminated successfully with warnings.

C:\>
```

Best of all, the export file ends up where it is supposed to be:

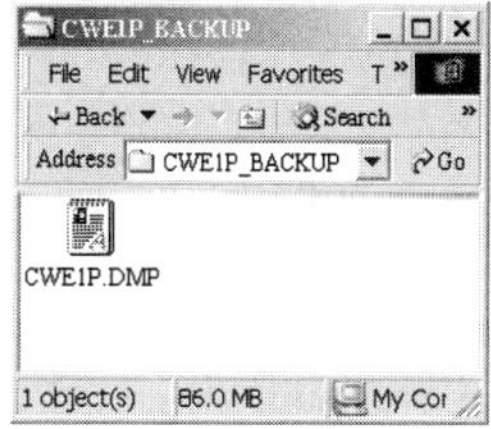

I imagine you're thinking, "That was easy!" and you're right, it was. All you really need to know is the *syntax*, and the basic syntax is clear. There is a lot more to the EXPORT utility, though, as you will find out if you go to the Oracle documentation.

The Import Step

As you have probably been thinking, the export step goes pretty easily. But you may also be thinking, "When I go to import the database, will I run into the same constraint considerations that we talked about in Chapters 3, 5, and 9? If I can't control how everything is loaded into the database, and the system tries to load a table that is dependent on another table that has not been loaded yet, will I have a problem?" Yes and No. When you load an entire database, you won't run into integrity constraint problems, because Oracle loads all the tables before loading the integrity constraints. But you're on the right track.

If you're loading data into existing tables, you can run into problems with constraints, and the import will result in rows not being loaded. This can happen because the tables aren't being loaded in the right sequence, so referential integrity kicks in and drops rows. Or you may run into duplicate keys in tables, and these rows will also be dropped.

So if you're loading into existing tables, it is advisable to disable constraints. You can do this simply by adding the `CONSTRAINTS = N` parameter when you run IMPORT. Once the database has been imported, you can reenable the constraints. To reenable, just use the following command:

```
SQL> alter table students
  2  enable primary key;
Table altered.
```

When would you load just one or several tables? When a table is damaged, or a programmer has deleted items that should not have been, or when an application runs wild and somehow posts incorrectly. Most of the time it will be the programming staff who will call and ask for a restore. Again, it will all come back to your backups!

Again, let's start learning how to use the IMPORT utility by running it from the command line. Once you're good at this, go ahead and create a parameter file, as we did with the EXPORT utility. Here's the basic syntax; it should look familiar:

```
>IMP <username/password>@INSTANCE FILE=<export file> FULL=Y
```

The following screen shows how to start IMPORT, and it also shows an error because we didn't specify "FULL":

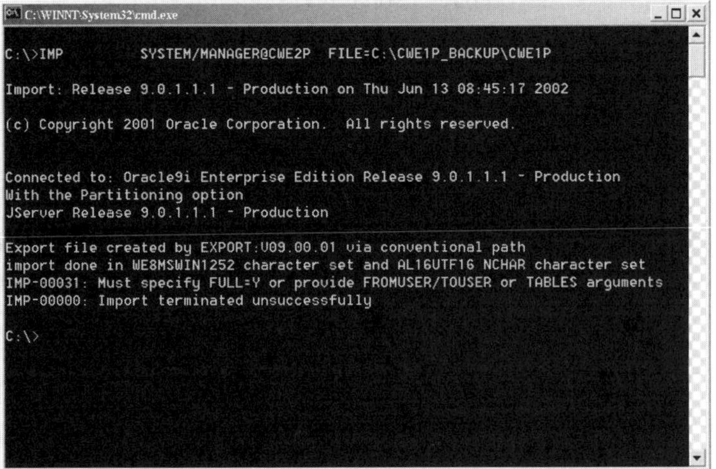

I'm showing you this error to make a point: IMPORT is not as forgiving as EXPORT, and you are better off using a parameter file once you're comfortable with this utility. One good reason to use a parameter file to avoid mistakes is that IMPORT, like EXPORT, cannot create a folder:

```
C:\WINNT\System32\cmd.exe
C:\>
C:\>
C:\>
C:\>
C:\>
C:\>
C:\>
C:\>
C:\>
C:\>
C:\>
C:\>
C:\>
C:\>
C:\>
C:\>IMP          SYSTEM/MANAGER@CWE2P  FILE=C:\CWE1P_BACKUP\CWE1P  FULL=Y
                         IGNORE = Y    DESTROY = Y
                           LOG = C:\CWE1P_BACKUP\IMPORT_TO_CWE2p.LOG

Import: Release 9.0.1.1.1 - Production on Thu Jun 13 10:01:55 2002

(c) Copyright 2001 Oracle Corporation.  All rights reserved.


IMP-00030: failed to create file C:\CWE1P_BACKUP\IMPORT_TO_CWE2p.LOG for write
IMP-00000: Import terminated unsuccessfully

C:\>
```

Note that if you specify `IGNORE = Y`, you won't see the dozens of screens with creation warnings such as "already exists." You can go to the log file for those. However, you will see SQL and Oracle errors:

```
C:\WINNT\System32\cmd.exe - IMP SYSTEM/MANAGER@CWE2P FILE=C:\CWE1P_BACKUP\CWE1P FULL=Y ...
Column 4 Impresora de inyecci≤n de tinta. en blanco y negro...
IMP-00019: row rejected due to ORACLE error 1
IMP-00003: ORACLE error 1 encountered
ORA-00001: unique constraint (OE.PRODUCT_DESCRIPTIONS_PK) violated
Column 1 2453
Column 2 E
Column 3 Inyecci≤n de Tinta C/4
Column 4 Impresora de inyecci≤n de tinta en color (con dos ...
IMP-00019: row rejected due to ORACLE error 1
IMP-00003: ORACLE error 1 encountered
ORA-00001: unique constraint (OE.PRODUCT_DESCRIPTIONS_PK) violated
Column 1 1797
Column 2 E
Column 3 Inyecci≤n de Tinta C/8/HQ
Column 4 Impresora de inyecci≤n de tinta en color. 8 pßgina...
IMP-00019: row rejected due to ORACLE error 1
IMP-00003: ORACLE error 1 encountered
ORA-00001: unique constraint (OE.PRODUCT_DESCRIPTIONS_PK) violated
Column 1 2459
Column 2 E
Column 3 LaserPro 1200/8/BW
Column 4 Impresora lßser en blanco y negro profesional. res...
IMP-00019: row rejected due to ORACLE error 1
IMP-00003: ORACLE error 1 encountered
ORA-00001: unique constraint (OE.PRODUCT_DESCRIPTIONS_PK) violated
Column 1 312
```

Use DESTROY to replace objects. DESTROY gets rid of any existing objects and is good for "refreshing" a database that will be used for testing and so forth. The danger with DESTROY is that *the IMPORT utility will finish successfully even if it doesn't import all rows*. It is important to go to the log!

```
C:\>
C:\>
C:\>
C:\>IMP        SYSTEM/MANAGER@CWE2P  FILE=C:\CWE1P_BACKUP\CWE1P  FULL=Y
                       IGNORE = Y    DESTROY = Y
                        LOG = C:\CWE1P_BACKUP\IMPORT_TO_CWE2p.LOG

Import: Release 9.0.1.1.1 - Production on Thu Jun 13 09:38:29 2002

(c) Copyright 2001 Oracle Corporation.  All rights reserved.


Connected to: Oracle9i Enterprise Edition Release 9.0.1.1.1 - Production
With the Partitioning option
JServer Release 9.0.1.1.1 - Production

Export file created by EXPORT:V09.00.01 via conventional path
import done in WE8MSWIN1252 character set and AL16UTF16 NCHAR character set
```

The DESTROY startup may take a couple of minutes because we specified IGNORE = Y, so any CREATE TYPE messages won't show. Notice that any system-created constraints are *not* ignored:

```
Column 1 2
Column 2 116
Column 3 bindms
Column 4 2
IMP-00019: row rejected due to ORACLE error 1
IMP-00003: ORACLE error 1 encountered
ORA-00001: unique constraint (AURORA$JIS$UTILITY$.SYS_C001414) violated
Column 1 2
Column 2 117
Column 3 publishjsp
Column 4 2
IMP-00019: row rejected due to ORACLE error 1
IMP-00003: ORACLE error 1 encountered
ORA-00001: unique constraint (AURORA$JIS$UTILITY$.SYS_C001414) violated
Column 1 2
Column 2 118
Column 3 unpublishjsp
Column 4 2
IMP-00019: row rejected due to ORACLE error 1
IMP-00003: ORACLE error 1 encountered
ORA-00001: unique constraint (AURORA$JIS$UTILITY$.SYS_C001414) violated
Column 1 4
Column 2 119
Column 3 repapi
Column 4 2          0 rows imported
. . importing table                    "SNS$INODE$"
```

Here's the last screen:

```
C:\WINNT\System32\cmd.exe
"IBUTE "MONTH" DETERMINES "TIMES"."CALENDAR_MONTH_DESC" ATTRIBUTE "MONTH" DE"
"TERMINES "TIMES"."END_OF_CAL_MONTH" ATTRIBUTE "MONTH" DETERMINES "TIMES"."D"
"AYS_IN_CAL_MONTH" ATTRIBUTE "MONTH" DETERMINES "TIMES"."CALENDAR_MONTH_NAME"
"" ATTRIBUTE "MONTH" DETERMINES "TIMES"."CALENDAR_MONTH_NUMBER" ATTRIBUTE "Q"
"UARTER" DETERMINES "TIMES"."CALENDAR_QUARTER_DESC" ATTRIBUTE "QUARTER" DETE"
"RMINES "TIMES"."END_OF_CAL_QUARTER" ATTRIBUTE "QUARTER" DETERMINES "TIMES"."
""DAYS_IN_CAL_QUARTER" ATTRIBUTE "QUARTER" DETERMINES "TIMES"."CALENDAR_QUAR"
"TER_NUMBER" ATTRIBUTE "YEAR" DETERMINES "TIMES"."CALENDAR_YEAR" ATTRIBUTE ""
"YEAR" DETERMINES "TIMES"."END_OF_CAL_YEAR" ATTRIBUTE "YEAR" DETERMINES "TIM"
"ES"."DAYS_IN_CAL_YEAR" ATTRIBUTE "FIS_WEEK" DETERMINES "TIMES"."WEEK_ENDING"
"_DAY" ATTRIBUTE "FIS_WEEK" DETERMINES "TIMES"."FISCAL_WEEK_NUMBER" ATTRIBUT"
"E "FIS_MONTH" DETERMINES "TIMES"."FISCAL_MONTH_DESC" ATTRIBUTE "FIS_MONTH" "
"DETERMINES "TIMES"."END_OF_FIS_MONTH" ATTRIBUTE "FIS_MONTH" DETERMINES "TIM"
"ES"."DAYS_IN_FIS_MONTH" ATTRIBUTE "FIS_MONTH" DETERMINES "TIMES"."FISCAL_MO"
"NTH_NAME" ATTRIBUTE "FIS_MONTH" DETERMINES "TIMES"."FISCAL_MONTH_NUMBER" AT"
"TRIBUTE "FIS_QUARTER" DETERMINES "TIMES"."FISCAL_QUARTER_DESC" ATTRIBUTE "F"
"IS_QUARTER" DETERMINES "TIMES"."END_OF_FIS_QUARTER" ATTRIBUTE "FIS_QUARTER""
" DETERMINES "TIMES"."DAYS_IN_FIS_QUARTER" ATTRIBUTE "FIS_QUARTER" DETERMINE"
"S "TIMES"."FISCAL_QUARTER_NUMBER" ATTRIBUTE "FIS_YEAR" DETERMINES "TIMES".""
"FISCAL_YEAR" ATTRIBUTE "FIS_YEAR" DETERMINES "TIMES"."END_OF_FIS_YEAR" ATTR"
"IBUTE "FIS_YEAR" DETERMINES "TIMES"."DAYS_IN_FIS_YEAR""
IMP-00003: ORACLE error 30371 encountered
ORA-30371: column cannot define a level in more than one dimension
Import terminated successfully with warnings.

C:\>
C:\>
C:\>
C:\>
```

Finally, always check the log, just in case.

Note

If you are importing into existing tables, turn the constraints off. When you import into a new set of tables, there is no problem because the tables are imported first, then the constraints. If the tables already exist, however, the load can run into problems if the tables are not imported in the proper sequence. That is, if the ANSWERS table comes before the QUESTIONS table in the export, there is the risk that a row or more of data in the ANSWERS table will be rejected because their matching referential integrity constraints in the QUESTIONS table haven't been loaded yet.

Note that the import will *not* overlie system-owned objects. Here's a quick refresher on how to look up constraints on a table:

```
select constraint_name,

from all_constraints
where table_name like 'QUEST%'
```

```
CONSTRAINT_NAME                C
------------------------------
SYS_C0021676                   C
SYS_C0021677                   P
SYS_C0021679                   C
SYS_C0021680                   C
SYS_C0021681                   P
SYS_C0021682                   R
SYS_C0021683                   R


SQL> desc all_constraints;
Name                           Null?    Type
------------------------------------------
OWNER                          NOT NULL VARCHAR2(30)
CONSTRAINT_NAME                NOT NULL VARCHAR2(30)
CONSTRAINT_TYPE                         VARCHAR2(1)
TABLE_NAME                     NOT NULL VARCHAR2(30)
SEARCH_CONDITION                        LONG
R_OWNER                                 VARCHAR2(30)
R_CONSTRAINT_NAME                       VARCHAR2(30)
DELETE_RULE                             VARCHAR2(9)
STATUS                                  VARCHAR2(8)

SQL> select * from all_constraints where constraint_name =
'SYS_C0021676';

OWNER                CONSTRAINT_NAME        C TABLE_NAME
--------------------------------------------------
SEARCH_CONDITION
--------------------------------------------------
R_OWNER              R_CONSTRAINT_NAME        DELETE_RU STATUS
-------------------------------------------------------------
SYSTEM               SYS_C0021676           C QUESTIONS_TYPE_DESC
QUESTIONS_TYPE_DESC IS NOT NULL

ENABLED
```

Database Instances

All shops have more than one database, unless all of the development and testing are done off-site. Normally you will have perhaps three or four "instances" of your database. You may have a simple, generic database that is a baseline for your system. This may be the original database product you purchased or created, and usually this copy is *not* modified. Then you will have an instance for your technical staff to work with; in fact you will probably have several such instances. Third, your users will have their own copy for acceptance testing, and finally, you will have a production instance.

Now remember that you will also be responsible for maintaining all upgrades from all your vendors—Oracle included. Sometimes you will need additional database instances to test these upgrades. So it is not uncommon for a shop to have more than four instances of a database at any one time. As DBA you will be the one who has to keep track of them—what state they're in, who has which rights to each one, and so forth. Make sure you keep good notes.

Fortunately, creating an instance is straightforward. We'll use import/export as an example.

1. Create the database, giving it your instance name, such as TEST or PREPROD.
2. Shut down the database you want to copy and bring it up in restricted mode. (This is why so many DBAs work weekends!)
3. Export the database.
4. Bring the original database back online.
5. Import the backup file to the new database.
6. There will be some errors as the system tries to create files that already exist. These are system files, so ignore the errors.
7. Check the logs for meaningful errors.
8. Test the new instance and release it for use.
9. Make sure you have a backup plan, especially if this is going to be a developmental database, or if it is going to require hours and hours of upgrades.

Warning

There is something called a **refresh** of a test instance. A refresh is useful when the test data is so out-of-date that it is no longer relevant. You can import just certain files, but most of the time refresh is an all-or-nothing proposition. Just remember to warn your customers that when you run the IMPORT utility just to bring the test database current, they will lose any data that they have entered because it will be overlaid with the database that you are importing. So if someone has favorite test cases out there, they will lose them and have to start over.

Modification and Tuning

I have already mentioned processes like increasing tablespaces, and adding and dropping tables. All DBAs do a lot more. The database is in your hands, and you will have to keep doing whatever it takes to keep it running smoothly. As you've seen by now, given all the typing mistakes you have undoubtedly already made, much caution and care must be given to working with the internals of the database. Hence usually only the DBA has the rights to create users, add or drop tables, change system parameters, and so forth. Although you may give your developers an instance or two to work in, you will keep the production instance and most others untouchable.

Most of the system changes you will make will revolve around tuning for performance improvements. These changes include things like deciding whether to use rollback segments or rollback tables, and how many archive logs to keep.

Let me put it another way. When the system really starts to slow down, or when backups start taking significantly longer than usual, the DBA is the person who will be called. I've mentioned creating temporary tablespaces for sorts as one way to improve performance, and there are others. However, the first thing the DBA does is analyze what's happening using the various Oracle tools and data dictionary views. With that information, the DBA can take actions to reduce processing bottlenecks, reduce seek times, and so forth. For example, the DBA might discover that one of the most used tables has an overabundance of integrity constraints, and upon analyis, the DBA may determine that some or many of them are not needed. Integrity constraints have the downside of reducing performance, and perhaps in some cases they should be minimized.

The same consideration applies to indexes. The existence of too many indexes on a table can have serious effects on performance when insert, update, and delete operations are carried out because Oracle must update the indexes at the same time. Performance analysis by the DBA can show whether there are too many indexes, and appropriate action can be taken.

The area of tuning is a true specialty. All I want to say here is that you must do your homework before installation to determine which installation parameters are best for your site. Do this by tapping expertise either within or without your organization. Also attend tuning classes; get some of the excellent, detailed technical books on tuning (Heidi Thorpe's *Oracle 8i Tuning and Administration* [Addison-Wesley, 2000] is a good example); and network with other DBAs and Oracle professionals by joining a local Oracle users group and attending conferences.

There is no magic wand I can give you to wave over your server. All I can say is to make sure you start out with enough disk space and memory, have a decent network in place, and make sure to put limits on your users so that they don't create runaway processes that will drag your system to a halt. After that, you just have to address each problem as it arises, analyzing it and then deciding what to do.

Note

Here's an important nugget of information for those who use Internet Explorer to download files: IE currently has the habit of downloading files first to a temporary file on your C: drive, and then copying the file over to the location you originally requested. For example, in the following scenario we started a download from Oracle, telling Oracle to send the file `92010NT_Disk3.zip` to the directory `D:\delete this folder`:

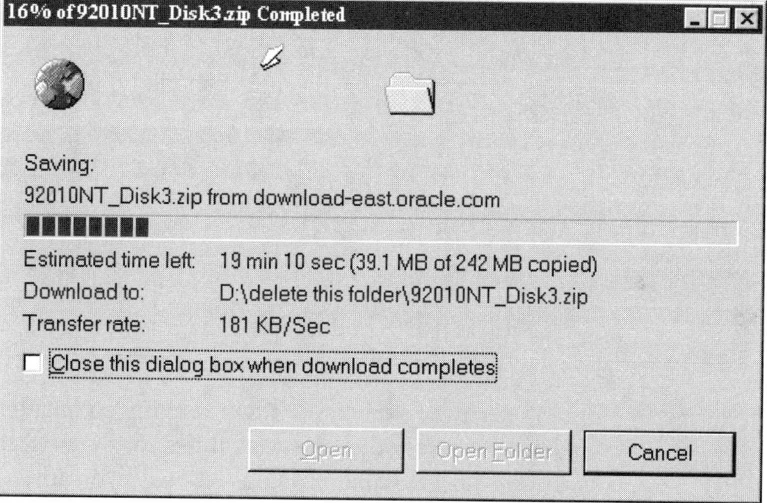

Although your disk light will be blinking during downloading, and the status bar above will seem to make things clear, *beware* that IE is really writing the file to the C: drive.

Continued

When the status bar reaches about 99 percent, you'll suddenly see this message:

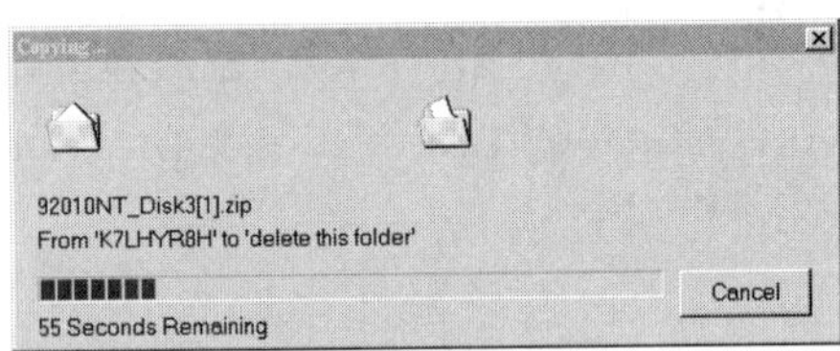

What this means is that IE is *now* copying the file from the temporary file on the C: drive (notice the internal name "K7LHY...") to the destination that you wanted.

Here's the problem with the way that IE does its downloading: If you check the space on your C: drive while this is going on, you will not see any changes in available space. If you do *not* have enough space on C:, IE will simply keep writing over what it *has* been able to download until it is finished. It will not tell you that you don't have any room. The net result is that you could spend hours downloading software, then run into a problem when you try to unzip it (you'll get the message that it is not a valid file type):

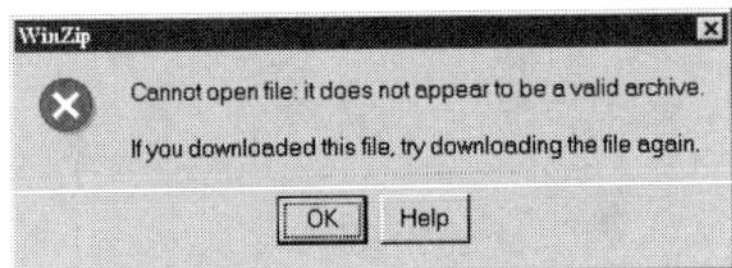

So if you use IE to download, *beware that space on your C: drive is important*!

Finally, here's one more thing for you to consider. In practice, as a DBA you will have very serious responsibilities for the ongoing successful operations of your database installation. You will need your own checklist for daily, weekly, monthly, quarterly, and so forth activities. You will be seen as the superoperator, troubleshooter, and all-around good person as you oil the wheels and air out the rooms to keep your shop running well. Your list of *mandatory* activities will include monitoring backups daily, checking logs for any problems, and checking the various relevant Web sites for alerts, new releases, warnings, and so forth. You will also have to spend time with your manuals because Oracle is constantly changing.

Chapter 13

Forms 6*i*

Now we'll have some fun. Actually, we'll have a slightly different kind of fun. This is where we start putting a lot of the parts together into something tangible for the non-techie. When we're done with this chapter, you'll have a real, functioning on-line GUI system that you can turn loose to your users.

Our goals here are to learn how to do each of the following:

- Install Forms 6*i*
- Create the GUI system
- Create a splash screen
- Create triggers and timers
- Customize the toolbar
- Use multiple tables with a form
- Add code to perform editing
- Deploy a new system

Installing Forms 6*i*

This installation will be so quick and easy for you that you'll almost do it in your sleep. Load the CD, run `setup.exe`, and you'll see the now-familiar Oracle Installer:

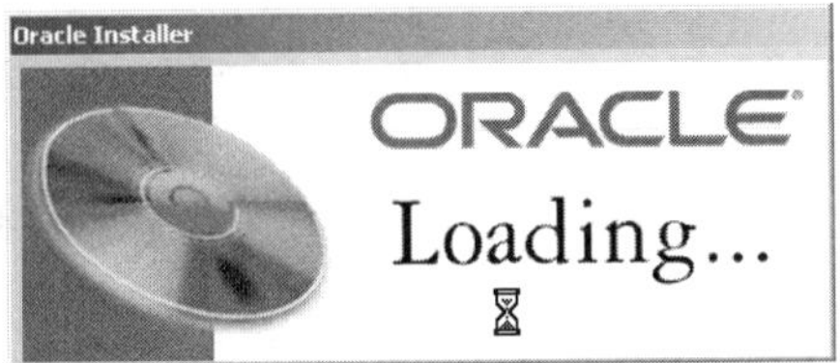

Check the defaults for the installation location, and make any necessary changes:

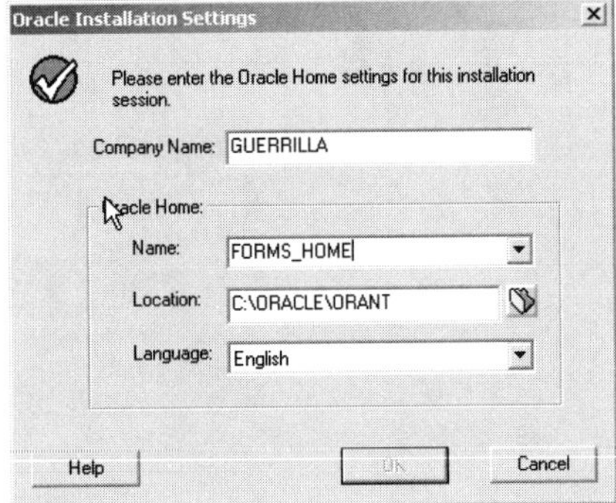

Accept the installation settings, and on the next screen select **Oracle Forms Developer**. Then specify a typical installation:

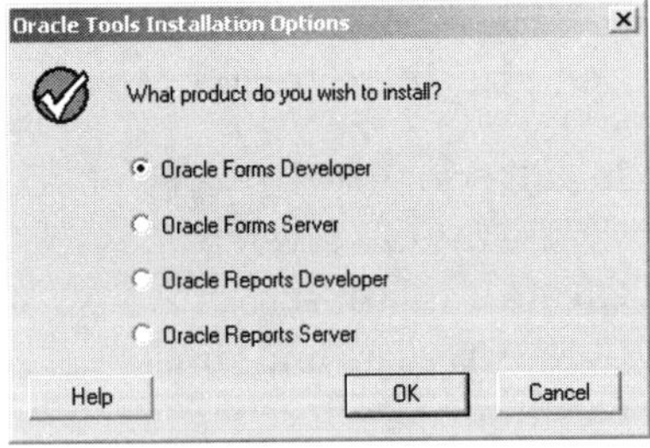

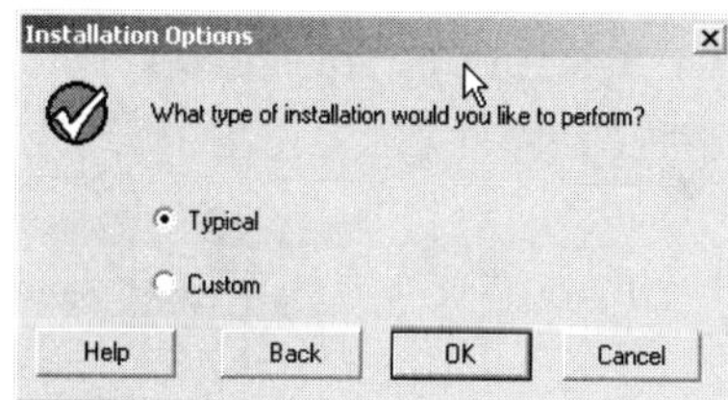

Skip the Forms Server installation:

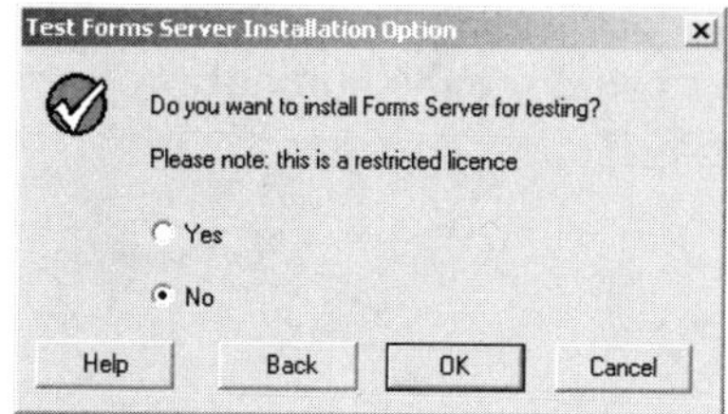

(Using a dedicated forms server is very common for performance reasons. For our purposes, however, we want to keep the installation as straightforward as possible.)

Various informational screens will appear:

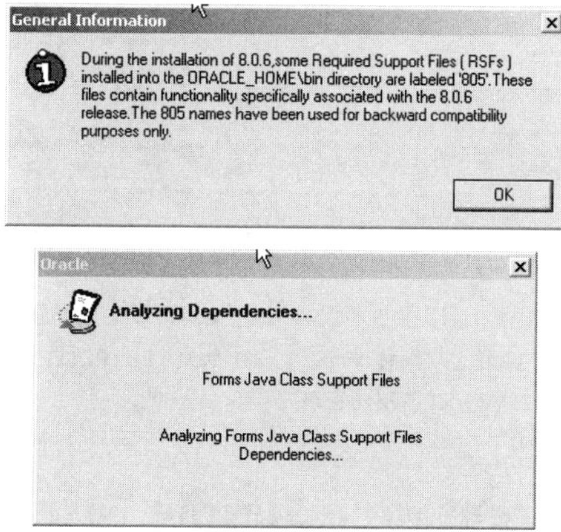

On the **System Support Files** screen, click **OK** to allow the installation of required Microsoft files:

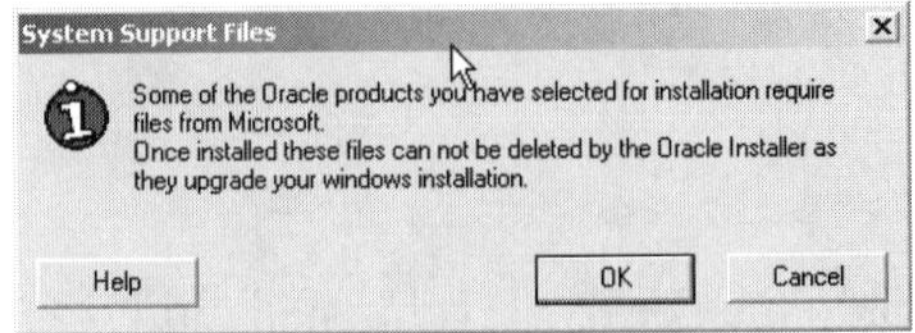

Next you'll see the familiar progress bar:

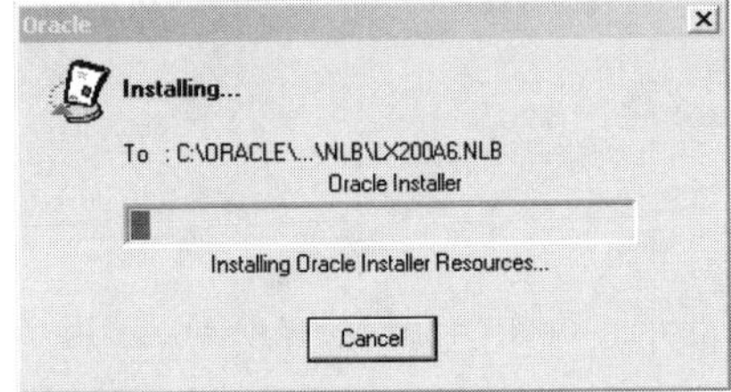

At the end of the installation you will see this message (if you don't have Adobe Acrobat Reader, now would be a good time to download it):

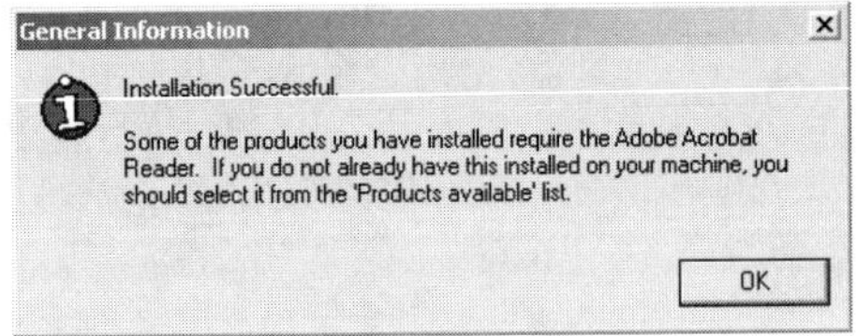

That's it. It's simple! Now all you have to do is make a shortcut on your desktop that will take you directly to the Form Builder executable: `ORANT\BIN\iFBLD60.EXE`.

Creating a Simple Form

Now that you have Forms 6*i* installed, we're going to create a quick and dirty form so that you can see some of the basic topology, geology, jargon, and concepts that you must have before we start getting fancy.

Here's what we're going to do:

- Build a form using the AUTHORS table only.
- Edit the form.

- Sneak in information on `.fmx` and `.fmb` files.
- Sneak in information on "ORA-xxx" and "FMB-xxx" errors.
- Run the form.

Then I expect you to go back and do the same thing to load some of the other tables! (But don't worry; I'll help you a bit.)

Start Forms 6*i* by clicking on its icon, select **Use the Data Block Wizard**, and on the wizard's welcome screen, click **Next**:

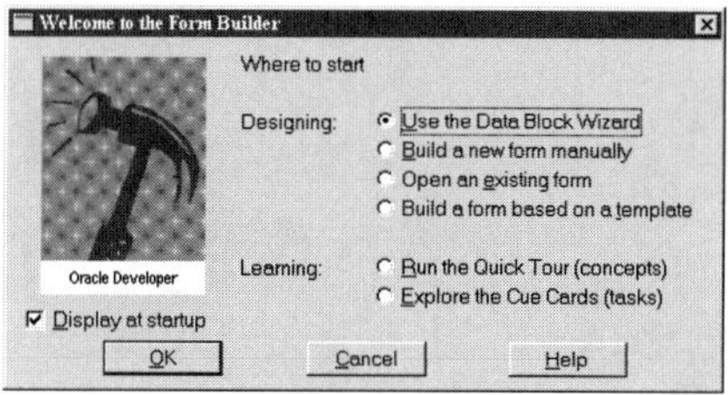

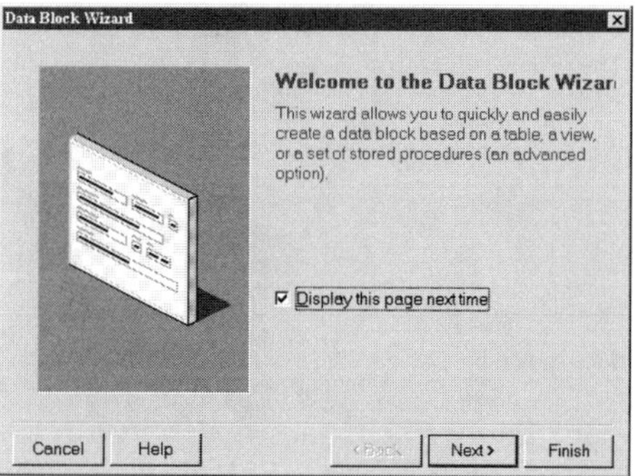

Select **Table or View**, and then browse to the AUTHORS table. (Note that you will be asked to log on before you'll be able to see any tables or views in the Guerrilla database. Use your System Administrator account.)

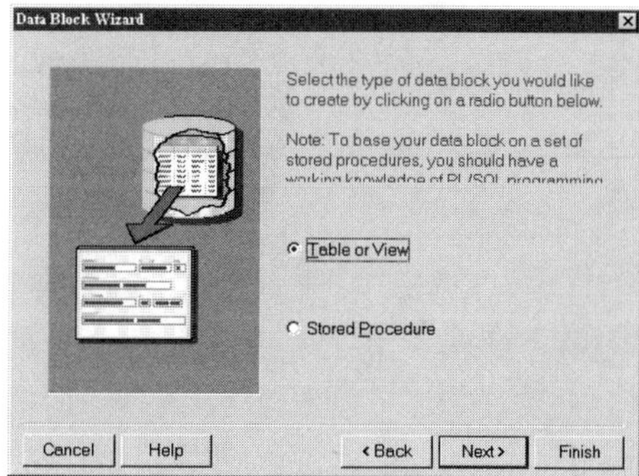

From the AUTHORS table, select both columns (**AUTHOR_ID** and **AUTHOR**), and make sure that **Enforce data integrity** is checked:

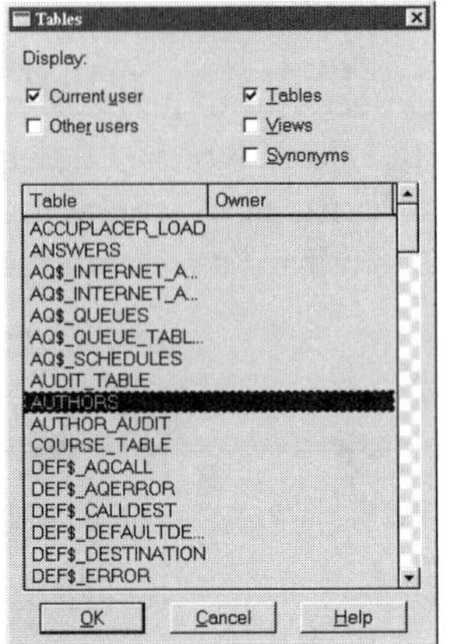

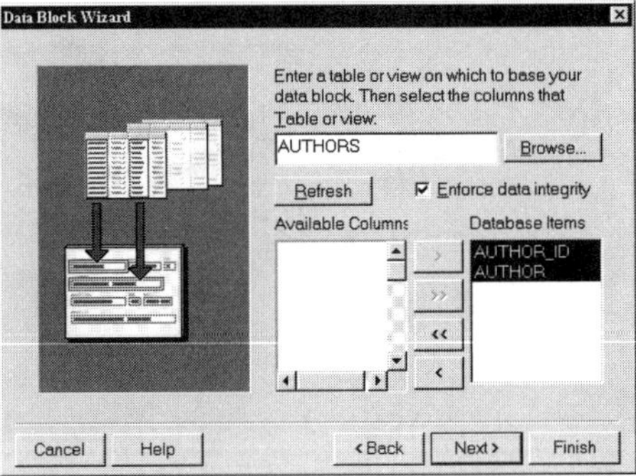

Call the Layout Wizard, and click past the welcome screen:

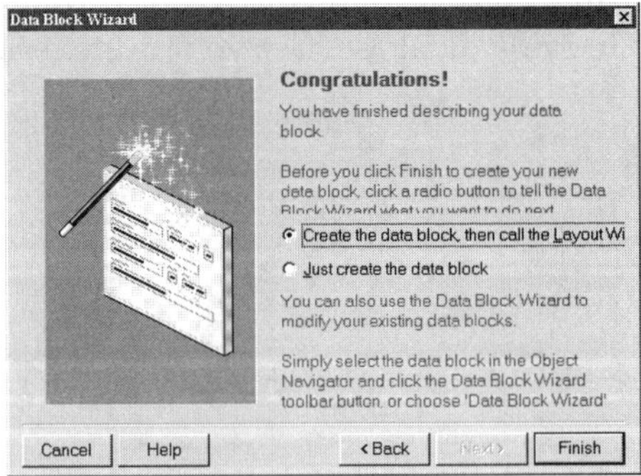

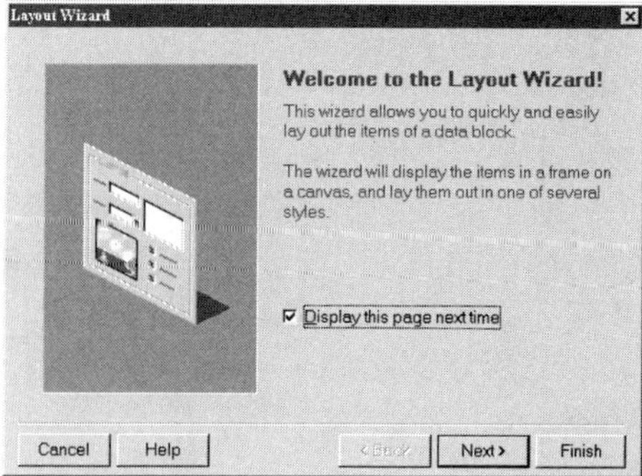

Take the **(New Canvas)** default, and again select both columns:

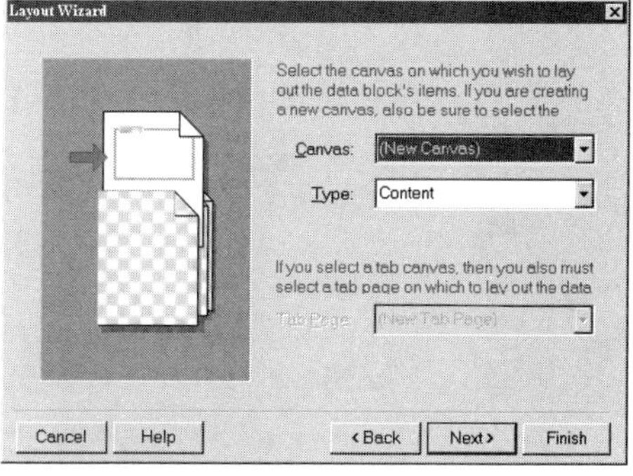

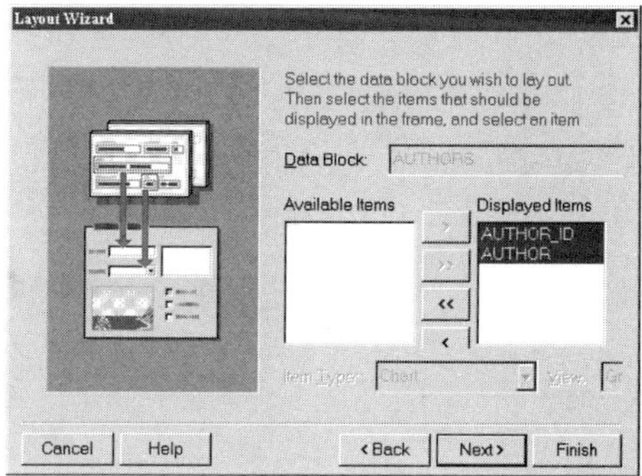

Because the screen you're building is simple, you can take the default display names or call them what you want. Then keep things simple by selecting **Form** for the layout style:

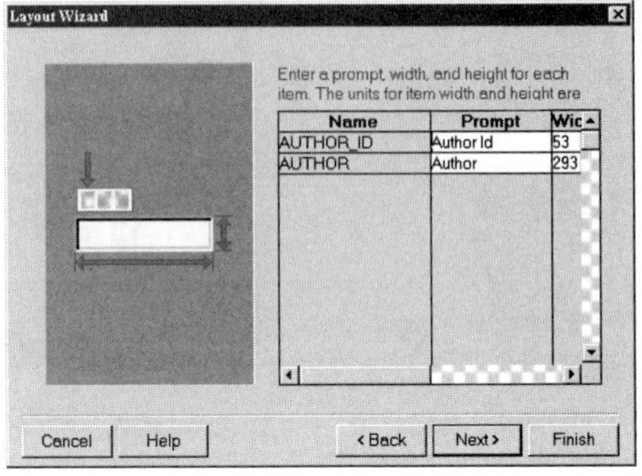

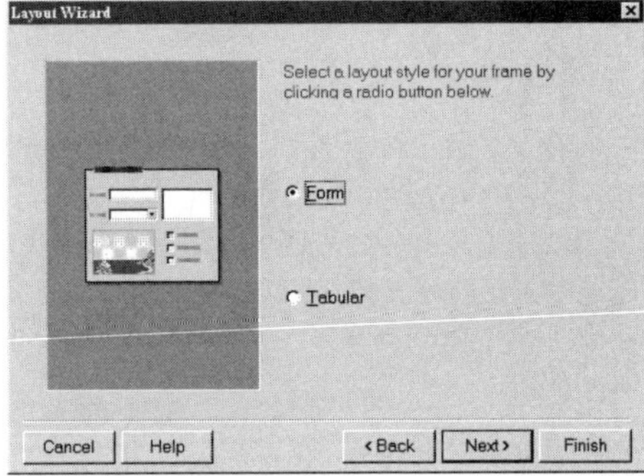

Give your new GUI screen a name, such as "Guerrilla Test Authors", and show only one record for now.

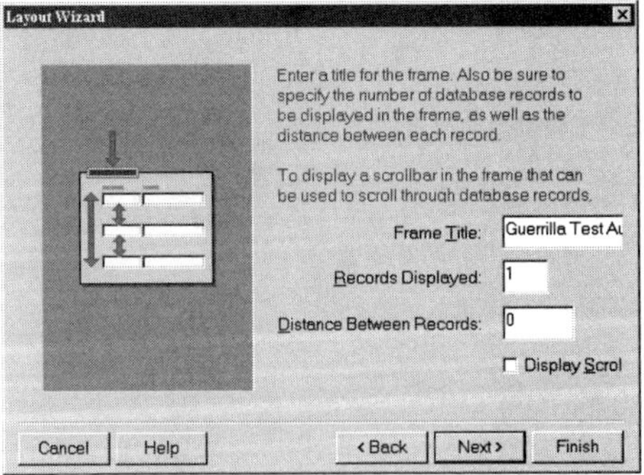

After accepting Oracle's praise, click **Finish**:

Now comes a rather complicated screen, **Object Navigator**—your friend for life! Don't panic; you'll be an expert at this by the end of this chapter:

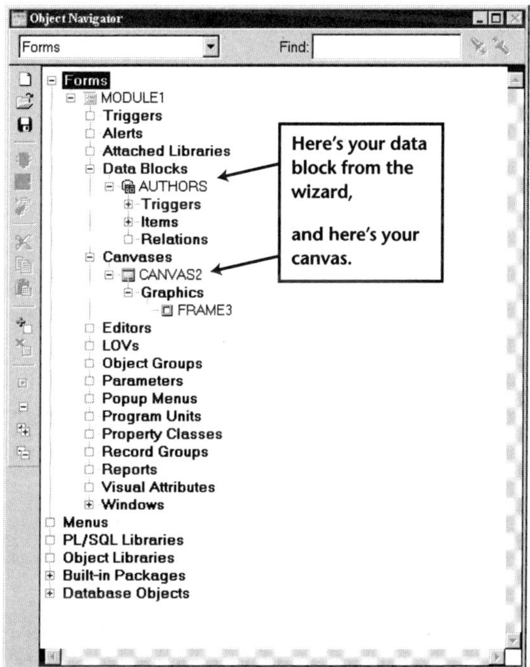

Note that sometimes you will get both the **Object Navigator** and the canvas screens, one on top of or partially covering the other. Forms 6*i* seems to remember how your screens looked the last time you were here, and it keeps the same format:

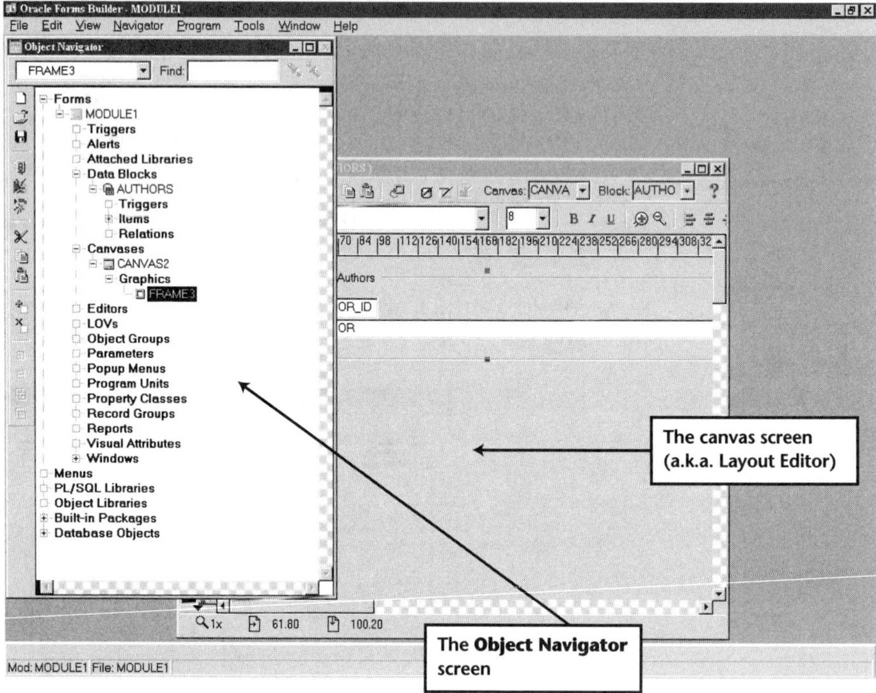

If you can see the canvas screen, maximize it to see a real, live, raw form that is almost usable. The canvas screen is where you will use your artistic ability and "paint" boxes, buttons, labels, and so forth—but not now.

Caution

You have actually built a simple form, and it will be live in a minute. But first, just a word of caution: Be very careful about hitting the upper-right X button to go back and forth. Hit the wrong one and you can lose everything! If you do happen to hit the wrong one, though, don't panic. Just repeat the steps outlined here.

Running the Form

Before we get too engrossed in all the Object Navigator and canvas details, let's run the form and see what the wizard gave us. No matter which screen you see—**Object Navigator** or the canvas—select **Program | Run Form | Client/Server**:

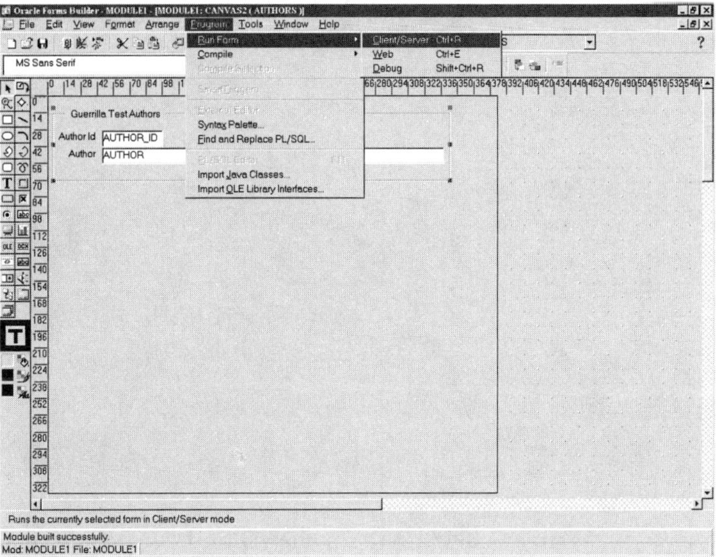

Because the wizard built this form, you should not get any compile errors. Instead you should see the runtime screen, which is the real, active form, ready for action:

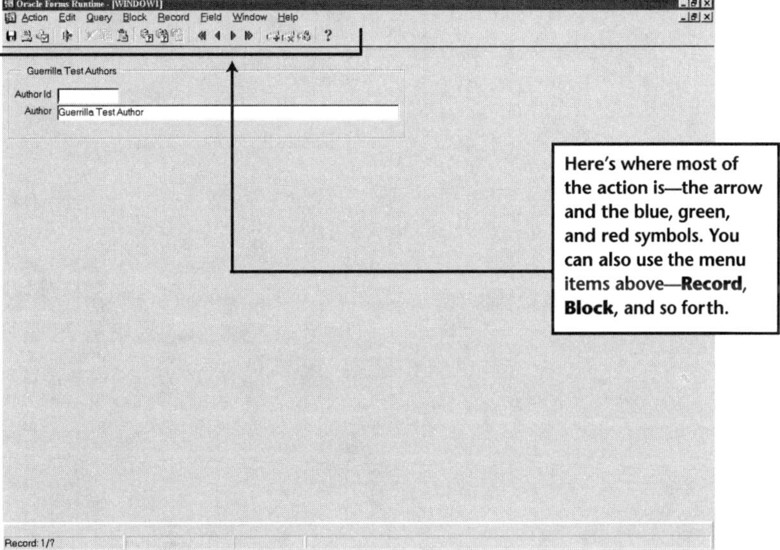

Using the icons or menu picks (**File**, **Edit**, and so forth) at the top of the screen, let's create our first author, using the brand-new AUTHORS table. Notice that the screen defaults to "Waiver Administration" for the **Author** field, which came from the way you built the table. (That was the default value, remember?)

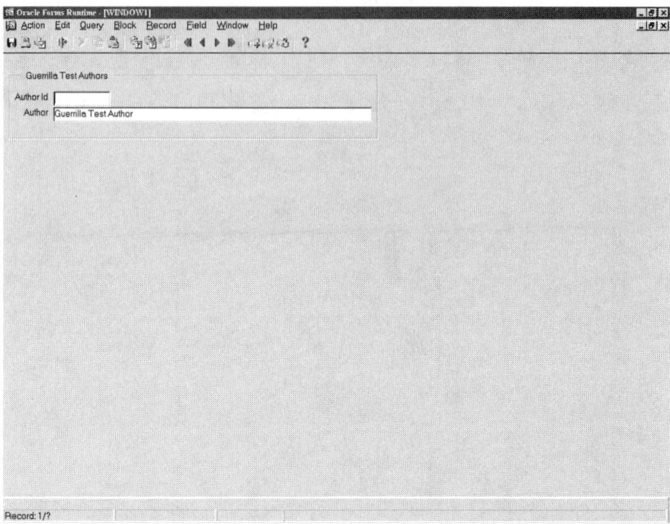

Enter "123456789" for the ID and "Test Guerrilla Author" for the name, and then click on the black diskette icon or select **File | Save** to save your entries, and you will see the message "Record: xx/yy" in the lower left-hand corner. (These numbers show how many records are currently in the table, and which record you're working on. If you've been practicing, you probably have already loaded several records into the table.)

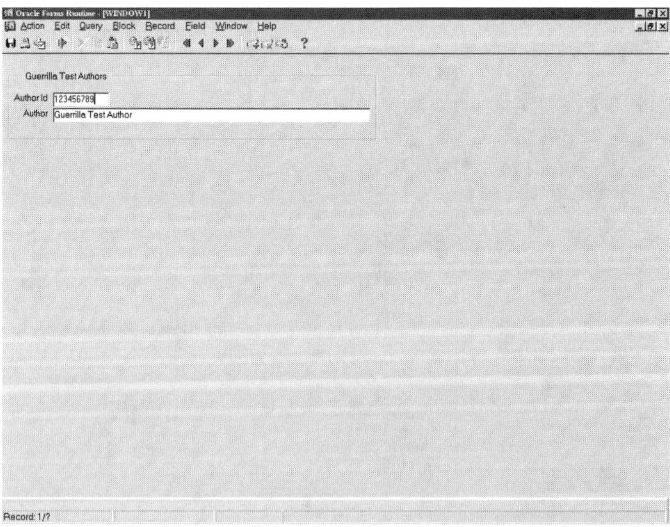

You have successfully entered your first data! Now enter two more test authors: Guerrilla Test Author2 and Author3.

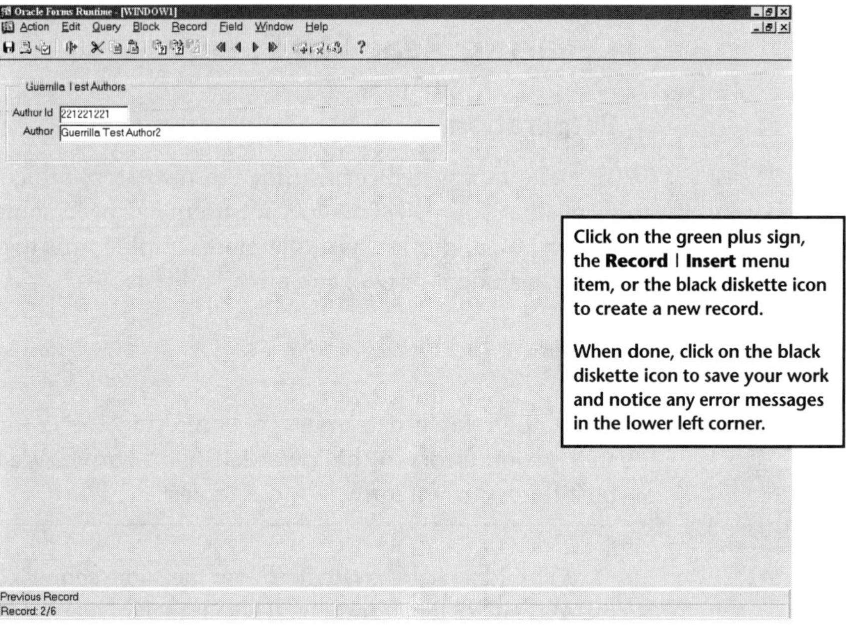

Oracle Forms Runtime - [WINDOW1]
Action Edit Query Block Record Field Window Help
Guerrilla Test Authors
Author Id 221221221
Author Guerrilla Test Author2
Click on the green plus sign, the Record | Insert menu item, or the black diskette icon to create a new record.
When done, click on the black diskette icon to save your work and notice any error messages in the lower left corner.
Previous Record
Record: 2/6

Now carefully exit, and then run the program again.

Note

Here's a quick navigation lesson. Once you're back in the form, if you use the blue arrows, you will not see your records. You have to run a query first. Just select **Query | Execute**, and the blue arrows will let you scroll through the records. Got it? The form defaults to **Add** or **Insert**, and if you want to look at what's already in the table, you have to change modes to **Query**.

If you have inserted or deleted data, or made any changes, and you have not saved those changes, Forms will ask you whether you want to save the changes when you exit:

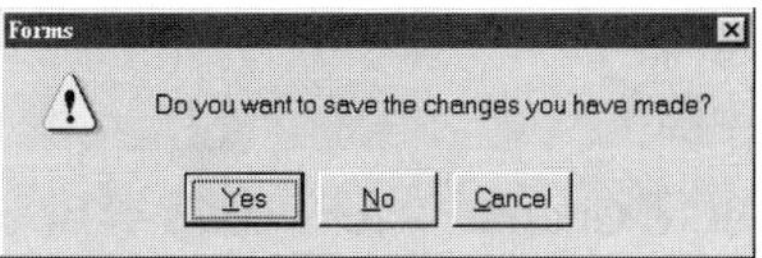

Because at this point it is hard to remember all that you have done, I strongly recommend that you save each record as you process it.

Creating Real GUI Forms

Preparation

To make our system usable for the next step, which is making the real GUI forms that you will show to your users, we need some data. Use what I've just shown you and make a couple more simple forms to enter some questions, answers, a student or two, and all the other tables.

Note

Remember: Table data must be entered in the correct sequence, or you will start seeing errors in the lower left-hand corner. We must not forget that we built referential integrity into our tables!

To build a usable system, follow the same sequence that we used in creating the AUTHORS table, and you'll be all set. However, you do not yet have any programs behind the scenes to check your work, so you'll have to keep good records of what you've entered, and from time to time go to SQL*Plus and run a SELECT `* from` *`<table-name>`* command to make sure you're linking the right tables:

Table-Loading Sequence
TEST_TYPE_DESC
TEST_ID
QUESTIONS_TYPE_DESC
AUTHORS
QUESTIONS
TEST_QUESTIONS_LINK
ANSWERS
STUDENTS
TEST_HISTORY
STUDENT_ANSWER_HISTORY

Note

Refer to Chapter 9 for details of how to load tables. Then write down what you will be loading, or follow the steps outlined here.

Let's take a quick walk through building the tables. First we have to load data into the TEST_TYPE_DESC table. Here's an example of using plain SQL*Plus and a quick and dirty form (which is called GUERRILLA TEST DESCRIPTIONS):

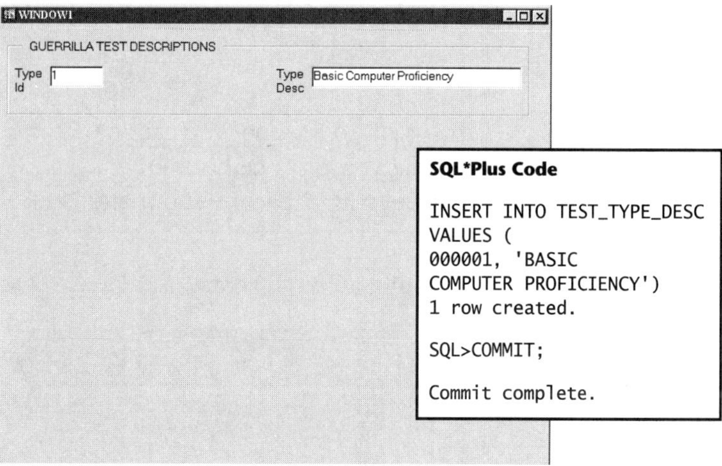

Or, if you still have the first canvas open, you can get fancy and add the GUERRILLA TEST DESCRIPTIONS form to that canvas:

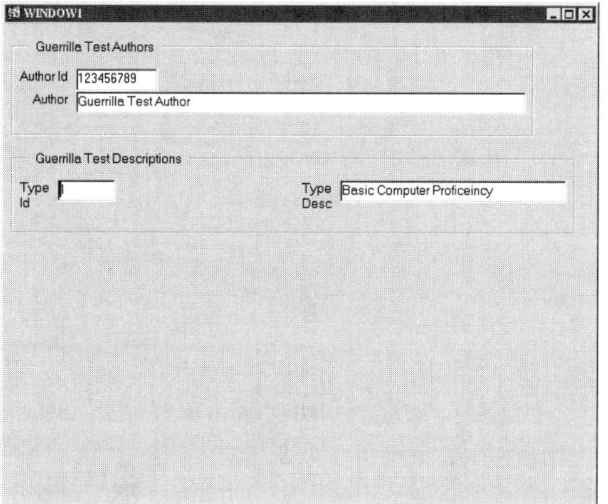

Tip

Here's a hint for the brave of heart: In Object Navigator, highlight **DATA-BLOCK**, click on **TOOLS | Data Block Wizard**, and off you go.

Note

If you're working on two new open forms and you haven't saved either of them with its own name, you will get an Oracle "FRM-30087" error when you try to run and compile the forms. Save and close one of them to end the conflict.

Note

Extra credit to anyone who caught the misspelling in the last screen shot. I suggest that you practice both entering and running queries in Forms to become proficient with the icons and menu items.

Now build a Test_ID entry. Again, use SQL*Plus and Forms:

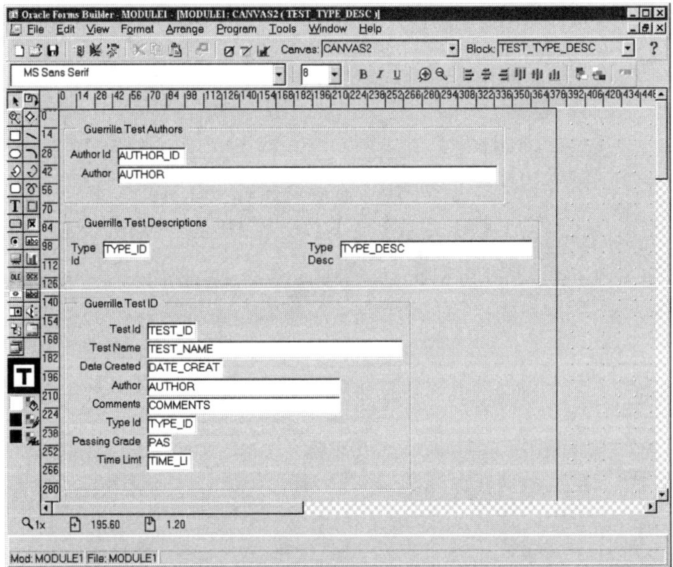

SQL*Plus Code

```
INSERT INTO TEST_ID VALUES (
000001, 'BASIC Knowledge I', '01-Mar-
02', 'Prof. J. Dean',
'To test basic DP', 000001, 70,02.00)

1 row created.

SQL>COMMIT;

Commit complete.
```

Components of Forms 6*i*

Now let's get acquainted with Form 6*i*'s components. If you're still at the run-time form, close it, and you should automatically be brought to the **Object Navigator** screen. It looks like a tree without leaves, or a verbal skeleton of some strange language.

Object Navigator

Just like the data dictionary, **Object Navigator** is your friend. Get familiar with it. It is the main sandbox for your development, and it is the tree-looking screen. The Object Navigator shown here is actually what you'll be building in a little while:

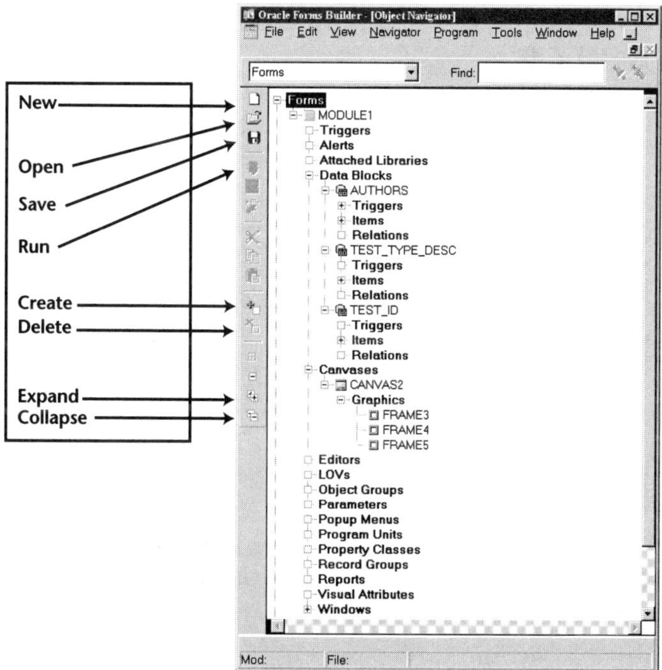

There are three more major sandboxes in Forms 6*i* you need to know about: the property palette, the canvas, and the PL/SQL editor.

Property Palette

If you right-click on most of the items in Object Navigator window, you'll get a pull-down menu, and one of the items will be **Property Palette**. The property palette is where you give your objects names, as well as pick colors, sizes, and so forth. It's like a blueprint with a lot of details that govern your objects.

Canvas

The canvas is where you will "paint" your GUI forms. It has plenty of editing, artistic, and other tools to help you create attractive, functioning forms.

PL/SQL Editor

As you will see shortly, you can build in plenty of code to handle all the editing, movement from form to form, warnings, and so forth that a good GUI system must have. Forms 6*i*, fortunately, has quite a few built-in tools to help you and make your life easier.

Got the general idea of how it works? Go ahead and try the same thing with some of the other tables, just to become really familiar with the basic steps and concepts. Be careful, though, to delete any new records that you add to the tables and don't want to keep around or have someone else see. For example, if you make up some strange names, or use names of coworkers, you may want to get rid of them as soon as you're done with your testing.

Steps in Creating GUI Forms

Here's where we start to work on our real GUI system. I hope the preceding brief discussion has gotten you excited. Let's keep that enthusiasm and get started!

Here are the steps we'll take:

1. Create a new folder for your project:
   `C:\GUERRILLA_Oracle\CWE1P_PROJECT`
2. Create the main form and canvas.

3. Create additional screens.
4. Create a splash screen.
5. Create triggers and a timer.
6. Change the pull-down menus.
7. Tie them all together.
8. Install the system.
9. Deploy the new system.

Warning

As we go along, I'm also going to sneak in building a couple of views.

There is quite a bit of detail in the following pages, and the only way to get through it and build your forms is just to get through it. I want to show you the final screens now so that you'll have a good picture of where we're going. With forms development, it's easy to get lost among the trees and canvases, so keep in mind that here's what you're going to make:

1. Splash

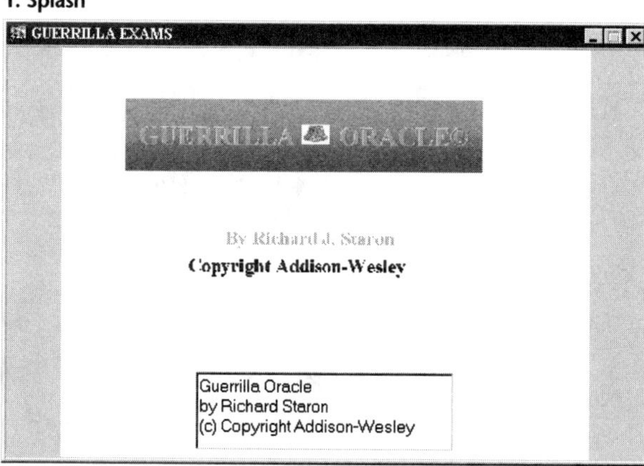

2. Main

Window
GUERRILLA ORACLE©
EXAMS
Administration
EXIT
By Richard J. Staron
Copyright Addison-Wesley
FRM-41810: Error creating menu.
Record: 1/1

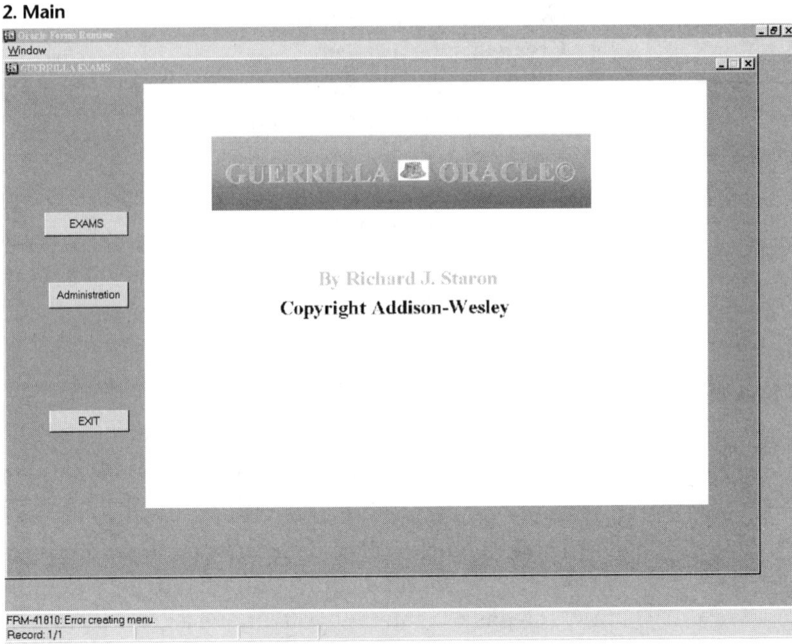

3. Select test

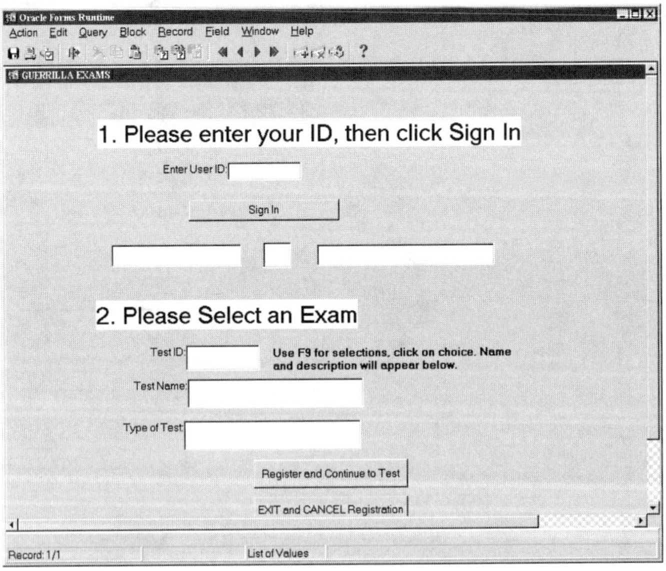

Oracle Forms Runtime
Action Edit Query Block Record Field Window Help
GUERRILLA EXAMS
1. Please enter your ID, then click Sign In
Enter User ID:
Sign In
2. Please Select an Exam
Test ID:
Use F9 for selections, click on choice. Name and description will appear below.
Test Name:
Type of Test:
Register and Continue to Test
EXIT and CANCEL Registration
Record: 1/1
List of Values

4. Take Test

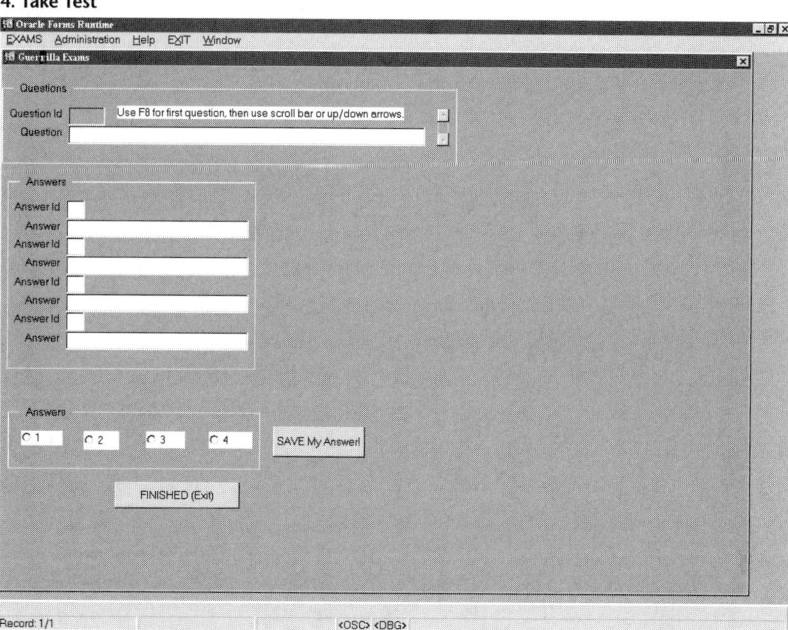

You may be thinking you can go ahead and get comfortable because all you have to do is create these four simple screens. Nothing to it, right? Well, as you'll see, a lot of work is involved in making what looks like simplicity itself. Just stay with it, go step by step, and you'll soon have your own version of these screens. Hopefully your sense of color and design will be better than mine!

OK, let's get started. Here's what we're going to build: first a splash screen (the one with the green "GUERRILLA ORACLE" splashed across it), then an opening screen, then the screen where you log in and select which test to take, and last, the actual test screen.

Splash Screen

Start Forms 6*i*, select **Build a new form manually**, and click OK:

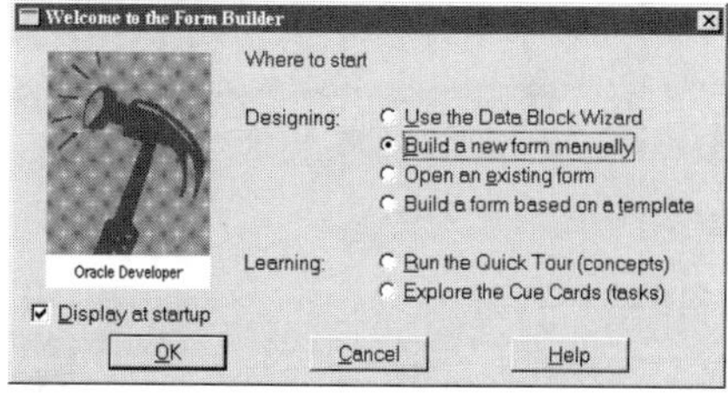

On the next screen change the name to "CWE1P_MAIN":

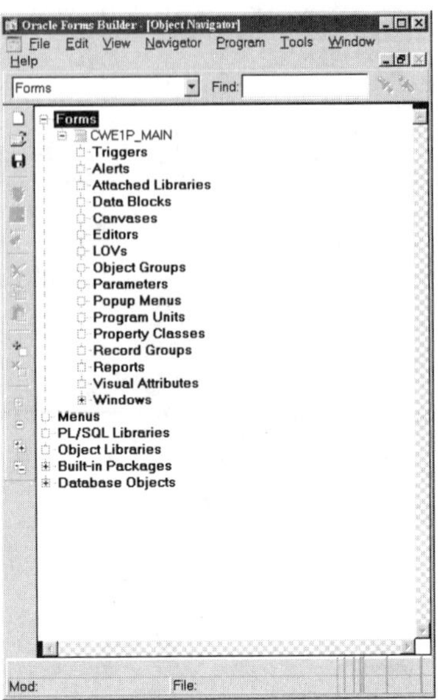

We want the form to fill the screen, so select **Triggers**, right-click and select **SmartTriggers**, then **PRE-FORM**, and type in the following: "SET_WINDOW_PROPERTY (FORMS_MIDI_WINDOW, WINDOW_STATE,MAXIMIZE);":

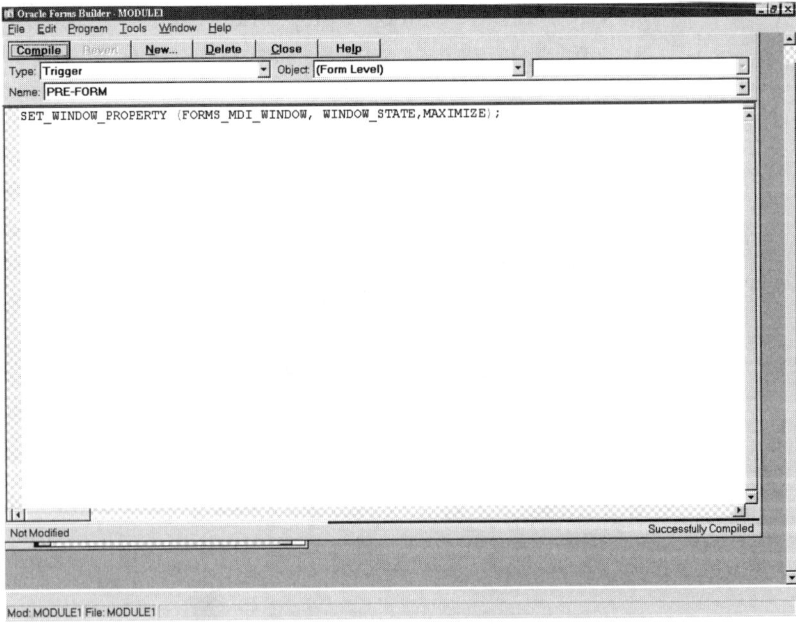

Now, click on the **Compile** button, and then when the compile is complete, click on the **CLOSE** button to close the form.

Canvas

Now let's create the canvas. Click on **Canvases** and then on the green plus sign or just double-click on **Canvases**, and change the name to "CWE1P_CANVAS":

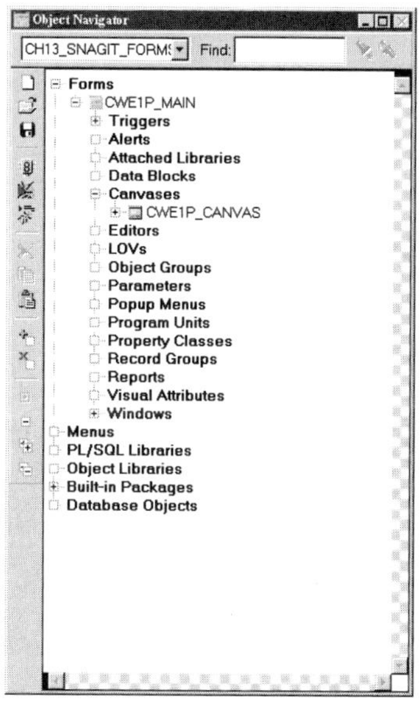

Now change the property palette: Right-click on the name, CWE1P_CANVAS, select **Property Palette** and then **Physical**, and change the Width to 580 and the Height to 375:

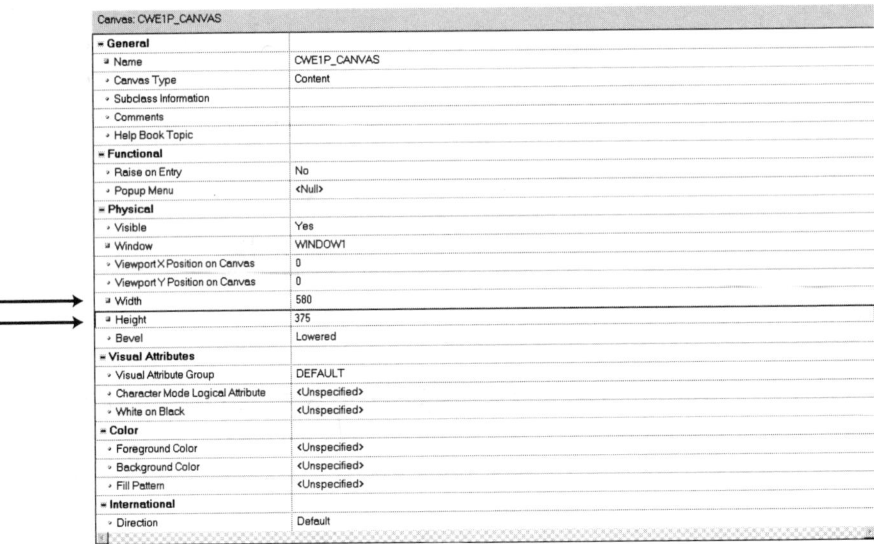

The last step in creating this main module is to configure the window node. Click on **Windows**, and a new entry will automatically be created. Change it to "CWE1P_WINDOW":

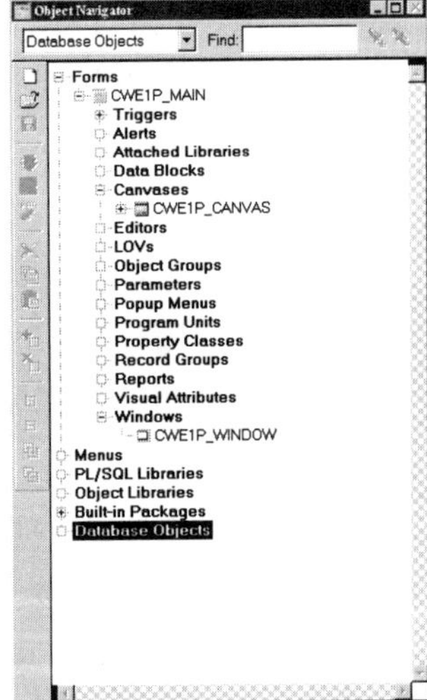

Do the same thing again—right-click on the name and select **Property Palette**—and change the properties as follows:

- **Title**: GUERRILLA EXAMS
- **Resize Allowed:** No
- **Maximize Allowed**: No
- **Width**: 580
- **Height**: 375

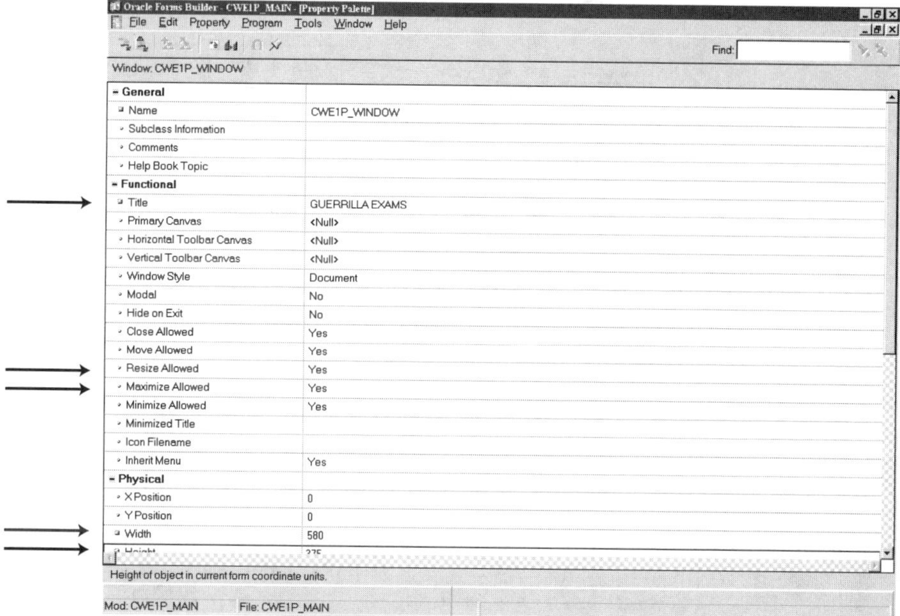

Save the form as `CWE1P_MAIN.fmb` in your `CWE1P_PROJECT` folder:

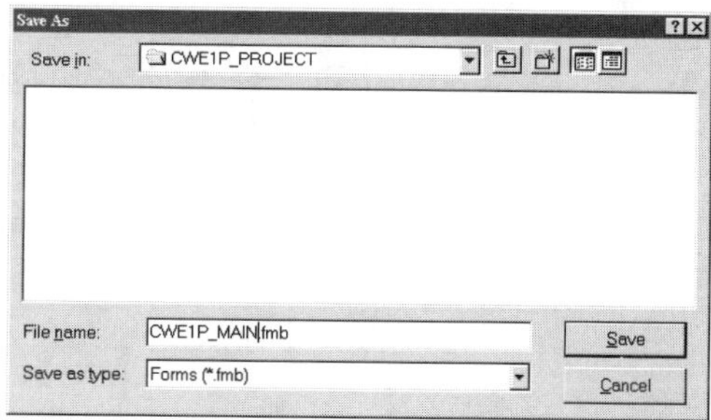

Buttons

Remember that our form has to have two buttons—**ENTER** and **EXIT**—along with our Guerrilla logo, and here's how we create those buttons.

Go back to the main **Object Navigator** screen, select **Data Blocks**, and click on the green plus sign. Then choose **Build a new data block manually** and change the name to "CWE1P_BLOCK":

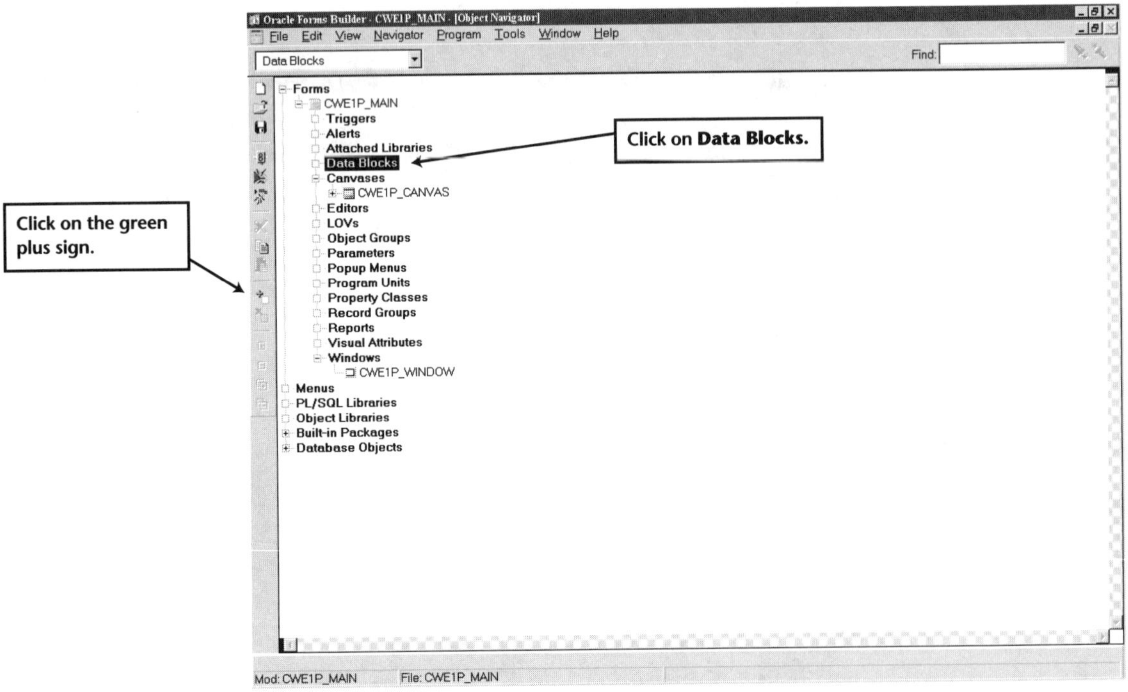

Click on **Data Blocks.**

Click on the green plus sign.

Select manual.

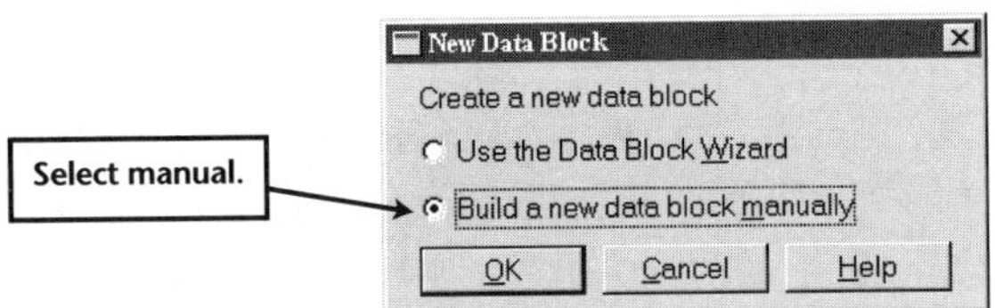

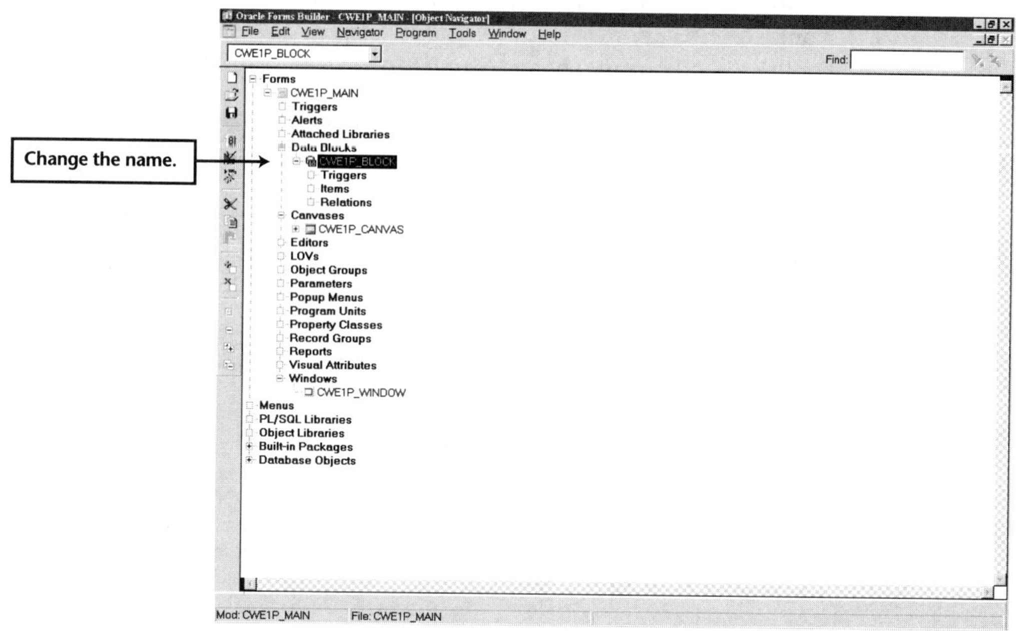

Now that we have our data block, let's add the buttons. Go back to CWE1P_CANVAS, double-click to open it, and then select the button icon and drop two buttons on the canvas:

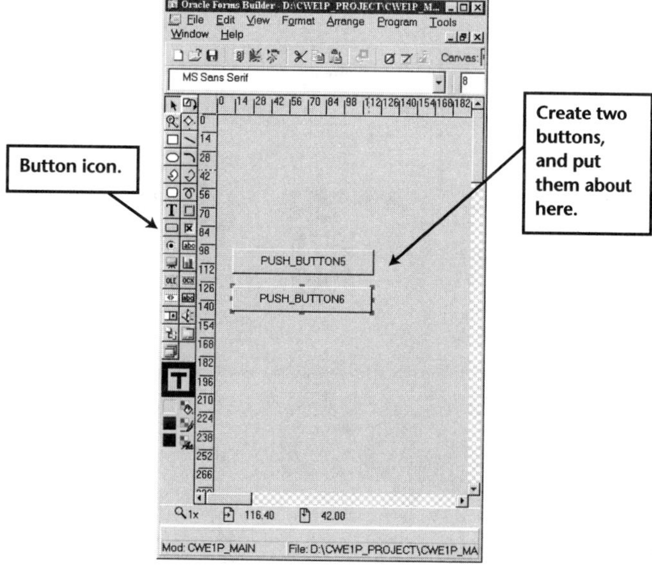

Ready for the property palette? First right-click on the first button and change **Name** to "ENTER_BUTTON", **Label** to "ENTER", **Width** to 63, and **Height** to 16. For the second button, change **Name** to "EXIT_BUTTON" and **Label** to "EXIT":

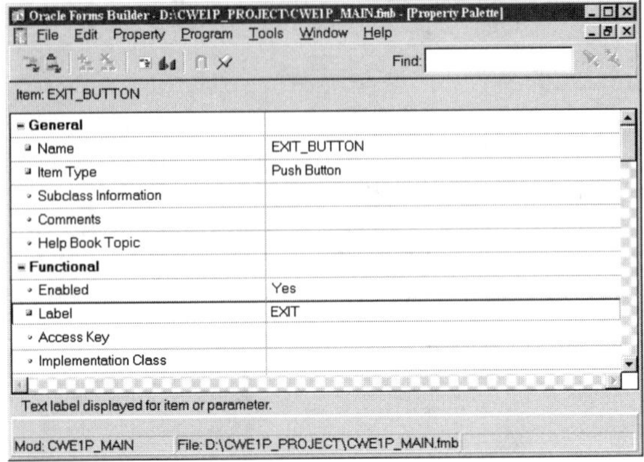

The result will look like this:

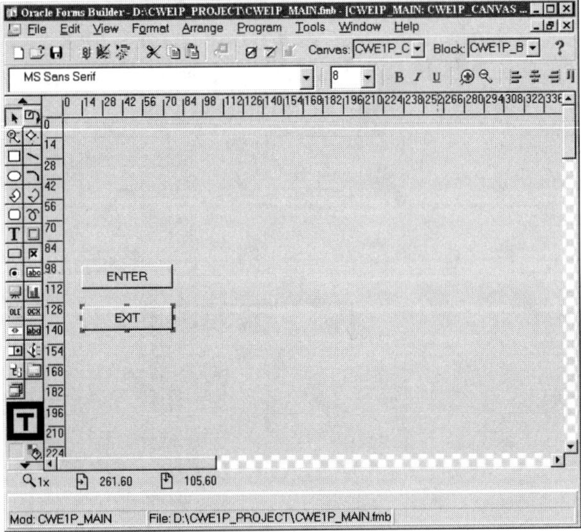

Images

Let's get our image. First make sure you are in Layout Editor. Next select **File | Import | Image...**:

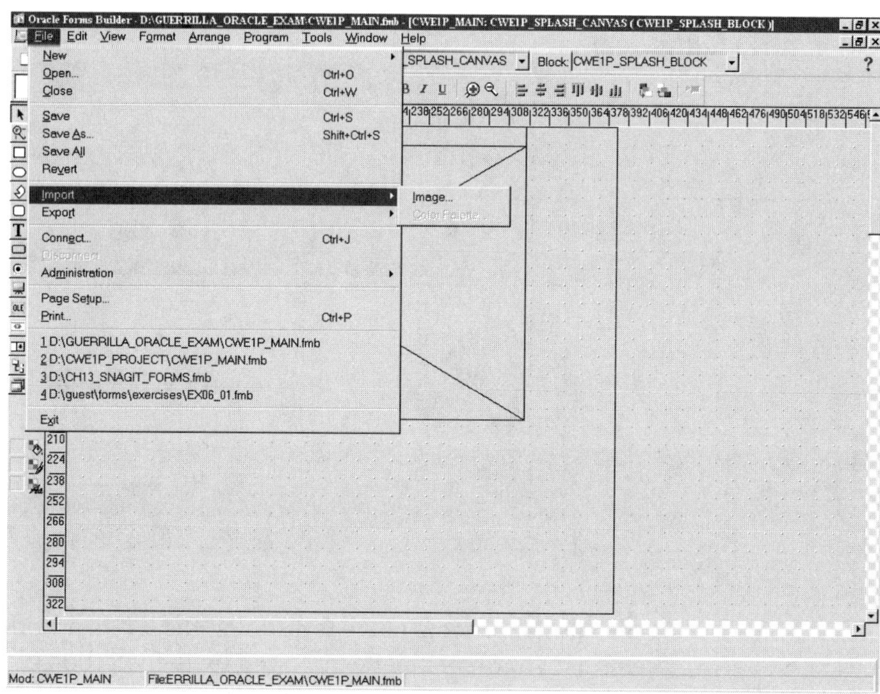

(The sample image is on the the book's CD for you. Once the image is on the canvas, you can resize it and move it around.)

Tip

This won't be the last time I say this: Save your work! You've done a little too much at this point to have to redo everything if you have a system failure, so save!

Now you can right-click on the image and then on the canvas and show your expertise with the property palette. Here's an example of what the canvas looks like after we resize the graphic, add some text, and change the canvas background color:

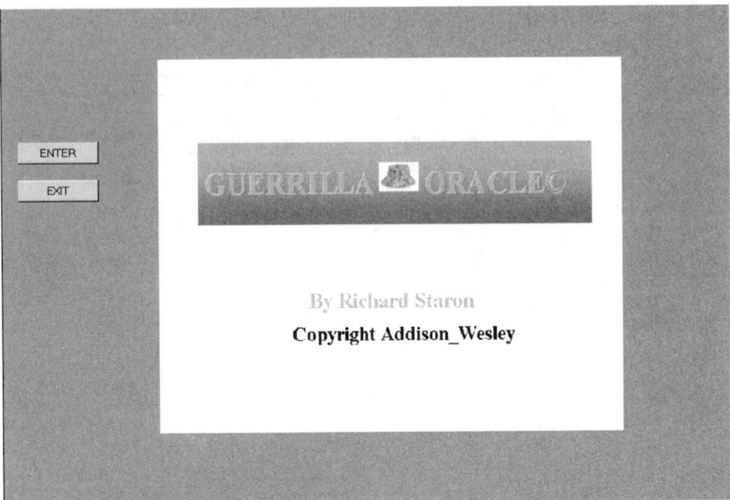
ENTER
EXIT
GUERRILLA ORACLE©
By Richard Staron
Copyright Addison_Wesley

Tools

Let's talk about some of the features on the left-hand side of the canvas. These items are your tool palette (accessed by the selection of **View | Tool Palette**), and they are what you use to add buttons, color, shapes, and so forth:

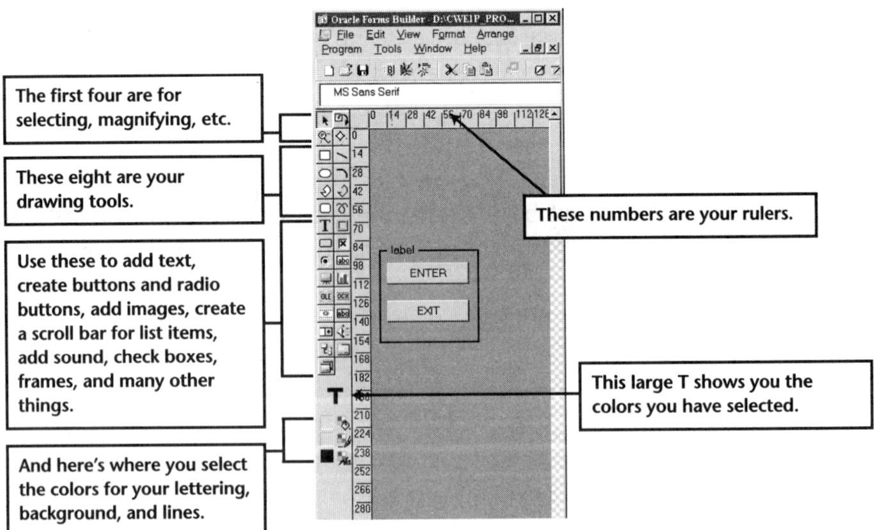
The first four are for selecting, magnifying, etc.
These eight are your drawing tools.
Use these to add text, create buttons and radio buttons, add images, create a scroll bar for list items, add sound, check boxes, frames, and many other things.
And here's where you select the colors for your lettering, background, and lines.
These numbers are your rulers.
This large T shows you the colors you have selected.
File Edit View Format Arrange
Program Tools Window Help
MS Sans Serif
label
ENTER
EXIT

Note

One thing I want you to do—at least for now—is select all the toolbars under the **View** menu when you're in Layout Editor working on a canvas. This way you'll have all the tools possible, along with the ruler and ruler guides.

OK, now what?, you ask. Well, I'm going to start sneaking in some more information. We have to let the users jump from one form to another, right? So how do we do this? We use what is called a **global variable**, and this variable will point to the home folder for the entire project. We create this global variable in the CWE1P_MAIN form by going back to the **Object Navigator** screen and selecting **PRE-FORM** under **Triggers**, just as we did a couple of minutes ago:

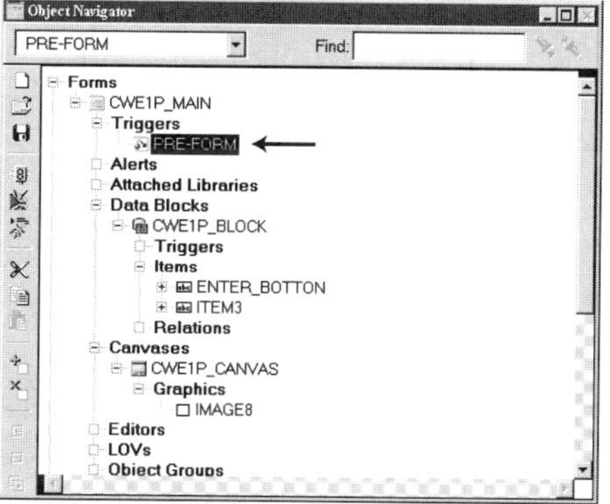

Then add the PL/SQL text:

```
:GLOBAL.project_path := 'D:\GUERRILLA_ORACLE\CWE1P_PROJECT';
```

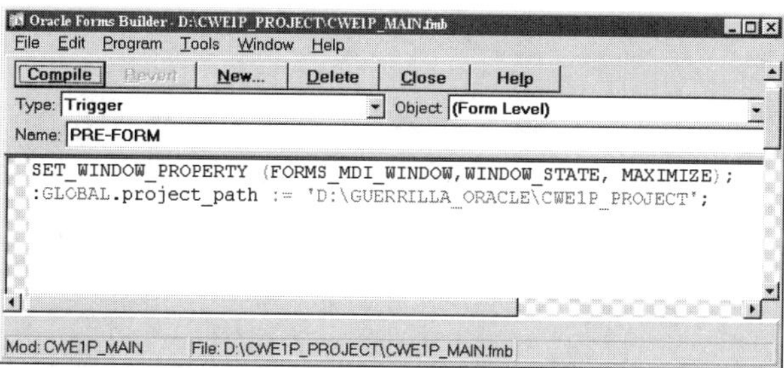

Compile and then close the form. (Any compile errors will be the result of missing single quotes or other missing syntax that is necessary.)

The Splash Screen

We are finally ready for the splash screen. Many systems display a logo screen when they start that disappears after a couple of seconds. It's like a "hello" to the user. Here's how to build one of these splash screens. (You should breeze through this because it's very similar to the form you just created. We'll add the three things necessary for a new window: the window, a canvas, and then a data block.)

Go back to your friend Object Navigator and do the following:

1. Make a new window called CWE1P_SPLASH.
2. Highlight **CANVAS**, click on the green plus sign, and rename your new canvas "CWE1P_SPLASH_CANVAS".
3. Click on **Data Block** and then the green plus sign, and select **Build a new data block manually**. Rename the new block "CWE1P_SPLASH_BLOCK".

Here's what your Object Navigator screen should look like:

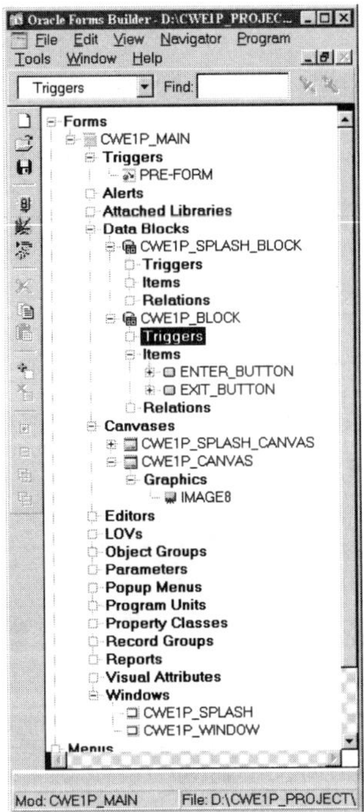

Bear with me. Here are the next steps. Open the property palette of CWE1P_SPLASH_CANVAS (under **CANVAS**) and do the following:

4. Make the title "GUERRILLA EXAMS".
5. Go down a few lines to the **Window Style** property, click next to property title and select **Dialog** from the list.
6. Make sure the value for **Hide on Exit** is "Yes".
7. Change the value for **Move Allowed**, **Resize Allowed**, and **Maximize Allowed** to "No". We do *not* want the user to play with the screen when it appears, so we're shutting off those features.
8. Center the screen by changing the X and Y positions to 120 and 100, respectively.
9. Now you have to fix the canvas, so close out of this window and select CWE1P_SPLASH_CANVAS.
10. Right-click and select **Property Palette;** change **Width** to 320 and **Height** to 200.

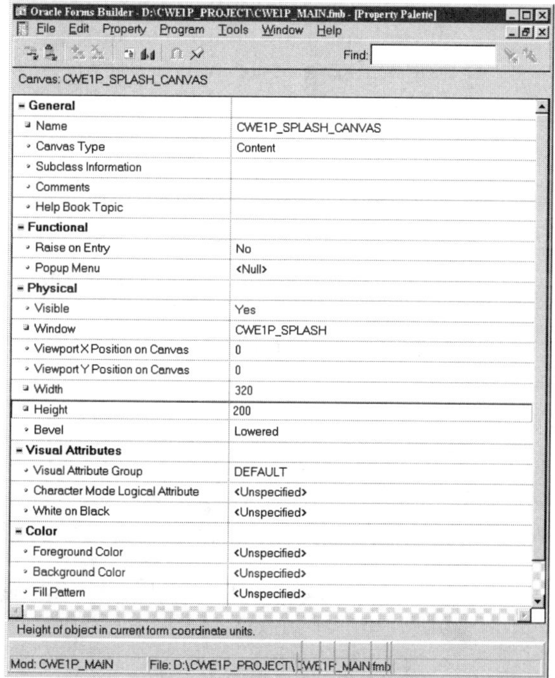

OK, you probably need a break, so take a short one, and then we'll get back to work.

Adding Image and Text to the Canvas

We now have to create a canvas that will have the graphical image and some text. There are some rules here, so just follow along and you'll be all set:

1. Go to CWE1P_SPLASH_CANVAS and double-click on it so that it opens up in Layout Editor. Notice that there is a white border inside. The reason is that you set the size to 320 x 200, remember? This is the area you have to work with for your image. *Don't go outside the white border!*
2. Pick the image item tool from the buttons on the left side, and draw a box inside the canvas that is just a little bit smaller than the canvas. You should have a big X within the white border on your canvas. (Make sure you pick the right tool. It looks like a projection screen with a blue picture on it.)
3. Right-click on your new image area (say, in the middle of the big X), select the palette, and change the name to "CWE1P_SPLASH_IMAGE".
4. Select **Sizing Style** (still in the property palette) and change it to "Adjust".
5. Make sure the X and Y positions are set to 0.
6. Change **Height** to 200 and **Width** to 320.
7. Under **Functional**, change **Sizing Style** to "Crop".
8. Close the property palette, staying in Layout Editor.
9. Now add a small box at the bottom of the image area. You can put it anywhere you want because it will contain just a couple lines of copyright information. Select the text icon (the icon with the "abc" in it) and draw the box so that your canvas now looks like this:

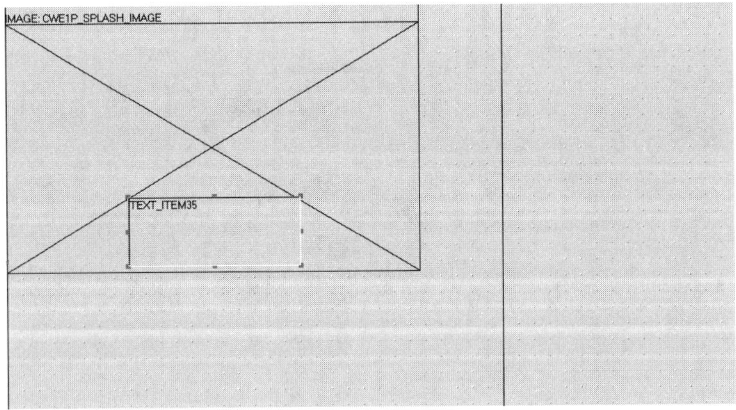

10. Your last step will be to set the variables in the property palette for your new box, so position the cursor somewhere inside the box, right-click, select **Property Palette**, and make the following changes:

- **Name:** CWE1P_SPLASH ITEM
- **Item Type:** Display item
- **Maximum Length**: 500
- **Background Color**: White
- **Font Name**: Arial

Your canvas should now look like this:

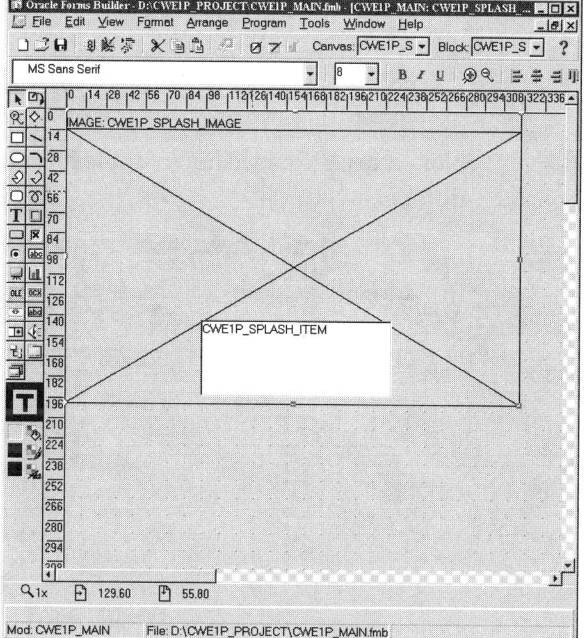

Displaying the Graphic

Now what you have is an area that can be used to display the splash image that you'll be loading with a trigger, and then hiding with another trigger. Isn't it amazing that something that will appear for only a few seconds has so many instructions?

Here we go. You'll be adding the PL/SQL code to grab and display the graphic and to fill in the little box at the bottom center:

1. **Select Tools | Object Navigator** and click on **PRE-FORM** under Triggers:

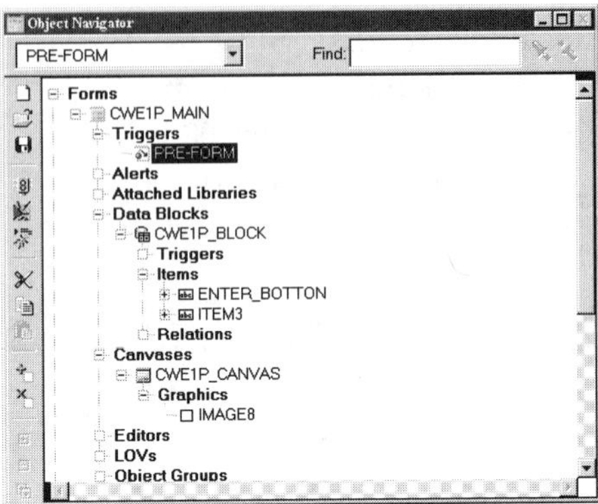

2. Now enter the code shown in the following screen shot and compile it (but don't exit yet!):

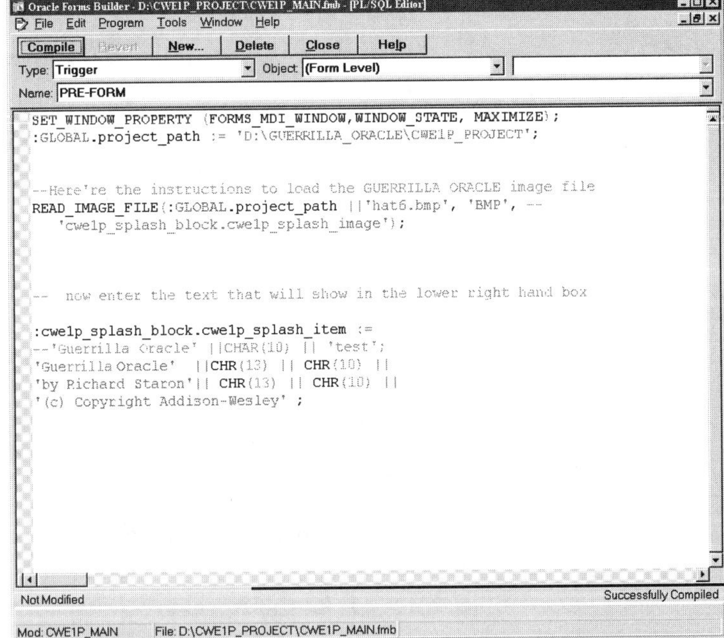

Note

I can't stress this enough: *Watch your syntax!* The little things like single quotes, semicolons, and so forth will trip you up. I have sometimes spent a lot of time debugging, when all the problem turned out to be was a missing single quote at the end of 'hat.bmp. You will find that Forms will accept bad syntax, compile it, and run it for you, even though it is nonfunctional.

All I can tell you is to check the Forms messages in the lower left-hand corner as you test your programs. The messages are usually small, and therefore easily overlooked, but they are your best source of information if your splash screen doesn't appear quite right.

So along with the admonition to save, save, save! let me add, *check your syntax!*

Building a Timer

Are you ready for the timer part? Let's build a form timer that will control how long your splash screen will display. This is just another bit of PL/SQL code that you'll add right where you left off:

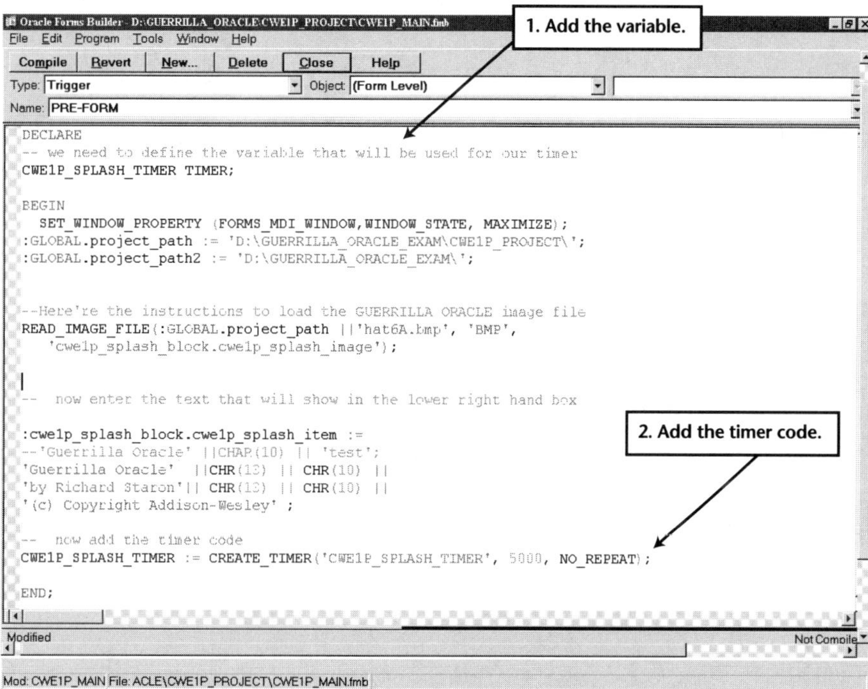

Good! Just a couple more steps and we'll test the thing. As you've probably imagined, we now have a trigger that will fire, but we need something to recognize the firing, and then do something about it. Those are our next two, and last, steps for the splash screen.

What we have to do is create another trigger that will go off when our timer trigger fires, and then, within our new trigger, tell it where to go next. So here's what we have to do:

1. Go back to Object Navigator.
2. Click on **Triggers**.
3. Click the green plus sign to create a new trigger.
4. When the box opens, select **WHEN-TIMER-EXPIRED**.

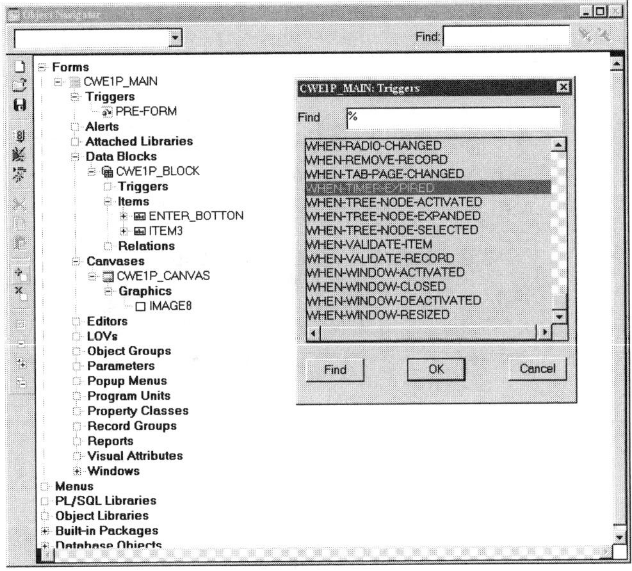

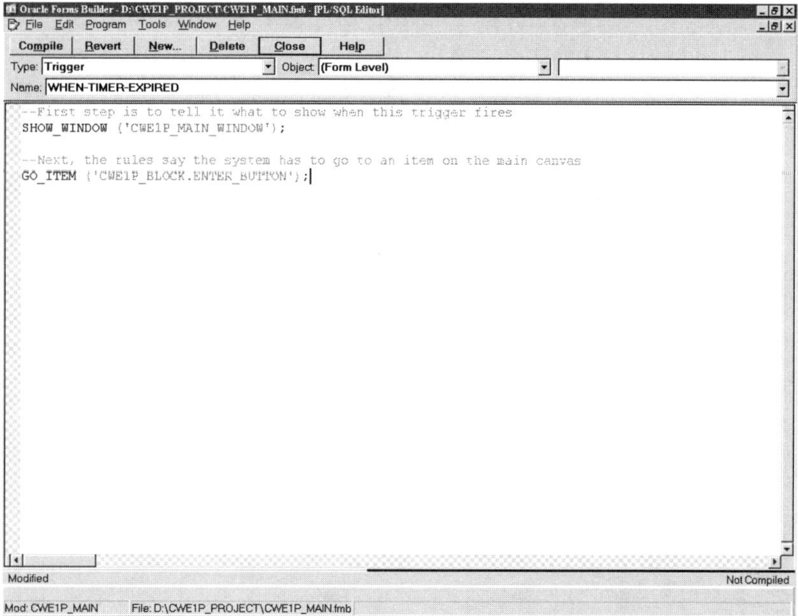

- Forms
  - CWE1P_MAIN
    - Triggers
      - PRE-FORM
      - WHEN-TIMER-EXPIRED
    - Alerts
    - Attached Libraries
    - Data Blocks
      - CWE1P_SPLASH_BLOCK
        - Triggers
        - Items
          - CWE1P_SPLASH_IMAGE
            - Triggers
          - CWE1P_SPLASH_ITEM
        - Relations
      - CWE1P_BLOCK
        - Triggers
        - Items
          - ENTER_BUTTON
          - EXIT_BUTTON
        - Relations
    - Canvases
      - CWE1P_SPLASH_CANVAS
        - Graphics
          - RECT34
      - CWE1P_CANVAS
        - Graphics
          - IMAGE8
    - Editors
    - LOVs
    - Object Groups
    - Parameters
    - Popup Menus
    - Program Units
    - Property Classes
    - Record Groups
    - Reports
    - Visual Attributes
    - Windows
      - CWE1P_SPLASH_WINDOW
      - CWE1P_WINDOW
- Menus
- PL/SQL Libraries
- Object Libraries
- Built-in Packages
- Database Objects

OK, you're saying, but how does Forms know which is the *first* form to display when the user starts the application? This is incredibly low-tech: *It's just the first one in the data block list*, so make sure your splash block is first! (To change the sequence, you can just drag and drop if necessary. But this is the only low-tech part of this process, so don't get too comfortable!)

Also make sure that all the subordinate items are where they belong. When working on very large systems, it's easy to get out of sync and create things in the wrong place, so double-check your work.

Let's test. The first time you compile, you'll probably get this message:

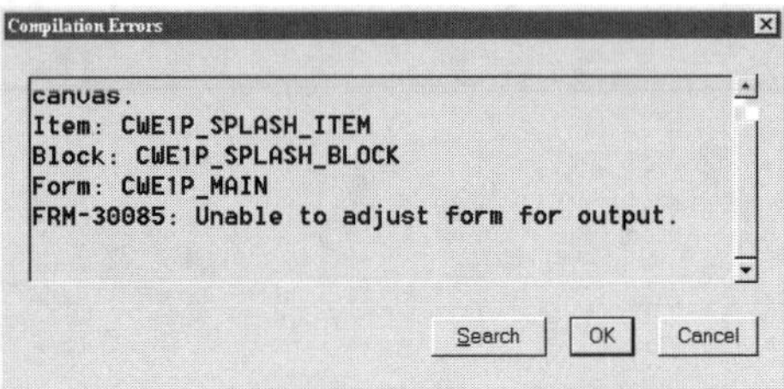

This usually means that when you placed the item on the canvas, it was outside the borders. Positioning can be tricky, so just go back to your splash canvas and move the item block or image block until you get it in the right place:

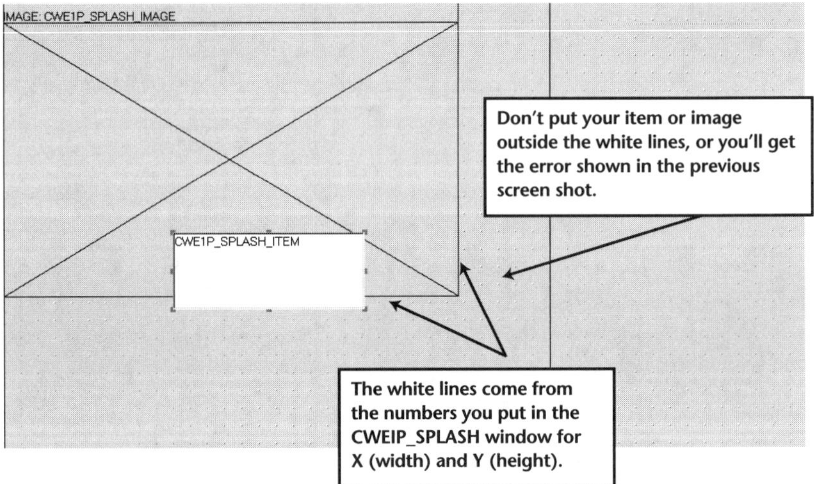

Now test your work: Select **Program | Run Form | Client/Server** and log on to any database:

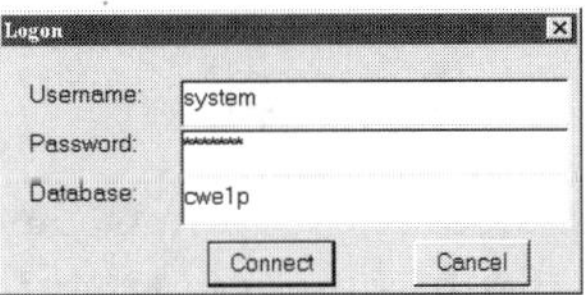

If everything is now working, your splash screen will appear, followed in five seconds by your main screen:

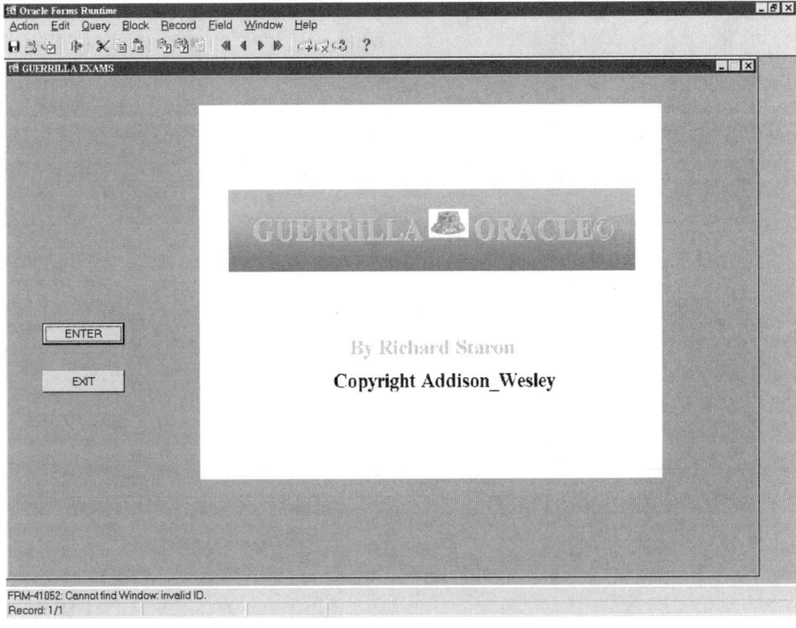

Since nothing is active yet, just click on the upper right X to get back to Object Navigator. Congratulations! Let's move on and make this thing come to life.

The Main Screen

So that we can add options like "Create exam," "Modify exam," "Run reports," and so forth sometime later, let's add another button: **Administration**. And while we're at it, let's change the **ENTER** button to **EXAMS**:

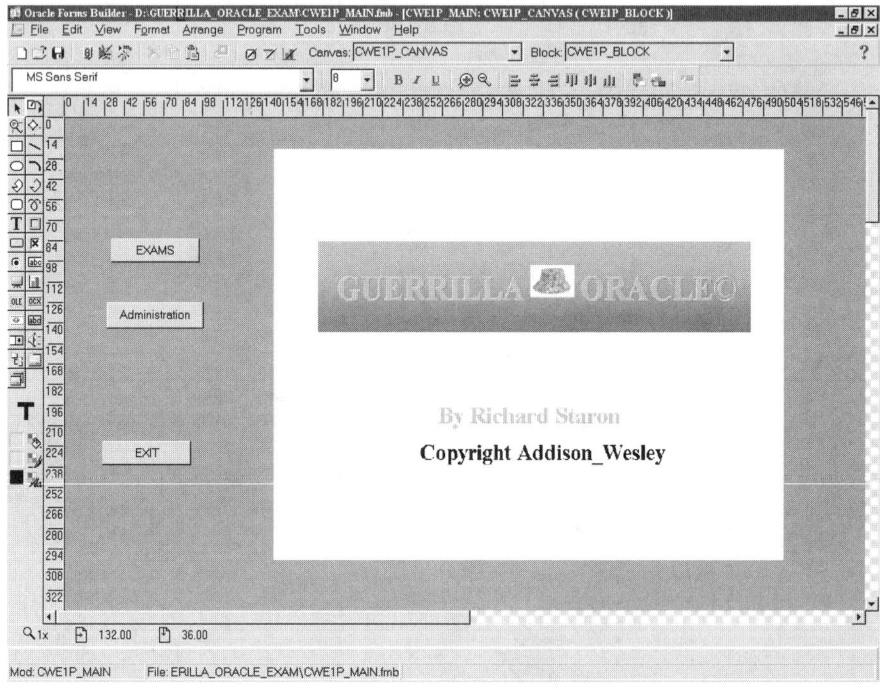

I know you'll want to run your creation from a shortcut. Here's how you do it: Create a shortcut, and then enter "D:\GUERRILLA_ORACLE\CWE1P_MAIN.fmx" in the **Target** field and "D:\GUERRILLA_ORACLE" in the **Start in** field:

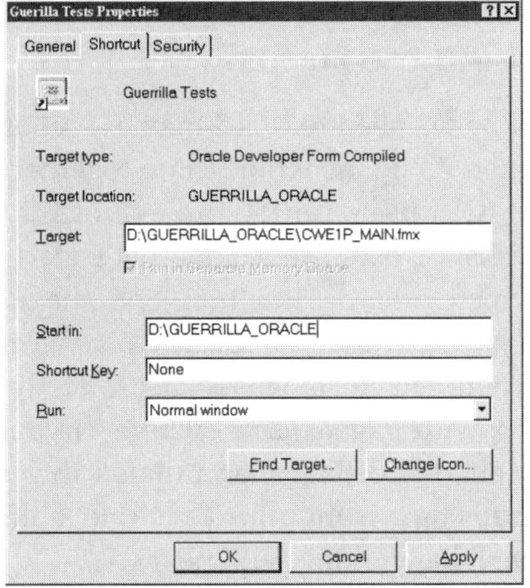

The icon probably won't work because your system does not have a program associated with `.fmx` files, so you'll have to make the connection.

You'll find the executable `(IFRUN60.EXE)` in the `ORACLE_HOME/ORANT/BIN` directory. Make the association (and *make it permanent*), and off you go!

Calling Forms from Forms

Now we'll learn how to call forms from forms. This is actually how systems are done: The user clicks on a button that triggers events that usually bring the user to another form.

We want our users to be able to do two things from the main form: exit or take a test. When a user clicks on the **EXAMS** button, the next screen has to be the user ID screen, where we check that the user is a valid user, and we prompt the user to select an exam. We also check whether the user has already taken that exam, and if so, prevent the user from going any further. If the user *can* take the exam, the next screen will be the warning that once the test has started, the user will be logged as having taken the exam, so this is the last chance to decide not to take the test.

If a user decides to take the test, the user record is updated and the exam questions are displayed. At the end the user hits the **FINISHED (Exit)** button, and the system calculates and displays the results, and then closes the test.

Using the Forms

Now we need to build the next set of forms and learn how to do some editing. Then I'll tie the whole thing together.

Our users can do three things from the main form: exit, do administrative tasks, or take the exams. Let's start with the sign-in screen for taking a test, which will be the first one the user will see after clicking on **EXAMS**. Remember that the forms we've worked with so far have been *data block forms*, where each form was related directly to one table. From here on, we'll be working with *unique forms*, where the data will be drawn from as many tables as needed and then manipulated through various SQL commands. A form that grabs data from more than one table is called a **control form**, and that's what we'll be working with next.

It's going to get interesting. I hope you realize by now that I'm taking you a step at a time into the rather intricate world of Forms. By now you have a good handle on using the wizard, and you should be comfortable with some of the basics of Object Navigator, so you're ready for another big step.

After deciding to take an exam, the user's next step is to choose a test. Here's what we're going to build next:

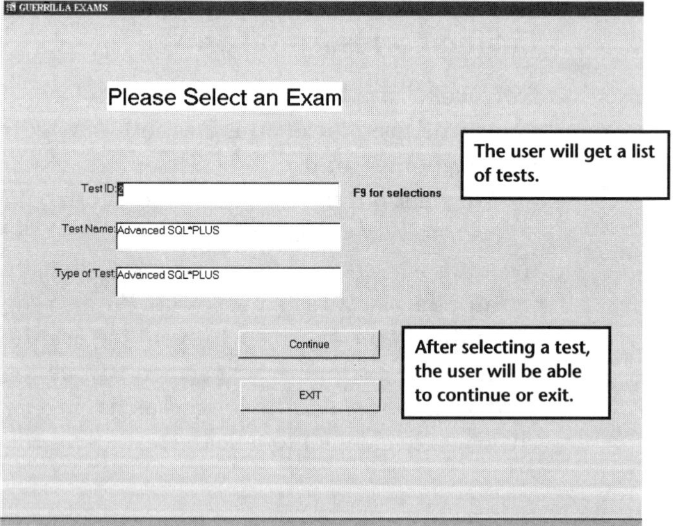

Hitting **F9** with the cursor in the **Test ID** box brings up a list of available tests, and the user can select one of them:

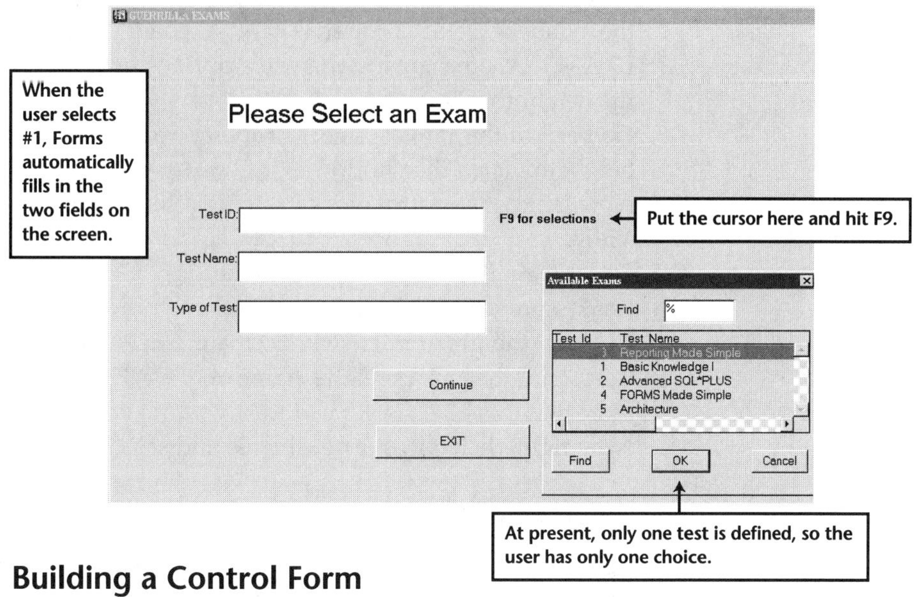

Building a Control Form

Note

Here is the overall sequence we'll follow to build a control form:

1. Build a new form.
2. Create the control block.
3. Have fun with Layout Editor!

To build a control form, start another Form Builder session. Next go through the following steps:

1. Click on **FILE | NEW | FORM** or highlight **FORM** and click on the green plus sign.
2. Rename the form from "MODULE1" to "CWE1P_SELECT_TEST".
3. Save the form in your `CWE1P_PROJECT` folder. You now have another `.fmb` record!
4. Click on **View**, and then **Visual View**.
5. Click on the plus sign next to **WINDOWS** to open the drop-down list. Now change the name of the default window to "CWE1P_SELECT_TEST_WINDOW".

6. Click on **CANVAS** and then the green plus sign to make a new canvas, and then rename it "CWE1P_SELECT_TEST_CANVAS".
7. Change the CWE1P_SELECT_TEST_WINDOWproperties: Right-click on the window, select **Property Palette**, change the name to "GUERRILLA EXAMS", the resize and max size options to "No", the width to 580, and the height to 375.
8. Go back to the canvas, select **Property Palette**, and change the width and height to match the window.
9. Now make the control block itself, by selecting **View** and then **Ownership View**.
10. Select **Data Blocks** under your new form: CWE1P_SELECT_TEST_FORM (make sure you're in the right form!).
11. Click on the green plus sign to create a new block, select the manual option, and then change the name to "CWE1P_SELECT_TEST_BLOCK". Note that this block is *not* tied to any particular table.
12. Now right-click on your new block, and select **Layout Editor**.

You should now be at this screen:

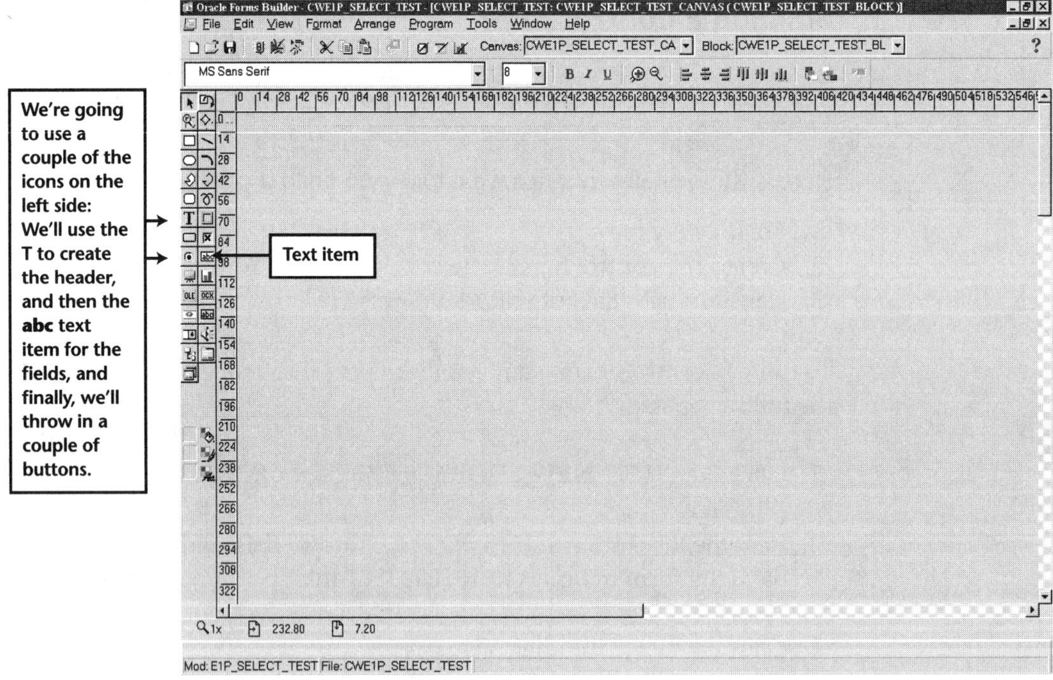

Building Screen Items

We're going to use some of the fantastic editing features to build the screen items, and then I'll show you how to create a list of values (LOV) so that the user can select the right exam.

Message Box

First select the giant **T**, and put the cursor somewhere at the top of the screen in the middle. You will see a small rectangular box. Change the font size to 18, and type in "Please Select an Exam". Your screen should look something like this:

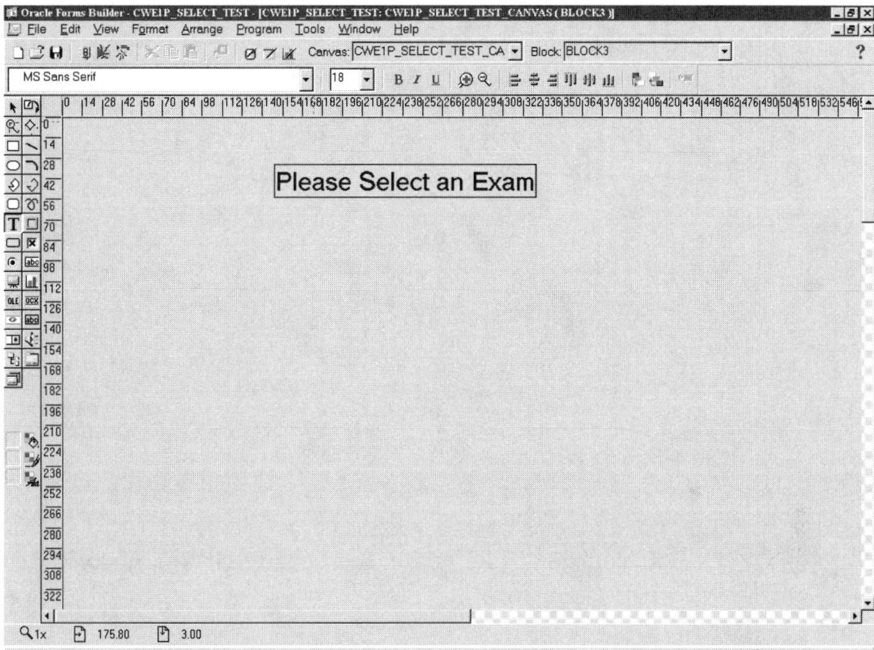

Now click on the text you have just typed in ("Please Select an Exam") until you see the black marks around it. Notice that at the very bottom of the tool palette on the left side of the screen are three colorful icons. If you put your cursor on them, the names **Fill Color** for the paint bucket, **Line Color** for the paintbrush, and **Text Color** for the "Aa" icon will appear. Right-click on the paint bucket, and change the color to white:

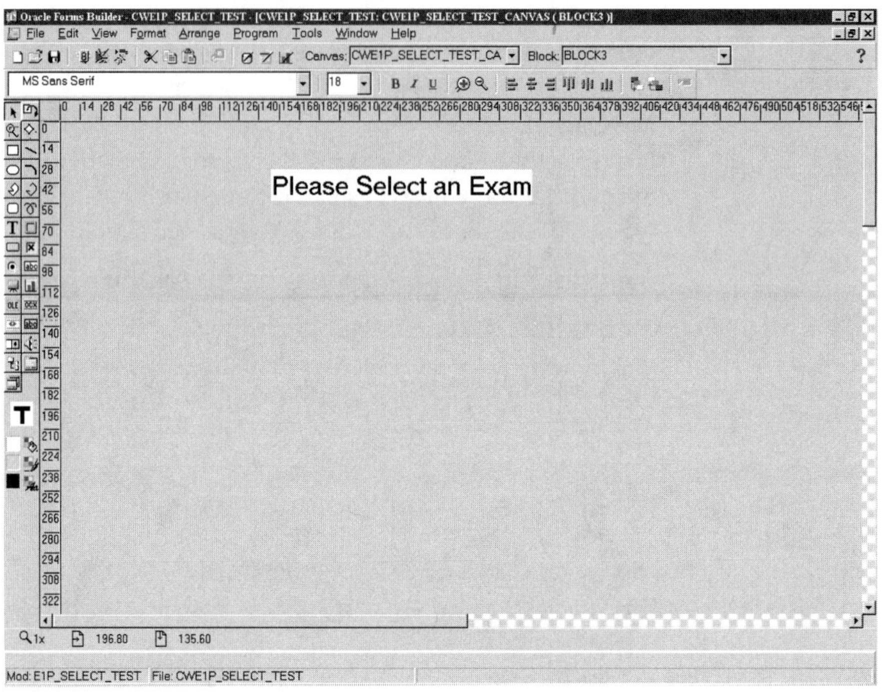

If you don't like white, then change it to any color that appeals to you. Just have some fun!

Data

Now we'll add the data fields. Change the font size back to 8, and then select the "abc" text item icon from the left side, and create three boxes. Then right-click on each box, select **Property Palette**, and make the following changes (you will have to scroll pretty far down to find the **Prompt** selection):

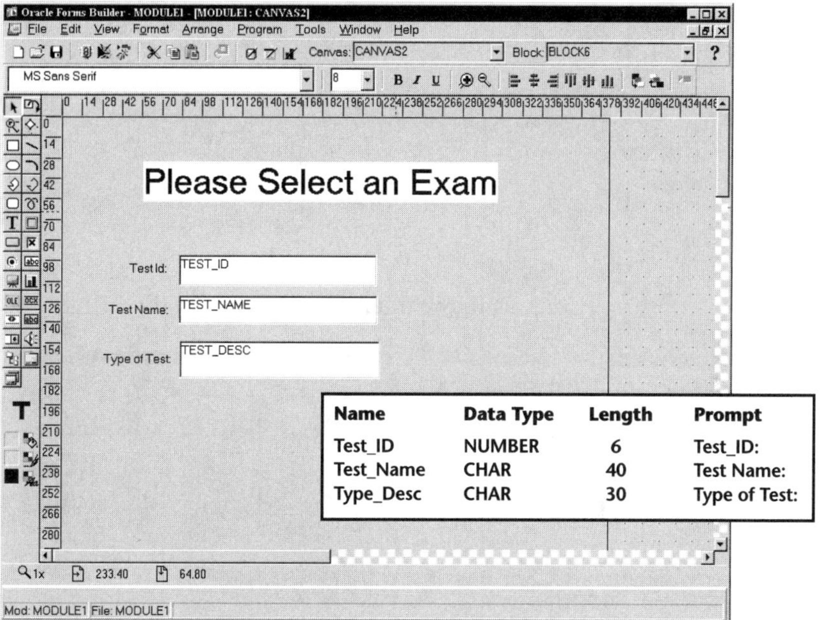

Name	Data Type	Length	Prompt
Test_ID	NUMBER	6	Test_ID:
Test_Name	CHAR	40	Test Name:
Type_Desc	CHAR	30	Type of Test:

What you have now done is tell Forms 6*i* that the boxes will be getting their data from fields from various tables. How do we get that data? First we'll let the system do it for us, by using a list of values. Then we'll return to the property palette for the three boxes we just created and we'll tell each box where to find its data.

To create a list of values (LOV), select **Tools | LOV Wizard**, and then **New Record Group based on a query**:

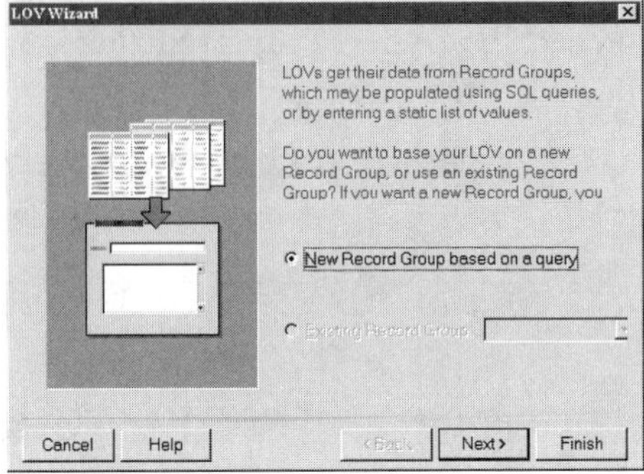

Connect to the database and type in the SQL query statement shown here:

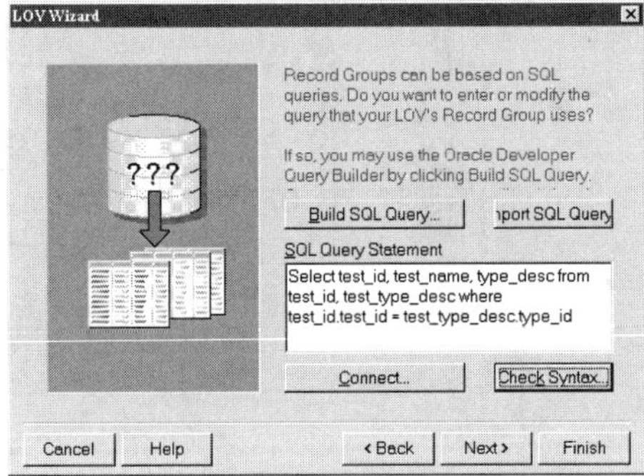

Click the **Check Syntax...** box, and you should see this message:

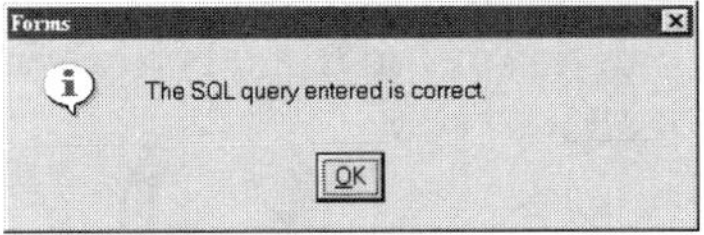

Click **OK**, select all three columns, and then fill in the **Return value** column:

1. Click on the first **Return value** box, for the column named Test_ID.
2. Click on the **Look up return item** box.

3. Select the correct column from the list (**CWE1P_SELECT_TEST_BLOCK. TEST_ID**), and it will pop into the **Return value** column.
4. Repeat steps 1 through 3 for the other two items (**TEST_NAME** and **TYPE_DESC**).

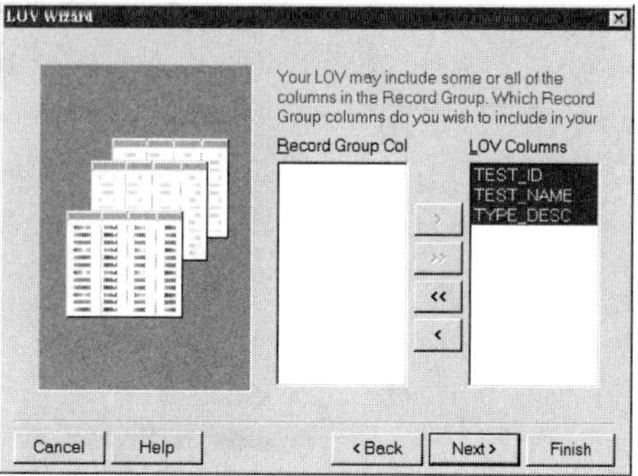

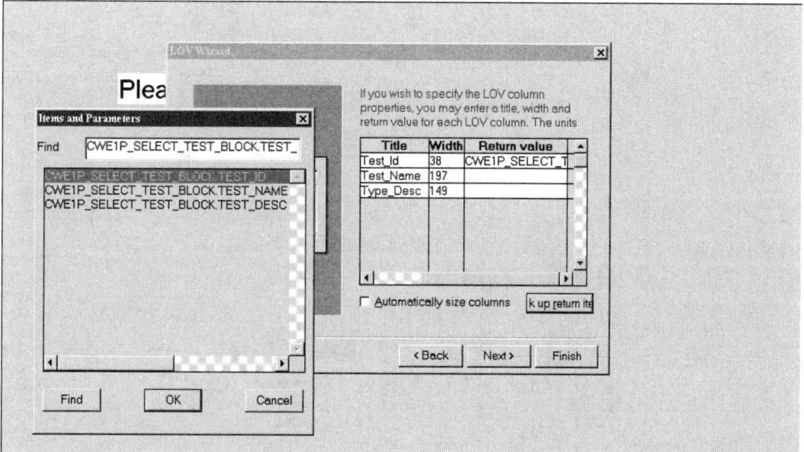

You have just told Forms 6*i* to return the data from these columns into these boxes on your new screen. Just make sure you match the fields, or the results will be confusing! Forms 6*i* *will* put the data where you tell it, so be careful.

Click **Next**, give your form the title "Available Tests", and then accept the 20-row default for retrieval of the data:

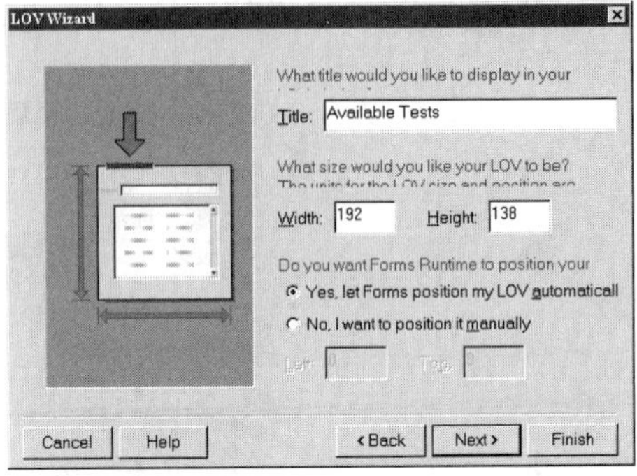

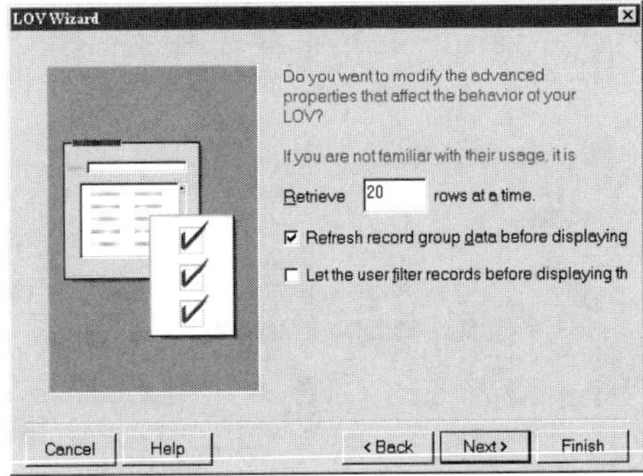

Lists of Values

Now we come to the LOV Wizard. It wants to know which item or items will have an LOV (list of values). Since we're going to give the test takers the ability to select a test, obviously we will want the list of values to be active for only the first selection, **TEST_ID**. So select only the **TEST_ID** column, and click **Finish**:

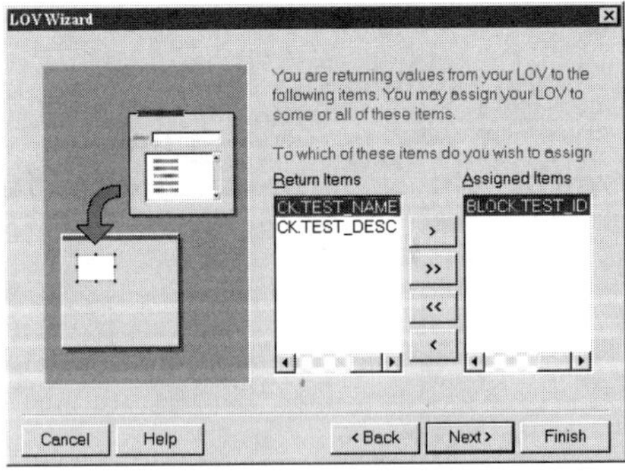

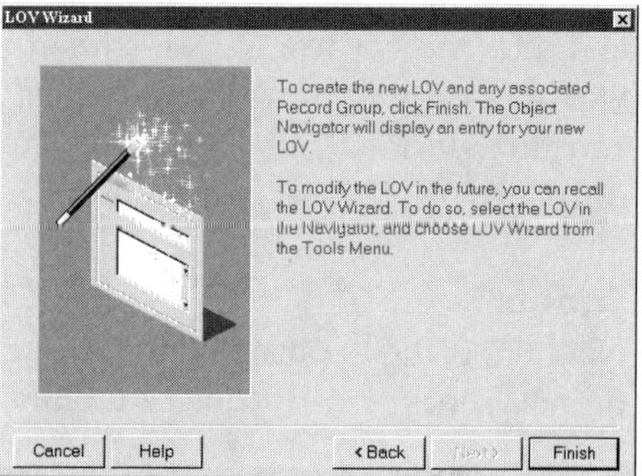

Now for the big test: running your new form. To do this, as you probably know by now, just select **Program | Run Forms | Client/Server**. And this is what you should see after you put the cursor in the **Test ID** box and hit **F9**:

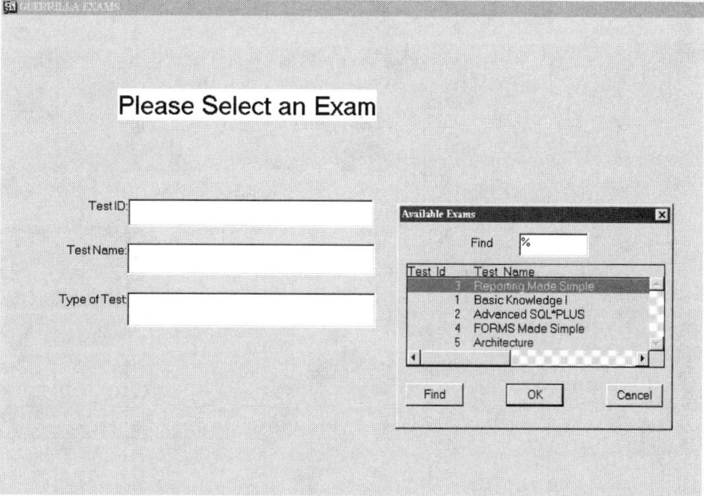

Now go have some fun. Return to Layout Editor. Right-click anywhere on your screen except in a text box, select **Property Palette**, and change the colors to anything you like. Do the same with the boxes: Go into the property palette and change some of the attributes to see what happens. Add a couple of buttons—**Continue**, **EXIT**, whatever you feel like. Just remember to periodically save your work. As you experiment, you will see how easy it is to correct mistakes. If you do end up with several conflicting lists of values, go to Object Navigator and delete them. Then just make a new LOV!

Congratulations! You have built another form. If you want, go back to SQL and add another test or two so that you can see that the list of values really works. Or if you're really ambitious, and we encourage this—create a quick and dirty form to enter new tests. You can probably make such a quick and dirty form in a matter of minutes now.

Triggers

Now I'm going to push you to take a rather big step. What I will have you do in the next series of instructions is modify what you've done so that it looks like this:

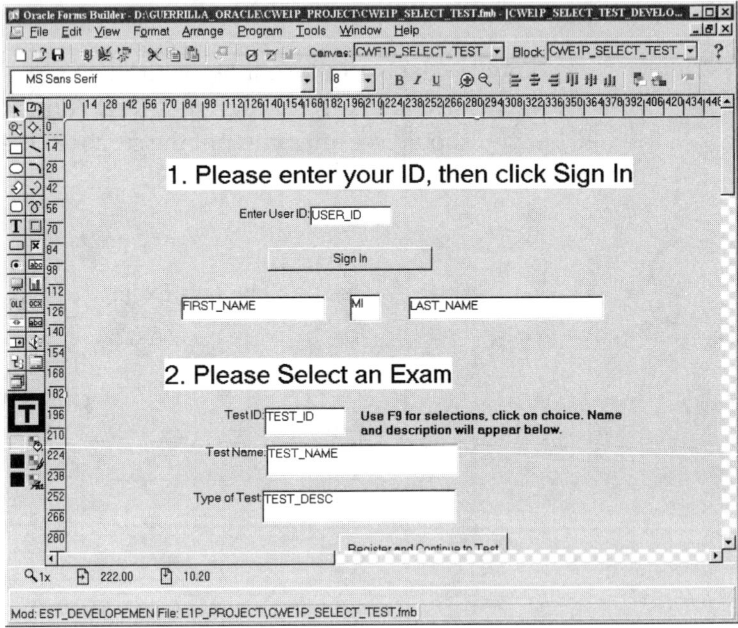

All we're going to do is add a few more fields at the top, add what's called a **trigger function**, and move the items around a bit. It's not as hard as it seems! The purpose is to check for a valid ID before letting someone register for a test. In other words, if you are not in the database, you cannot take an exam, and you will get an error (shown in the lower-left corner) if your ID is not valid. Here are the steps:

1. Move the existing items to the bottom of the screen to make space at the top. Then add a couple of new items at the top:
2. Create four new text items, for user ID, first name, middle initial, and last name; a text field that says, "1. Please enter your ID, then click Sign In"; and a new button labeled **Sign In**. You should know how to do this.
3. Arrange the parts into a symmetrical, eye-pleasing layout.
4. Make the necessary changes to the property palette for each of the items:

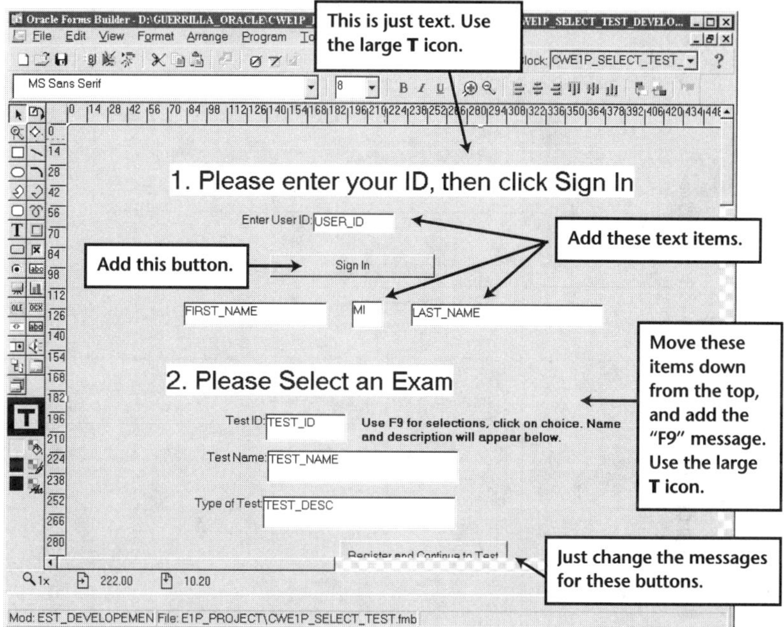

Item	Name	Size	Prompt
User_ID	User_ID	9, NUMBER	Enter your user ID:
First_Name	First_Name	15, CHAR	*no prompt*
MI	MI	1, CHAR	*no prompt*
Last_Name	Last_Name	20, CHAR	*no prompt*

For example, here's the property palette for User_ID:

General	
Name	USER_ID
Item Type	Text Item
Subclass Information	
Comments	
Help Book Topic	
Functional	
Enabled	Yes
Justification	Start
Implementation Class	
Multi-Line	No
Wrap Style	Word
Case Restriction	Mixed
Conceal Data	No
Keep Cursor Position	No
Automatic Skip	No
Popup Menu	<Null>
Navigation	
Keyboard Navigable	Yes
Previous Navigation Item	<Null>
Next Navigation Item	<Null>
Data	
Data Type	Char
Maximum Length	30
Fixed Length	No
Initial Value	

Name: USER_ID

Data	
Data Type	Number
Maximum Length	9
Fixed Length	No
Initial Value	
Required	No
Format Mask	
Lowest Allowed Value	
Highest Allowed Value	
Copy Value from Item	
Synchronize with Item	<Null>
Calculation	
Calculation Mode	None
Formula	
Summary Function	None
Summarized Block	<Null>
Summarized Item	<Null>
Records	
Current Record Visual Attribute Group	<Null>
Distance Between Records	0
Number of Items Displayed	0
Database	
Database Item	Yes
Column Name	
Primary Key	No
Query Only	No

Data type = number, maximum length = 9

Font Spacing	Normal
Prompt	
Prompt	Enter User ID:
Prompt Display Style	First Record
Prompt Justification	Start
Prompt Attachment Edge	Start
Prompt Alignment	Start
Prompt Attachment Offset	0
Prompt Alignment Offset	0
Prompt Reading Order	Default
Prompt Color	
Prompt Foreground Color	black
Prompt Font	
Prompt Font Name	MS Sans Serif
Prompt Font Size	8
Prompt Font Weight	Demilight
Prompt Font Style	Plain
Prompt Font Spacing	Normal
Help	
Hint	
Display Hint Automatically	No
Tooltip	
Tooltip Visual Attribute Group	<Null>
International	
Initial Keyboard State	Default

Prompt = Enter User ID:

Now that you have added the text items, have changed the label names in **Property Palette**, and have played around with sizes and positions, you are ready to take action. Just right-click on the **Sign In** button, select **SmartTriggers | WHEN-BUTTON-PRESSED**, and enter this code:

❶ **Important:** The names you use here have to match the names you put into the property palette for each item. For example, we called the middle-initial box "MI" in the property palette.

❷ A colon is needed in front of the block name.

```
select f_name, M_I, L_Name
into :cwe1p_select_test_block.first_name,
 :cwe1p_select_test_block.MI, ❶
 :cwe1p_select_test_block.last_name

 from students
 where students.student_id = :cwe1p_select_test_block.user_id; ❷
```

You also have to go back to Object Navigator and change the name of the button you just created. Just click on it and change it to "Sign_In":

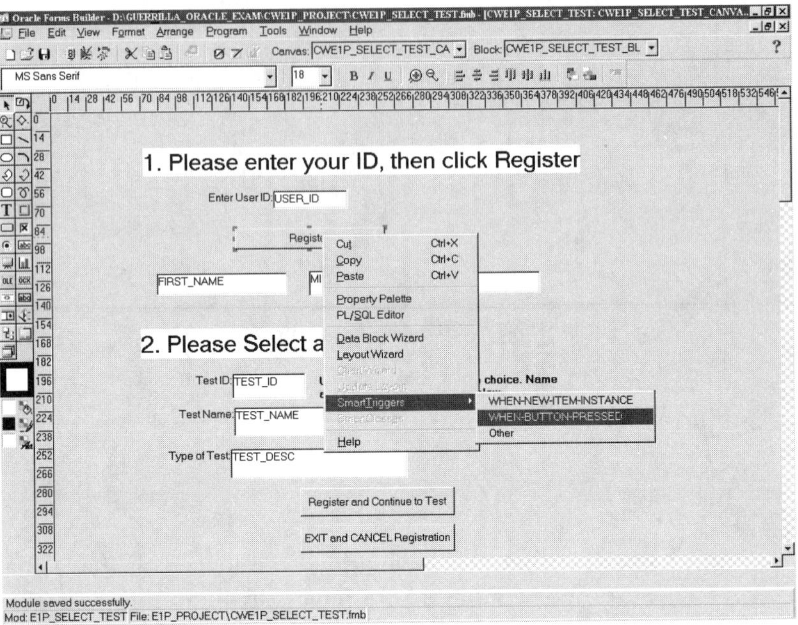

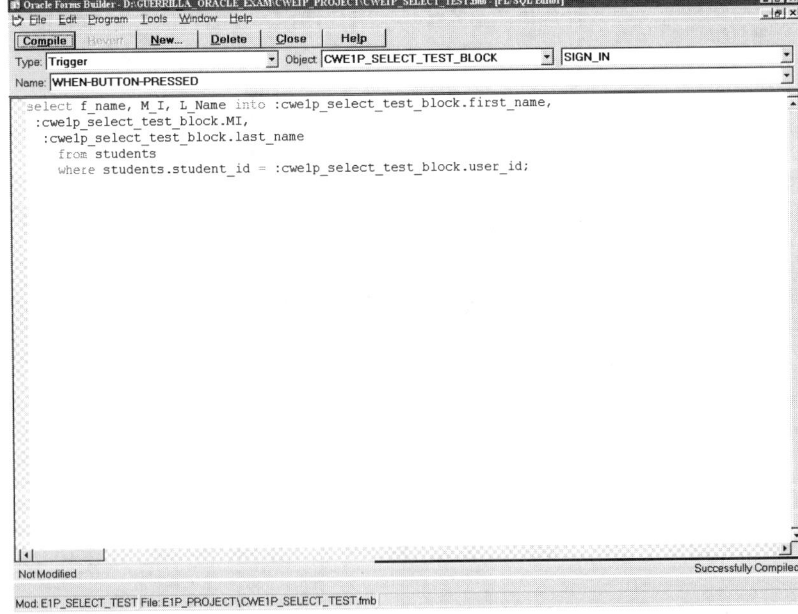

This is the type of error you get when your names do not match what you put into the property palette:

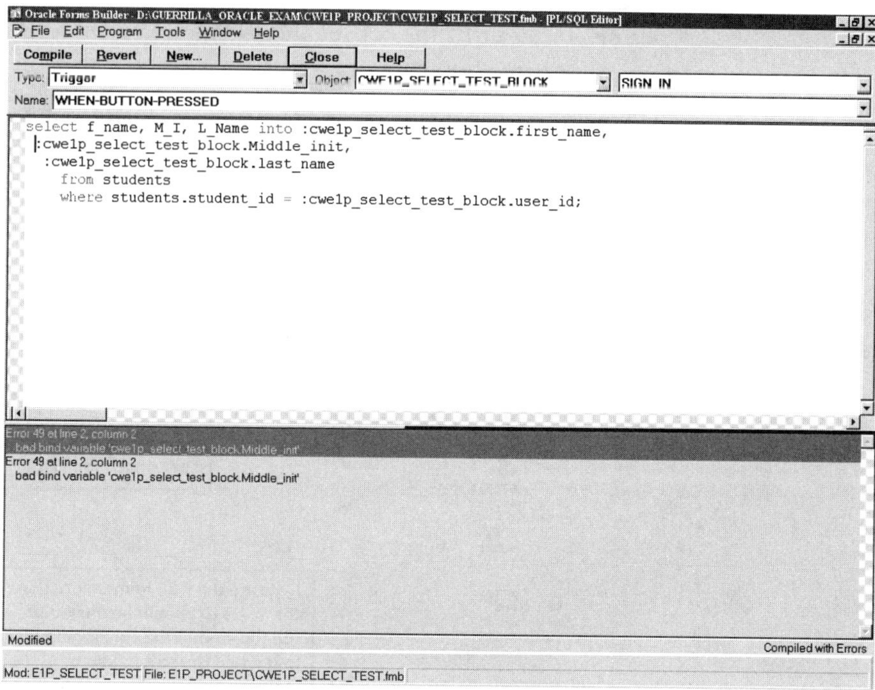

When you're done, click on **Compile**, clean up any errors (you will have spelling errors), and then hit **CLOSE**. OK, you're probably asking, where did these funny names come from?

If you go back to your friend Object Navigator, you will see your data block and the names of the items that you just created. Your names may be different from what is shown, but that's OK. Note that you should move the **USER_ID** item to the top of the items list so that the cursor defaults there when the screen opens:

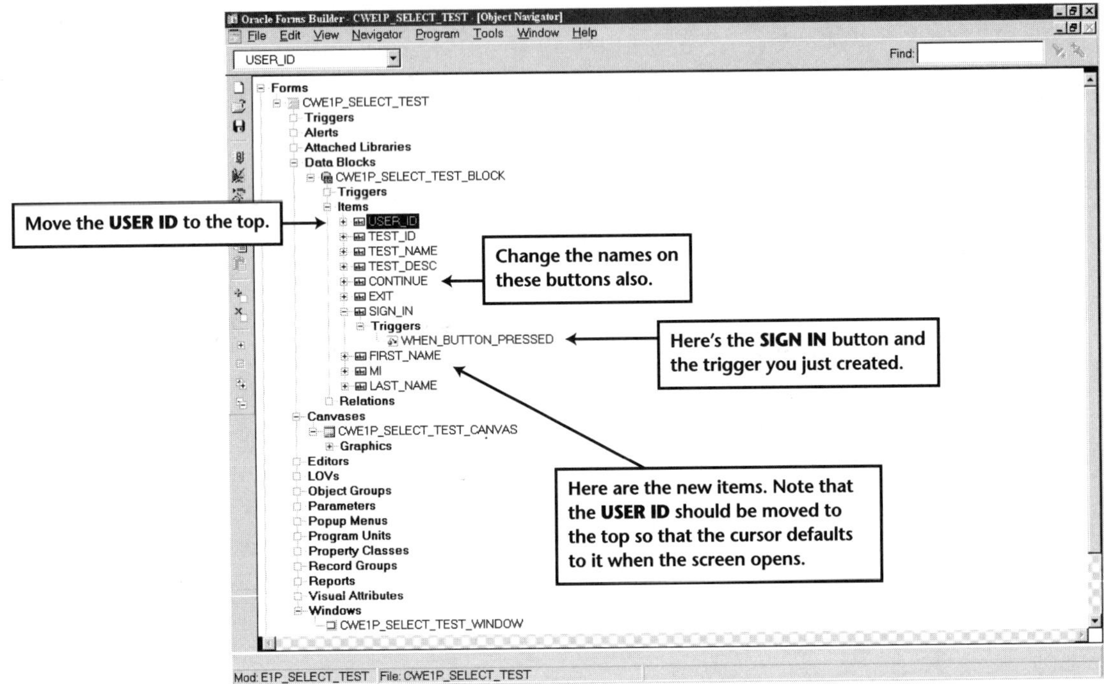

Note

Working with Forms is *complex* but very rewarding! Just stick with it, and you'll get it eventually. As I've said already, you will have many, many errors, most of the time as a result of syntax problems. Be patient.

I'm trying to give you some experience with the major parts of Forms in this chapter, and you're about halfway there. Don't give up!

Let's move on and finish this screen. The next step is to test, so select **Program | Compile | Client/Server**. Now enter an ID, hit the **Sign In** button, and see what happens. If the ID is not nine digits long, you should get an error message in the lower left-hand corner telling you that the field is not completely filled. If the ID is not valid, you should see an error referring to an "unhandled exception," followed by an "ORA-xxx" error message:

Oracle Forms Runtime
Action Edit Query Block Record Field Window Help
GUERRILLA EXAMS

1. Please enter your ID, then click Sign In

Enter User ID: 123456

Sign In

2. Please Select an Exam

Test ID: Use F9 for selections, click on choice. Name and description will appear below.

Test Name:

Type of Test:

Register and Continue to Test

EXIT and CANCEL Registration

FRM-40203: Field must be entered completely.
Record: 1/1

Oracle Forms Runtime
Action Edit Query Block Record Field Window Help
GUERRILLA EXAMS

1. Please enter your ID, then click Sign In

Enter User ID: 423123456

Sign In

2. Please Select an Exam

Test ID: Use F9 for selections, click on choice. Name and description will appear below.

Test Name:

Type of Test:

Register and Continue to Test

EXIT and CANCEL Registration

FRM-40735: WHEN-BUTTON-PRESSED trigger raised unhandled exception ORA-01403.
Record: 1/1

Note

You're right—our original design had the students create their own record. However, the specs have changed, and the director now wants only those already in the database to be able to take the test. Good eyes for those who caught this change! This is how the real world operates.

OK, I tricked you a bit. Now you have to go back to SQL*Plus and enter a couple of valid users, some tests, questions, and so forth. This should be easy for you now. If it isn't, check the CD for scripts on building and loading the tables. I do not give you a script to load users; I figure that's where you can be really creative and add your friends and others. You have to have a valid user in your database for the sign-in to work properly.

When it does work, you'll see the user name. Then the user will go to the **Test ID** field, hit **F9**, select the test from the drop-down list, and decide whether to continue. Here's what it looks like when all the parts are working:

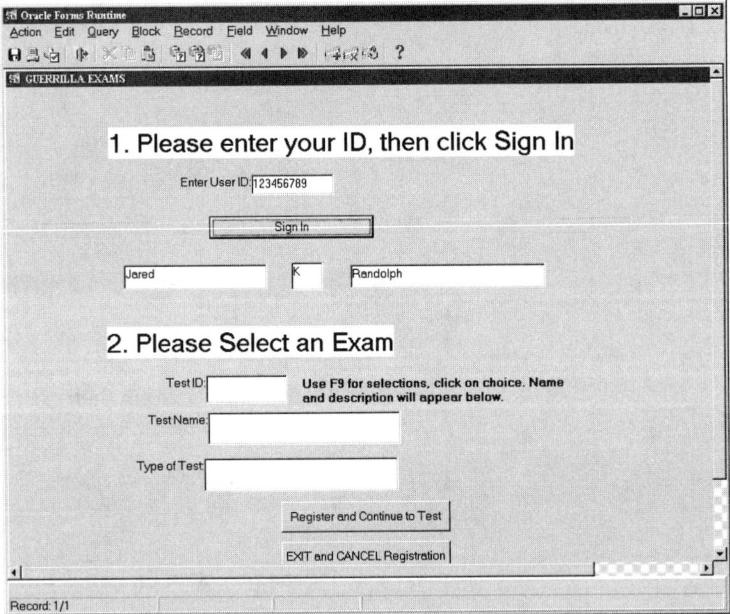

All we have left is to program the two buttons: **Register and Continue to Test** and **EXIT and CANCEL Registration**.

For registration we want to add a record that this person started this test. To exit, we just want to end the program because so far nothing has been written to the student's record. So again, we use smart triggers. Exit is easy, but the "continue" screen needs somewhere to go, and right now we don't have another screen. We will in a couple of minutes though. So let's wrap up the **EXIT** button. Go back to Layout Editor, right-click on the **EXIT** button, select **SmartTriggers | WHEN_BUTTON_PRESSED**, and type "EXIT_FORM;" (note the semicolon!):

Compile, hit **Close**, then test. Click on the **EXIT** button, and the form should simply close. Now to the more complicated part.

Don't forget to save your work!

Handling Errors

At this point, you're probably wondering what we're going to do about error messages. For our purposes, we're going to let Forms display them in the lower left corner. You can go to the Oracle error manual pages (all 2,000 of them!) to look up the "ORA-xxx" errors, and use Forms help for Forms ("FRM-xxx") errors. Although there is more than enough horsepower in Forms to build in error-handling code, I am not going to cover that in this book. It is somewhat complex, even more complicated than what we've covered so far!

But you're right. A fully functioning system has to trap errors and produce clear messages, and I advise you at some future time to obtain some of the Forms 6*i* reference manuals on the market and work with the PL/SQL code and logic to handle errors. For now, let's get moving.

Creating the Test Form

We have only a couple more things to do. We're going to add another canvas because we're out of room on this one. The new canvas will be for the actual test—yes, we've finally gotten that far! The last step will be to change some of the toolbars and what you see at the top of the screen.

Note

In creating the "take test" canvas, you're going to learn about master–detail relationships, one of the neatest features in Forms 6*i*. What this means is that you will have a master table in a data block, and on the same canvas will be a detail block that is linked to the master. We're going to use this relationship to tie the questions and answers together. Each question has four possible answers, so the question is the master, and the answers are the details.

Make sure you're in your SELECT_TEST form. If not, open it. Then do the following steps:

1. Create the canvas: Go to Object Navigator, highlight **Canvases**, and then click on the green plus sign to create a new canvas. Then change the name to "CWE1P_TAKE_TEST_CANVAS":

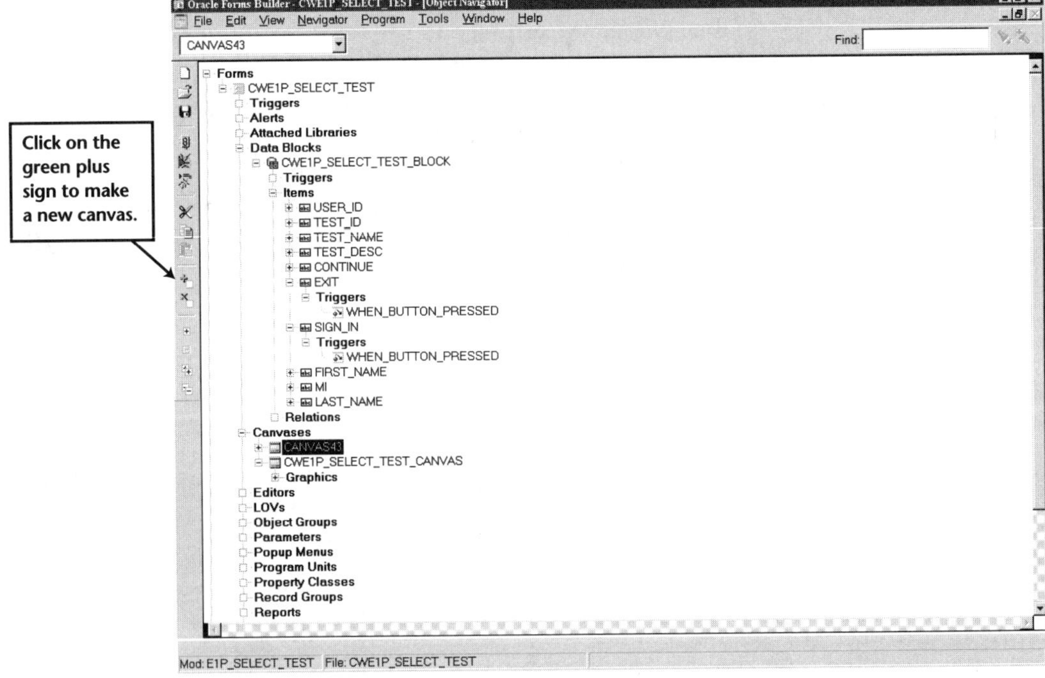

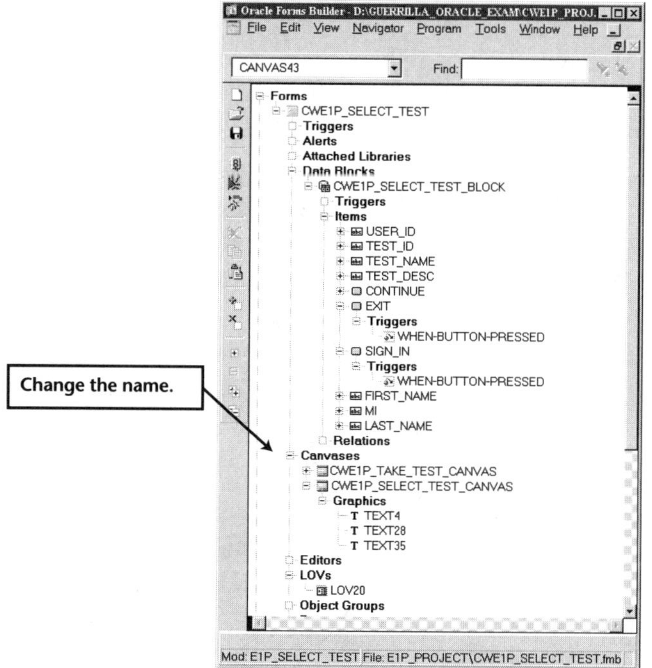

Tip

The order of the canvases doesn't make any difference. Data blocks, however, are displayed in the order they appear in Object Navigator.

---

2. Left-click on the new canvas to get into Layout Editor. Make sure that at the top, in the canvas display, it says "CWE1P_TAKE_TEST_CANVAS". If it doesn't, change to the correct canvas, or else you're in for a big, nasty surprise in a couple of minutes!

Here's what we're going to build: a screen where the user selects a question at the top, the possible answers automatically display at the bottom, and the user clicks on an answer choice and then hits **SAVE My Answer!** When done, the user just clicks the **FINISHED (Exit)** button to exit the form:

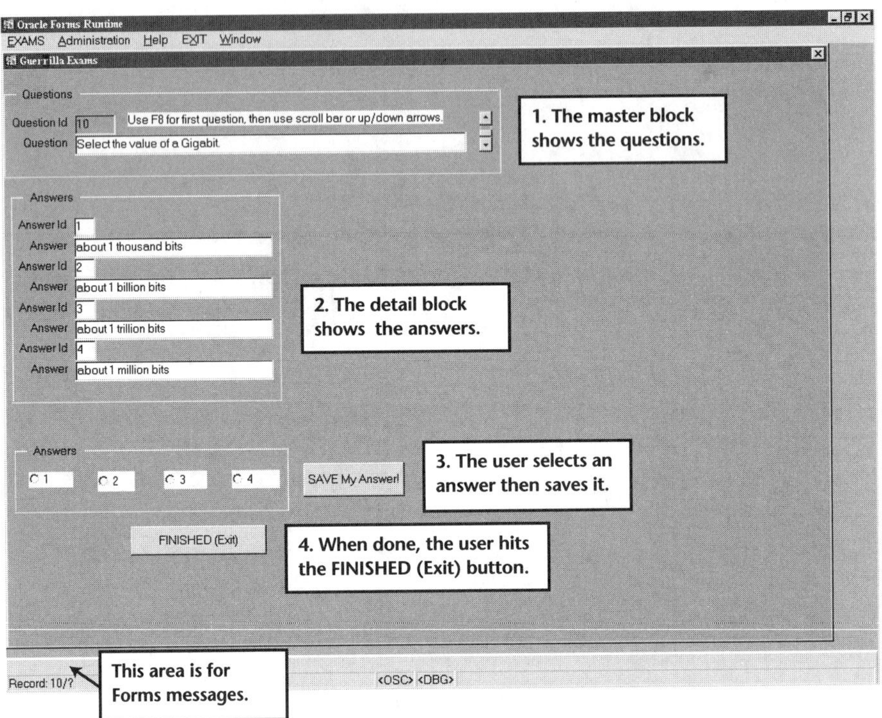

You can see that there are four main parts, plus the artistic efforts to add colors and graphics if desired:

1. Create the master block and the **F8** query function.
2. Create the detail block and link it to the master block.
3. Create the four radio buttons so that the user can make a selection.
4. Create the "FINISHED" button, which is really a glorified exit button. (All you have to do is put the ending time into the file for this user for this test.)

The Master Block

You're in Layout Editor, right? Select **Tools | Data Block Wizard**, skip the welcome screen, and select **Table or View**:

Save your work!

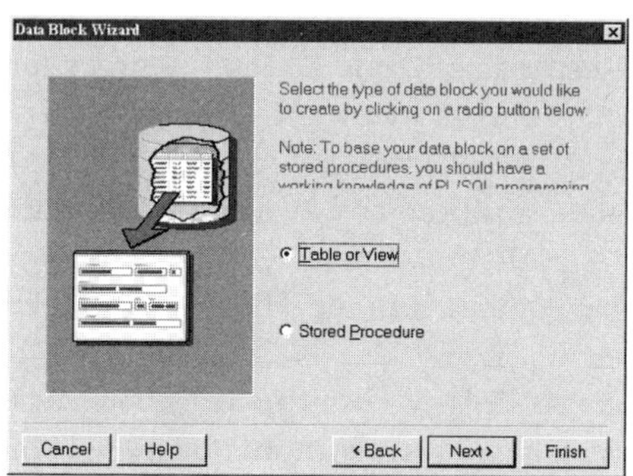

Now I'm going to stop you in your tracks. Because these tables are for display only, and because we want to keep things simple, you now have to go to SQL*Plus and create two views: one for questions and one for answers. You see, we're *not* going to update either the QUESTIONS or the ANSWERS table here, so let's make two views out of tests, questions, and answers and come up with columns that link the two together. Then, create a public synonym for the view—use the same name. The syntax is as follows:

```
CREATE OR REPLACE VIEW VQUESTIONS2

  as select question_id, question, test_id from questions,
        test_id, test_questions_link
  where test_id = link_test_id and
  question_id = link_question_id;

Create public synonym vquestions2 for vquestions;
Synonym created

View created.
```

Now add values to the TEST_QUESTIONS_LINK table. This is the table, remember, that ties the tests and questions together:

❶ The three values represent test number, question number, and weight.

```
SQL> insert into test_questions_link values (
  1,1,1); ❶

1 row created.
```

Keep going to add all ten questions for Test 1. Of course, you can add as many questions as you want, as long as you have these in your QUESTIONS table. (If you have already loaded more than one test in the TEST_ID table and feel very creative, go ahead and load additional values to the TEST_QUESTIONS_LINK table.)

Note that if you try to add the same record twice, or a record that does not have a match in the TEST_ID and QUESTIONS tables, you will get constraint errors. Remember these? These are the primary key and referential integrity constraints we built in way back when. Obviously it would be a disaster if there were tests without questions! For example, you get an error if you enter:

❷ Duplicate key error.

```
SQL> run
  1* insert into test_questions_link values (1,8,1)
insert into test_questions_link values (1,8,1)
*
ERROR at line 1:                                     ❷
ORA-00001: unique constraint (SYSTEM.SYS_C002978) violated
```

And if you try to add a record in which the question number is greater than what's in the QUESTIONS table, you will get another error:

❸ Referential integrity violated! Record not in QUESTIONS table!

```
SQL> run
  1* insert into test_questions_link values (1,8,1)
insert into test_questions_link values (1,8,1)
*
ERROR at line 1:                                     ❸
ORA-00001: unique constraint (SYSTEM.SYS_C002978) violated
```

Once you're done, go back to the Data Block Wizard and just follow the instructions on the screen.

Select the view you just created, **VQUESTIONS2**, and the two items (**QUESTION_ID** and **QUESTION**), hit **Next**, and uncheck the **Auto-join data blocks** box:

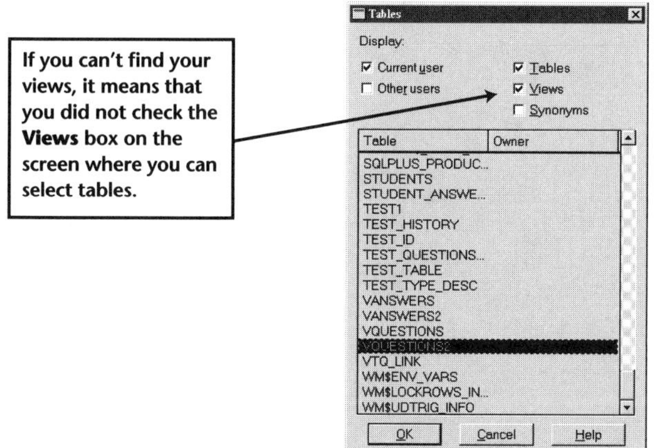

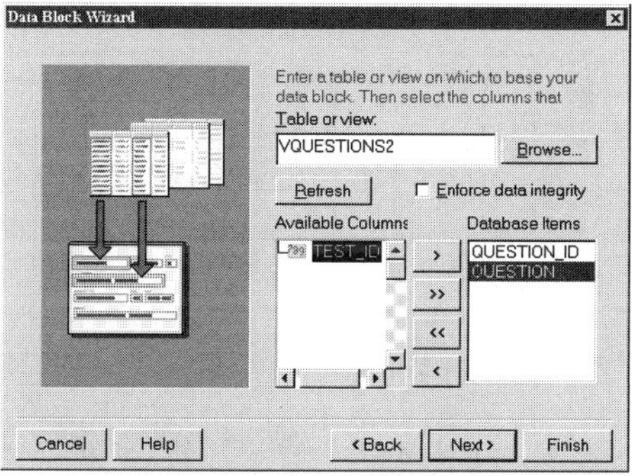

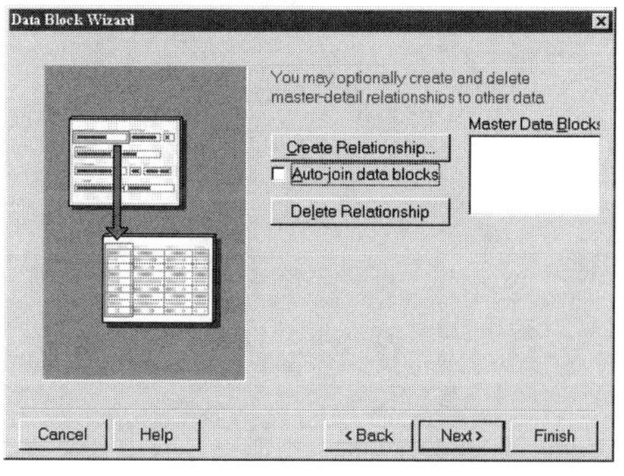

Go to the Layout Wizard by selecting **Create the data block, then call the Layout Wizard**; skip the welcome screen; and then make sure you select the test canvas. This is very important!

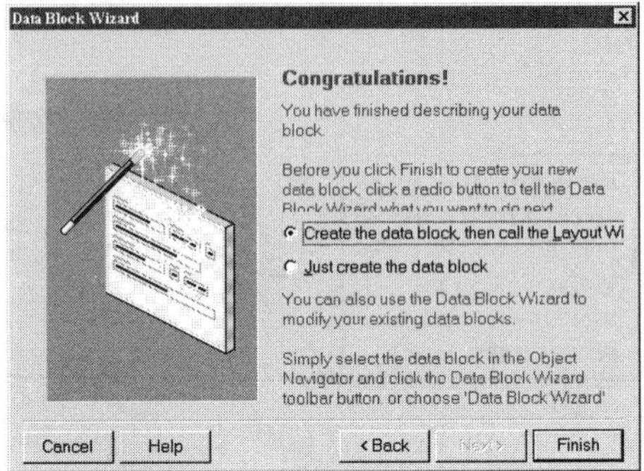

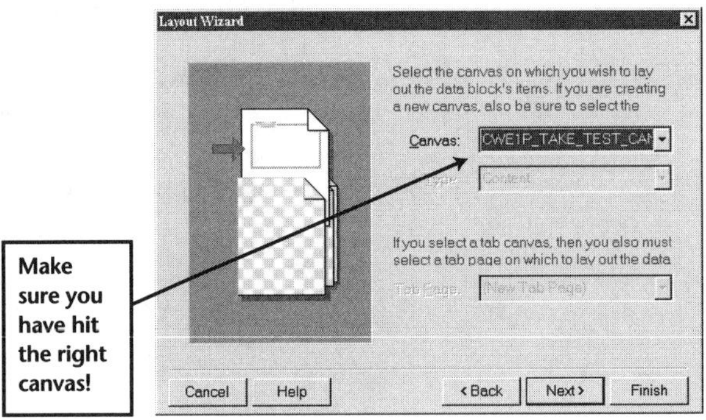

On the next two screens, select both items and accept the default sizes:

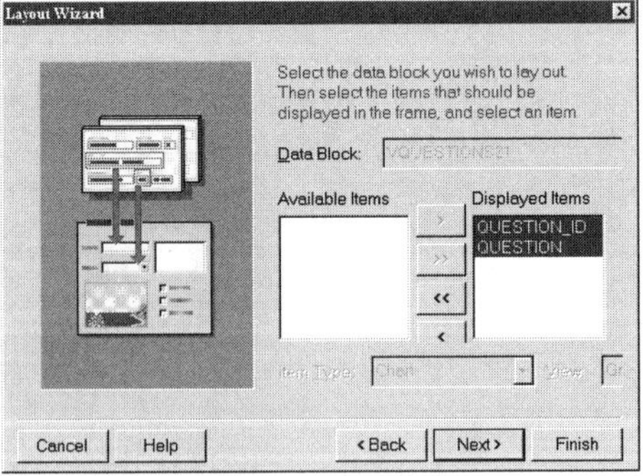

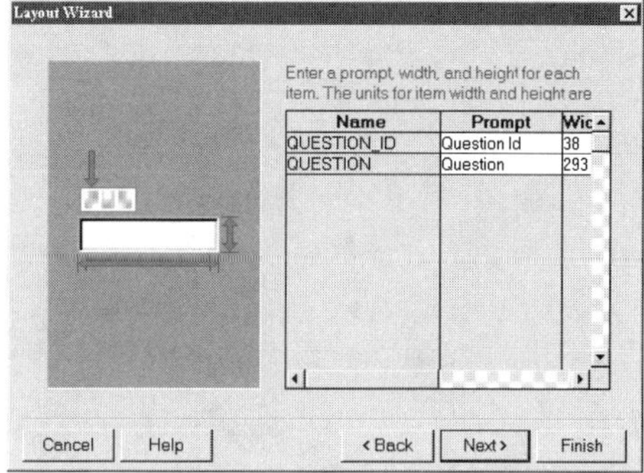

Then select **Form**, give it the title "QUESTIONS" and one record to display, click on **Display Scrollbar**, then accept the congratulations, and hit **Finish**:

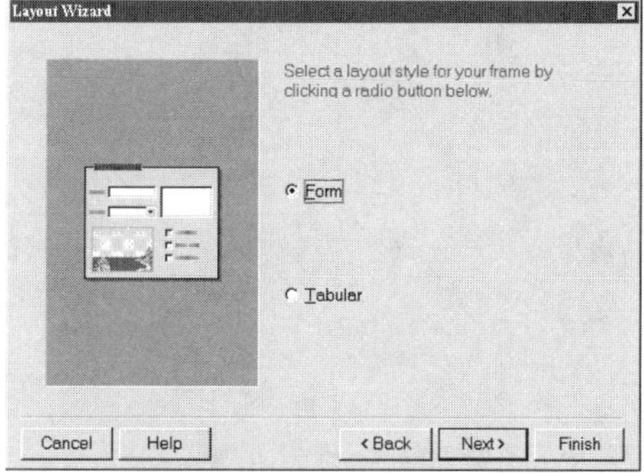

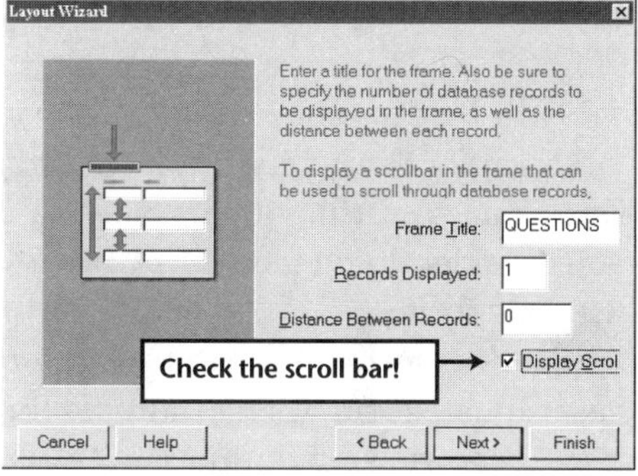

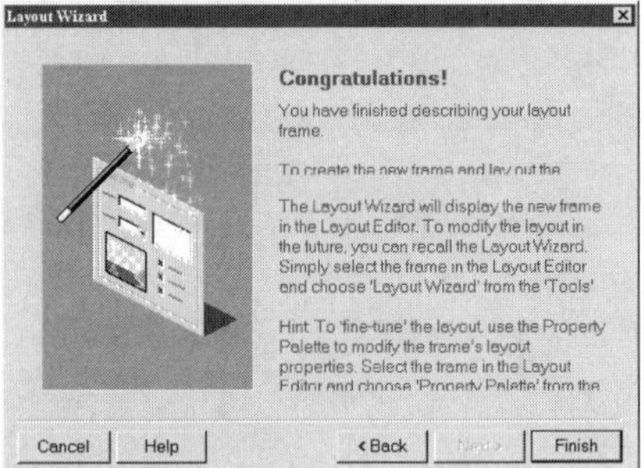

Your new canvas now looks like this:

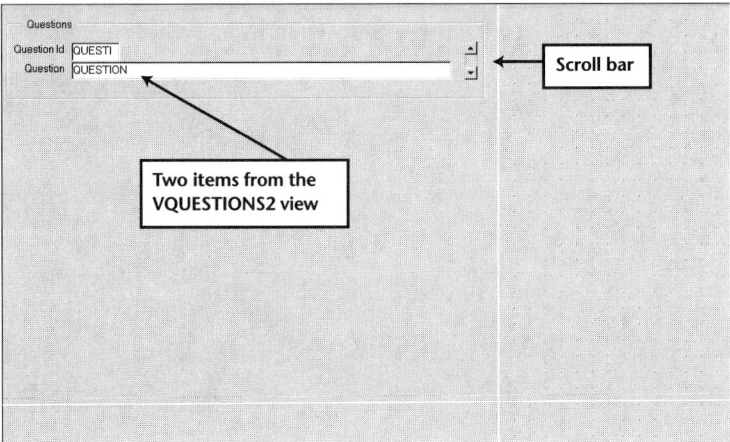

I'm sure that now you want to test, but first you have to go back to the SELECT_TEST canvas and activate the last button.

Now here's something to consider. When I work with forms, I create a new test form for every screen. This way I can test my logic, layout, block relationships, and so forth without blowing up the working form. I recommend that you consider doing the same. Once you have things working, just redo them in the main form.

Another technique is to use multiple forms instead of having multiple canvases in one form. Using multiple forms is great when you have several programmers working on the same system. It's also excellent when a particular application lends itself to being divided into several major parts. But that's advanced Forms 6*i*; I just want to get you started and enthused!

Here's another editing hint. When you create data block items on a canvas, you usually want to move them around a bit. That's fine, until you actually resize the entire block by pulling on one of the corners. Then the items will jump back to their original places. To prevent this, click on the block's outline, then on **Property Palette**, and change **Update Layout** to "Manually":

Save your work!

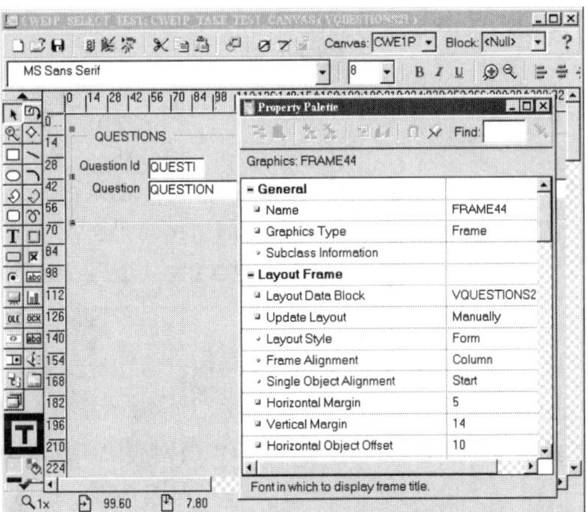

If you go into Object Navigator, your form should look like this:

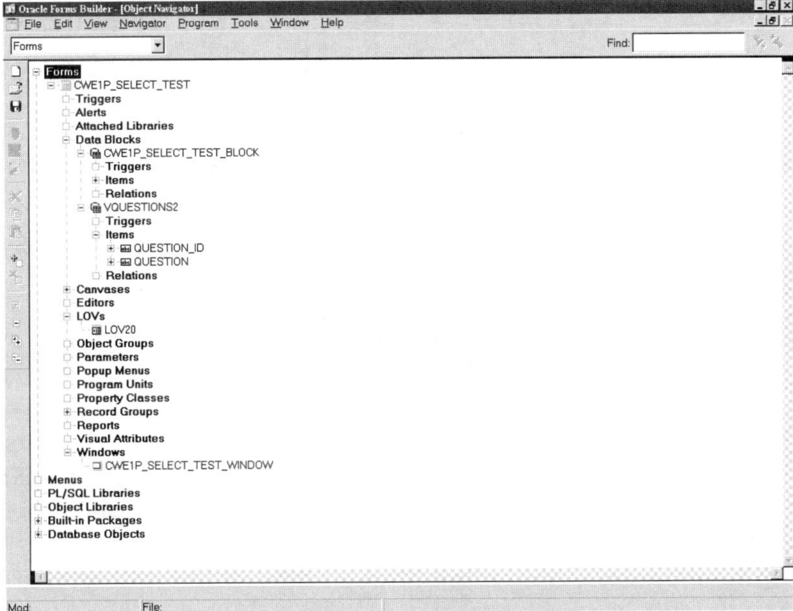

Go back to the SELECT_TEST canvas in Layout Editor. It's easy: At the top of the screen, the block (and canvas) that you're in is shown. Just use the down arrow next to the Canvas box to get a list, click on **SELECT_TEST**, and you'll go right back to that canvas.

Now right-click on the **Continue** button, select **SmartTriggers | WHEN-BUTTON-PRESSED**, and type "GO_ITEM ('vquestions2.question_id');". Compile, then close and test.

Tip

If you get an error like "Error 357 at . . . Table, View" or "Sequence reference 'vquestions2.question_id' not allowed in this context", most likely you did not put the single quotes around the vquestions2.question_id command.

You should now be able to click on the **Continue** button and go to the new canvas, where you can click on **F8** and see the questions. Congratulations, you're close to being done! If you put the cursor in the **Question Id** field and hit **F8**, here's what you should see:

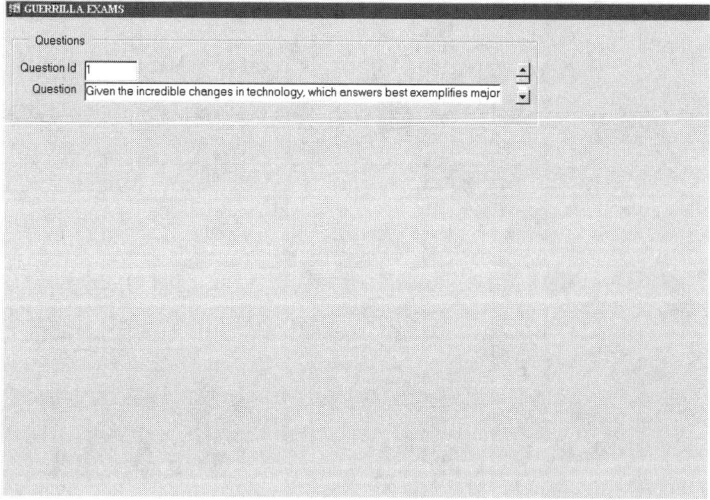

You can also now use the up and down arrows, and the **Page Up** and **Page Down** keys. Have fun running your form. (Note that you should see only ten questions—more if you've been very creative!) Now exit this screen, and let's move on.

The Detail Block

The next step is to add the detail block, which will be really easy now that you've done the master. Go back to the TAKE_TEST canvas, start up the Data Block Wizard, and this time select . . . uh oh, I forgot! *Go back to SQL and create a view from ANSWERS: Create or replace view VANSWERS2 as select answer_question_id, answer_id, answer from ANSWERS.* Now create a public synonym for the view, using the same name as the view. Run the new view, and 40 rows should be returned—10 questions, each with 4 answers. (If you've added more answers to the ANSWERS table, you will, of course, get more results.)

Done? OK. We're going to use the Data Block Wizard again. So get into Layout Editor and, as always, check the top of the screen to make sure you have the right canvas:

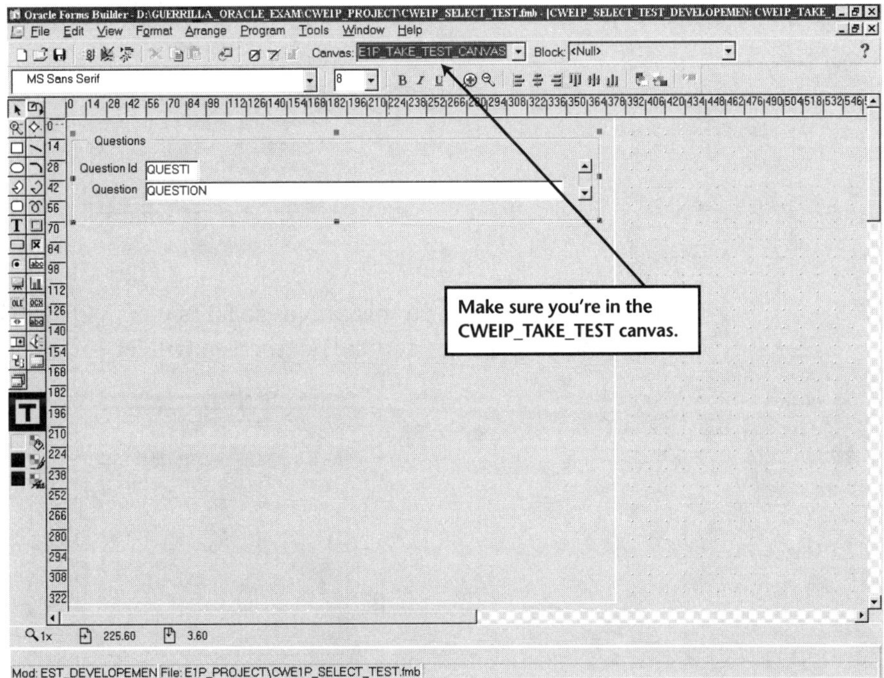

Now just click on **Tools | Data Block Wizard | Table or View** and select your new view, VANSWERS2, and all three columns.

On the next screen, uncheck the **Auto-join data blocks** box, and click on **Create Relationship....** Then on the **Relation Type** screen, choose **Based on a join condition**:

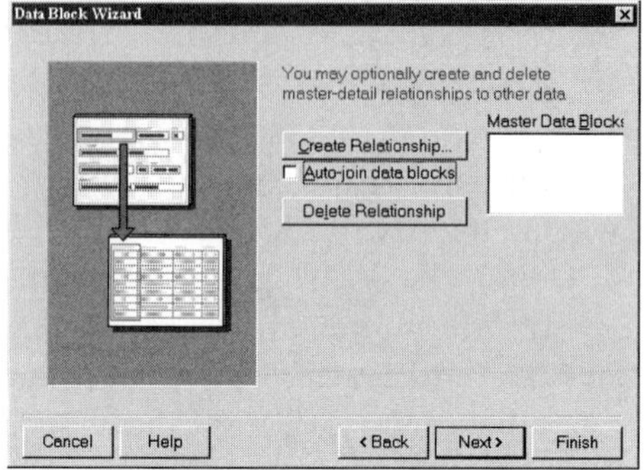

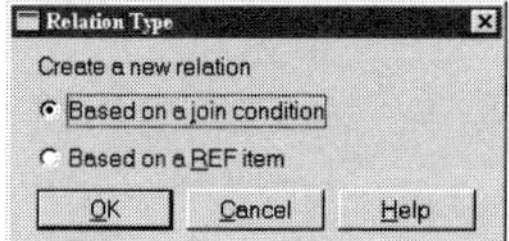

The only other table on this canvas so far is your VQUESTIONS2 view, so select that when it pops up, and the next screen will let you build the relationship:

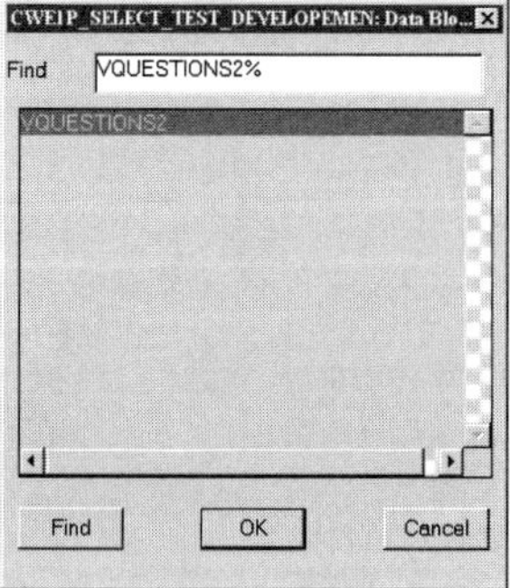

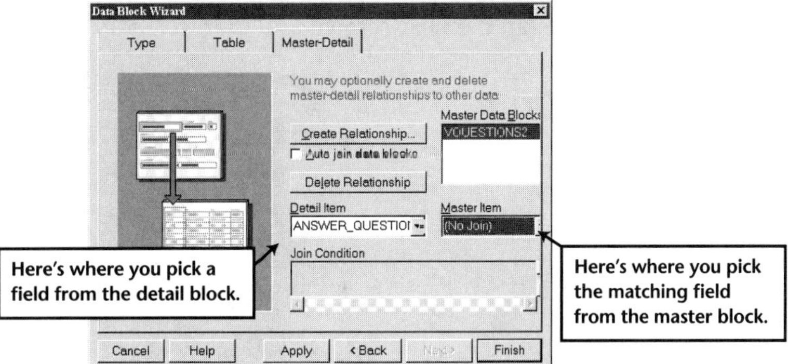

Remember that we want to tie all the answers to each question. So we create a join by picking **ANSWER_QUESTION_ID** for the detail item, and then picking **QUESTION_ID** for the master item. Forms 6*i* then creates the code:

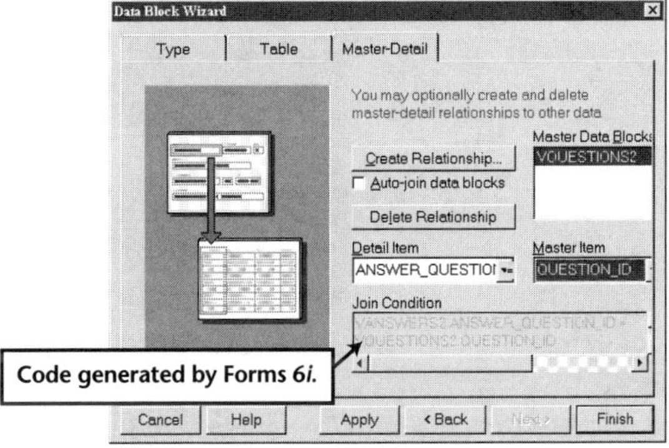

Click **Finish**, go to the Layout Wizard (this should look a little familiar by now), and just be careful to stay on the correct canvas:

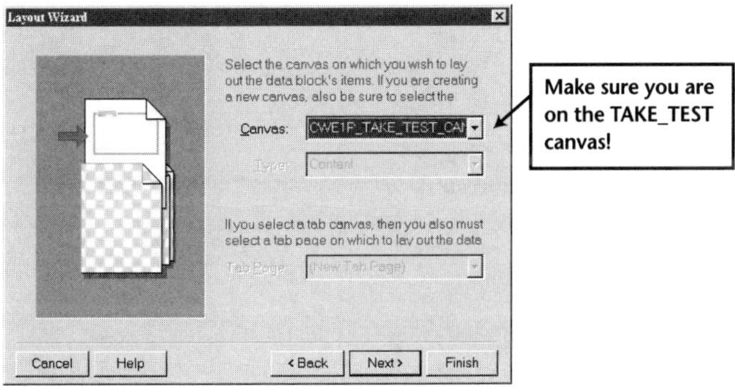

We want to show only two of the items, so select **ANSWER** and **ANSWER_ID**, skip the next screen, and then select **Form**:

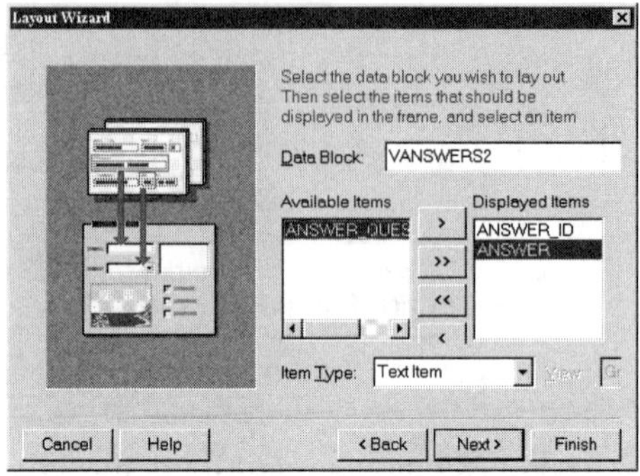

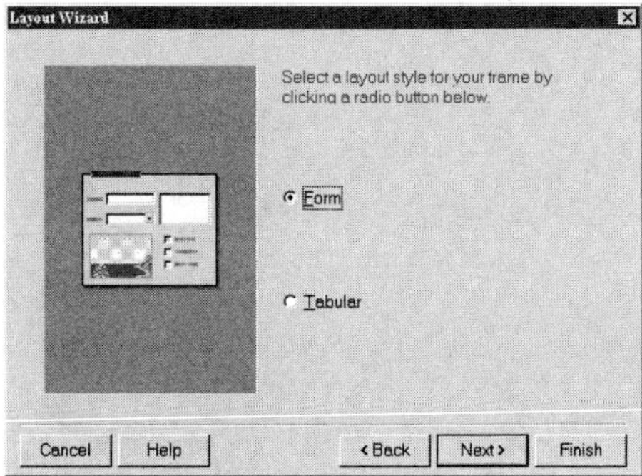

Give the form the title "Answers", with four records showing:

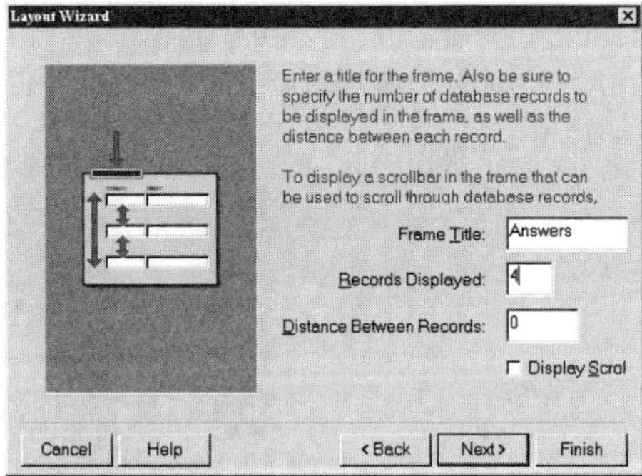

Then accept the congratulations offered, and your canvas should look like this:

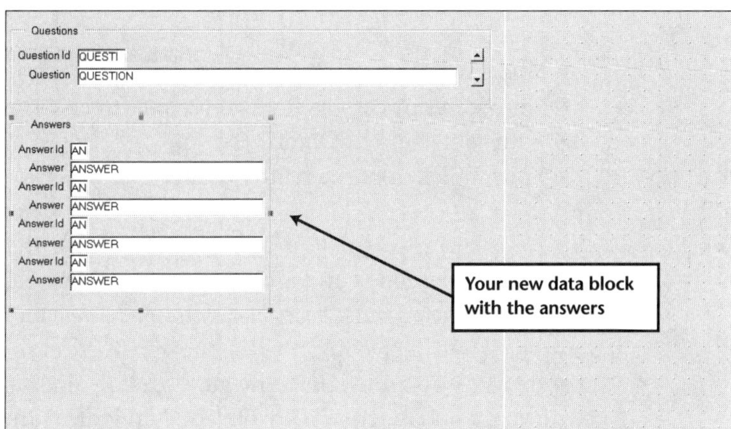

You can go ahead and test by selecting **Program | Run | Client/Server**. Remember? When you get to your new canvas, make sure the cursor is in the **Question Id** field, then hit **F8**, and you should get the first question with its answers below. (Notice that I added instructions for **F8**.)

OK, you're saying, what if this doesn't work? I've been telling you to test at every step, so you know that the only change you've made is to add the detail block. To test what you did in building the relationship, go to SQL*Plus and run the same code to see what results you get. Here are several things that can cause problems:

- You have canvas items outside the boundaries.
- Some of your canvas items have incorrect settings.
- Your views are not valid.
- Your tables don't have any data.

As a last resort if you just cannot resolve the problems, you can always delete the new block and all its items and start again. Be warned, however, that you must also *go into Object Navigator and delete the data block information*. For example, if we just couldn't get the master detail to work, we could stay in Layout Editor and delete the new detail block containing the answers. We would then have to go to Object Navigator and *delete the data block VANSWERS2*. We do this by highlighting the block and then clicking on the red X in the left-hand column of icons:

Save your work!

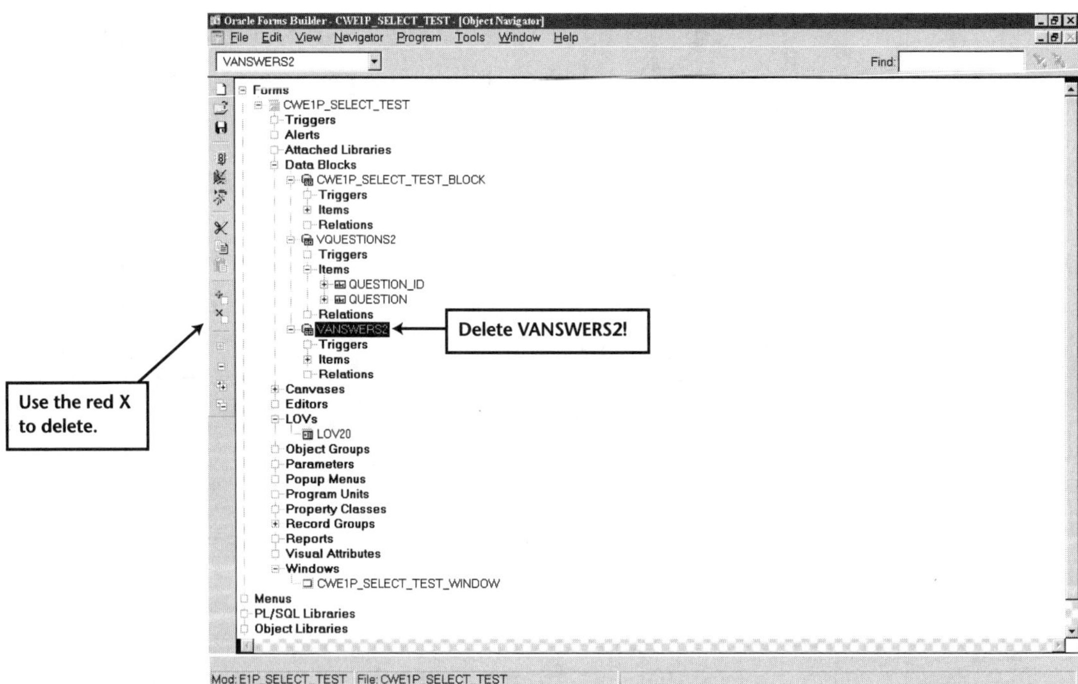

Tip

An easy way to get to Layout Editor for a canvas is simply to click on the canvas when you're in Object Navigator.

Buttons

What's left with this canvas? We have to add the button to finish, add the instructions to use **F8**, and most importantly, give the users a way to select an answer. Here's where I'll introduce you to what's called a **radio button group**.

Groups such as radio buttons or drop-down lists are handy when there are a limited number of choices. Radio buttons are great for five or fewer selections, and by nature they are mutually exclusive; that is, the user can click on only one of them. You then take that value and write it to the database, as you'll see, and you now have a record of the student's answers for each question for this particular test. See how it's all coming together? Building an Oracle system is like getting a long freight train moving: It takes time, but once it's rolling, it goes sweetly.

Let's create the last data block. Again, make sure you're on the right canvas (TAKE_TEST), and select the Data Block Wizard. This time the table is STUDENT_ANSWER_HISTORY, where you'll select only one field: **STUDENT_ANSWER**. On the next screen, uncheck **Auto-join data blocks**. If you see data from your previous work when you created a join relationship, just click the **Delete Relationship** button:

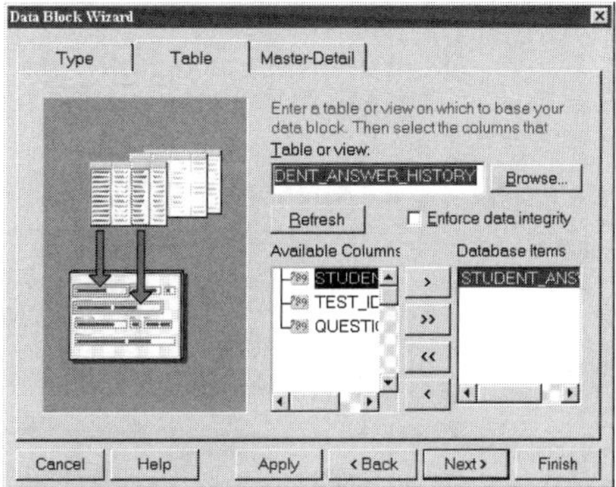

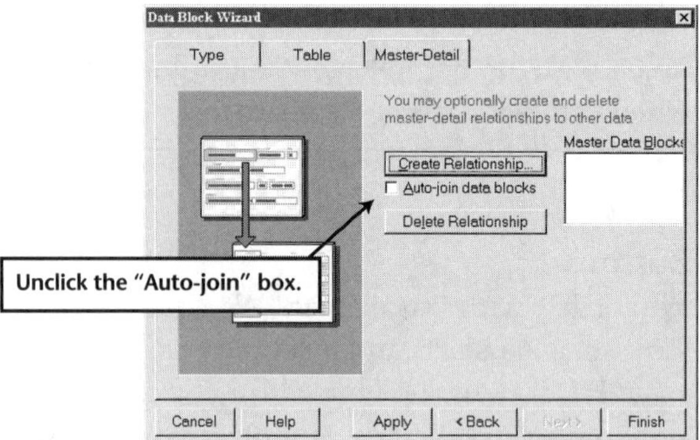

Go on to the Layout Wizard; the canvas is TAKE_TEST_CANVAS. Change the data block to VANSWERS2, then select the one field, and this time change **Item Type** to **Radio Group**, giving it any title you like:

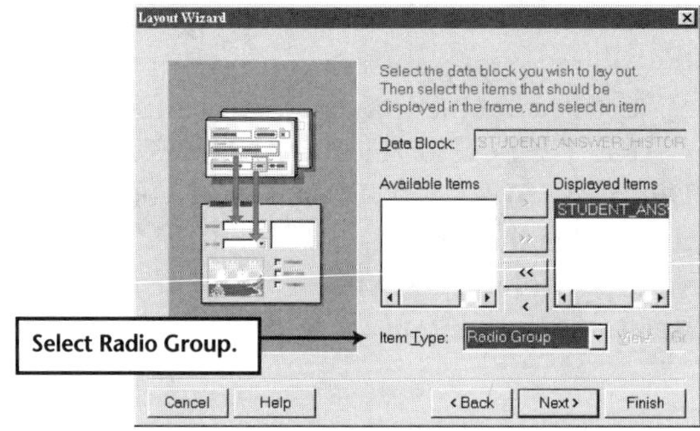

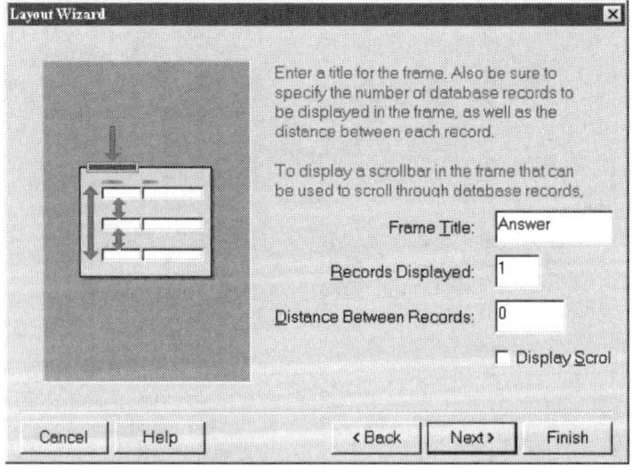

The canvas now has a funny-looking line for the new block, so just pull on the black tabs to expand it:

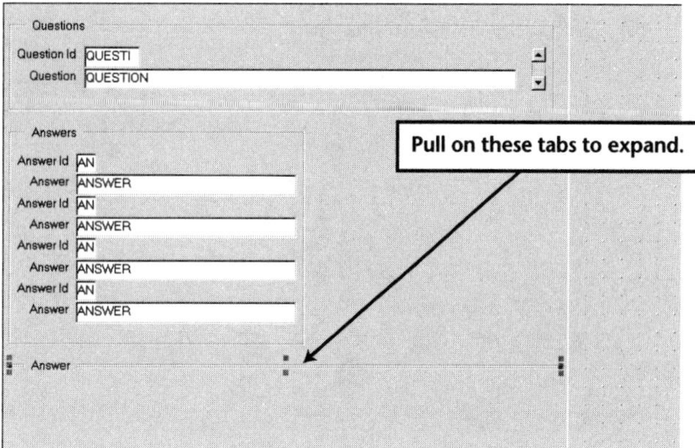

Now add the radio buttons by clicking on the icon, then putting the cursor (which is now a crosshatch), in the new block. You will be asked which radio group you want to place the button in. Click **OK** to select **STUDENT_ ANSWER**, and you will then see the new radio button in the new block:

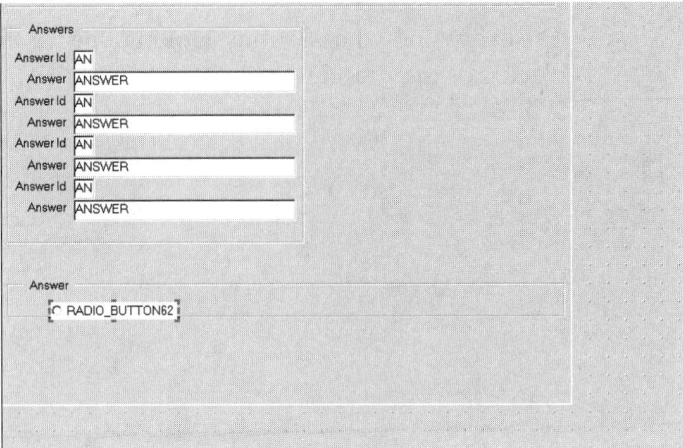

Now add three more radio buttons, and change the properties of each:

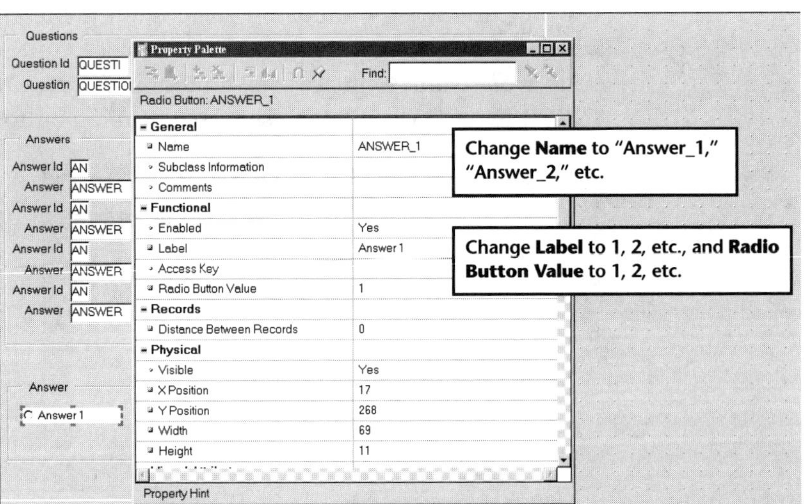

Here's what your canvas should look like:

Now we set the initial value. Again, this is done in the property palette, so go back to Object Navigator and find the radio button group. It has a symbol next to it that looks like two small circles arranged vertically:

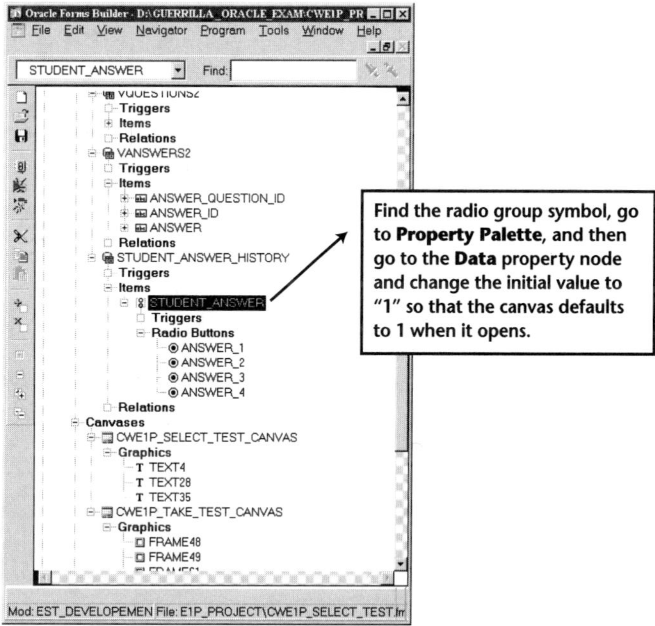

Next add a command button named **SAVE!** or **SAVE My Answer!** and create a smart trigger for **WHEN_BUTTON_PRESSED** that has the following code (which deletes any previous answer for this question and replaces it with the new answer):

```
DELETE STUDENT_ANSWER_HISTORY
where
student_answer_history.test_id =
:cwe1p_select_test_block.test_id
and
student_answer_history.student_id =
:cwe1p_select_test_block.user_id
and
student_answer_history.question_id =
vquestions2.question_id;

insert into student_answer_history    values (

:cwe1p_select_test_block.user_id,:cwe1p_select_test_block.test_
id,
   :vquestions.question_id,
   :student_answer_history_block.student_answer);

COMMIT;
```

Your data block names may be different.

Oracle Forms Builder - D:\GUERRILLA_ORACLE\CWE1P_PROJECT\CWE1P_SELECT_TEST.fmb

File Edit Program Tools Window Help

Compile Revert New... Delete Close Help

Type: Trigger Object: STUDENT_ANSWER_HISTORY_BLOCK PUSH_BUTTON66

Name: WHEN-BUTTON-PRESSED

```
DELETE STUDENT_ANSWER_HISTORY
where
student_answer_history.test_id =     :cwelp_select_test_block.test_id
and
student_answer_history.student_id = :cwelp_select_test_block.user_id
and
student_answer_history.question_id = :vquestions2.question_id;

insert into student_answer_history values (
   :cwelp_select_test_block.user_id,:cwelp_select_test_block.test_id,
   :vquestions2.question_id,
   :student_answer_history_block.student_answer);

COMMIT;
```

Watch the colons (:)!

Notice that the syntax is the block name followed by the item name in the block.

Not Modified Successfully Compiled

Mod: EST_DEVELOPEMEN File: E1P_PROJECT\CWE1P_SELECT_TEST.fmb

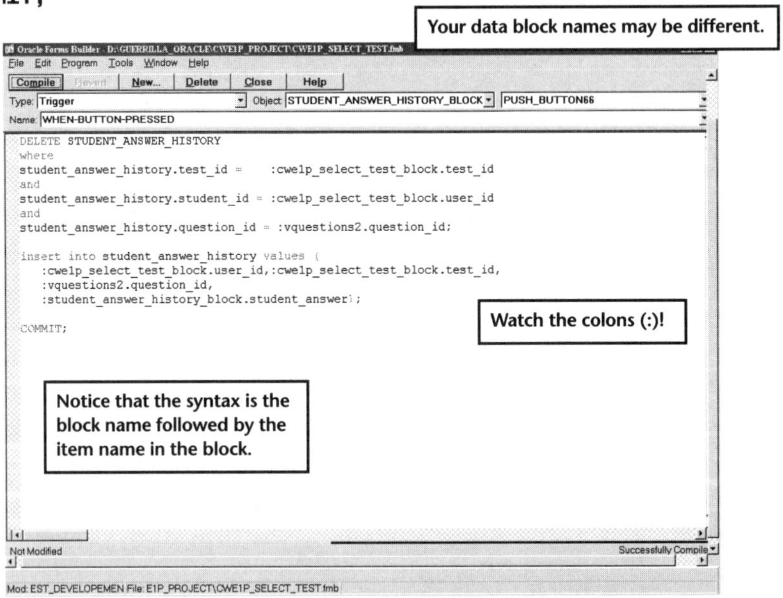

Tip

Some of your block names may be different, so just make changes if you get syntax errors.

Tip

A message like "STUDENT_ANSWER_HISTORY not defined" means simply that you are not logged onto the database. Hence, Forms 6*i* cannot find the table. Log on and you'll be all set.

Save your work!

The last step is to add the "FINISHED" button at the bottom of the canvas. You should know how to do that by now, so create the button, rename it, and add the following code for a smart trigger for **WHEN_BUTTON_PRESSED**:

```
-- Notice that we've hard-coded the test results. In a
-- production
-- system you would have a routine to calculate the actual score
-- and so forth. My goal here is to show you how to update the
-- student record. Here would be your routine to calculate the
-- score and total test times.

-- Now update the record for this student for this test.

UPDATE  test_history
  SET SCORE  = 100,
    END_TIME = '113011'
  WHERE
     test_history.test_id = :cwelp_select_test_block.test_id
     and
     test_history.student_id =
:cwelp_select_test_block.user_id;

COMMIT;
```

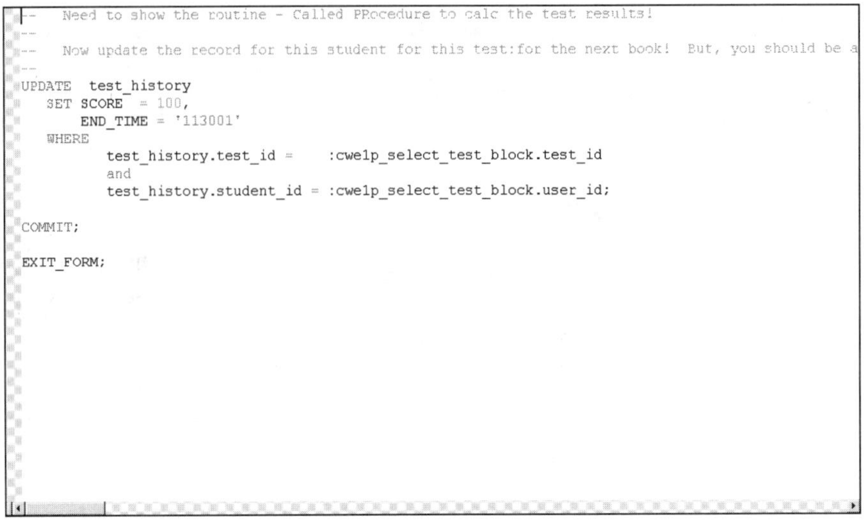

```
--   Need to show the routine - Called PRocedure to calc the test results!
--
--   Now update the record for this student for this test:for the next book!  But, you should be a
--
UPDATE  test_history
   SET SCORE  = 100,
       END_TIME = '113001'
   WHERE
          test_history.test_id =    :cwelp_select_test_block.test_id
          and
          test_history.student_id = :cwelp_select_test_block.user_id;

COMMIT;

EXIT_FORM;
```

Don't forget to go back to Object Navigator and change the names of your new buttons to make them more readable. You don't have to, but it is good practice.

Tracking IDs

There's just one more step. For testing purposes, we have not kept track of student IDs taking a test. Remember the rule—only one shot at a test? As you've surely realized by now, we have not enforced that rule simply for ease of testing. When your system is done, you will have to add the following code on the SELECT_TEST canvas, under the **Register and Continue to the test** button trigger:

```
--  Create a new record for this student for this test. Remember
--  that the
--  rules are that a student can only take a test once!
--  You should add a routine to check if there is a student
--  record
--  for this test, and if so, throw up a message to stop the
--  user from
```

```
--  continuing. That's for the next book! But, you should be
--  able to try it on your own.
--
insert into test_history values (
                :cwe1p_select_test_block.test_id,
                :cwe1p_select_test_block.user_id,
                0,
                sysdate, '091500', '0', 'Main Lab'
                     );
go_item ('vquestions.question_id'); ❶
```

❶ This line already existed. Remember?

What about a duplicate record? When a user tries to take enter a test that he or she has already taken, Forms 6*i* throws up an error message in the bottom left corner—we've seen this already—so you do not have to process for errors!

Note

You're probably wondering what is going on with these views. Why did we wait until now? Are more coming? You see, views are pretty straightforward, yet they can become very sophisticated. Instead of showing them to you as an isolated exercise, I put them here so that you could get an idea of the kind of processing they're good for. Let me give you another example. Suppose that you want to show all the questions and their answers, but not allow anyone to see questions greater than, say, 100 because those are for advanced students. You would create a view like this:

```
create or replace view QA_VIEW
    as (select question_id, question, answer_id, answer
    from questions, answers
    where answer_question_id = question_id and question_id <
101);
```

Now anyone in your department who has rights can simply run this view and get a list of all questions and answers, without being able to change anything! So a view is a great way to combine selective data from various tables for your customers.

Linking the Forms

Let's see where we are. By now you should have two forms and a couple of icons for the splash screen and main screen (if you added other icons, that's OK):

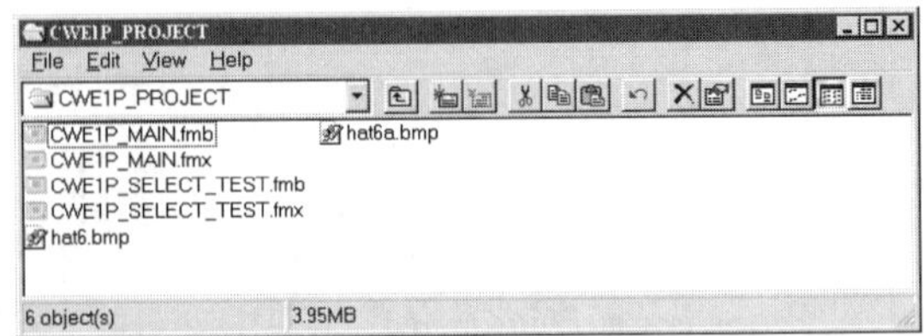

The `.fmx` files are the compiled programs that are run, and the `.fmb` files are the source files that you work with in Object Navigator and Layout Editor.

I'm showing you this because we're getting close to finishing, and it should be on your mind that somehow we have to tie the two forms together. You already know how to go from one canvas to another within a form. Now I'll show you how to jump from form to form. Then we have to finish up some of the buttons, and finally, change the top toolbars and menu bars.

Forms *6i* provides several ways to navigate among various forms:

- **`CALL_FORM`** immediately jumps to the next form; it can pass parameters.
- **`OPEN_FORM`** opens another form, but it doesn't immediately jump to it.
- **`NEW_FORM`** opens another form and immediately closes the one it came from.

We're going to use `CALL_FORM` to get to the CWE1P_SELECT_TEST form, and you already know about the `EXIT_FORM` trigger we'll put on the main screen. As you've probably imagined, we can also close specific forms as needed. The command that we would use in the trigger is `CLOSE_FORM`.

Let's change the main canvas now and add a trigger to jump to the CWE1P_SELECT_TEST form, as well as a trigger to exit in case the user decides not to take a test.

Start Form Builder. Select **Open an existing form**, and then **CWE1P_MAIN.fmb**:

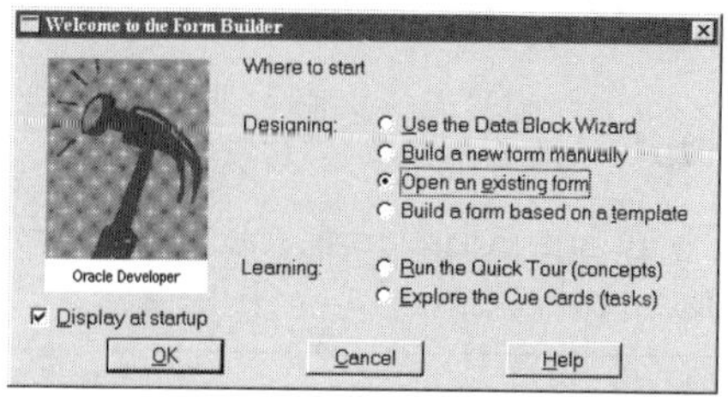

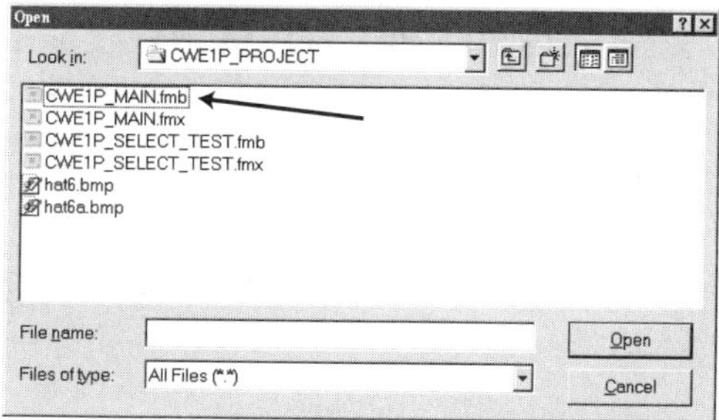

Then open CWE1P_CANVAS with the three buttons:

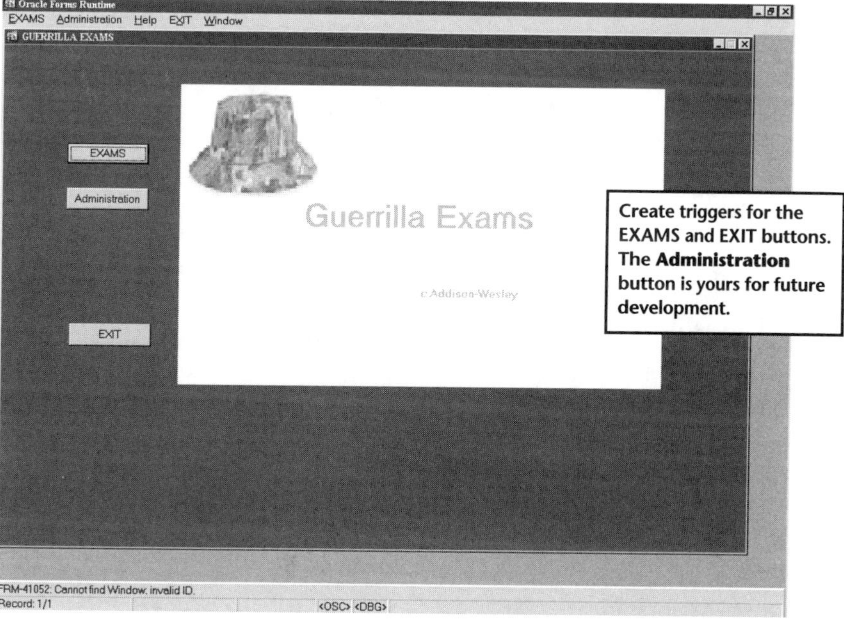

Remember how to create a trigger? Right-click on the **EXAMS** button, select **SmartTriggers | WHEN-BUTTON-PRESSED**, and type "CALL_FORM (:GLOBAL.PROJECT_PATH | | 'CWE1P_SELECT_TEST');".

Note

If you put your icons into another folder, you will have to declare another global path.

To add another global path, go to Object Navigator for the CWE1P_MAIN form, select the **PRE-FORM** trigger, and enter a second global path:

Save your work!

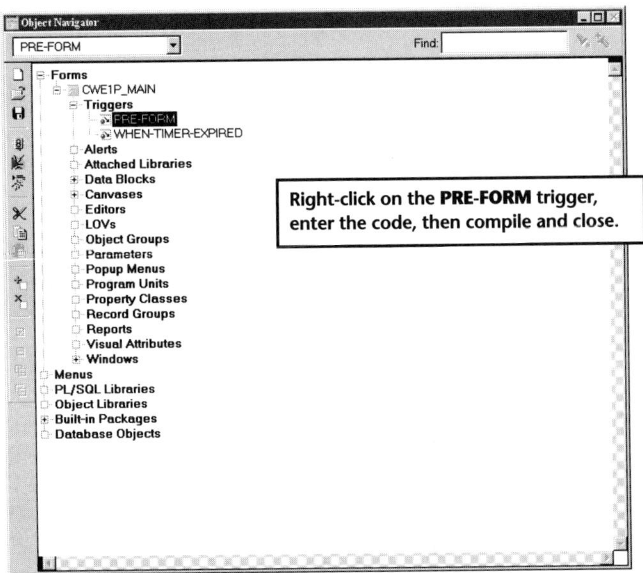

```
DECLARE
-- we need to define the variable that will be used for our timer
CWE1P_SPLASH_TIMER TIMER;

BEGIN
  SET_WINDOW_PROPERTY (FORMS_MDI_WINDOW,WINDOW_STATE, MAXIMIZE);
:GLOBAL.project_path := 'D:\GUERRILLA_ORACLE_EXAM\CWE1P_PROJECT\';
:GLOBAL.project_path2 := 'D:\GUERRILLA_ORACLE_EXAM\';

--Here're the instructions to load the GUERRILLA ORACLE image file
READ_IMAGE_FILE(:GLOBAL.project_path ||'hat6A.bmp', 'BMP',
   'cwe1p_splash_block.cwe1p_splash_image');


--  now enter the text that will show in the lower right hand box

:cwe1p_splash_block.cwe1p_splash_item :=
--'Guerrilla Oracle' ||CHAR(10) || 'test';
'Guerrilla Oracle'  ||CHR(13) || CHR(10) ||
'by Richard Staron'|| CHR(13) || CHR(10) ||
'(c) Copyright Addison-Wesley' ;

--  now add the timer code
CWE1P_SPLASH_TIMER := CREATE_TIMER('CWE1P_SPLASH_TIMER', 5000, NO_REPEAT);

END;
```

If you need to, type in the "project_path2" global path.

Now just add the EXIT_FORM code for the smart trigger for the **EXIT** button, and test. You should be able to get to the CWE1P_SELECT_TESTform and take an exam. (Forget how? First create the button and change the name to "EXIT". Then right-click on the button, select **SmartTriggers WHEN_BUTTON_PRESSED**, type in "EXIT_FORM;"—don't forget the semicolon!—and then compile and close. Now run a quick test.)

Note

Again, this reminder: **Save your work** at every step of the way. That's why Oracle has put the diskette icon everywhere!

If you run into problems, take a close look at the errors in the bottom left corner. Sometimes there's an error in your new global path. Often the problem is just a misspelling or a missing comma. It is interesting that the trigger function picks up a lot of the syntax errors, but not all of them. If you get a message like "Procedure or Function xxxx not declared", usually either you have missed a colon (:) or you have misspelled the name of a block.

We're in the home stretch now. All we have to do is clean up the top of the screen—that is, work on the menus.

Menus

This is the final piece, and it is what will make your screens look absolutely professional. I'll show you how to replace the Forms menu bar at the top of the screen with your own. Instead of the default items—such as **Action, Edit, Query, Block**, and so forth—you will have items that match some of the things the user can do on your screens, and only those things!

These are the steps:

1. Create a menu module.
2. Create the menu items (parent and child items).
3. Activate the items.
4. Put the menus on the CWE1P forms.

> **Note**
>
> Custom menus can be attached only to a form, not a specific canvas. Thus some forethought is required to make sure everything works together.

Creating a Menu Module

Let's start with some of the main ideas. A **menu item**, contrary to what you may be thinking, is the entire set of horizontal menu selections across the top of the screen. Any **menu module** can have several menu items that are attached to different screens.

A menu item has both parent and child items, as you will see. And a menu module is a distinct object, not a form. We will save our menu module as `CWE1P_MENU.mmb`. (Yes, the related `.mmx` file is the compiled module!)

Here are the steps for creating a menu module:

1. Start Forms.
2. On the welcome screen, select **Cancel**.
3. Go to Object Navigator.
4. Click on the **MODULE1** node and delete it by clicking on the red X (we don't need a form).

5. Select the **Menus** node, click the green plus sign, and rename the node "CWE1P_MENU".
6. Now select the **Menus** node under your new CWE1P_MENU node, again click the green plus sign, and rename it "CWE1P_MAIN_MENU".
7. Save `CWE1P_MENU.mmb` in the `Oracle_Guerrilla` folder:

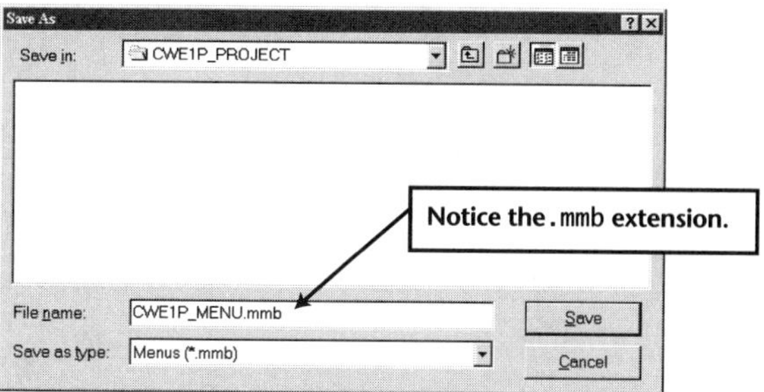

Your **Object Navigator** screen should look like this:

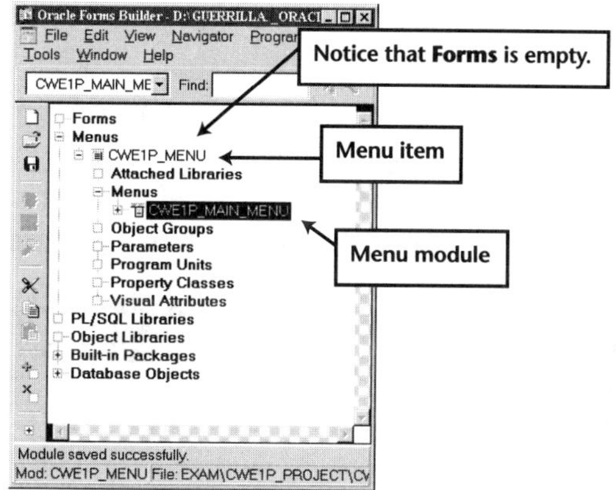

Creating Menu Items

Now we go to the menu editor to build the contents of our first menu item. Just double-click either the menu module icon or the menu item icon, and the editor screen will appear:

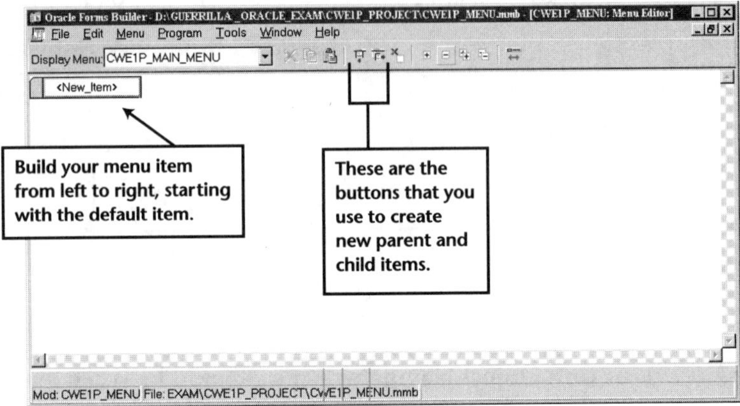

The rules are pretty simple: The highest level, or parent, items are created first, from left to right.

Just select the default menu item (**<New_Item>**), and double-click on the button that has an arrow pointing to the right:

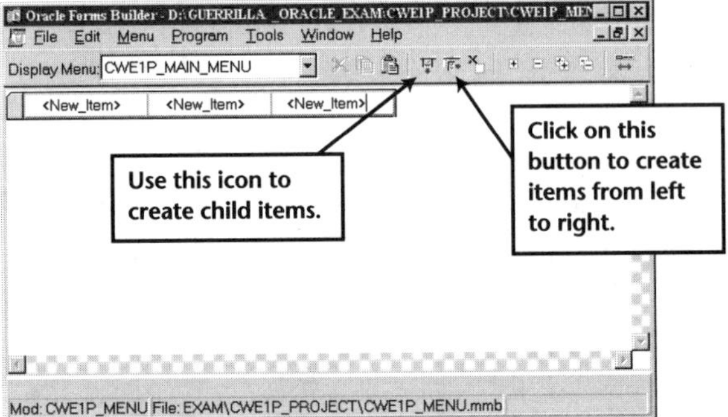

Now just highlight the items one at a time and change the names by right-clicking on each item, selecting **Property Palette** (remember that from your work with forms?), and changing the label:

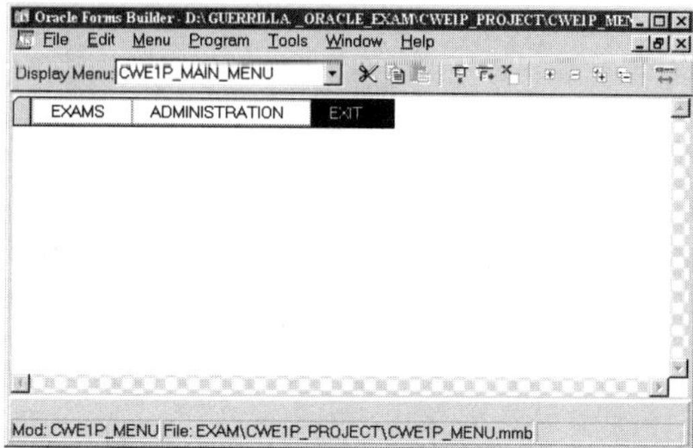

Although we don't have any child items for **ADMINISTRATION**, we can add them now; we just won't activate them. Highlight the **ADMINISTRATION** item, then click several times on the icon that has an arrow pointing downward and change the labels:

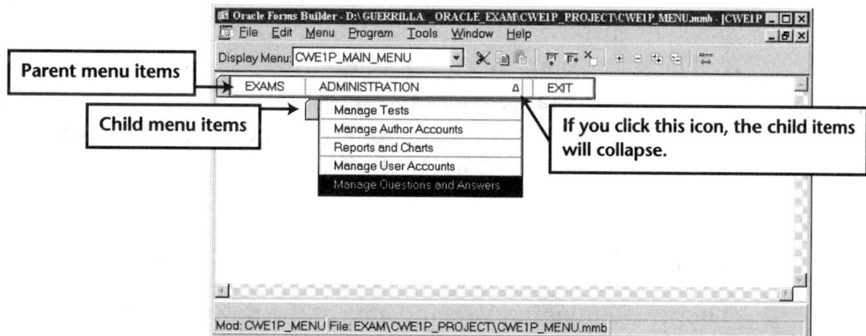

You may have noticed that in the property palette, under the **Functional** node you have choices for some of the variables:

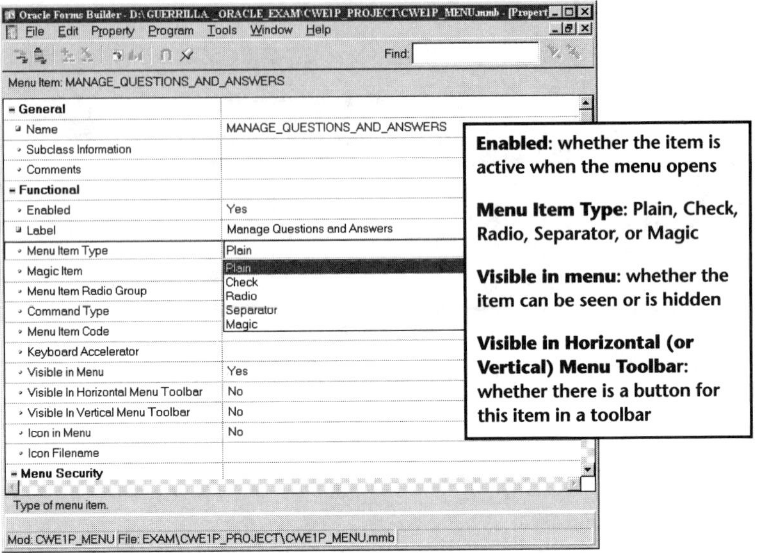

All menu items are **Plain** by default, which means that they have text labels, and a trigger will fire when the user selects any Plain item. This is the most common type. **Check** means that the item has a property that can be disabled or enabled. **Radio** means that the choices are like radio buttons: Only one can be selected at a time. **Separator** means just that: This item is a separator bar in the menu. **Magic** refers to specific types that are predefined in Forms: **Cut**, **Copy**, **Paste**, **Clear**, **Undo**, **About**, **Help**, **Quit**, and **Window**. Some of these can have user code associated with them.

Note

I hope you're getting a good idea of the power of Forms. Although I am just introducing you to Forms for our purposes of presenting the guerrilla exams, it would be great if you took the initiative and expanded your expertise by experimenting with these other features.

Let's use a Magic type. Go to the **Exit** menu item, open **Property Palette**, and change **Menu Item Type** to "Magic" and **Magic** to "Quit":

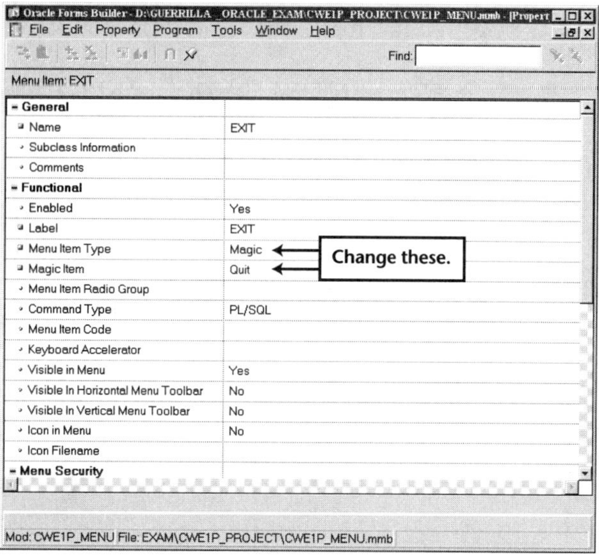

OK, you've seen what's missing. Go ahead and add the **Help** parent menu item. (And in the **Functional** node of its property palette, don't forget to change **Menu Item Type** to "Magic" and **Magic Item** to "Help".)

Now just a couple of sentences on **access keys**, those keys that you can hit instead of clicking on a menu item. For example, you can type "X" for **Exit**. All menu items have the first letter as the default access key. If you want to change the default for a particular item, go to that item's property palette (yes, again!) and put an ampersand (&) in front of the letter you want. For example, to make "X" the access key for **Exit**, type in "E&XIT". When that menu item is highlighted, the user can either hit the **X** key or click on **Exit** to exit.

Activating the Menu Items

Let's activate the menu items we just created and bring one of our screens to life. For our first screen, the **ADMINISTRATION** items are not enabled. You can just change the value in the property palette for those menu items to "Enabled", but I'm going to show you how to pop up a message instead. Just create a trigger for each **ADMINISTRATION** child item that has this code (right-click on the menu item, then select **PL/SQL Editor** to create the PL/SQL code):

```
MESSAGE ('This item is not active at this time');
```

The **EXIT** button is easy: Just create the trigger to EXIT_FORM. The **EXAMS** selection has to call the main form, so create a trigger that says

```
CALL_FORM (:GLOBAL.PROJECT_PATH||'CWE1P_main.FMX');
```

Your **Object Navigator** screen should now look like this:

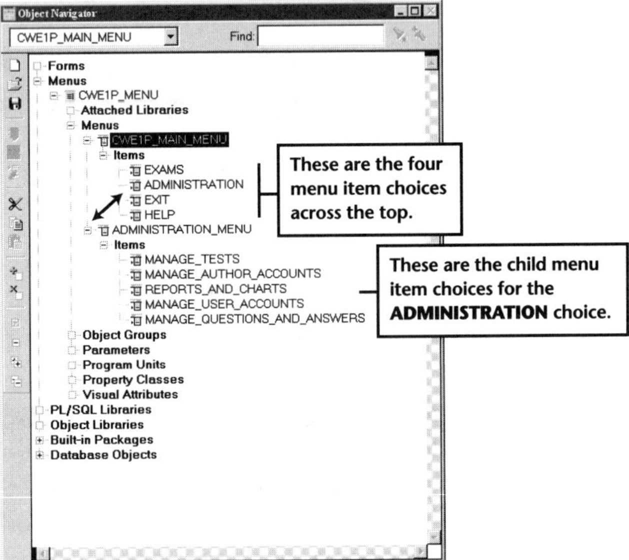

The next big step is to compile. Now don't just run off and try to compile the menu like a form! Instead, select **File | Administration | Compile** and correct any errors.

Eventually, or immediately if you've lucked out, you will see the message "Module built successfully" in the lower left-hand corner. Once you get this message, you're ready to move on.

Tip

One of the most important things to remember is that every time you make a change to a menu, you have to compile the menu, then go to the form that uses it and compile that form also. If you don't, you will get what look like very strange errors. So get in the habit of the following steps: *change menu, compile menu, go to form, compile form, test form.* This little mantra will save you a lot of headaches.

Adding Menus to a Form

Now we tie the menu to a form:

1. Close your menu and open your main form (CWE1P_MAIN)—yes, go back to **Object Navigator**—and open the property palette for the form. Then change the **Menu Module** item to the full path:

```
D:\GUERRILLA_ORACLE_EXAM\CWE1P_PROJECT\CWE1P_MENU:
```

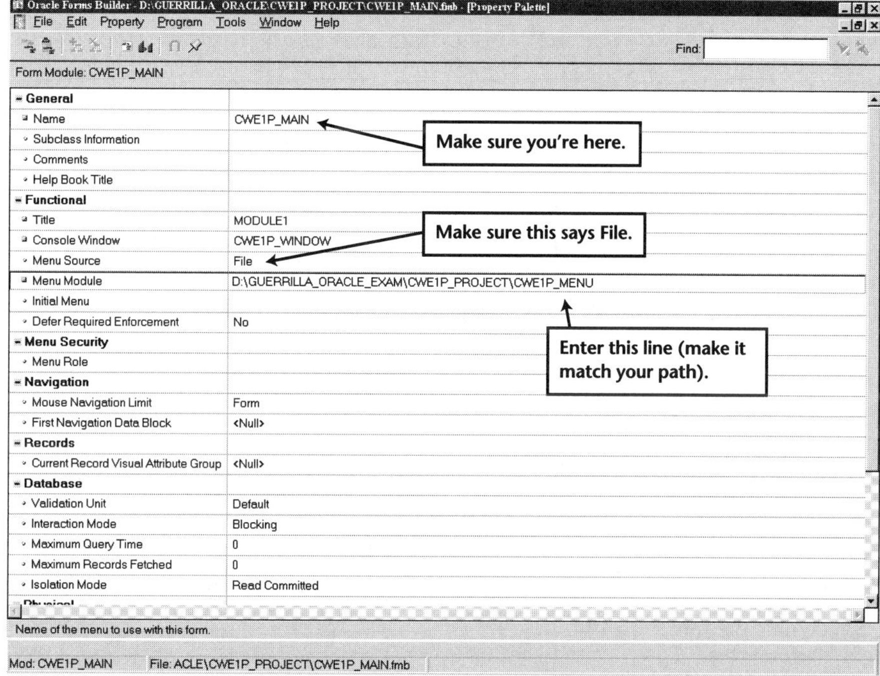

Tip

The global path variable does not work here, so be careful if you ever move your menu files.

We've reached the last step! To make your project look professional, you have to have a custom menu for your last two canvases—the ones where the student selects and then takes the test, remember? This is the `SELECT_TEST.fmb` form that we created a little while ago, and this is the form that needs the custom menu.

Note

Remember, custom menus can be tied only to a form, not a canvas.

This step is a little complex because it has two canvases, or two screens. So we have to make sure that the menu item we create fits both. That is, both the screen where the user selects the test and the screen where the user takes the test will have the same menu item you make.

The only menu item that seems to comfortably fit both screens is the non-functioning **HELP** item, right? We can't really run code from menu items. Menu items have to hop to a form, and we want the user to make choices on the screens, such as which test, which answer, and so forth. So about the only thing that makes sense is some kind of help item. Everything else is already on the canvases because you did such a great job.

You should know the drill by now. You have to create one new menu item that will be called **HELP**. Then right-click on the item, then on **Property Palette**, and disable the item by entering "No" in the **Enabled** field of the **Functional** node:

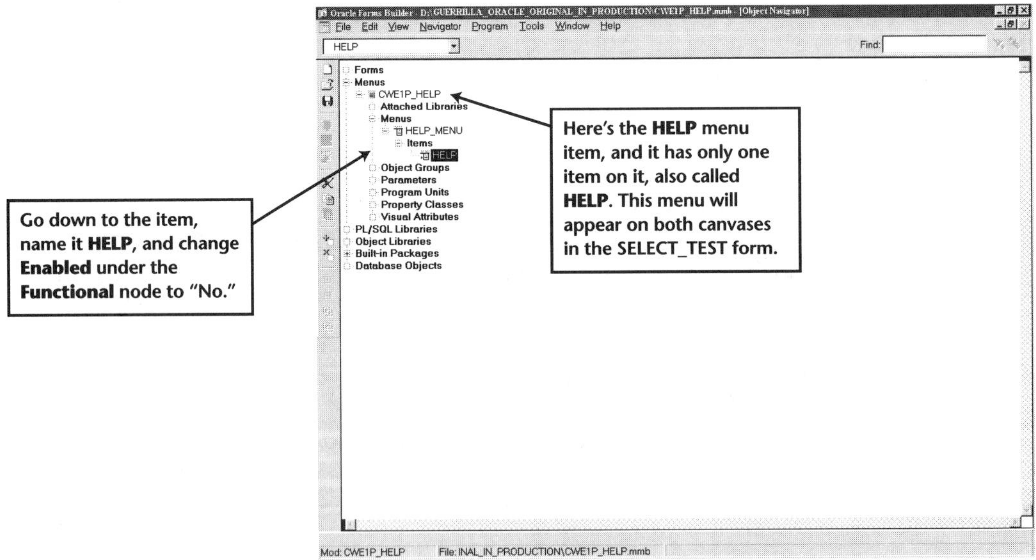

Warning

You must *save* each one of the menu items: **File | Save As <name>!** And you must compile each one!

Here's what your GUERRILLA_ORACLE folder should look like:

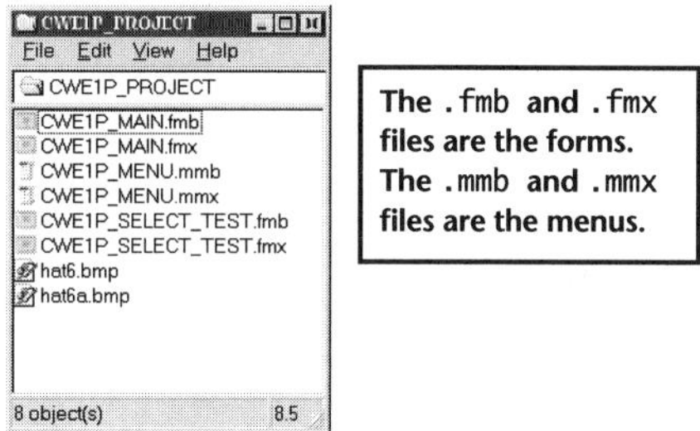

Finally, we have to attach the menu items to the form. You know how to do this: Go to the form, select **Property Palette**, go down to the **Functional** node, and for **Menu Module** type the path: "D:\GUERRILLA_ORACLE\CWE1P_PROJECT\CWE1P_HELP":

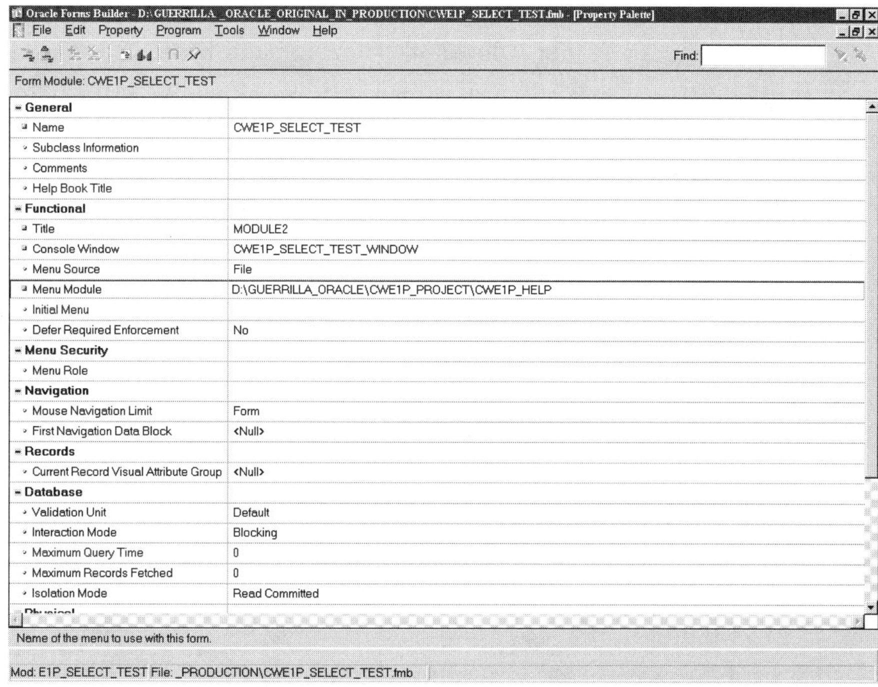

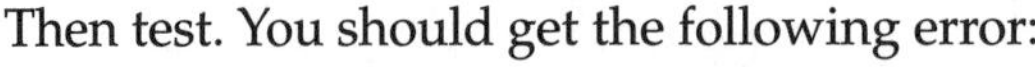

Then test. You should get the following error:

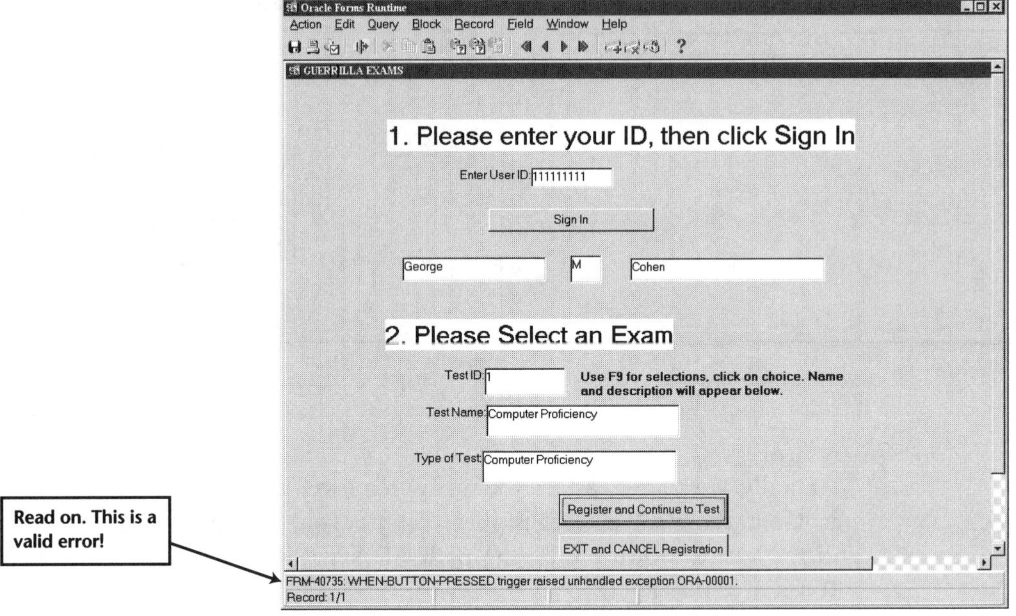

At first it looks like your system has failed. However, if you check the Oracle error, you'll find that your system has worked perfectly. An "ORA-00001" error means that you have violated a unique constraint. Remember that a person is allowed to take an exam only once? Well, we already have a record for this user for this test, so we *should* get an "ORA-00001" error, and we did. So it's working!

To continue testing, either delete the history record for this person or create a couple of new users. However, notice that the menu has changed to the simple one you created. You always get a **Window** item, and all we wanted was a nonfunctioning **Help** item.

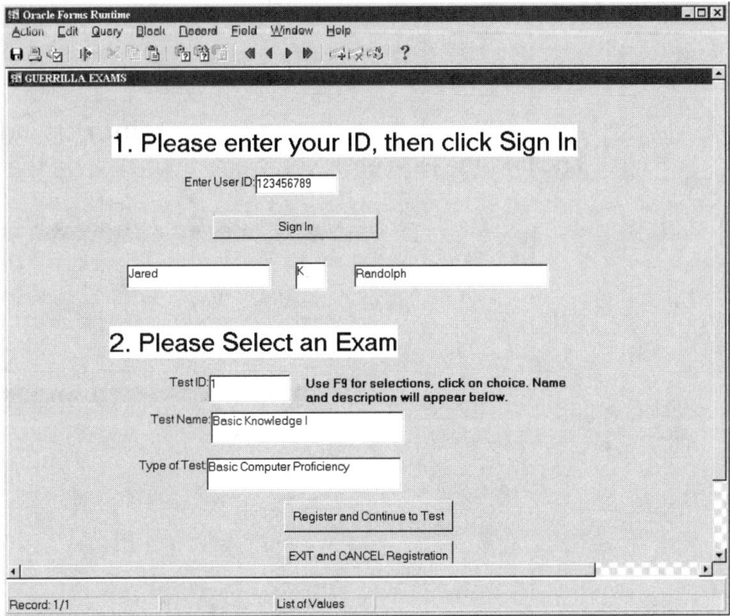

So there it is. You have your running system, using all the major components of Forms 6*i*. Because there is so much more in Forms, I strongly encourage you to get a couple of books and refine your system. Add the administration functions, error handling, security, toolbars with icons, and pop-up menus.

Congratulations! You've mastered some of the intricacies of Forms 6*i*. Go show off what you've done.

One Last Tip

Always build your forms and menus a piece at a time. Add one thing, compile, then test and debug. Do too many things at once, and you're dead! Forms is just too complex to rush through.

OK, One More Tip

You can find all the "FRM-xxx" errors in the Help index. Just go to **Help | Topics** and find the FRM error you want, then click on the error to get the explanation:

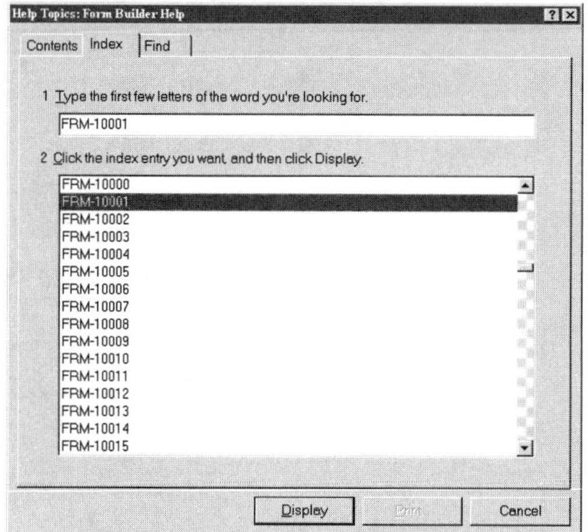

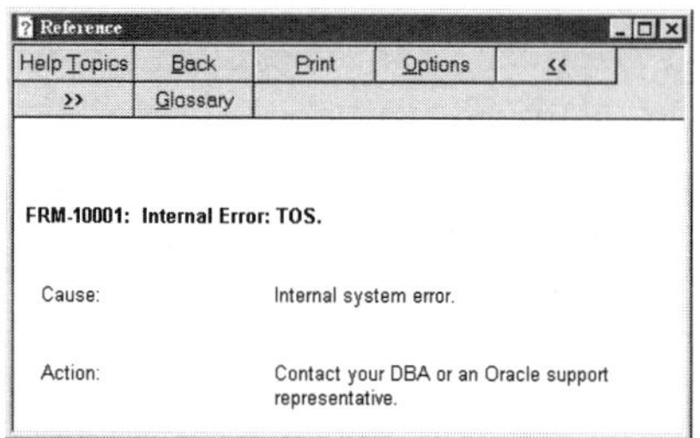

For information on Forms 6*i* security issues, see Appendix A.

Chapter 14

Guerrilla Toolbox

This chapter could easily become an entire book, series of books, movie or possibly TV show!, and you may be the one to do it. However, I hope that you take these pages and make them the start of your own binder of tools and tips. Add to it as you learn from list servers (especially http://otn.oracle.com—Oracle Technical Network), conferences, local Oracle user groups, and other good reference materials. And make yourself a promise that you won't stop learning until you're certified as brain-dead!

Here's what we're going to cover:

- Reporting made simple
- Queries

- Sequences
- Date handling
- Playing with letters
- Number functions
- Some interesting verbs
- Triggers
- Feeding other systems
- Linking to Access

Simple Report Writing

Hopefully you've learned by now that I tend to lure you into things by telling you not to worry and just follow the instructions. Well, using the built-in SQL tools will let you build simple reports, but with a bit of practice you can actually create pretty sophisticated reports.

Note

Most shops usually use a third-party tool such as Brio, SQR, or Crystal Reports for the bulk of their report generation. Users can easily learn some of these, IT staff can use others for intricate reports, and all of them fit nicely in the Oracle environment.

However, be aware that Oracle has released a significantly improved Oracle Discoverer. Discoverer presents a different model for users to access the database data, along the idea of having "workbooks" that contain the data for individual business areas. I encourage you to investigate this tool further.

We are going to jump right into using the power of SQL*Plus. Take a look at the following report, which shows the very first customer for the "Guerrilla Oracle Waiver Exam Testing Institute":

```
Sat Jan 19                                                  page    1
                          All Tests Taken
Test Identification       Student Identification      Location
------------------------  --------------------------  -------------------
1                         222222222                   Main Lab

                          Guerrilla Exams
```

And here's the SQL*Plus code:

```
rem
rem            Tests Taken report
rem    written by Jerome Engles
rem
rem  purpose:  this is an ad hoc report to list all tests taken,
rem  by type of test
rem
```

❶ Use the broken vertical bar for a separator.

```
set headsep |  ❶
```

❷ ttitle = top title; btitle = bottom title

```
ttitle 'All Tests Taken'  ❷
btitle 'Guerrilla Exams'
```

❸ Three columns for the report, using the table column names

```
Column TEST_ID          heading  'Test Identification    '  ❸
Column TEST_ID          format  999999999
Column STUDENT_ID       heading  'Student Identification    '
Column STUDENT_ID       format  999999999
Column LOCATION         heading  'Location'  format a30
```

❹ Break when Test_ID changes

```
Break on TEST_ID  ❹
```

❺ Page formatting

```
Set LINESIZE    80  ❺
Set PAGESIZE    55
Set NEWPAGE     0
```

❻ Start of spooling

```
SPOOL C:\TEST.LST  ❻
```

❼ Notice that each column has a SELECT statement.

```
SELECT  TEST_ID, STUDENT_ID, LOCATION  ❼
        FROM
           TEST_HISTORY
        ORDER BY TEST_ID;
```

❽ End of spooling

```
End of spooling  ❽
```

Here's how things match up:

❶ System-generated date.

❷ ttitle

❸ Columns

❹ Data from table

❺ btitle

```
Sat Jan 19 ❶                                                   page   1
                          All Tests Taken ❷
Test Identification       Student Identification        Location ❸
_____________________     ___________________________   _________________
1                         222222222                     Main Lab ❹

                          Guerrilla Exams ❺
```

From this simple example you should have the general idea, so let's look at some rules:

By convention, the **headsep** (head separator) character is the broken vertical bar, but if your keyboard doesn't support it, you can use another key. Just be careful not to use something that may appear in one of your headings. The head separator tells the system to put the heading on more than one line. You'll see this in the next example, where we expand our simple report.

You can add comments either with the `rem` command at the beginning of the line, or by enclosing them within these keystrokes:

```
/* ... */
```

You can use this notation anywhere!

Calculations

The calculation verbs available are basically the same ones you use in programming: AVG, COMPUTE, COUNT, MAX, MIN, NUM, SUM, STD, and VAR.

To produce totals, use the BREAK ON command followed by a COMPUTE statement. In the next example you'll see simple totals. BREAK ON is used to tell Oracle when to skip a line or lines, or start a new page. BREAK ON can take four conditions:

1. **BREAK ON <column name> skip 1**. When the value in the column changes, your report will skip a line.
2. **BREAK ON ROW skip 1**. Every time the value of the row changes, your report will skip a line.
3. **BREAK ON PAGE**. Every time a page is filled, your report will jump to a new page.
4. **BREAK ON REPORT <commands>**. When the report ends, it will produce totals.

Using the BREAK ON command gets you into advanced reporting. With it you can produce reports, for example, that will list all the exams someone has taken; show the class dates, grades, hours, and then total hours; skip two lines; and go on to the next person. At the end, it can skip to a new page and then print total hours for everyone. As with any other programming tool, you will have to use BREAK ON, make mistakes, learn the nuances, and keep practicing until you're comfortable.

Finally, you can create pseudocolumns, make calculations using columns, and get pretty fancy with your reports. (A pseudocolumn is a column that really isn't in the table, such as SYSDATE.) I refer you to further documentation on using the power of SQL*Plus reporting.

Let's look at our earlier report, now that it has some totals and uses two tables. We've added the student last name. We also wanted a count for the number of students who have taken the various tests available. Since we ran the first report a couple of minutes ago, several more students have taken various exams. Here's the new report:

❶ Totals from the BREAK ON

```
Mon Jan 21                                                page 1
                          All Tests Taken
Test Id     Student Id     Location          Student Name
-------     ----------     ---------------   ---------------
  1         111111111      Science Lab       Cohen
            222222222      Main Lab          Williams
            333333333      CVS Office        Champagne
            444444444      High School       Klien
            555555555      Training Rm 300   Sanpletic
-------     ----------
  5              5 ❶

  2         111111111      Science Lab       Cohen
            222222222      CVS Office        Williams
            333333333      Off site          Champagne
            444444444      Lab 554           Klien
            555555555      Training Rm 50    Sanpletic
-------     ----------
  5              5

and so on . . .
```

And here's the SQL*Plus script for this report:

❶ Notice the use of the head separator.

❷ Skip two lines after a break.
❸ Totals.

❹ Get the student last name from the student table by matching the student ID.

```
rem
rem              Tests Taken report
rem    written by Jerome Engles
rem
rem  purpose:  this is an ad hoc report to list all tests taken,
rem  by type of test
rem
set headsep |  ❶
ttitle 'All Tests Taken'
btitle 'Guerrilla Exams'
Column TEST_ID            heading  'Test|Id '
Column TEST_ID            format  999999999
Column STUDENT_ID         heading  'Student|Id    '
Column STUDENT_ID         format  999999999
Column LOCATION           heading  'Location'  format a20 trunc
Column L_Name             heading 'Student|Name' format a30 trunc

Break on TEST_ID skip 2  ❷
compute count of test_id  on test_id  ❸
compute count of student_id on test_id
Set LINESIZE    80
Set PAGESIZE    55
Set NEWPAGE     0
SPOOL C:\TEST.LST
SELECT  TEST_ID, TEST_HISTORY.STUDENT_ID, LOCATION, L_NAME
       FROM
          TEST_HISTORY, STUDENTS
          WHERE TEST_HISTORY.STUDENT_ID = STUDENTS.STUDENT_ID  ❹
       ORDER BY TEST_ID;

SPOOL OFF
```

And here's what the report looks like if the user selects "1" for the test ID (only one student has taken that test so far):

All GUERRILLA EXAM Tests Taken As of
APRIL, 15, 2002 SYSTEM;

Test Id	Student Id	Location	Student Name
1	111111111	Main Lab	Cohen
1	1		

Here's one other important note on Oracle Reports: You can use variables. Suppose you wanted to do something like let your users enter which test they want to report on. Here's how you would do it: In your script, add the PROMPT and SELECT statements, and you will get just the test that your user specifies:

❶ Prompt the user.

❷ Use what was entered to qualify the SELECT statement.

❸ Note this rule: The variable must be in single quotes and start with an ampersand when it is used in a SELECT statement.

```
ACCEPT XTEST  PROMPT  'Enter Test ID: '  ❶

SELECT  TEST_ID, TEST_HISTORY.STUDENT_ID, LOCATION, L_NAME  ❷
      FROM
         TEST_HISTORY, STUDENTS
         WHERE
            TEST_ID = '&XTEST'  ❸
           AND
         TEST_HISTORY.STUDENT_ID = STUDENTS.STUDENT_ID
      ORDER BY TEST_ID;
```

Now for the sake of completeness, and because you're probably scratching your head, here's the script modified to show the current date and user in the title. Notice that to do this, we had to:

- Create two special columns with the tag NEW_VALUE
- In our SELECT statement, format and print SYSDATE
- Get the user ID and print it

❶ Notice the NEW_VALUE tags.

❷ Notice the formatting and use of SYSDATE and user.

```
rem
rem              Tests Taken report
rem    written by Jerome Engles
rem
rem  purpose:  this is an ad hoc report to list all tests taken,
rem  by type of test
rem

set headsep

ttitle  center      'All GUERRILLA EXAM  Tests Taken As of '
skip 1 -
       center       XTODAY '  '  XUSER ;  SKIP 3

btitle 'Guerrilla Exams'
column XTODAY NEW_VALUE XTODAY noprint format a1 trunc   ❶
column XUSER NEW_VALUE XUSER noprint format a1 trunc
Column TEST_ID            heading  'Test|Id '
Column TEST_ID            format  999999999
Column STUDENT_ID         heading  'Student|Id    '
Column STUDENT_ID         format  999999999
Column LOCATION           heading  'Location'  format a20 trunc
Column L_Name             heading 'Student|Name' format a30 trunc

Break on TEST_ID skip 2
compute count of test_id  on test_id
compute count of student_id on test_id

Set LINESIZE   80
Set PAGESIZE   55

ACCEPT XTEST  PROMPT  'Enter Test ID: '
SPOOL C:\TEST.LST
SELECT  TEST_ID, TEST_HISTORY.STUDENT_ID, LOCATION, L_NAME,
     TO_CHAR(SYSDATE, 'fmMONTH, DD, YYYY') XTODAY,   ❷
     USER XUSER
   FROM
     TEST_HISTORY, STUDENTS
       WHERE
```

```
        TEST_ID = '&XTEST'
        AND
    TEST_HISTORY.STUDENT_ID = STUDENTS.STUDENT_ID
    ORDER BY TEST_ID;

SPOOL OFF;
```

What's going on? NEW_VALUE is an Oracle construct that lets you put a variable, such as SYSDATE, into `ttitle` or `btitle`. SYSDATE is the current date automatically maintained by Oracle. The format is DD-MMM-YY—for example, 04-JUN-03. (Remember the pseudocolumn I mentioned earlier, when I gave SYSDATE as an example?) NEW_VALUE moves what you take in the SELECT ... TO_CHAR ... statement into the NEW_VALUE column. In effect, it is a column that you make on the fly; it exists only as long as you run the script, and it really isn't part of any table. Notice that the name of the column, XTODAY, appears in several places—that is, in the column definition and in the SELECT statements. Here's the output from the script:

```
                    All GUERRILLA EXAM  Tests Taken As of
                 ❶  JANUARY, 25, 2002  WAIVER_DEV2;  ❷

Test Id        Student Id       Location            Student Name
-------        ------------     ----------------    ----------------
  1  ❸         111111111        Science Lab         Cohen
               222222222        Main Lab            Williams
               333333333        CVS Office          Champagne
               444444444        High School         Klien
               555555555        Training Rm 300     Sanpletic
-------        ------------
  5               5
                                Guerrilla Exams
```

❶ Notice the date.

❷ The user is WAIVER_DEV2

❸ Only Test 1 was selected for this run.

There's another SQL*Plus reporting tool that is very useful for quick and dirty scans of the database. For any mainframe or DOS programmers out there, this tool is similar to a line editor or the old Edlin tool. It's called the **command-**

line editor, and you run it from the SQL> prompt. Remember, if you don't save your work, it disappears when you exit SQL!

Type in a standard SELECT command, such as

```
1* SELECT STUDENT_ID, L_NAME, SSNUM from STUDENTS
```

Student Id	Student Name	SSNUM
123456789	Randolph	123456789
222222222	Williams	222222222
111111111	Cohen	111111111
333333333	Champagne	333333333
444444444	Klien	444444444
555555555	Sanpletic	555555555
666666666	Levin	666666666
777777777	Corsu	777777777

Now we want to add the first name. Just use the LIST command, followed by the CHANGE command:

❶ List the commands first.

❷ Then use the CHANGE command. Use a special character to show the start and end of what you want to change. In this case it's the slash (/).

```
SQL> LIST ❶
  SELECT STUDENT_ID, L_NAME, SSNUM from STUDENTS

SQL> CHANGE /SSNUM/SSNUM,F_NAME ❷
  1* SELECT STUDENT_ID, L_NAME, SSNUM,F_NAME from STUDENTS

SQL> LIST
  1* SELECT STUDENT_ID, L_NAME, SSNUM,F_NAME from STUDENTS
```

If your script is on multiple lines, just type "LIST xx", where "xx" is the line number you want to change:

```
SQL> LIST
  1  SELECT STUDENT_ID,
  2  L_NAME,
  3  SSNUM,F_NAME
  4  from
  5* STUDENTS
```

To add the state, edit just line 3:

❸ List the line you want.

```
SQL> LIST 3  ❸
  3* SSNUM,F_NAME
```

(Or just type in "3".)

❹ Append the new column.

```
Now use "APPEND":
SQL> append, state  ❹
      3* SSNUM,F_NAME , state
```

❺ Check your work with another list.

```
   SQL> list  ❺
  1  SELECT STUDENT_ID,
  2   L_NAME,
  3  SSNUM,F_NAME , state
  4  from
  5* STUDENTS
```

Here are some other useful commands:

- **DEL** lets you delete the current line or any other line that you specify.
- **INPUT** lets you add a whole new line.
- **/** lets you run the commands after making changes.

Queries

Now we enter the world of queries. A **query** is what you do with a SELECT command. Queries can be simple or complex. In a simple query, you might ask for information from one table—for example, SELECT TABLE_NAME from ALL_TABLES. In a complex query, the SELECT statement is qualified by conditions such as WHERE or by the use of union, join, or other such construct. Let's investigate these a little further.

In a **join**, columns selected from two tables on the basis of a key match—primary to foreign—are connected:

❶ Note the use of LIKE.

```
SELECT L_NAME, TEST_ID from STUDENTS, TEST_HISTORY
WHERE STUDENTS.STUDENT_ID = TEST_HISTORY.STUDENT_ID
AND STUDENTS.L_NAME LIKE '%Klie%'  ❶
```

This join connects the STUDENT_ID columns in both tables:

L_Name	Test_ID
Klien	1
Klien	2
Klien	3
Klien	4
Klien	5

You can join unrelated columns in what is called a **non-key join**. Suppose that you wanted to see if any author had the same name as any student. You could write a SELECT statement matching the two columns. (Non-key joins are not common, but you should know that they are possible.)

Outer joins can be left-handed or right-handed. Are you confused? Well, here's how an outer join works. We would use an outer join if we wanted all rows in a column when we joined tables, even those without a match on both tables. For example, some students in the STUDENTS table will not yet have taken an exam. Suppose that we want to list all students, along with the exams they have taken. If we do a normal join,

```
WHERE STUDENTS.STUDENT_ID = TEST_HISTORY.STUDENT_ID
```

we will get only the students that have taken exams. To get *all* students, we have to write our query like this (this is a *left* outer join):

```
WHERE STUDENTS.STUDENT_ID(+) = TEST_HISTORY.STUDENT_ID.
```

We would use a *right* outer join to do something like finding all the tests, including those that have not been taken:

```
WHERE TEST_HISTORY.TEST_ID = TEST_ID.TEST_ID(+)
```

Now as long as we're talking about joins, what is a union? A **union** is a way of combining similar data from several tables. If you wanted to send a mailing to everyone in your STUDENTS table who had also taken exams, or only to those who had not ever taken an exam, or to everyone in both tables, but you did not want to send two letters to them, a union would be the tool for you.

To get everyone listed in both tables, use the simple UNION statement:

```
SELECT STUDENTS.STUDENT_ID from STUDENTS
UNION
SELECT TEST_HISTORY.STUDENT_ID;
```

And here's the list you will get:

❶ In our test tables, only five students have taken tests so far, but the union lists all students from both tables without repeating any names.

Student_ID
111111111
123456789
222222222
333333333
444444444
555555555
666666666
777777777

❶

To get students who are in the STUDENTS table and not in the TEST_HISTORY table, use the MINUS command:

```
SELECT STUDENT_ID from STUDENTS
MINUS
SELECT STUDENT_ID from TEST_HISTORY;
```

Here are the results:

❷ Students not in the TEST_HISTORY table.

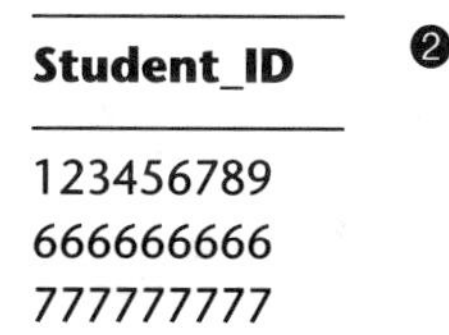

Student_ID
123456789
666666666
777777777

❷

And you guessed it, to get only names in *both* tables, use INTERSECT:

```
SELECT STUDENT_ID from STUDENTS
INTERSECT
SELECT STUDENT_ID from TEST_HISTORY;
```

Here's the resulting report:

❸ Only those students who are in *both* tables.

Student_ID ❸
111111111
222222222
333333333
444444444
555555555

Putting the Date in the Spool File Name

You've probably noticed that the preceding examples give the spool file a simple name. Sometimes you want to create the spool file with the current date in its name, for obvious reasons. One way to do this is to add another column, then build your spool file name by concatenating the date and the name:

❶ Create a column to hold the variable XSPOOLNAME.

❷ By setting TERM OFF, you fool the system into using XSPOOLNAME instead of prompting you for a name.

❸ Build the full spool file name.

❹ Now spool your output to it.

❺ Here's a simple SQL command.

❻ End by turning spooling off.

```
col filename new_value XSPOOLNAME  ❶

set term off  ❷

select to_char(sysdate, 'mondd') || 'PERSONS.txt' XSPOOLNAME
from dual;  ❸

spool c:\&XSPOOLNAME  ❹

select * from person_table;  ❺

spool off;  ❻
```

OK, how fancy can we get with the spool file name and dates? Here's an example of another script that has not only the date, but also the time and the type of application (GL). This script is also on the book's CD:

```
REM
REM      Here's a nifty little script to use the current date
REM      and time as an output file name
```

```
REM
REM      There's actually quite a bit going on here.  First,
REM      the SCAN ON command is used to
REM      make sure our setup will handle substitution variables
REM      Second, a variable is created - FILEDATE.
REM      Third, we load FILEDATE with the current date and
REM      time
REM      Now we set the SPOOL FILE to FILEDATE by using the
REM      substitution symbol '&'
REM      Then we just continue processing, and finally turn
REM      spooling off.
REM
REM     Note that you can add other text to the spool file
REM     name, such as "GENERAL LEDGER" and
REM     so forth by just adding additional concatenations. I
REM     put the "GL" both at the beginning and at the
REM     end to show you that you can append additional text
REM     anywhere:
REM
REM   SELECT
REM      'GL'||TO_CHAR(SYSDATE,'YYYYMMDDHH24MI')||'GL'||'.TXT'
REM      filedate from dual;
REM      and the spool file name is:  GL200208280952GL.TXT
REM
REM
REM  Step 1:  Set "scan on" to make sure that your setup will
REM      use substitution variables
SET SCAN ON
REM  Step 2: Create the variable
      COLUMN FILEDATE  NEW_VALUE  FILEDATE
REM  Step 3: Load the date and time
      SELECT
'GL'||TO_CHAR(SYSDATE,'YYYYMMDDHH24MI')||'GL.TXT' FILEDATE FROM
DUAL;
REM  Step 4: Set the SPOOL FILE
      SPOOL C:\&FILEDATE;
```

```
REM  Step 5: Continue processing
     Sdate_takenELECT FNAME from STUDENTS;
REM At the end, turn spooling off
     SPOOL OFF;
```

Date Handling

It's time to look at what we can do with dates. This is another huge topic, so we're going to cover just the basics. As you become more sophisticated with your reporting and programming, you will just jump for joy at what you can do in Oracle with dates. In fact, you can become a hero of the list servers if you develop this specialized expertise. In any event, you can become a big person on campus because almost all SQL programming classes play with dates, and many homework assignments require figuring out clever date manipulations. Once word gets out that you can do these, you'll have free coffee and tofu for life!

To start, first you must simply accept the fact that to Oracle, a date is a real data type, and that Oracle includes with a date the hours, minutes, and seconds. Now don't get too worried; Oracle also gives you the tools to work with all these parts.

Got it? When you define a date column, Oracle stores all this—MM,DD, YY,HH,MM,SS—and then gives you tools to format the data into what you want for your report, screen, or whatever. The two tools are `TO_CHAR` and `TO_DATE`:

1. **TO_CHAR** converts an Oracle date into a character string.
2. **TO_DATE** converts a character string or number into an Oracle date.

Usually you will use an Oracle date column, so that's what we'll use in our examples. Now Oracle gives us more than 40 ways to format a date column, so you can go as wild as you'd like. I'll cover the most common ones here.

Let's take our TEST_HISTORY table. We have a Date_Taken column that we want to appear on our reports. To satisfy everyone, however, we have to be able to print that date in various formats. Here are a couple of examples:

To show all the test dates for a student in MM/DD/YY format, use this code:

```
SELECT TO_CHAR(DATE_TAKEN, 'MM/DD/YY')
from TEST_HISTORY
WHERE
STUDENT_ID = 111111111 order by date_taken;
```

Here's the resulting report:

❶ Don't mind the heading; we just didn't specify a name.

TO_CHAR(❶
01/22/02
02/14/02
04/21/02
05/21/02

Here's how to clean up this simple listing above to change "TO_CHAR" to a real heading:

❷ In this script we have created a real column name—Date_Taken—by putting it right after the SELECT command. You can do this with any column you select.

```
SELECT '  '||TO_CHAR(DATE_TAKEN, 'MM/DD/YY') DATE_TAKEN   ❷
 from TEST_HISTORY  WHERE STUDENT_ID = '111111111'
 ORDER BY DATE_TAKEN
```

and here are the results:

DATE_TAKEN
01/22/02
02/14/02
04/21/02
05/21/02

Here are a couple more results using different formatting commands:

❶ Notice the format for month, day, and year here, and the results below.

❷ This is an example of getting the dates for a student for particular exams.

```
SELECT TO_CHAR(DATE_TAKEN, 'Month, DDth, YYyy')  ❶
from TEST_HISTORY
WHERE
STUDENT_ID = 111111111
and TEST_ID in (3,4)  ❷
```

And here's the resulting report:

TO_CHAR
May   , 21ST, 2002
April , 21ST, 2002

In the next example, look at the "fm" in front of "Month". It takes out the spaces between the month name and the comma:

```
SELECT TO_CHAR(DATE_TAKEN, 'fmMonth, DDth, YYyy')
from TEST_HISTORY
WHERE
STUDENT_ID = 111111111
and TEST_ID in (3,4)
```

Here's the resulting report:

TO_CHAR(DATE
May, 21ST, 2002
April, 21ST, 2002

To get the hours, minutes, and seconds, just add them to the SELECT statement:

```
SELECT TO_CHAR(DATE_TAKEN, 'fmMonth, DD, YYyy, HH:MM:SS')
from TEST_HISTORY
WHERE
STUDENT_ID = 111111111
and TEST_ID in (3,4)
```

The resulting report looks like this:

TO_CHAR(DATE_T
May, 21, 2002, 4:5:18
April, 21, 2002, 4:4:8

Note

Do you remember that DATE is a unique Oracle data type? If you want to do any calculations on a string, first you have to turn it into a date, then do the manipulation. But, and here's the tricky part, the string must be in one of the 40 plus acceptable Oracle date formats. If it isn't, Oracle cannot turn it into a date.

Here's what you can do with the date column:

- Add months. For example, the following code:

❶ We want to calculate the date for this person's next exam, which should be three months after taking Test 1.

```
SELECT ADD_MONTHS(DATE_TAKEN, 3) NextExam ❶
from TEST_HISTORY
WHERE STUDENT_ID = 111111111
and TEST_ID = 1
```

results in this report:

NextExam
22-APR-02

- Subtract months (just add the minus sign). For example, the following code:

```
SELECT ADD_MONTHS(DATE_TAKEN, -2)StudyTime
from TEST_HISTORY
WHERE STUDENT_ID = 111111111
and TEST_ID = 1
```

gives this result:

StudyTime
22-NOV-01

Other commands you can use are LAST_DAY, MONTHS_BETWEEN, NEXT_DAY, GREATEST, and LEAST. The SQL code is similar to the examples just given:

- `Select` **LAST_DAY** `(DATE_TAKEN) END_MONTH from ...`
- `Select` **MONTHS_BETWEEN**`(SYSDATE, DATE_TAKEN) LastExam from ...`
- `Select` **NEXT_DAY**`(DATE_TAKEN, 'MONDAY') NewWeek from ...`
- `Select` **LEAST**`('21-MAR-02', DATE_TAKEN) OLDEST from ...` (**GREATEST** has the same format.)

Note

The examples here show just the format for the commands. They may or may not make sense if you use the TEST_HISTORY file, but they will give you an idea of the syntax.

One last note: You can use dates in your WHERE clauses. You can subtract two dates, and you can use the BETWEEN or IN operator, but be very careful using the LEAST or GREATEST command. LEAST and GREATEST work only if you first convert the dates using the TO_DATE command.

Way back in Chapter 9 we talked about how you will not always get information in the format you really want. This is especially true of dates. Many systems keep dates in the format MM/DD/YY, and now you know that Oracle keeps the date in the format DD-MON-YYYY. So what can you do? If you try to load the date as is, it will fail. In the preceding paragraphs you saw some of the incredible formatting that Oracle allows, and you can use some of the same logic to handle incoming dates.

Let's say that you're loading a history file containing all the tests that everyone has taken, in the standard format MM/DD/YYYY. To get the data into Oracle format, just do this when you define the field in SQL*Loader:

```
TEST_DATE       DATE    'MM/DD/YYYY'
```

Oracle will now store the dates in its native DD-MON-YYYY format. To accommodate what your users are accustomed to, you can use the TO_CHAR commands to format the dates back to the other format when you're reporting the information.

Note

Here's an important note: I strongly suggest that from now on you always use YYYY whenever you have control over dates. Some systems will take a date such as 06/15/02 as June 15th, 1902, instead of 2002. To avoid any problems, get in the habit of always using all four digits for the year.

I want to complete something that you've probably been wondering about since the last chapter: How do we really go about calculating the start and end times for the test? Oracle actually includes the time when you specify a column type of DATE, so you don't have to put it there. But how do you get access to it? Again, the various date formatting commands are at your disposal. For example, if you wanted to look at the test start times, you would just use this command:

```
SELECT TO_CHAR(DATE_TAKEN, 'DD/MM/YYYY, HH:MI:SS')
TEST_DATE_TIME from TEST_HISTORY;
```

And these would be the results:

TEST_DATE_TIME
14/02/2002, 04:35:41
15/06/2002, 01:25:36
27/06/2002, 10:23:33
07/09/2002, 11:47:36
22/01/2002, 12:00:00
21/05/2002, 12:00:00
21/04/2002, 12:00:00

So there are two ways to capture the times: (1) use SYSDATE for both, or (2) extract the time from SYSDATE and store it in a separate column.

Sequences

What are sequences, and why are they used? A **sequence** is an automatic numbering tool that is very useful when you're inserting rows in a table and want to have one of the columns automatically filled in with sequential numbers. Suppose you were loading an AUTHORS table from a spreadsheet, or even manually, and you needed to have a unique, numerical identifier for each author as the rows were inserted. You could manually type in a number, or you could use the Oracle sequence feature to help you. The syntax is easy:

1. Create the sequence using the SEQUENCE command.
2. Use it with an INSERT statement.

Here's an example of sequence creation:

```
CREATE SEQUENCE AUTHOR_SEQ  increment by 1 start with
333333334;
```

You can start anywhere and increment by any amount, and you can specify a maximum amount. If you increment by a *negative* number, the sequence will be descending.

Here's how we use a sequence:

```
INSERT INTO AUTHORS
            VALUES (AUTHOR_SEQ.NextVAL, 'Dr. Guerrilla');
```

And here's what the AUTHORS table contains:

Author_ID	Author
123456789	Guerrilla Test Author
333333334	Dr. Guerrilla ❶
111111111	Guerrilla Test Author2
222222222	Guerrilla Test Author3
333333333	Waiver Administration

❶ **333333334 is the one that came from the INSERT statement using the Create SEQUENCE AUTHOR_SEQ command shown above.**

To delete a sequence, use the DROP command—that is, DROP SEQUENCE AUTHOR_SEQ, for example. That's it.

Manipulating Letters and Numbers

Strings

This section takes us into the area of **strings**, which are simply sequences of things, like the letters in this sentence or your name. In the course of your work you'll have to play with strings, and fortunately SQL comes with several good editing tools to help you:

- **CONCAT**. This command, or ||, is used to concatenate several strings. For example, either of the following two commands:

  1. `SELECT L_NAME||F_NAME from STUDENTS` ❶
  2. `SELECT CONCAT (L_NAME,F_NAME) from STUDENTS;`

  yields this report:

CONCAT(L_NAME,F_NAME)
RandolphJared
WilliamsJacob
CohenGeorge
ChampagneAlice
KlienMarisha
SanpleticMartha
LevinDonald
CorsuFrank

❶ Use the broken vertical bar to concatenate strings.

- **LOWER**. For example, the command `LOWER ('GUERRILLA ORACLE')` produces "guerrilla oracle".
- **UPPER**. For example, the command `SELECT UPPER(L_NAME) from STUDENTS` produces all student names in uppercase letters.
- **INITCAP**. For example, the command `SELECT INITCAP(LOWER(L_NAME))`❷ `from STUDENTS;` gives the following:

Randolph
Williams
Cohen
Champagne
Klien
Sanpletic
Levin
Corsu

❷ Notice that you have to use both INITCAP and LOWER to get the first letter of the last name as an uppercase letter.

- **LENGTH**. For example, the command `SELECT LENGTH(L_NAME) from STUDENTS` gives the length of each last name.

- **SUBSTR**. This command is used to get a piece of a string. For example, the command `SELECT SUBSTR(L_NAME, 3,5) from STUDENTS;` yields this result:

SUBST
ndolp ❸
lliam
hen
ampag
ien
nplet
vin
rsu

❸ **The SUBSTR command above took part of the last name: It started at position 3 and went for the next five characters.**

- **SOUNDEX**. This fun command looks for strings that sound like the string you're using to compare. (Note that spelling does count!). Here's an example:

```
SELECT L_NAME from STUDENTS
       WHERE SOUNDEX(L_NAME) = SOUNDEX('willyams');
```

  This command returns the name "Williams". But be aware that SOUNDEX assumes American English! Results are not predictable with other languages, especially with foreign names.

- **INSTR**. This command is used to look for the location of a particular character in a string. For example, the command `SELECT L_NAME INSTR(L_NAME, 'A') from STUDENTS` gives these results:

L_Name	INSTR(L_Name,'A')
Randolph	0 ❹
Williams	0
Cohen	0
Champagne	0
Klien	0
Sanpletic	0
Levin	0
Corsu	0

❹ **Notice zero hits for *A*. Now try it with a small *a*.**

Here's the same SELECT statement, but using a small *a*:

```
SELECT L_NAME INSTR(L_NAME, 'a') from STUDENTS;
```

The results look like this:

❺ Now you can see the position of the first occurrence of the letter *a* in each last name in the table.

L_Name INSTR(L_Name,'a')	
Randolph	2
Williams	6
Cohen	0
Champagne	3
Klien	0
Sanpletic	2
Levin	0
Corsu	0

❺

The INSTR command is extremely useful when you're searching the database for particular patterns, names, invalid strings, and so forth. You'll probably be using it a lot.

For our final discussion of strings, we're going to take a look at four more tools that you can use to manipulate a string or set: LPAD, RPAD, LTRIM, and RTRIM. (You already know that SUBSTR lets you find a piece of a string.)

The PAD twins—R and L—let you add characters to the (guess where?) right and left ends of a string. By default the characters are spaces, but you can use anything. Common uses of RPAD and LPAD are to add periods or dashes to help the user read across a line. Here's an example:

```
SELECT RPAD(L_NAME,40,'.'), F_NAME from STUDENTS;
```

This command produces the following report:

❻ We used RPAD to add periods to the right of the last name.

RPAD(L_Name,40,'.') F_Name	
Randolph..................................	Jared
Williams..................................	Jacob
Cohen......................................	George
Champagne..............................	Alice
Klien.......................................	Marisha
Sanpletic.................................	Martha
Levin.......................................	Donald
Corsu......................................	Frank

❻

Now let's look at the TRIM twins: LTRIM and RTRIM. These commands are used to remove characters at the ends of strings, such as quotation marks. Here are a few examples:

- `SELECT **RTRIM**(TEST_NAME, '"') from TEST_ID;`
  This command gets rid of the quotation mark at the end of a string. (Note that the double quote is enclosed within single quotes.)
- `SELECT **RTRIM**(TEST_NAME, 'Ph.D') from TEST_ID;`
  This command drops "Ph.D." from the end of a string.
- `SELECT **LTRIM**(**RTRIM**(TEST_NAME, 'Ph.D"') '"') from TEST_ID;`
  This command gets rid of quotation marks at the beginning and end of a string, as well as "Ph.D." at the end. Notice that we're modifying both ends here: LTRIM gets rid of the quotation mark on the left, and RTRIM takes care of "Ph.D." and the quotation mark on the right. Just be careful with your parentheses.

More Functions for Working with Strings

TRANSLATE

Suppose you wanted to modify last names by changing certain characters. You would use the Oracle TRANSLATE command as in this example:

```
SQL>  1* select translate(L_NAME, 'R', 'x') from students
```

Here are the results:

TRANSLATE(L_NAME,'R'
xandolph ❶
Williams
Cohen
Champagne
Klien
Sanpletic
Levin
Corsu

❶ Notice that "Randolph" is now "xandolph". No other names were changed because there weren't any more capital Rs.

❷ Notice that this command says to replace any capital *R* with a blank space. That's how it works: Specify the character(s) you want to replace with what you want them replaced with.

You can use this technique to eliminate characters by putting blanks in the TRANSLATE command:

```
SQL> SELECT TRANSLATE(L_NAME, 'R', ' ') from STUDENTS   ❷
```

The results look like this:

TRANSLATE(L_NAME,'R'
andolph ❸
Williams
Cohen
Champagne
Klien
Sanpletic
Levin
Corsu

❸ Notice that "Randolph" is now " andolph".

DECODE

DECODE is an interesting function. I use it to reverse financial transactions where a duplicate journal entry has to be made but the sign has to be reversed. Here's the general syntax:

DECODE (value, if it is this1(a), then change it to this1(b), if it is this2(a), then change it to this2(b), . . . else change it to this)

Here's an example:

DECODE(voucher_sign, '+', '−', '−', '+', 'D','C', C', D', 'Z');

Change + to −
Change − to +
Change *D* to *C*
Change *C* to *D*
Else make it a *Z*

DECODE can be a very powerful tool when used with other functions. Such programming gets rather complex, and I refer you to more detailed documentation on DECODE. What I have shown you here will more than suffice for most of your normal work, but for those who are curious and have taken a liking to such functions, go and look deeper.

Number Functions

In this short section I'm going to introduce you to some of the more common mathematical functions that are used in normal business environments. For the serious mathematicians out there, be aware that there is much, much more horsepower in Oracle math functions than we're going to cover here, and more in-depth references are available when you need them.

We're going to take a look at AVG, COUNT, MAX, MIN, SUM, GREATEST, and LEAST. Before we start, keep in mind these two things:

1. We use the normal math symbols (+, –, *, /) when specifying any calculations. Here's an example:

   ```
   Select FEES, FINES, PARKING, FEES + FINES + PARKING TOTALS
   from registration_record;
   ```

2. NULL is *not* zero. It is a special Oracle construct that means that the field is empty. This is important.

NULL

Let's digress a bit and talk about NULL. In Oracle, as I have mentioned, NULL means "empty"; it does *not* mean zeros or spaces. It is an intrinsic feature, and when you run the DESC command on a table, one of the headings will be "NULL?". For example, this command:

```
SQL> desc temp_person_table;
```

yields the following results:

Name	Null?	Type
Person_ID		NUMBER(12)
Hours		NUMBER(9,2)
Run_Date		DATE

Here none of the columns are set to NULL, which is standard. However, there are some important considerations with NULL values.

First, any mathematical computation that uses a NULL value ends up staying null. For example, the following code inserts data for a particular person into COURSE_TABLE with a NULL value for HOURS, and then increases the hours for that person:

❶ Notice NULL value in the 'insert' command.

```
SQL> RUN
  1  INSERT into COURSE_TABLE values (
  2* 987654321, 16, '12-APR-02', 'Satellite', 65.25,null) ❶
1 row created.

SQL> RUN
  1* UPDATE COURSE_TABLE set hours = (hours +12) WHERE PERSON_ID
= 987654321
1 row updated.
```

Now take a look at the HOURS value for person 987654321. You would expect 12 hours, but it is still NULL. Run a simple SQL statement to select everything from the COURSE_TABLE:

```
SQL> select * from course_table;
```

The results look like this:

PERSON_ID	COURSE_ID	DATE_TAKE	LOCATION	GRADE	HOURS
987654321	16	12-APR-02	Satellite	65.25	
222222222	2	15-JAN-02	Home Office, Lab 12	81.5	18

Now that you know how NULL values work, think about other implications. Other math activities, such as AVG, SUM, MIN, MAX, and COUNT will skip any NULL columns, possibly making the results meaningless. You could do a count on all the rows in a table, then do a count on just one column, and get different results. The reason is that COUNT will count all rows but will skip NULL columns!

You can test for NULL values, but you must use the correct syntax. Instead of the equal sign and so forth, you must use the following general syntax: "If Person_ID IS NULL . . . (do something)", or "If Person_ID IS NOT NULL . . . (do something)".

Now let's take a look at the test scores to date for all students:

❷ So far, we have 25 students who have taken Guerrilla Waiver exams, with scores ranging from 22 to 100.

SCORE		
98	88	100
90	32	100
50	75	100
87	22	100
92	98	80
93	90	100
79	91	100
72	80	100
		100

❷

Suppose that the director of training comes to you and wants a quick synopsis of the scores—no details, just a summary. Here's where you can combine math functions and deliver a neat, quick, easily understood overview. Just use the following SELECT command:

```
SQL> SELECT AVG(SCORE), COUNT(SCORE), MAX(SCORE), MIN(SCORE),
SUM(SCORE)
  2  from TEST_HISTORY;
```

And here are the results:

AVG(SCORE)	COUNT(SCORE)	MAX(SCORE)	MIN(SCORE)	SUM(SCORE)
84.68	25	100	22	2117

❸ Notice the GROUP BY statement. We must use this because we're asking Oracle to give information on a group of rows, not just one row. Any time we ask for such a function as SUM, COUNT, or AVG, we must include the GROUP BY clause.

Note the use of the various math commands, and when the director comes to you and says she would like a breakdown so that she can see which exam is getting the lowest score, you refine the SELECT command like this:

```
SELECT TEST_ID, AVG(SCORE) from TEST_HISTORY GROUP BY TEST_ID;  ❸
```

The results look like this:

TEST_ID	AVG(SCORE)
1	84.6
2	60.8
3	94.6
4	90.8
5	92.6

Now that the director can see the average scores, she asks you to show details for Test 2. Just keep refining your SELECT statement, as here:

```
SQL> SELECT STUDENT_ID, SCORE from TEST_HISTORY
         WHERE TEST_ID = 2
```

Now we get these results:

STUDENT_ID	SCORE
111111111	50
222222222	32
333333333	22
444444444	100
555555555	100

Since you've done such a good job getting the information so quickly, the director now wants to see how student 111111111 has done on *all* tests. By now I'm sure you can figure out the SELECT command for that!

But what I want you to realize is that you have really created a group of queries that should become standard reports that the director can run whenever she wants. So go ahead and create the scripts, using standard coding, as well as prompting the user for input, such as which test or which student. In going through these rather simple exercises, you will have discovered what is valuable to your users.

Some Interesting Verbs and Adverbs You Should Know

In the preceding pages I've used some SQL statements without really explaining them. I guessed that you could figure out the purpose and syntax from the context and examples. However, here's a little more information on the GROUP BY (and HAVING), ORDER BY, and WHERE clauses.

GROUP BY

Here's the important thing to remember: When you want to combine a group function (such as COUNT, AVG, or SUM) with an individual function such as SELECT L_NAME (with L_NAME being an individual item), you have to use the GROUP BY statement. Otherwise, get ready for "ORA-xxx" errors that say something about "not a group function."

And here's one more important syntax item:

❶ You must match your SELECT and GROUP BY items.

❷ You have two SELECT items, so you must have two GROUP BY items. Also whatever you put in the COUNT statement must also appear in your SELECT statement.

```
        ↓
SELECT TEST_ID, SCORE, COUNT(TEST_ID) from TEST_HISTORY GROUP ❶
BY TEST_ID, SCORE ❷
     ↑
```

How do we use this feature? Suppose you have to produce a list of student scores by test, but you do not want to repeat duplicate scores. Running the preceding SELECT command will produce the following results:

❸ Notice that the COUNT column shows duplicate scores for a test, and ❹ the SCORE column shows the actual scores, all arranged in test ID order.

TEST_ID	SCORE ❹	COUNT(TEST_ID) ❸
1	75	1
1	80	2
1	90	1
1	98	1
2	22	1
2	32	1
2	50	1
2	100	2
3	87	1
3	88	1
3	100	2
4	72	1
4	90	1
4	92	1
. . . and so on		

Now suppose you wanted to list only the failing scores. Now you use the HAVING command, like this:

❶ Notice the use of HAVING.

```
SQL> SELECT  TEST_ID, SCORE, COUNT(TEST_ID) from TEST_HISTORY
GROUP BY TEST_ID,
     score HAVING score < 70;  ❶
```

Here are the results:

Test_ID	Score	COUNT(Test_ID)
2	22	1
2	32	1
2	50	1

Remember that HAVING is a group function and works only when you're using the GROUP BY command! Here's the error you get if you go after something with the HAVING statement that is *not* in your GROUP BY clause:

❷ Since SCORE is not in the GROUP BY clause, you get this error.

```
1  SELECT  TEST_ID, SCORE, COUNT(TEST_ID) from TEST_HISTORY
GROUP BY TEST_ID
  2* HAVING score < 70
HAVING score < 70
       *
ERROR at line 2:  ❷
ORA-00979: not a GROUP BY expression
```

ORDER BY

Now let's add the ORDER BY function. As you've seen, the GROUP BY clause is used to group things together. It does not change the way items sort. Suppose you now needed to be able to list the scores in descending order by test ID. Here's where you add the ORDER BY statement, and notice that you can have more than one item in it:

```
SQL> SELECT  TEST_ID, SCORE, COUNT(TEST_ID) from TEST_HISTORY
GROUP BY
             TEST_ID, SCORE
  HAVING score > 70
  ORDER BY TEST_ID, SCORE
```

❸ There's a lot going on here. First of all, we want only scores greater than 70—hence the HAVING statement. Then, to show the scores in ascending order within TEST_ID, we added the ORDER BY phrase. And don't forget, we're using a COUNT function, so we get a total for any duplicate scores.

You're seeing a pretty powerful set of functions here that will help you look really good to your users whenever they ask you for information like this!

Here are the results: ❸

TEST_ID	SCORE	COUNT(TEST_ID)
1	75	1
1	80	2
1	90	1
1	98	1
2	100	2
3	87	1
3	88	1
3	98	1
3	100	2
4	72	1
4	90	1
4	92	1
4	100	2
5	79	1
5	91	1
. . . and so on		

WHERE

Finally, we have the `WHERE` clause. Think of `WHERE` as a gate or filter. It qualifies the rows that are returned, as in these examples: `WHERE SCORE > 70` or `WHERE TEST_ID = 1`. One of the most important uses of the `WHERE` clause is to prevent what is called a *Cartesian product*, which is just a way of saying that you can end up with huge results if you join tables and do not use a `WHERE` clause. For example, if we wrote a `SELECT` statement that selected all rows from STUDENTS and all rows from TEST_ID, and there were 500 rows in the STUDENTS table and 50 rows in the TEST_ID table, we would end up with 25,000 rows of rather useless data. (For you skeptics, go ahead and run `Select * from students, test_id`, and you will see that you will get back not the sum of the rows in both tables, but the result of multiplying the numbers of both tables! Do it now and get it out of your system. *Do not do it* when your systems are in production, or you'll bring them to their knees.) But beware; it happens. So use the `WHERE` clause whenever possible to prevent such situations, as well as to produce meaningful results.

You can also use various operators with the WHERE clause, such as:

- WHERE SCORE BETWEEN 70 AND 100;
- WHERE SCORE = 90 OR SCORE = 80 OR SCORE = 70;
- WHERE EXISTS (SELECT SCORE FROM TEST_HISTORY WHERE SCORE >99);
- WHERE SCORE IN (99,98,97,96);

Triggers

Because the term *trigger* is not the least intuitive, your first impulse probably is to ask simply, "What?" Well, a **trigger** is a superb tool that lets us do something every time something else happens. Every time you add a new student, for example, you can have a trigger fire so that an e-mail is sent to Marketing with the student information for mailing lists. Or every time someone gets a perfect score on a test, a report can be created for the director or instructor.

Get the idea? In many businesses and universities these triggers are all-important. Human Resources always wants to know anytime someone changes name, address, and so forth. So you would put triggers on those columns in the database. Whenever any rows with the flagged data change, such as in an INSERT, UPDATE, or DELETE operation, certain other things will automatically happen, such as an e-mail being sent to Human Resources, a report being printed, or emergency notification being sent to someone.

Triggers can act on rows or statements. **Row triggers** fire every time a row is changed in a table. **Statement triggers** fire *once* for each statement. For example, if you added 20 students to the STUDENTS table, one statement trigger would fire. But if you set up the trigger as a row trigger, you would get 20 trigger firings.

There are four triggers for rows and statements: INSERT, UPDATE, DELETE, and INSTEAD OF. And for all except INSTEAD OF, you can specify before or after. These options provide 14 possible triggers.

We create a trigger like this:

```
CREATE OR REPLACE TRIGGER STUDENT_CHANGE
AFTER INSERT OR UPDATE ON STUDENTS
FOR EACH ROW
BEGIN
  IF INSERTING THEN
       INSERT INTO AUDIT_TABLE VALUES (SAUDIT_SEQ.NEXTVAL,
'INSERT');
  ELSE
```

```
        INSERT INTO AUDIT_TABLE VALUES (SAUDIT_SEQ.NEXTVAL,
'UPDATE');
  END IF;
END;
```

In this example we have told Oracle to create an entry in AUDIT_TABLE anytime the STUDENTS table is updated or a row is inserted. Notice how we slipped in another sequence!

Now let's take a look at how triggers are really used. If you want to monitor a table, you will want the before and after information, or at least the before information. Oracle gives us handy keywords—NEW and OLD—to use when we're writing to an audit table or something similar.

Let's create a simple audit table for authors:

```
CREATE TABLE AUTHOR_AUDIT  (
  AUDIT_NO        NUMBER(9),
  AUDIT_DATE      DATE,
  AUDIT_ACTION    VARCHAR2(10) CHECK (AUDIT_ACTION IN('UPDATE',
                      'INSERT')),
  AUDIT_AUTHOR_ID NUMBER(9),
  AUDIT_AUTHOR    VARCHAR2(30)
              );
```

We've already created the sequence AUDIT_SEQ. So let's create a trigger to update the AUTHOR_AUDIT table when a record is inserted or changed:

```
CREATE OR REPLACE TRIGGER AUTHOR_TRIGGER
  AFTER INSERT OR UPDATE
  ON AUTHORS
  FOR EACH ROW
  BEGIN
    IF INSERTING THEN
          INSERT INTO AUTHOR_AUDIT   VALUES
      (AUDIT_SEQ.NextVal, SYSDATE, 'INSERT', ❶
     :NEW.AUTHOR_ID, :NEW.AUTHOR); ❷
    ELSE
        INSERT INTO AUTHOR_AUDIT   VALUES
      (AUDIT_SEQ.NextVal, SYSDATE, 'UPDATE',
     :OLD.AUTHOR_ID, :OLD.AUTHOR);  ❷
    END IF;
 END;
```

❶ Notice in the next lines that we'll be using a sequence.

❷ Notice the colon before OLD and NEW.

In this example, we are writing to AUDIT_TABLE any new information on an INSERT, and the old information on an UPDATE.

Caution

Creating a trigger requires great attention to detail. If anything is misspelled or left out, for example, the only message you will get is, "Warning: Trigger created with compilation errors." This can be rather frustrating, and all I can tell you is to go back and check your spelling and your use of parentheses, semicolons, and so forth. One misspelled word or one missing semicolon will cause this error, and all you can do is take your code apart piece by piece until you find the culprit. Maybe someday Oracle will enhance its error messages. Obviously the compiler found a problem, but it just isn't designed yet to give us details.

What happens when we do an INSERT or UPDATE operation? Let's look at an example:

```
    INSERT INTO AUTHORS   VALUES   (
    AUTHOR_SEQ.NEXTVAL, 'Harry Pottingham')
1 row created.
```

AUDIT_NO	AUDIT_DAT	AUDIT_ACTI	AUDIT_AUTHOR_ID	AUDIT_AUTHOR
2	24-JAN-02	INSERT	333333336	Harry Pottingham

Here are the contents of the AUTHOR_AUDIT table:

Yes, you can have three triggers stacked in one script. Here's the code:

```
/*  TRIGGER CREATE SCRIPT
    for three activities  */

CREATE OR REPLACE TRIGGER AUTHOR_TRIGGER
AFTER INSERT OR UPDATE OR DELETE     /*  monitor inserts and
updates  */
ON AUTHORS
FOR EACH ROW
BEGIN
  IF INSERTING THEN   /* for an INSERT, get the NEW values  */
```

```
        INSERT INTO AUTHOR_AUDIT   VALUES
    (AUDIT_SEQ.NextVal, SYSDATE, 'INSERT',
  :NEW.AUTHOR_ID, :NEW.AUTHOR); END IF;

 IF UPDATING THEN        /*   for an UPDATE, then get the OLD
values   */
        INSERT INTO AUTHOR_AUDIT   VALUES
    (AUDIT_SEQ.NextVal, SYSDATE, 'UPDATE',
  :OLD.AUTHOR_ID, :OLD.AUTHOR);  END IF;

 IF DELETING THEN        /*   for a DELETE get the OLD values
*/
        INSERT INTO AUTHOR_AUDIT   VALUES
    (AUDIT_SEQ.NextVal, SYSDATE, 'DELETE',
  :OLD.AUTHOR_ID, :OLD.AUTHOR);  END IF;

END;
```

You can add error processing using the EXCEPTION statement. There are three parts to handling exceptions: (1) building the DECLARE statements, (2) adding the IF... logic, and (3) creating the EXCEPTION section. Here's the same script again, modified just for inserts with exception routines:

❶ First the DECLARE section . . .

❷ . . . then the logic to check the positions 9, 10, and 11 of the user name to see if any of them equal "BUS" or "bus" . . .

❸ . . . and then at the end, the actual exception handling.

```
CREATE OR REPLACE TRIGGER INSERT_AUTHOR
    BEFORE   INSERT  ON AUTHORS
DECLARE  ❶

  NO_AUTHORITY  EXCEPTION;

BEGIN
  IF SUBSTR(USER,8,3) <> 'BUS'   ❷
    THEN RAISE NO_AUTHORITY;
  END IF;

  IF SUBSTR(USER,8,3) <> 'bus' ❷
    THEN RAISE NO_AUTHORITY;
  END IF;

 EXCEPTION   ❸
  WHEN  NO_AUTHORITY
```

```
    THEN
      RAISE_APPLICATION_ERROR (-20001, 'User NOT authorized');
END;
```

If all goes well, an unauthorized user will get the following message:

```
          *
      ERROR at line 1:
      ORA-20001: User NOT authorized
      ORA-06512: at "SYSTEM.INSERT_AUTHOR", line 10
ORA-04088: error during execution of trigger
'SYSTEM.INSERT_AUTHOR'
```

That's it for triggers! But let me say one more thing. Triggers can impede performance, and in busy shops they can quickly fill up audit tables. If you ever want to stop a trigger, just use the ALTER command (notice that you can take action against a specific trigger or against all triggers in a specific table):

- ALTER TRIGGER audit_trigger DISABLE;
- ALTER TABLE AUTHORS DISABLE ALL TRIGGERS;

To start a trigger, use the same command with ENABLE:

- ALTER TRIGGER audit_trigger ENABLE;
- ALTER TABLE AUTHORS ENABLE ALL TRIGGERS;

(By the way, the BEGIN...END coding you've done for trigger processing is PL/SQL code!)

Feeding Other Systems

I guarantee that once word gets around that there's a database with student, test, and historical information, you'll get requests to pull data and load it into a spreadsheet or something similar. Because most programs will accept a comma-delimited file, all you have to do is create an output file with commas between each field, and either a single or double quote for the character or non-numeric data. Here's a sample script:

```
rem   Script to create a comma-delimited file
rem   from the student records
rem   for use in office spreadsheets.
```

❶ The spool file will have the comma-delimited output.

❷ Check the notes below on the use of single and double quotes. The rules are quite strict.

```
set heading off
set pagesize 0
set feedback off
set echo off
SPOOL C:\STUDENT_SSN.DAT   ❶ T

SELECT
''''||L_NAME||''''||','||SSNUM ❷
FROM STUDENTS;

SPOOL OFF;
```

What you have to remember is that there are rules for quotes: If you need a single quote, you have to use four single quotes to get one. If you need a double quote, you must do this: `'"'`—that is, a single quote then a double quote then a single quote. Notice that the comma is also put in single quotes.

Here's the output file for the sample script I just showed you:

❸ Notice the comma after the name and the single quotes around the name.

```
'Randolph',123456789 ❸
'Williams',222222222
'Cohen',111111111
'Champagne',333333333
'Klien',444444444
'Sanpletic',555555555
'Levin',666666666
'Corsu',777777777
```

So go ahead, pull all the data that anyone needs from any of the tables. Just be mindful of getting your quotation marks straight!

Linking to Access

Many shops use Microsoft Access for reporting as well as data manipulation. Fortunately, only a couple of steps are required for tying Access to your Oracle database.

The first step is to start Access, open an existing or new database, and then go to **File | Get External Data | Link Tables...**:

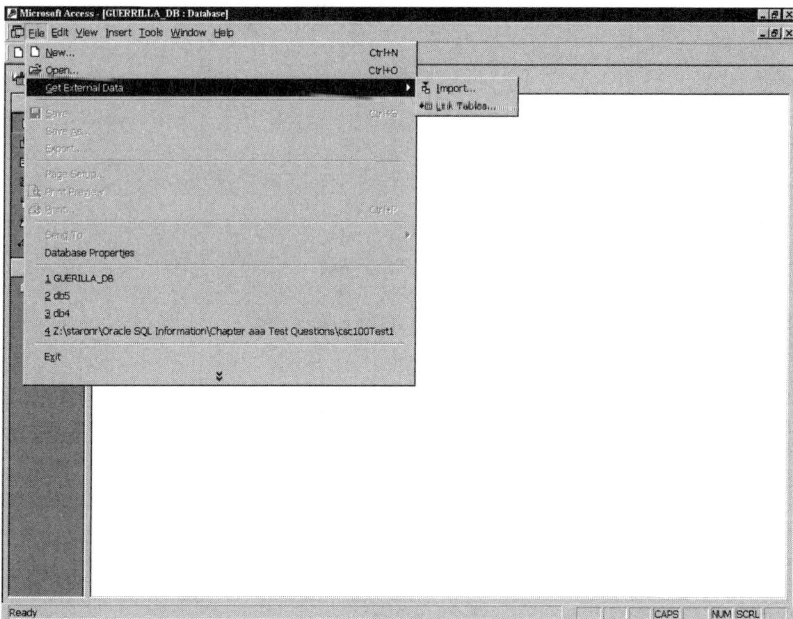

On the next screen, go to **Files of type** at the bottom and scroll down to the ODBC databases:

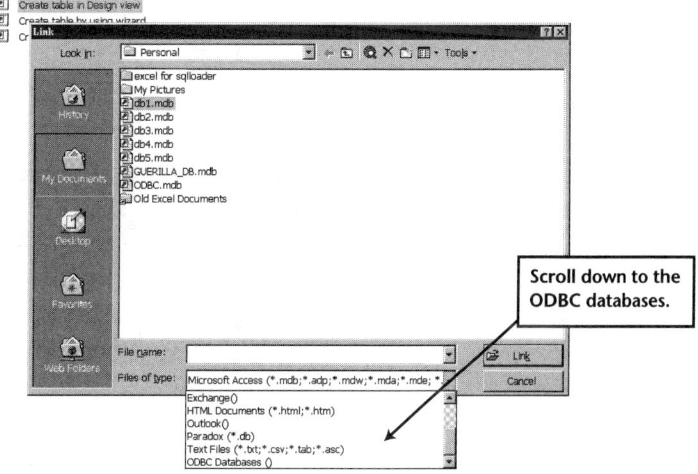

The next screen has two tabs. Select **Machine Data Source**:

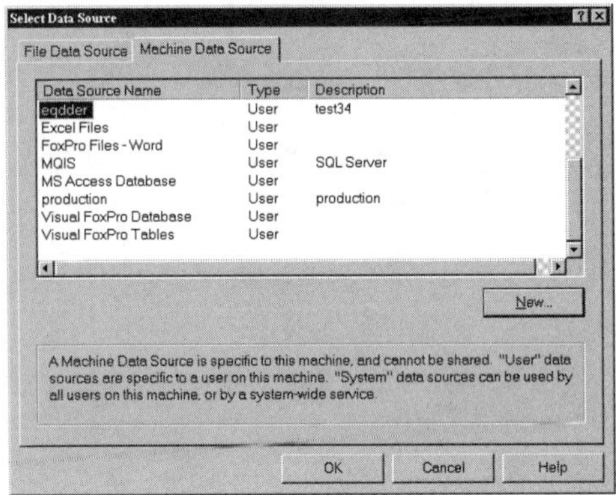

The first step is to add the CWE1P database, so click on **New...**, and then select **User Data Source**:

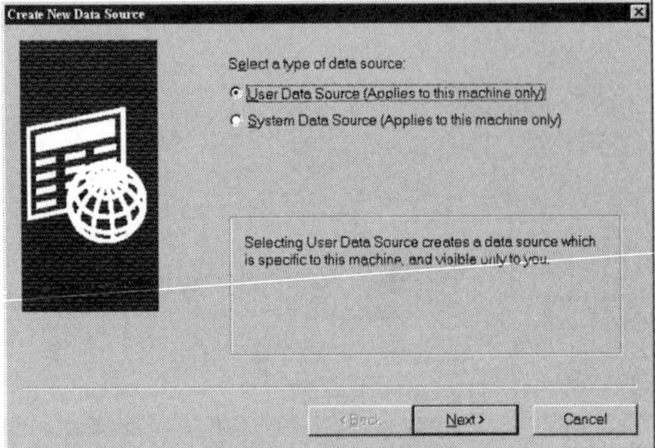

Now scroll down and find the **Microsoft ODBC for Oracle** driver:

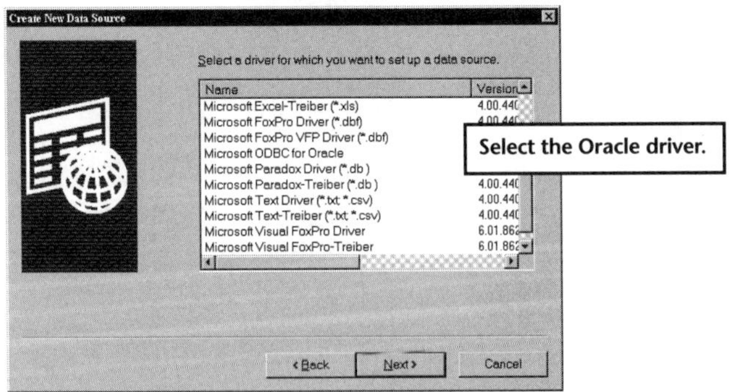

Click **Finish**, and enter the logon information:

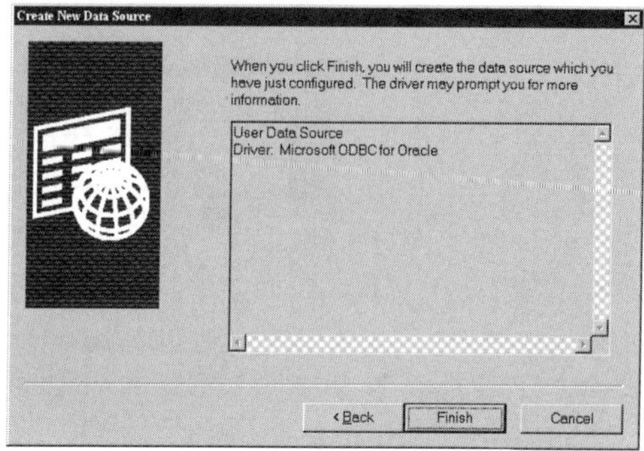

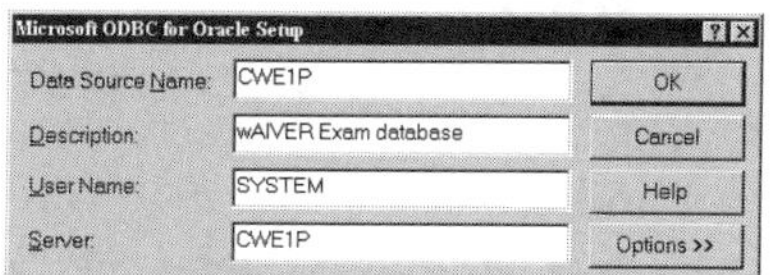

You will now see **CWE1P** in the list:

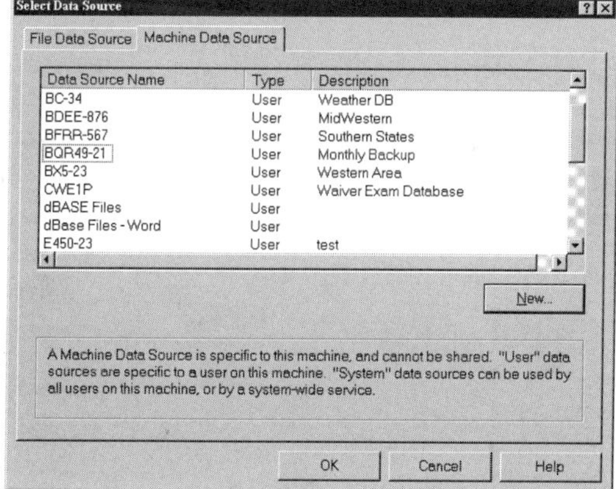

Go to the tables, click on **CWE1P**, enter your logon information, and you will see a list of the CWE1P tables that you can access:

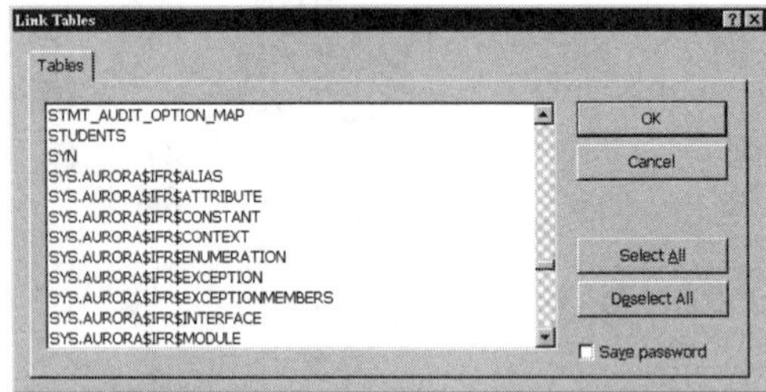

*i*SQL*Plus

Once you have a 9*i* database running, with the Oracle HTTP Service active, you get an additional feature: *i*SQL*Plus. This is Oracle's way of letting you perform SQL programming over the Web. And lest you start getting nervous, this is a real gift because there is nothing you have to do.

To test your sytem, just go to your Web browser, type in the IP address of your database server followed by "ISQLPLUS", and you will get the login screen:

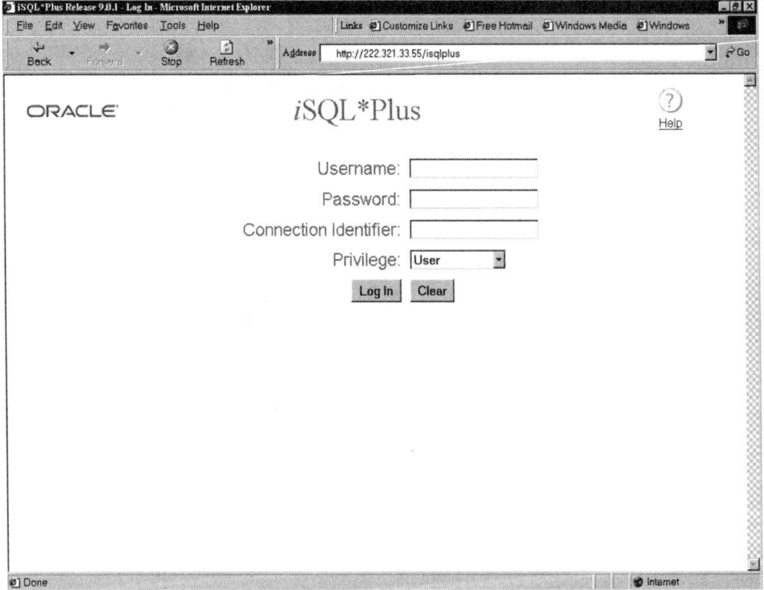

Next you'll see the work screen:

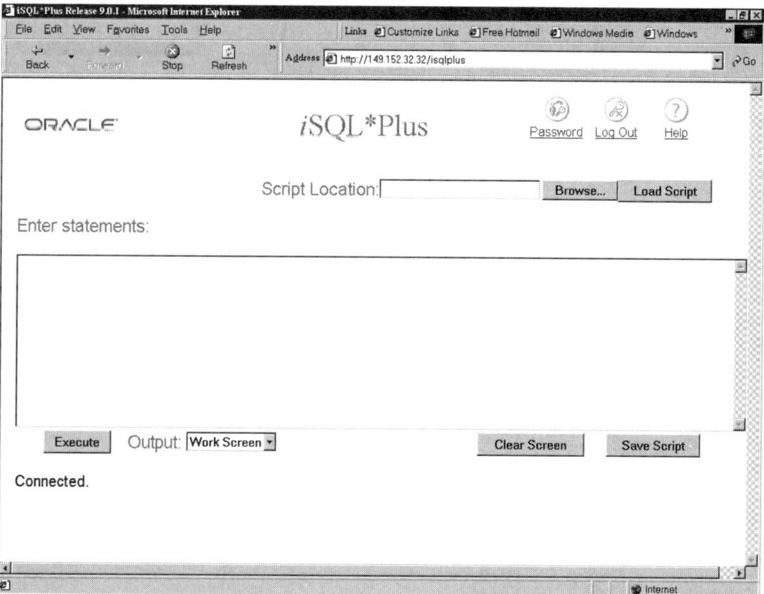

If you type in the simple command "select * from students;" and then hit the **Execute** button, in a few seconds you will get the results at the bottom of the screen:

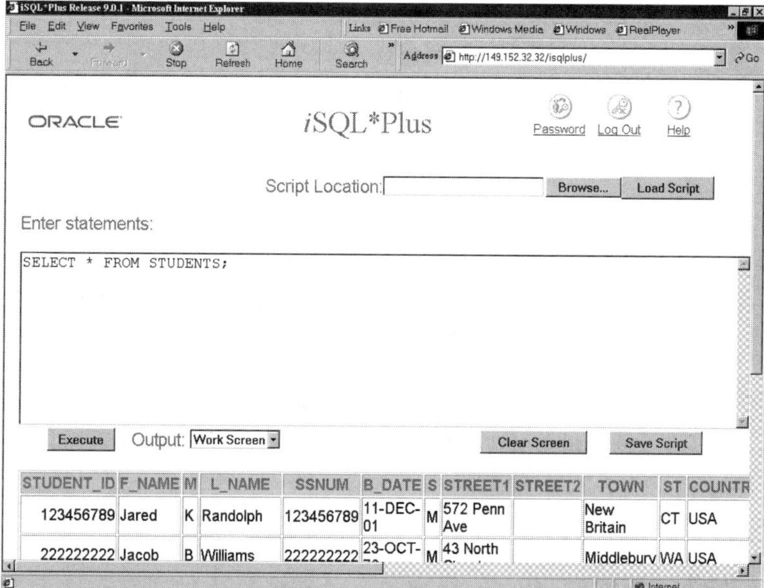

What is attractive about this method is that it is a true GUI interface with automatic column formatting. Notice that *i*SQL*Plus makes the columns very easy to read. (At the present time you cannot stretch or compress the columns.) Under the **Output** drop-down list, you can display your results in their own window or save them to a file. You can also save your scripts using the **Save Script** button, as well as run any script using the **Browse...** and **Load Script** buttons in the upper right area of the screen.

What are the advantages? First of all, your network folks will be happy because this method does not raise the random port assignment issue that requires special consideration if you have a firewall. (For those who are interested, Oracle usually listens on port 1521 or so, but it can reply on any port when you come to the server remotely. This flexibility makes firewalls choke. There are products available to handle the problem, but they do require installation and support.) Second, it is a GUI interface, hence easier than the SQL> command-line prompt. Third, all you need is a browser. Nothing else has to be installed on the client!

So here's another fine Oracle tool. Have fun with it!

In this chapter you have been introduced to the incredibly complex yet wonderfully challenging world of SQL*Plus and PL/SQL. (Entire books are dedicated to just one or two of the topics mentioned here!) Keep going, get yourself some good reference books, start collecting interesting scripts, and see what you can do with the waiver database tables. Practice, practice, practice!

Tip

Here's one thing to add to your own Oracle toolbox. This is one of those annoying things that periodically pop up, and you forget what to do. Every once in a while you're going to get the "Input truncated to 13 characters" error message when you run SQL commands from the SQL> prompt. Evrything will look good, and I guarantee you won't find any errors in your code. It's just a little quirk in SQL*Plus processing: Your script doesn't have a carriage return after the last line. That's all it is! Just go to the end of the last line in your script, hit **Delete**, hit **Enter**, save the script, and it will work fine. Most new programmers run into this problem, and knowing what to do will make you look smart!

In a sentence, then, if you get the error message "Input truncated to 13 characters" when running SQL*Plus, just add a carriage return to the very end of your script.

Chapter 15

The Web!

Getting your forms on the Web takes us now into new territory. If you've gotten this far, you've already done a load of guerrilla work, so tackling another mini-guerrilla task will be nothing!

We're going to move away from the world of the Oracle database, SQL*Plus, and the database server world, to the world of browsers, "middle tier," and a host of new terminology (such as *applet*). You can do it, and believe me, when you're done, you'll be rather proud.

To make the quantum leap from your client/server–based application to the world of the Web, you have to do several things:

- Acquire a very basic understanding of what's going to happen and why.
- Install Oracle9*i* Application Server (9*i*AS).
- Slightly modify your forms application and move it to the 9*i*AS server.

Regarding the Web technology, I'm going to give you just enough information here so that the next couple of pages make sense. To make your system work, and then to support it, you have to know some of the architecture, buzzwords, and how the parts fit together.

Briefly, here's what a **three-tier system** is:

1. A client PC with a browser
2. A Web server somewhere that the client PC talks to
3. A database somewhere from which the Web server, or middle tier, grabs information and passes that information to the client

Because Oracle has given us a pretty good tool for creating three-tier systems, without much ado we're going to create one ourselves.

Let's see what we already have. We all have a client PC with a browser, right? We've already created a significant computer waiver exam database. And we've created a rather nice Forms-based GUI system for the user. What's next? Right! Build the **middle tier**, the Web server.

As I said, Oracle has handed us a great product, 9*i* Application Server, that we can use for our Web deployment. 9*i*AS is the latest in a series of Web products. It is Oracle's attempt to bundle all the parts into one package. One major feature is that 9*i*AS includes the Apache Web server, the de facto industry standard. In addition, 9*i*AS does automatic configurations and provides an easy way to test the installation.

Let's get started. In a nutshell, here are the steps:

1. Install the 9*i*AS Server software with Web features.
2. Test the software.
3. Test a quick and dirty form.
4. Test the client PCs.
5. Modify our forms system.
6. Move our forms to the Web server.

I'll explain the details as we go along. Remember, we're going after the missing piece—the middle tier. This tier has to listen to both the client and the database server, and then do work for both. In effect, it is the middleman in the entire schema.

Warning

Unlike Oracle Web, the 9*i*AS server has to be on its own machine. *Do not put it on the same server with your database!* If you do, it won't work and you'll end up having to redo everything.

Also make sure that no other Oracle products are installed. If you have any doubts, take a look at your registry under **Local Machine | Software**, and also scan your drives looking for "Oracle," "ORA," or "ORAINST." Again, if there are any other products or residue, you will run into all kinds of problems during the installation. If necessary, completely rebuild your server. That's what I did!

Before you do anything with 9*i*AS, you need a server, whether NT or W2K. So build or find one, and make sure it has nothing on it. You do *not* want to run any other Oracle or office-type applications with your 9*i*AS server, or serious Web degradation will happen.

Now install your licensed 9*i*AS CD, start it up, and after the standard, gray Universal Installer screen, you'll see this:

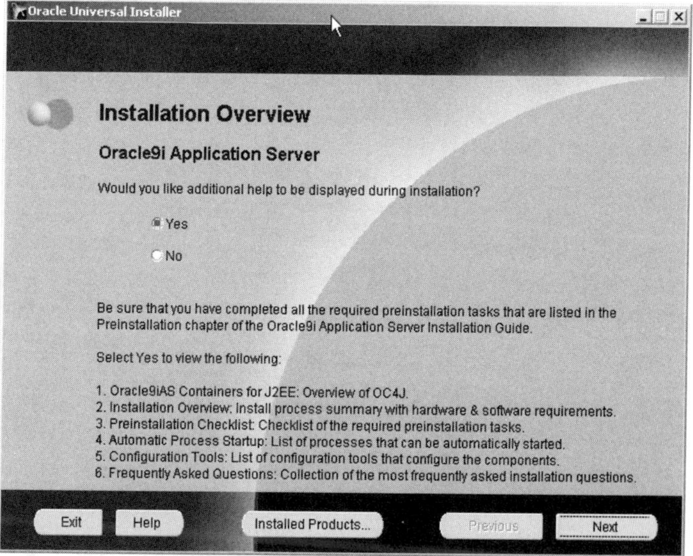

If you select **Yes**, you'll get a bit more documentation as you go through the installation. Hit **Next**, and you'll see the standard **Welcome** screen, then a brief status bar followed by the selection screen. Choose the full-blown system, **Enterprise Edition**, to get the Forms server components:

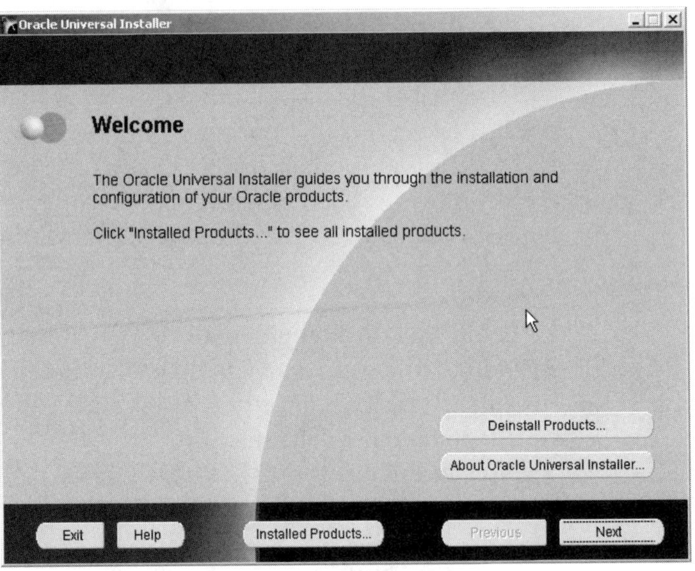

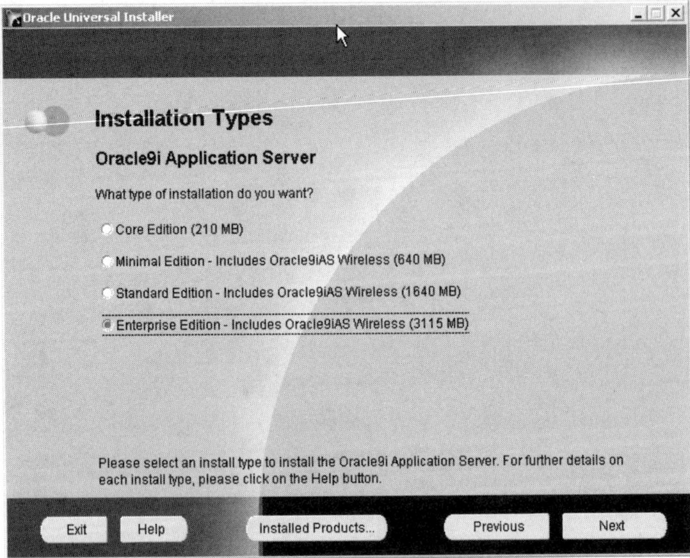

Warning

Notice that you need 3GB of disk space!

Next take the default directories for the various 8.06 and 8.07 components:

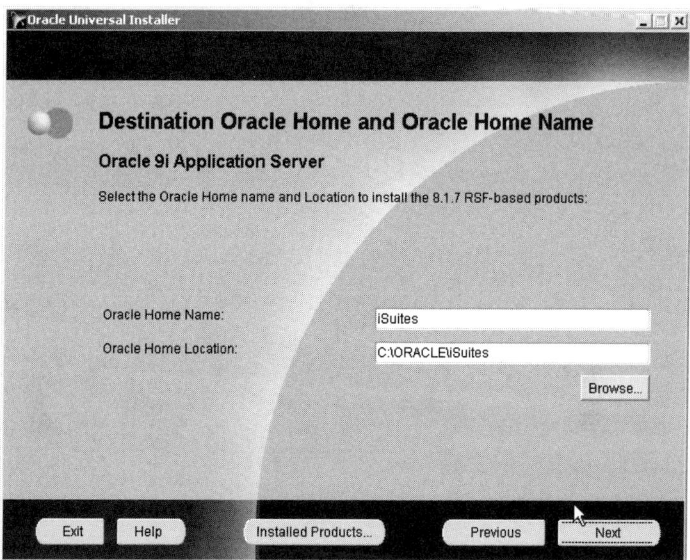

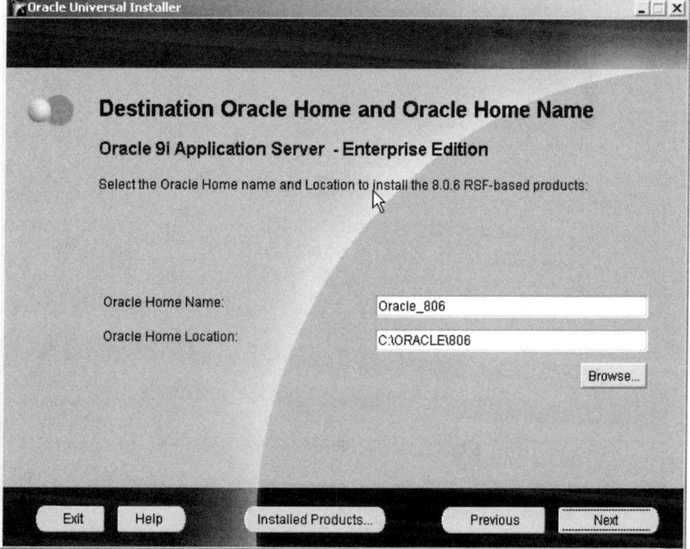

For now, just select two products to install: (1) **Oracle9iAS Forms Server and Oracle9iAS Reports Server** and (2) **Oracle HTTP Server in SSL Mode**:

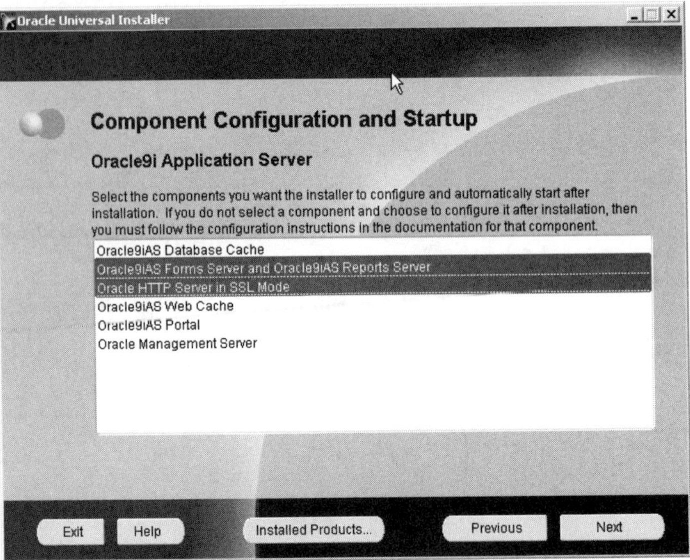

Then for the next couple of minutes, watch the installation screens and status bars:

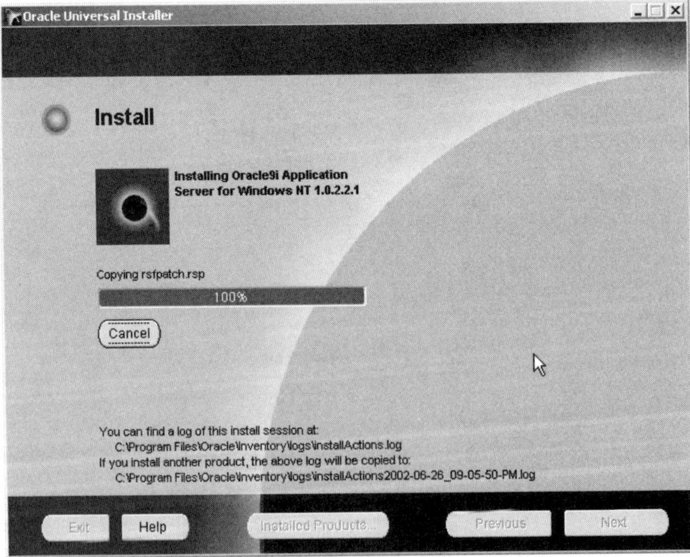

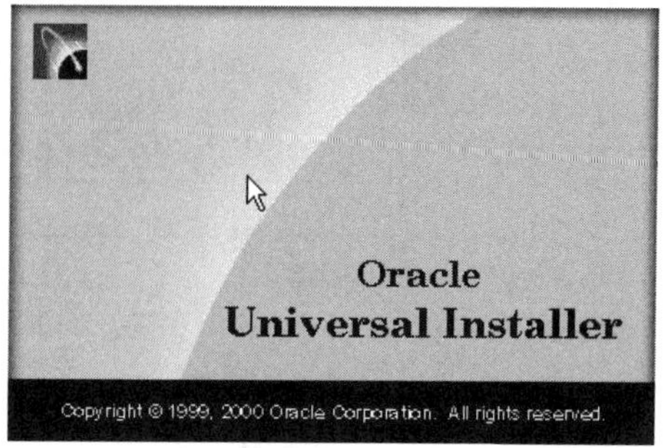

Note that CPU usage may hit 100 percent or close to it at times:

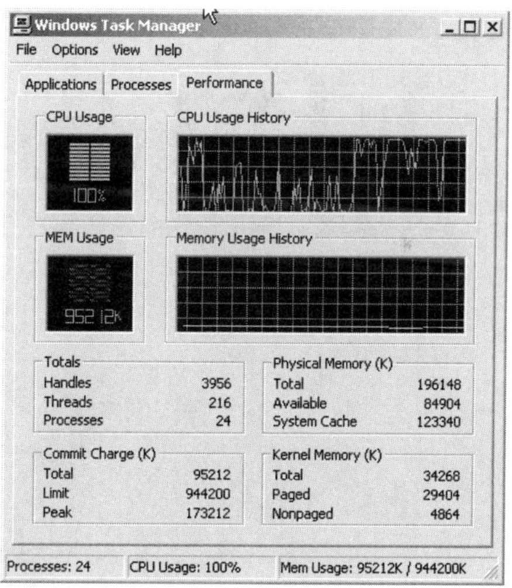

Take the defaults for the portal screens, since we're not installing the portal product.

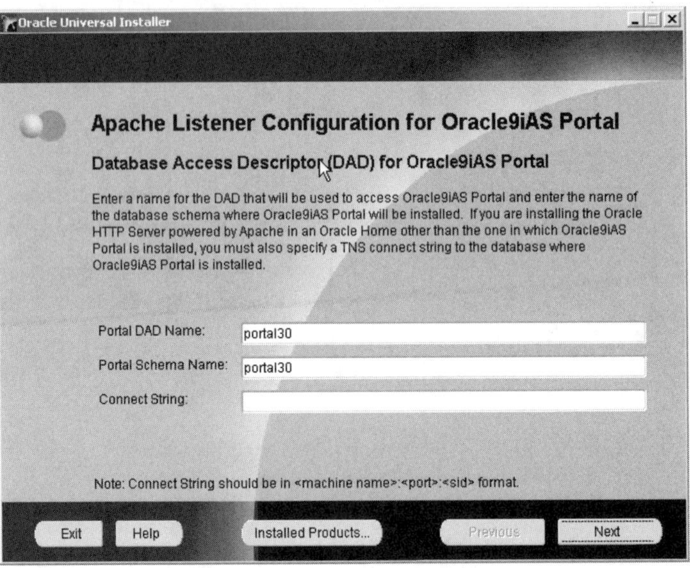

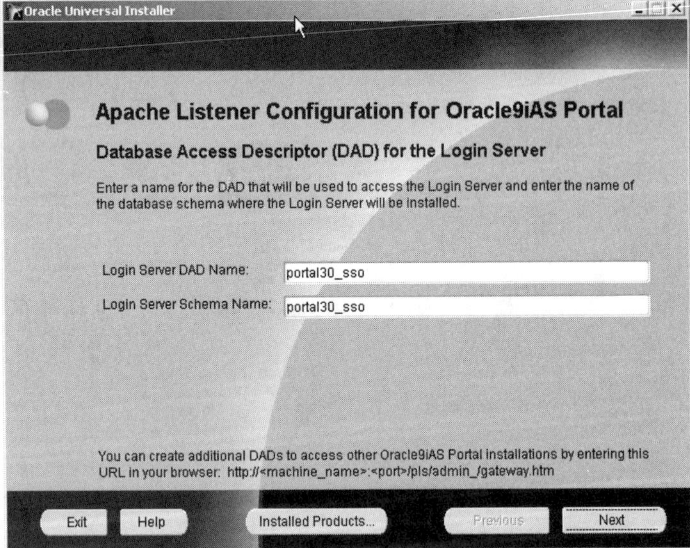

Skip over the "Wireless Edition" screens:

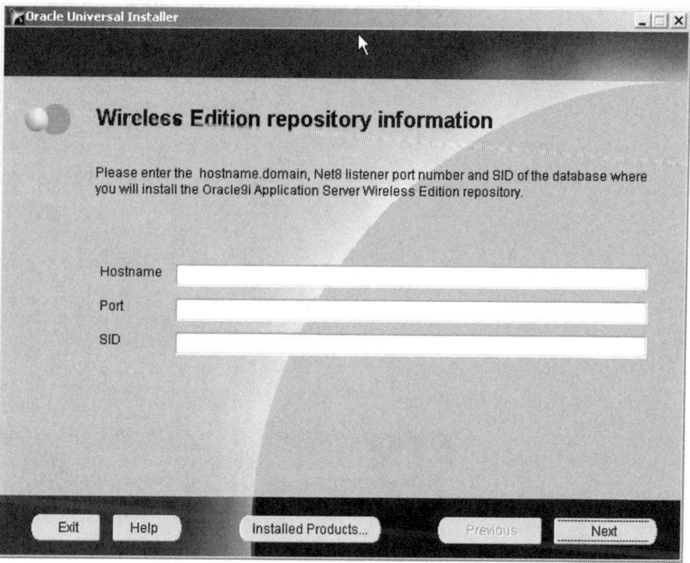

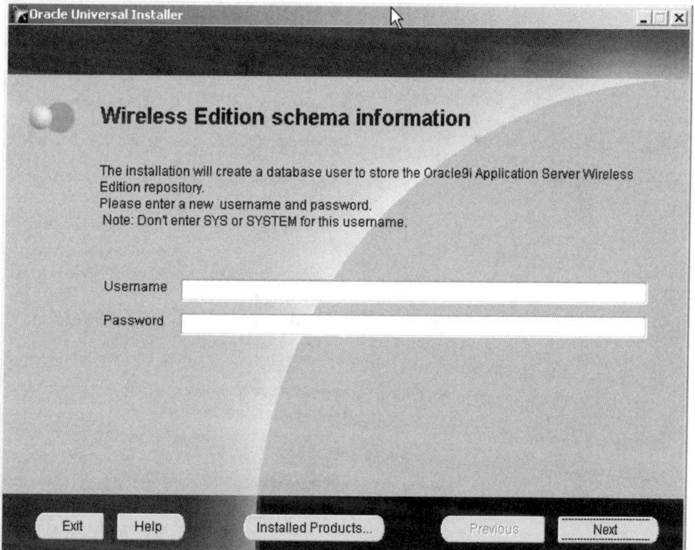

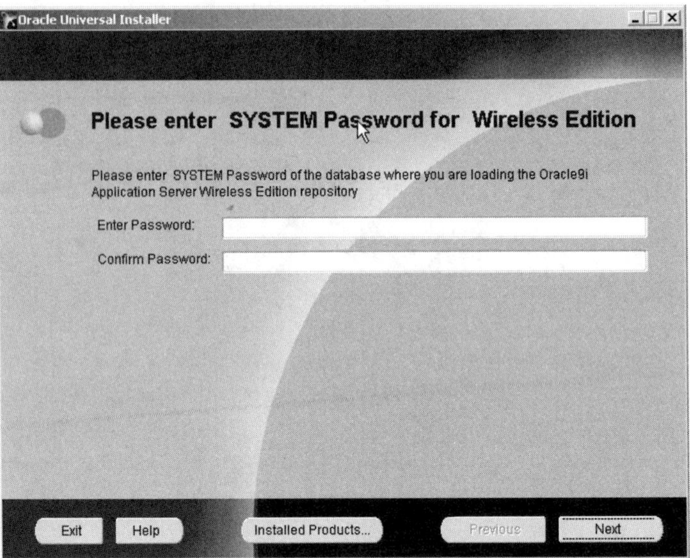

On the **Summary** screen, notice the Apache Web server, HTTP, and Forms server entries. (If these entries are not shown, go back and start over. These are about the only things we want from 9*i*AS for our purposes.)

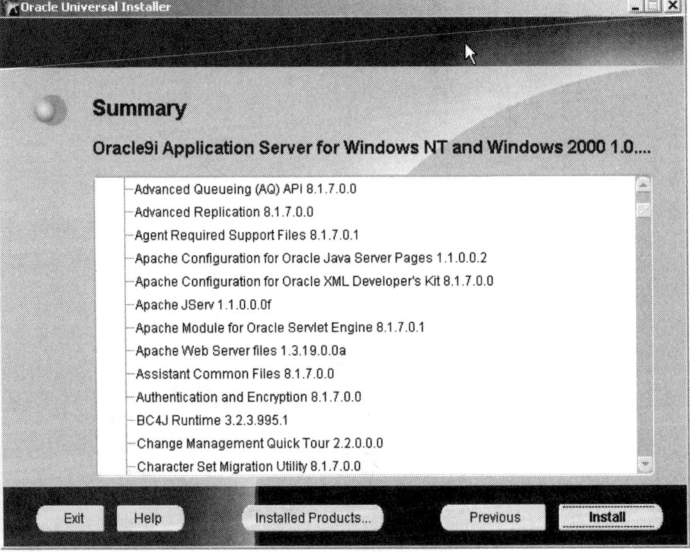

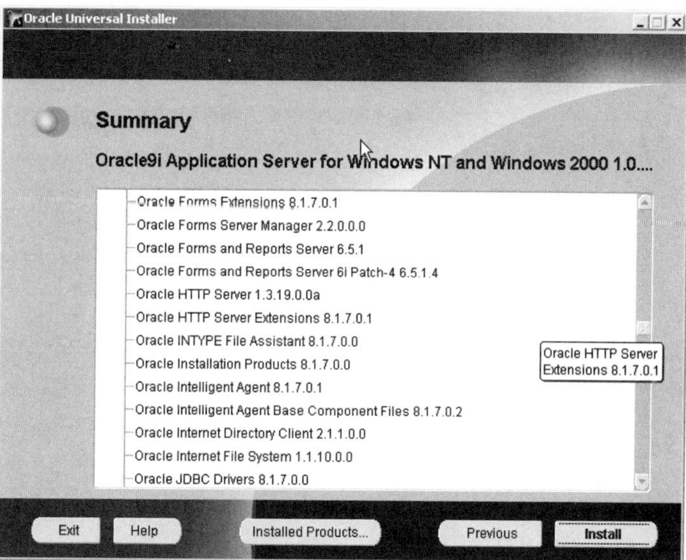

Now click on **Install**, and the fun will begin. This can take some time, and you will see "Copying" and then "Installing" messages flashing constantly. (It may seem as if the system has stalled, but just be patient.)

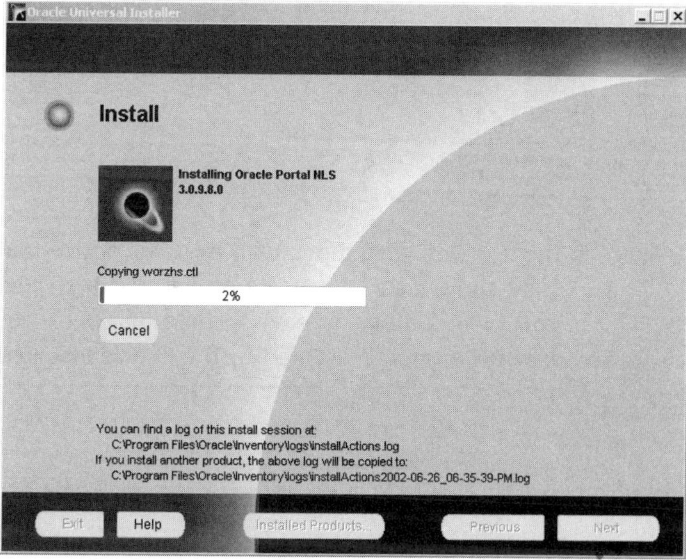

Toward the end of the installation the screen will refresh a couple of times, and various displays will appear:

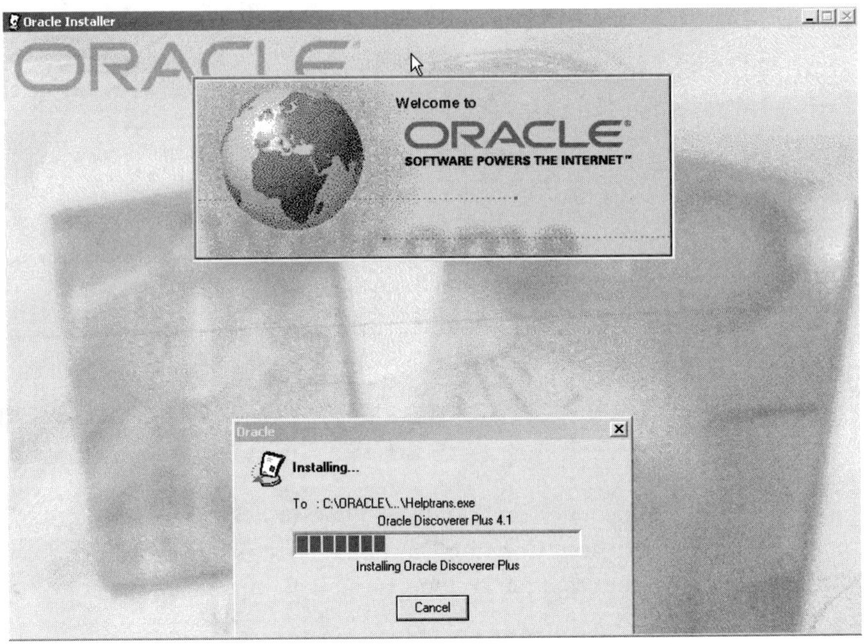

Note

Those of you with supersharp eyes will notice that the screens change between using the Oracle Universal Installer and the Oracle Installer. This causes problems only if later you have to deinstall, because the Universal Installer *cannot uninstall* products installed by the Oracle Installer!

Notice that even though you did not select the portal package, some portal components will be installed:

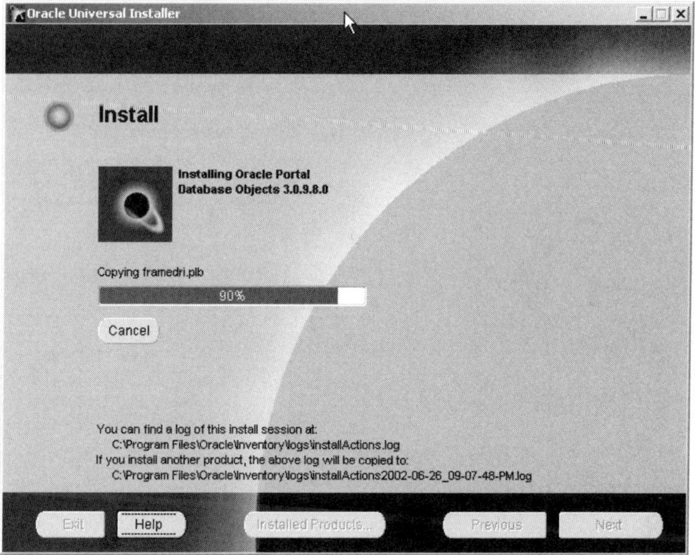

The installer will stay at **100 percent** for a bit, while it wraps up the installation. *Just leave it alone.* The final screen gives you a chance to add additional features (I suggest just taking a look at what has been installed, and then hitting **Exit**):

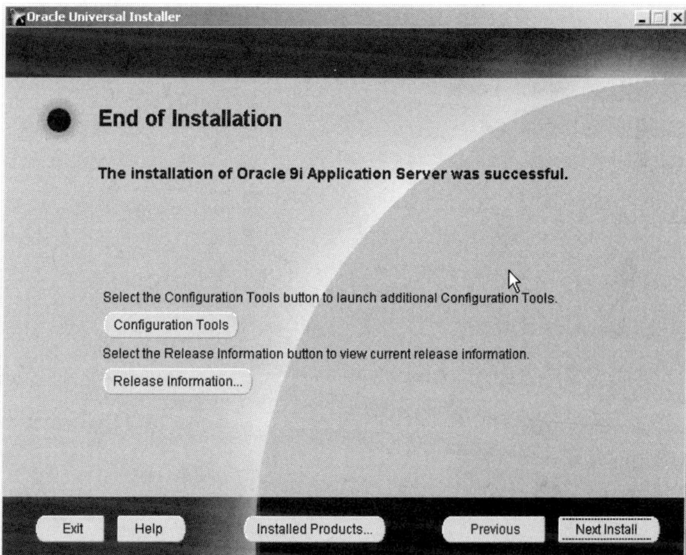

Since we do not want any additional features, just exit by clicking **Close**:

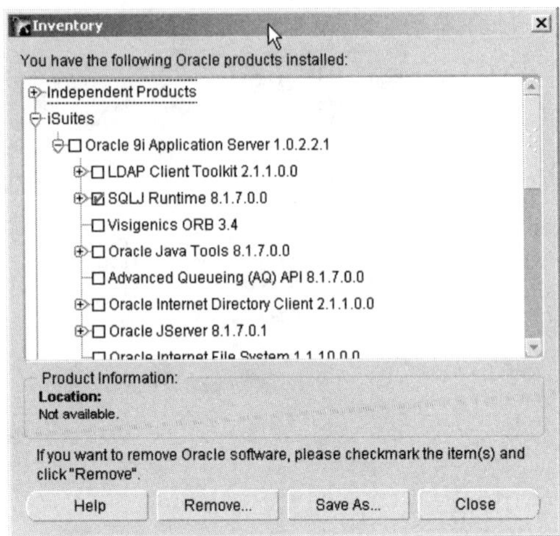

Now check your **Programs** directory and notice all the new Oracle programs:

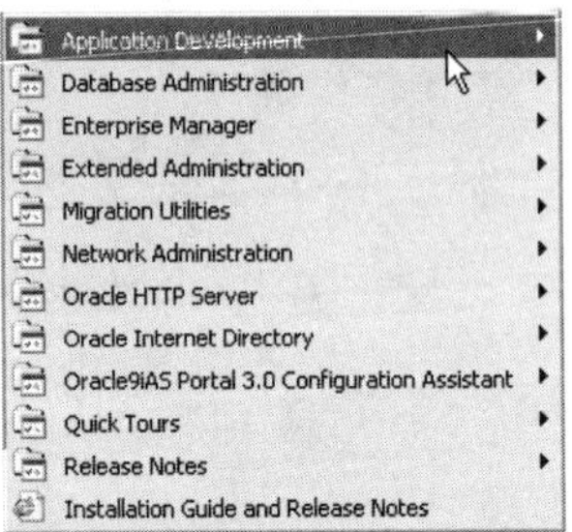

Note also that you now have new services for the Oracle tasks you just installed:

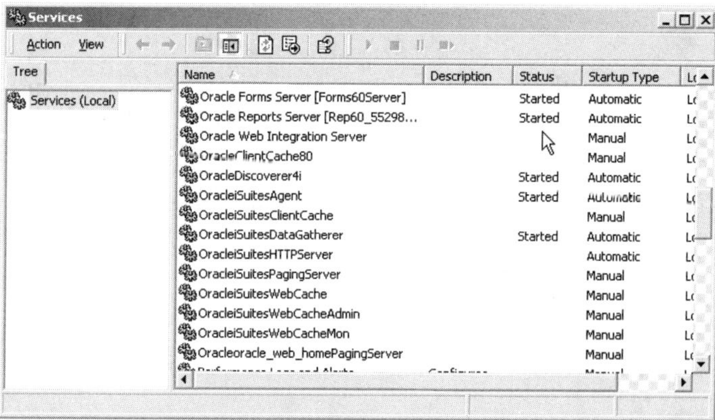

Now *test* your work. Oracle provides a neat tool for this purpose. Just go to **Start | Programs | Forms 6i | Run Form on the Web**, and then take the defaults and run the test form:

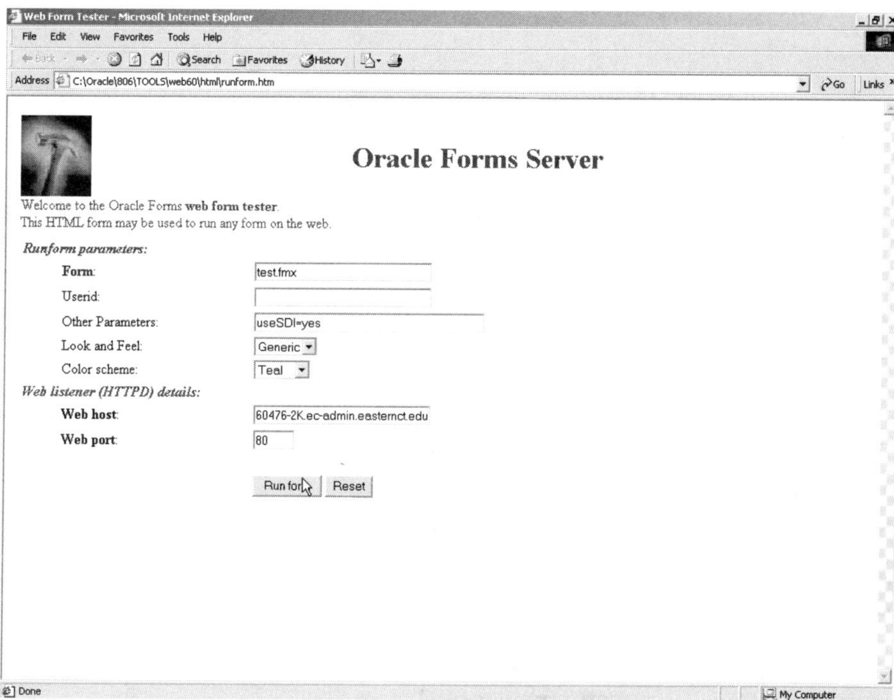

You should see the following message:

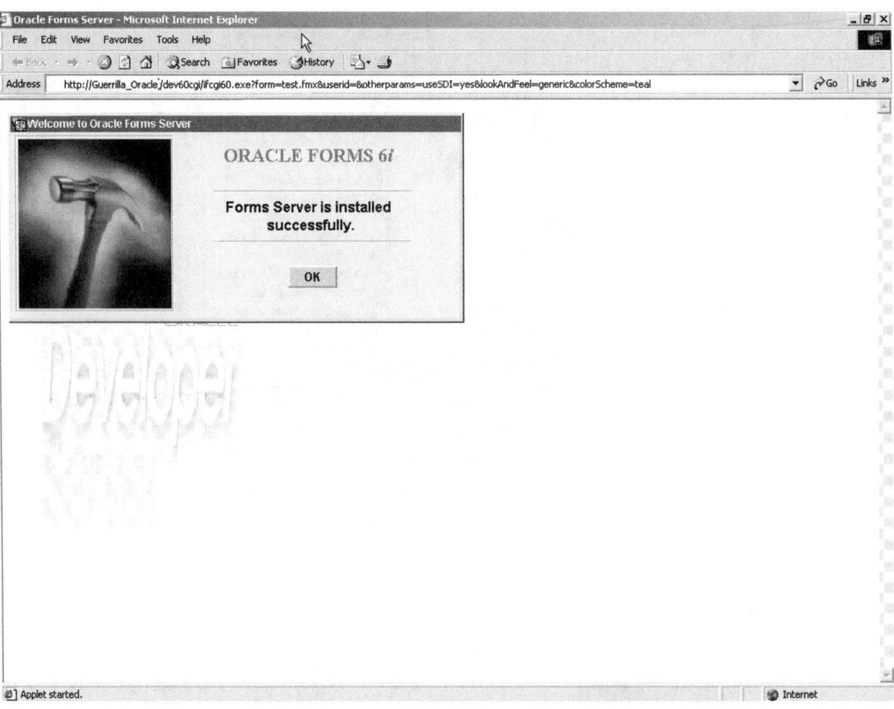

That's all there is to building a basic 9*i*AS server that will manage our forms on the Web. As many of you know, quite a bit goes into making this product so solid and easy to install—items such as HTML, Java, configuration files, and a host of other things. But using and modifying these are topics for another time; these are some of the things that will be covered in the next book. What I want to do here is get you going on using the Web without too much confusion or head banging. *If you have received the message shown in the last screen shot, you're almost there!*

Take a moment and look at the URL in the previous test screen. You'll see the Web server name, followed by a series of parameters. Every parameter means something:

❶ The "http:" portion points to the server.

❷ This is the path to the `.fmx` program.

❸ The question mark indicates that variables follow.

❹ These are parameters that the system will use to find the `.fmx` file and then paint the screens.

http://Guerrilla_Oracle/ ❶
dev60cgi/ifcgi60.exe ❷
? ❸
form=test.fmx
&userid= ❹
&otherparms=useSDI=yes
&lookAndFeel=generic
&colorScheme=teal

Tip

For added testing, I suggest that you now build a quick and dirty form using one table, run it, fix errors, and then compile it. When it's ready, move it (the `.fmx` file) to the Web server (`<ORACLE HOME>/FORMS60`), test it on the server, and then *run your new form again on a client PC.*

To test, use the same URL but *use your form name* instead of "TEST.FMX", and test on all operating systems that will access your forms. If it works, read on in the text. Otherwise debug your program until it runs cleanly. Then read on. (One reason I want you to run a test on a local PC is to make sure that the local broswer is 9*i*AS compatible. Using Internet Explorer, version 5 or higher, is *required*. Check the Oracle documentation for more details if necessary. Also you'll feel good if your test works the first time, and this will give you a confidence boost to continue.)

Here's an example of a quick and dirty form that was created through use of only the STUDENTS table. It was called `WEBTEST.fmx`. We just used its name instead of `TEST.fmx` once we moved it into the `<ORACLE HOME>/FORMS60` directory. Here's the URL, using a made-up IP address:

```
http://111.111.11.11/dev60cgi/ifcgi60.exe?form=webtest.fmx&useri
d=&otherparms=useSDI=yes&lookAndFeel=generic&colorScheme=teal)
```

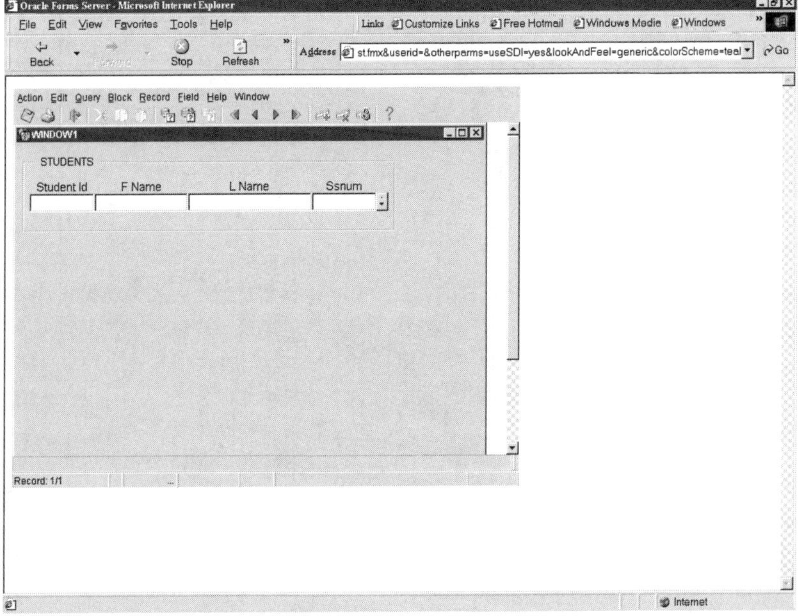

Note

Oracle 9*i*AS is very Java-oriented, and it defaults to using Java programs for the Web interface. The first time a client PC tries to run a forms program, you may get a screen asking if you want to install JInitiator. Say yes, and then just take the defaults as the product is installed. There is a lot more to this, but installing JInitiator is enough for now.

The last step, as I said, is to tweak the forms you've developed. Splash screens are handled differently on the Web (actually they become part of the Web configuration files, but that is beyond the scope of this chapter). So all we're going to do is to disable the logic for the splash screen and remove the screen.

What do we do? We have a very successful client/server system running, and we don't want to make the programming too complicated. What I suggest for this book is that you copy `CWE1P_MAIN.fmb` as `WEBCWE1P_MAIN.fmb`. Then make your changes to the "web" file. Why? This way you will maintain the integrity of your client/server product. After your copying, your Guerrilla Oracle folder should look like this:

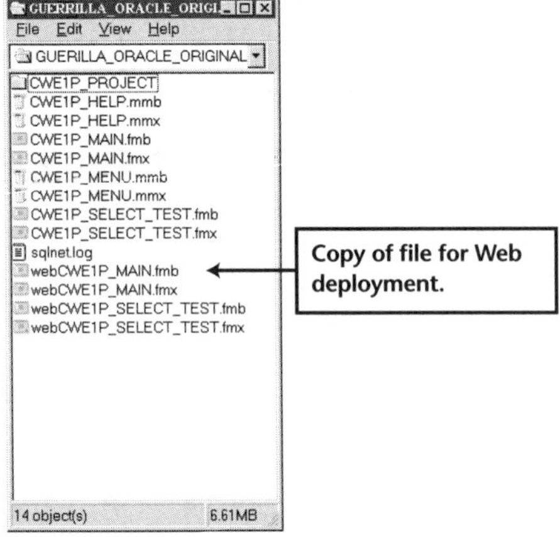

Now remove the splash screen, including the timer code and triggers. This is easy:

1. Open the `WEBCWE1P_MAIN.fmb` file, and remove the `WHEN_TIMER_EXPIRED` trigger, the `CWE1P_SPLASH_BLOCK` block, and the `CWE1P_SPLASH_CANVAS` canvas:

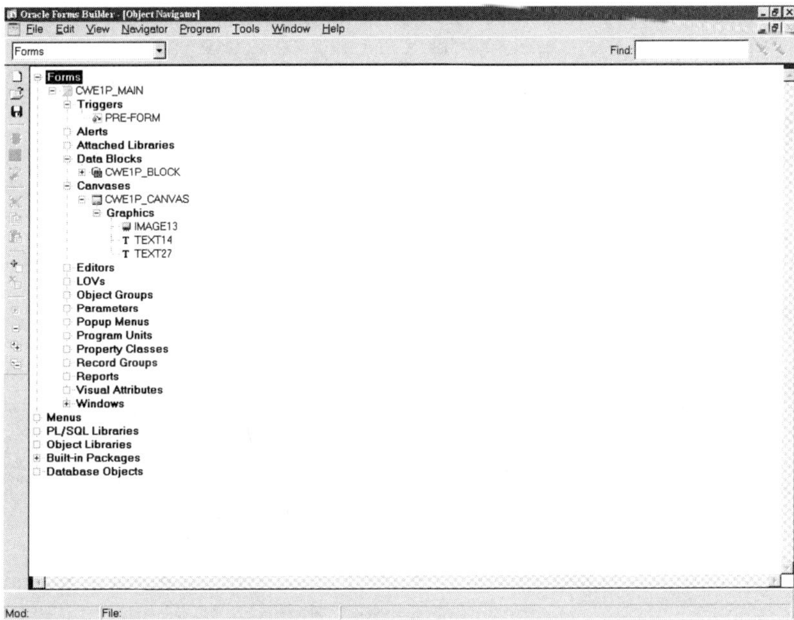

2. Change the code in the `PRE-FORM` trigger to disable the splash screen and trigger:

```
DECLARE
-- For the WEB, do not use a SPLASH Screen and TIMER, so comment out
-- the instructions.  Keep the code for the GLOBALS.
-- we need to define our variable that will be used for our timer:
--  CWE1P_SPLASH_TIMER TIMER;
BEGIN
  set_window_property (forms_mdi_window, window_state,maximize);
:GLOBAL.project_path  := 'D:\GUERRILLA_ORACLE\CWE1P_PROJECT\';
:GLOBAL.project_path2 := 'D:\GUERRILLA_ORACLE\';

--Here're the instructions to load the GUERRILLA ORACLE image file
--READ_IMAGE_FILE(:GLOBAL.project_path ||'hat6.bmp', 'BMP', --
--   'cwe1p_splash_block.cwe1p_splash_image');

--  now enter the text that will show in the lower right hand box
--:cwe1p_splash_block.cwe1p_splash_item :=
--'Guerrilla Oracle' ||CHAR(10) || 'test';
--'Guerrilla Oracle'  ||CHR(13) || CHR(10) || --
--'by Richard Staron'|| CHR(13) || CHR(10) ||
--'(c) Copyright Addison-Wesley' ;

--now add the TIMER code
--CWE1P_SPLASH_TIMER := CREATE_TIMER('CWE1P_SPLASH_TIMER', 5000, NO_REPEAT);
END;
```

3. Run the form in client/server mode, and fix any errors.
4. Compile, run again in client/server mode, and save the form.

Note

I can't emphasize enough how important it is to *compile and save*. In fact, if you don't see your changes, the reason is that you did not compile the forms in the correct order. Basically, you have to compile from the bottom up. It never hurts anything to compile your program, so if in doubt, just compile right up the ladder: first the canvas, then the data block, then the entire form. Also compile all canvases while you're at it. And don't forget to compile the WEBCWE1P_MAIN form because you've changed the form that it calls.

---

5. Now run everything in client/server mode. The normal function keys will still work. Fix any errors.

Now how do we get this thing onto the Web? All we have to do is copy the `.fmx` and `.mmx` files to your new Web server. But here's where it gets a little tricky. The general rule is to put your main `.fmx` module into the `<ORACLE HOME>/FORMS60` directory. Why? Because that's the default spot. (For those of you who are experienced at working with the Web, you can put the files anywhere as long as you have the path specified in the registry under `FORMS60PATH`. I'll get into much more on this in the next book.)

However, remember that we have globals that point to `D:\GUERRILLA ORACLE`? Well, we had two choices. For our Web files we could change the globals to point to somewhere else, or we could just make a `GUERRILLA ORACLE` folder on the Web server D: drive and put all the other files there. To keep things simple, I suggest that you do make a folder on the D: drive, and put a full copy of the `GUERRILLA ORACLE` folder there. If you have the `.fmb` files, don't worry; they won't hurt anything. When you're all done with your testing, you can delete the `.fmb` and `.mmb` files.

You have now done two things:

1. Copied the `WEBCWE1P_MAIN.FMX` folder over to the `FORMS60` directory on the Web server.
2. Created a copy of the Guerrilla Oracle folder on the Web server D: drive (or you've changed the globals to point to another drive on the Web server).

You're ready to test!

Note

There is one other very important step: Check the keyboard file on the Web server. Oracle has a file (`fmrweb.res`) that it uses to map the keyboard. However, this map assumes that the keyboard emulates the VT-100. What this means is that some PC function keys may not work unless you change the map file. However, Oracle has included another keyboard map file (`fmrPCweb.res`) designed for the 101-key PC keyboard.

If you find that the function keys **F8** and **F9** do *not* work, go to the Web server, look in the `<ORACLE HOME>/FORMS60` directory, and find the file `fmrweb.res`. Rename it `original_fmrweb.res`. Now find the file `fmrPCweb.res` in the same directory, make a copy of it, and then rename it `fmrweb.res`. The function keys should now work fine.

To test, go back to the Web server and choose **Run Form on the Web** under **Start | Programs | Forms 6*i***, and put the name—"WEBCWE1P_MAIN.FMX"—on the form. You should see the main **Guerrilla Exams** screen. If not, you'll get a form error, and you can look it up (remember—under **Help** in Forms, type in "FRM", and you'll get a list of all error codes). Most likely you'll run into misspellings or something similar. Just make *one* change at a time, or you're asking for trouble.

Now for the grand finale, run your form from a client PC:

1. Open your browser.
2. Here's the URL to start with:

http://<your Web server address> ❶
/dev60cgi/ifcgi60.exe
?form= WEBCWE1P_MAIN.FMX ❷

❶ **Plug in your IP address.**

❷ **Then make the "?form=" section refer to *your* `MAIN.fmx` form.**

And here's what the URL should look like in your browser:

```
http://<your IP address>/dev60cgi/ifcgi60.exe?form=webcwe1p_main.fmx
```

3. If you see a message to load JInitiator, install it.

4. First the "loading applet" message appears. Next the Oracle logon screen appears, followed by the Guerrilla Oracle main screen:

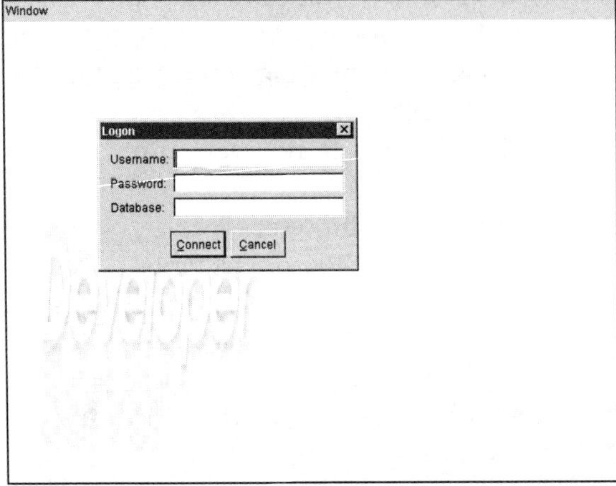

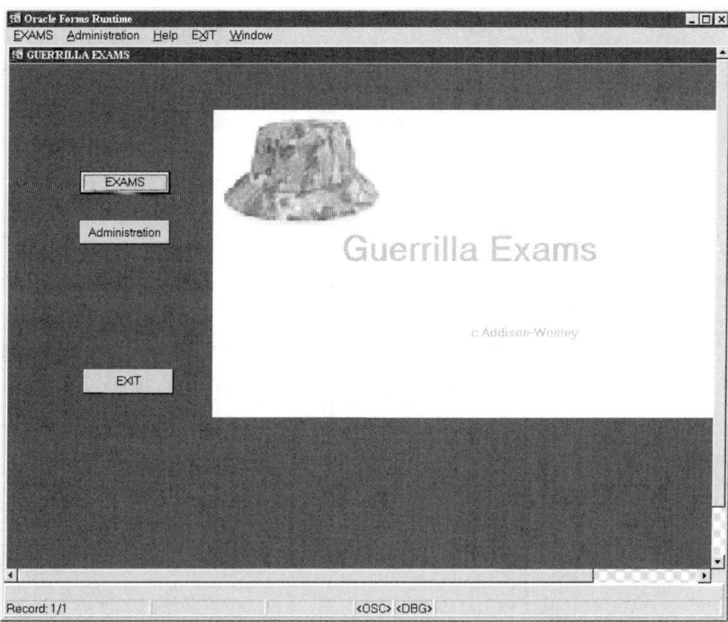

Select **EXAMS**, enter the necessary data, and you should then see the "take test" screen. After you enter a test ID, hit **F9** and the pop-up list will appear. Select the test you want:

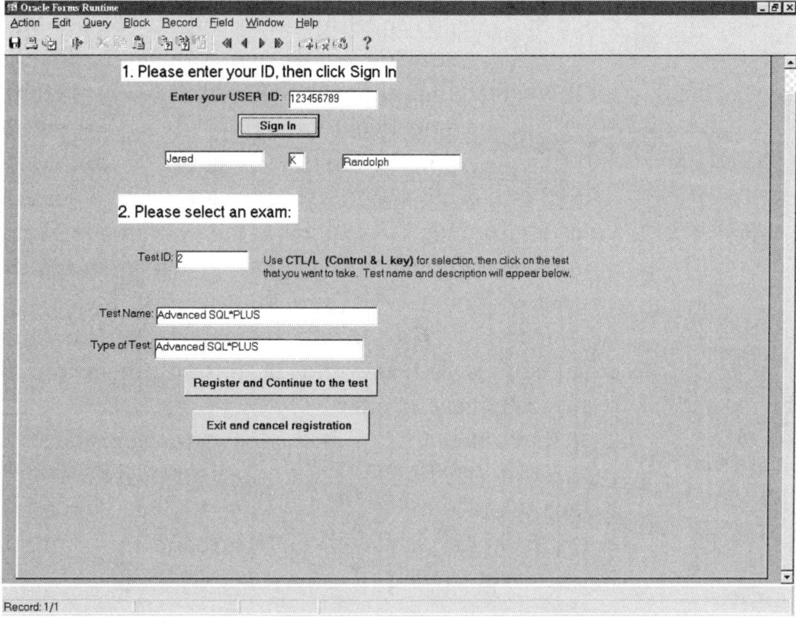

Click **Register and Continue to the test**, and the actual exam screen will appear:

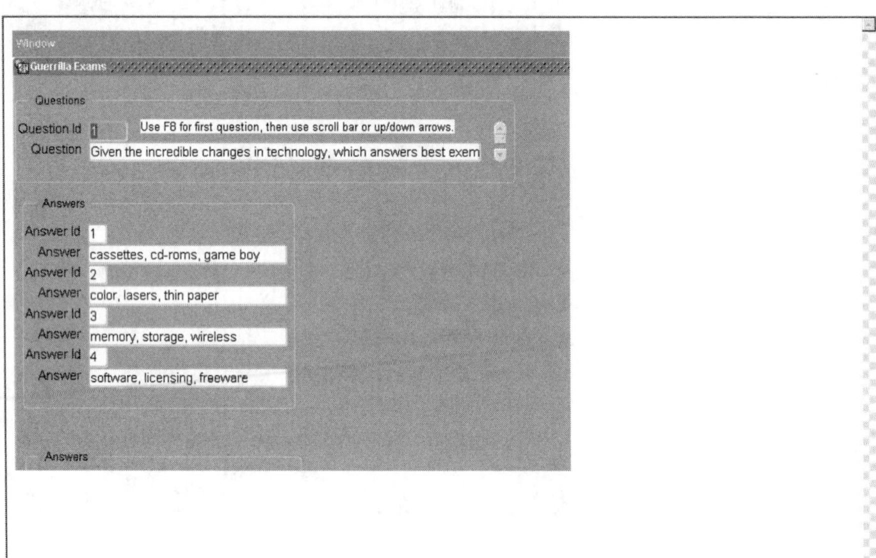

Put the cursor in the **Question Id** block, hit **F8**, and the first question will appear. Use the scroll bar to go through all the questions.

Did you notice that we also tweaked the message on the "take test" screen to tell the user to use **F8** and the scroll bar? Good. Make those changes on your own screen. I also suggest that you now go back and create another menu bar for this screen that has only a few items, such as **Help**, **Save**, and **Exit**.

Also I strongly—very strongly—advise that you actually take a waiver test and try everything before turning your system loose. You may find some odds and ends that need correcting; you may find some things that are quirky in your environment. Try to make the system as bulletproof as possible because your users will push it to its limits. There are some shortcomings in the system I've shown you, but I'm sure you will take the examples and enhance them to fit your own design and environment. I've given you the basics; now go to specific manuals on forms and dig through them to make your Guerrilla waiver exam system even better!

What's that I hear? Is it the graduation march? Well, you may not have realized it yet, but you're at the end of the book. Congratulations! I don't have any profound quotes or wise sayings. You've shown incredible tenacity and intellectual acuity to have reached this point, and I hope your journey has been rewarding.

Appendix A

Forms 6*i* Security

Throughout this book, I've said that ultimately we would be applying security to the *forms*, not the user. This would protect our database because users would not have rights to the tables, hence could not change anything if they were to get to a SQL prompt and log in.

Here's how we're going to do this (four quick steps):

- Create a universal user—WAIVER_USER—with basic capabilities.
- Create a powerful role—we'll use the WAIVER_DEV_ROLE.
- Assign that role to our MAIN MENU.
- Assign that role to each MENU ITEM.

1. First, create a general user that will be used by everyone taking an exam. Refer back to Chapter 8 for a refresher on Roles, Profiles, and Users. Now

create the user 'Waiver_User' with the same password, unlimited logons, tablespaces, and so forth. Limit the time to 2 hours, then grant basic rights such as create session. If you have a general ROLE, then grant that role to WAIVER_USER. Now log on to the database as that user, correct any problems, and make sure the user cannot see any of the Waiver tables.

2. Start FORMS, and select your CWE1P_MENU.MMB module. Highlight CWE1P_MENU, right-click and select Property Palette. Then, change USE SECURITY to YES :

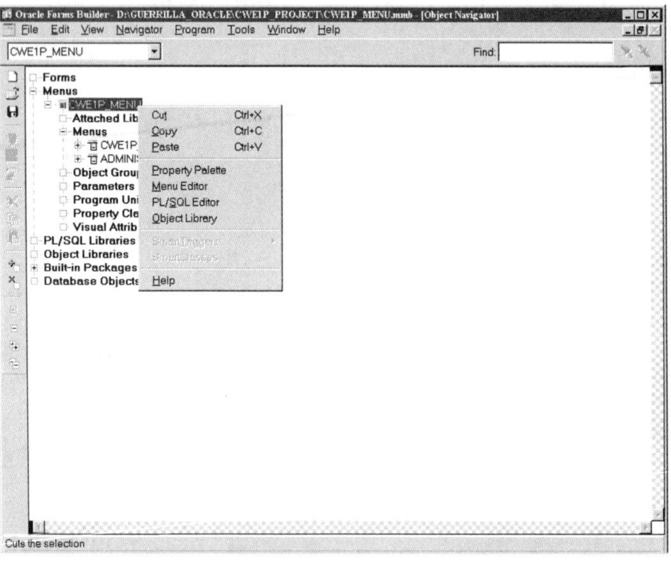

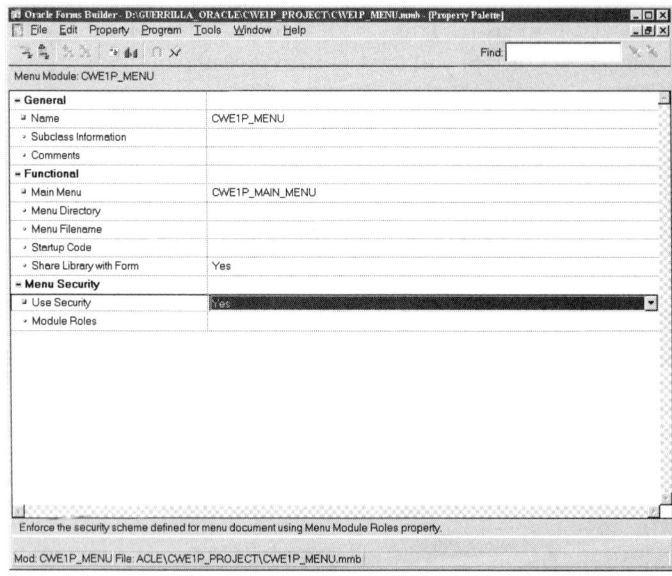

3. Now, click on the MODULE ROLES, and you'll see "More" to the right. Click on More, and in the box that appears, enter the WAIVER_DEV_ROLE that you created back in Chapter 8. This role should have very powerful rights to all tables. If you didn't create it properly, you'll know shortly!

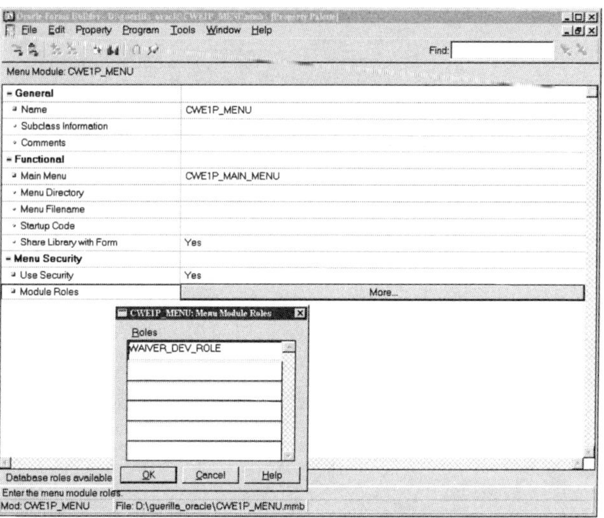

4. Finally, add the same ROLE to the four menu items: Exams, Administration, Exit, and Help. Double click to open the CWE1P_MAIN_MENU, click on Exams, then hold the shift key down and click on HELP so that all four items are highlighted. You're going to make the change to all four at the same time. Now right-click, select Property Palette and the "? Item Roles", click on "More", click "OK" to the Multiple Objects box, and enter the Role:

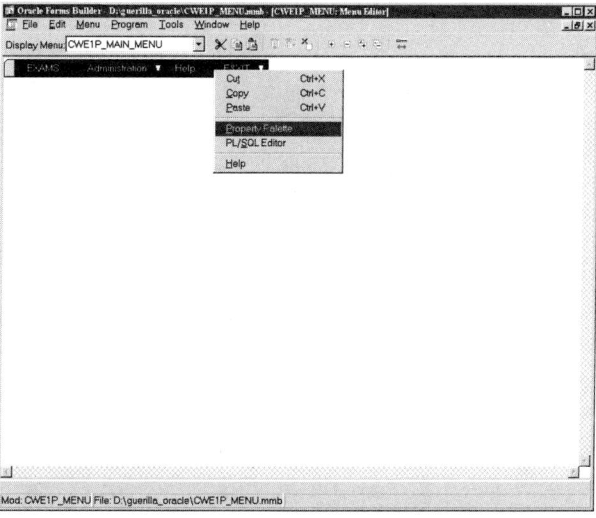

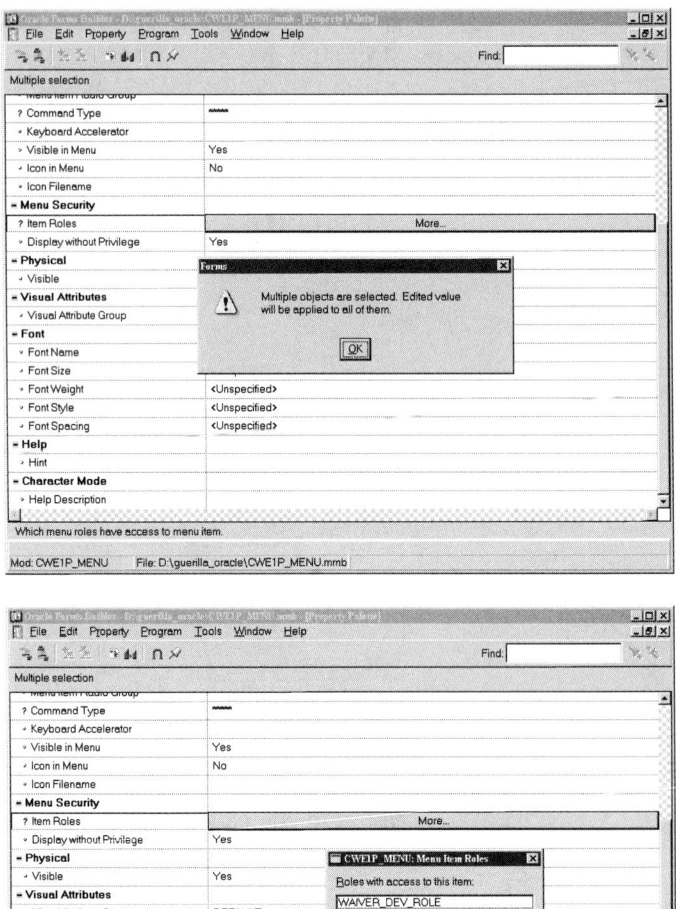

Of course, you could have completed each menu item one at a time. Since there aren't any more menus, compile your MENU module, then compile your FORMS, and you're ready to test with your generic user ID.

Bibliography

In addition to the specific sources listed here, refer to the various Oracle Corporation manuals, such as *Oracle9i Database Administrator's Guide*, Release 1 (9.0.1). For Oracle manuals, go to http://otn.oracle.com/docs/content.html and http://download-east.oracle.com/otndoc/oracle9i/901_doc/nav/docindex.htm. And, above all, go to http://otn.oracle.com and join this immense, free Oracle resource.

Anderson, C., and Wendelken, D. (1997). *The Oracle® Designer/2000 Handbook*. Reading, MA: Addison-Wesley.

Feuerstein, S. (1997). *Oracle PL/SQL Programming*, 2nd ed. Sebastopol, CA: O'Reilly.

Feuerstein, S., Dye, C., and Beresniewicz, J. (1998). *Oracle Built-in Packages*. Sebastopol, CA: O'Reilly.

Koch, G., and Loney, K. (1997). *Oracle 8: The Complete Reference*. New York: McGraw-Hill.

Lewis, J. (2001). *Practical Oracle8i™: Building Efficient Databases*. Boston: Addison-Wesley.

Lulushi, A. (2001). *Oracle Forms Developer's Handbook*. Upper Saddle River, NJ: Prentice Hall.

Morrison, M., and Morrison, J. (2002). *Enhanced Guide to Oracle* 8i. Boston: Course Technology.

Silberschatz, A., Korth, H. F., and Sudarshan, S. (2002). *Database System Concepts*, 4th ed. Boston: McGraw-Hill.

Thorpe, H. (2001). *Oracle8i™ Tuning and Administration: The Essential Reference*. Boston: Addison-Wesley.

Index

Note: *Italicized* pages refer to tables/figures.

A

B

C

D

E

F

G

J

K

L

M

Q

R

S

W

POWERED BY
Safari
TECH BOOKS ONLINE

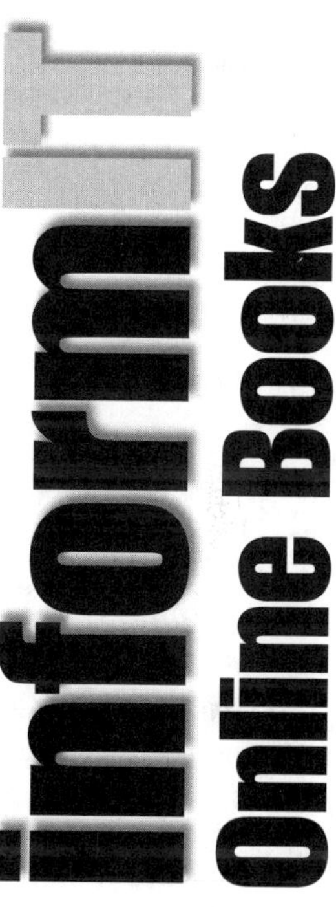

informIT
Online Books